# LITERARY STYLE: A *Symposium*

# LITERARY STYLE:
## A Symposium

*Edited and (in part) translated by Seymour Chatman*

1971
OXFORD UNIVERSITY PRESS
LONDON AND NEW YORK

# ACKNOWLEDGMENTS

I WISH to thank the other members of the organizing committee for their help—Roman Jakobson and Thomas Sebeok (who, unfortunately, could not participate) and René Wellek, Stephen Ullmann and Roland Barthes (who could), as well as those who have helped me in the work of editing the manuscript—Whitney Blake, James Raimes, Nicholas Fraser, and Harry Bishop. I am particularly grateful to Harold Mosher, Jr., for his labor and advice on the translations. I am sure all participants join me in thanking The Rockefeller Foundation, and particularly John Marshall and Gerald Freund, for helping to make our stay at the Villa Serbelloni comfortable and profitable. I owe thanks to the John Simon Guggenheim Foundation and to the University of California Humanities Institute for financial support during my editorial labors.

S.C.
Berkeley
April 1971

# CONTENTS

# EDITOR'S INTRODUCTION

THE SYMPOSIUM ON LITERARY STYLE took place in late August 1969 at the Villa Serbelloni under the kind auspices of the Rockefeller Foundation. It is difficult to imagine a more tranquil and delightful site or more congenial and stimulating company. The participants felt a remarkable unanimity of purpose. Despite differences in terminology and background, it was clear that everyone was talking about the same thing, and in ways that were mutually comprehensible, if not always mutually acceptable.

Such unanimity could not have been the result of environment or company alone. It surely reflects a growing sense of a coherent field, of the acceptance of a body of principles and terminology; and part of the excitement that suffused the discussion must have stemmed from recognition of that fact. Modern literary stylistics, drawing upon several disciplines—linguistics, literary criticism, literary history, theory of literature—has in recent years developed methods of analyzing texts and characterizing literary language and forms that is disciplined and replicable, without losing a refreshing diversity: there is the Russian Formalist-Jakobsonian school, the French *structuralistes*, influenced by the Russians, the Czechs, and Hjelmslevian linguistics, the British School, in the tradition of J. R. Firth, the American School with its debt to the New Criticism and to Bloomfieldian and Chomskian linguistics and more recently to linguistic philosophy, the inheritors of the Continental and particularly the Spitzerian stylistic tradition, and so on. Many of the assumptions of these schools can be found implied or asserted in the following pages; what is remarkable is how much agreement is reflected in the papers and discussion, and how even the disagreements sharpen rather than diffuse the issues. Many of these, of course, are not new: the debate between monists and dualists for example (see the discussion of Barthes' paper) goes back to Plato and Aristotle. But the terminology (the metalanguage) and hence some of the conceptualizations outfit fresh attacks on time-honored questions.

The Symposium was originally thought of as a successor to the 1958 Style in Language Conference at Indiana University,[1] and in fact was called at the outset the Second Style in Language Conference. But it soon became clear that there were enough differences to suggest the need to avoid treating one as a sequel of the other. For one thing, the Bloomington Conference was very much interdisciplinary. Not only linguistic and literary scholars were invited but also folklorists, psychologists, anthropologists, and philosophers, and "style" was taken in the broadest possible sense: not only literary style was discussed but linguistic style and indeed the whole area of what psychologists call "individual differences." For another, the Conference was attended only by Americans, while the organizers of this Symposium were anxious from the very outset to make it as international as possible. (Ten European nations were in fact represented, three of them in the Eastern zone.)

The participants chose their own topics, and it is my task to arrange these in a way that best reflects the sense of cooperation and focus of the Symposium. It is to be hoped that the order chosen does do that, without at the same time concealing the breadth of interest which necessarily characterizes any discussion of style. The papers tend to group themselves according to whether the predominant concern is with theory or practice. The theoretical group in turn seems to split into three sub-groups: (1) those concerned with definition of the term (Barthes, Miles) or with the general role of style (Todorov); (2) those concerned with the relation of style to nearby disciplines (linguistics: Enkvist; aesthetics: Wellek; psychology: Milic; content and discourse analysis: Doležel; philology: Uitti; semantics: Ullmann); and (3) those concerned with specific stylistic features (phonology: Fónagy, Levin, Wimsatt; syntax: Weinrich; illocutionary speech acts: Ohmann). The "practical" papers tend rather to center around corpora: the style of a whole period (Zumthor), of a genre (Starobinski), of individual authors or works (Hasan, Halliday, Niculescu, Sayce). The word "tend" is very important here, since it will become clear to the reader that this categorization does not always hold up; the "theoretical" papers contain plenty of illustrations, in several cases focusing at length on a single text (Doležel, Weinrich); whereas the "practical" papers contain important theoretical insights, often argued at length and even at times independently of the analysis itself. (This is particularly true of the papers by Hasan and Halliday, which could, therefore, with equal logic, appear in the theoretical group.) In the totality there is provided, I think, a very fair epitome of the field of stylistics today, and it is clear from discussions and papers that theory and practice were mutually informative.

A word about the details of the organization of the Symposium. Abstracts of all papers were written and circulated, and the papers themselves were presented *in toto* during the actual sessions (ten in all). Each paper was discussed for approximately an hour, and the discussion was tape-recorded. An exact typescript was made, but I have presumed to rearrange the discussions in logical order, on the assumption that the actual temporal sequence of speakers in free discussion is random (whoever gets his hand up first speaks first), and hence not the most edifying arrangement. Further, I have taken it upon myself to summarize, rather than to quote comments directly, and to delete the names of all discussants except the author of the paper in question. My reason for doing so is to preserve the sense of focus without losing the pace of the discussion by including the extra verbiage and occasional confusions of *viva voce* sessions. An interpretation seems preferable to an exact record, since the record would then have to be examined by each speaker, who would feel the usual temptations to alter, amend, ramify, and so on. I have found in earlier experience that after the introduction of different terms and second thoughts, discussants often seem to be talking *past* each other, or even in different rooms, at different conferences. I am willing to risk charges of personal bias or misinterpretation to avoid the suggestion of such misfiring. I am gratified to say that the great majority of participants to whom I sent my account accepted it immediately; in the one or two cases where they did not, I have rearranged it to their liking. In general, I have interpreted the discussion as an adversary or antagonist-protagonist encounter, the challenger speaking first and the defender responding. I trust that my use of such tags as "The question was raised whether . . ." and "The next speaker wondered if . . ." will be self-evident to the reader, and that he will be able to note without difficulty the appearance of a new participant and the reappearance of the author of the paper.

It would be presumptuous to attempt to summarize in a brief introduction the richness and complexity of this Symposium. But perhaps I can give the reader some sense of its unity and focus by noting certain persistent themes in the discussion. They are perhaps best formulated by these questions:

1. *What is style?* As everyone knows, "style" is an ambiguous term. Among other things, it has been used to refer to the idiosyncratic manner of an individual or group; or to a small-scale formal property of texts (in the language alone, or additionally in other attendant systems like meter); or to a kind of extra or heightened expressiveness, present in non-literary language as well; or to a decorum based on social or cultural context; or to any one of a number of other concepts.[2] Several participants were concerned with this polysemy: Ullmann's paper, for example, opens with a sketch of different senses of the word; Ohmann's shows how his account of the syn-

tactic aspects of the style of a passage from Beckett's *Watt* would be accommodated by various theories of style; Sayce points out the difference between linguistic and literary stylistics; and so on.

The sense most widely inferred in the proceedings is style as a formal property of a text. Guiraud, for example, speaks of it as "the specific form of the text," and for Miss Miles one of the functions of stylistic analysis is that of "distinguishing elements and relations in a text." Todorov warns, however, that simply identifying style with coherence, that is "form, structure, totality, a unique and harmonious assemblage of several more general categories within the particular work" would make the term otiose. Ohmann shows the inadequacy of typical stylistic-formal analysis, pointing out that the illocutionary as well as the locutionary dimension of language is subject to stylistic variation. Zumthor notes the inapplicability of the old ornamentalist conception of style to the medieval lyric, and Starobinski argues that the form-content dichotomy is unviable for autobiographical genres. Barthes revives the monistic view of the relationship between form and content in a new and interesting way: not that "style is meaning" (as in Wanning, Wimsatt and Beardsley), but rather that meaning itself is only one form ("style," "code") among others.

But style is seen not only as a function of small-scale, but also of large-scale form (a use of the term first proposed, to my knowledge, by Archibald A. Hill). Enkvist speaks of how linguistics can aid in the analysis of "the way in which sentences are strung together into large units and into discourse." Doležel is not only theoretically but also practically concerned with how to account for "the organization of textual units in a temporal sequence." Weinrich discusses the textual function of the article in French, arguing that "there is no reason to stop syntactic (and hence stylistic) research at the magic border of the sentence." And Halliday's functional theory of language finds the "textual" to be one of the important functions to be accounted for, one that includes "the establishment of relations between sentences."

The notion of style as the manner of an individual or group is also explicitly and implicitly referred to. Guiraud says that "Each author has his own language—which his readers must learn." Miss Miles argues that the stylistics of manner is radically comparatist: "The very concept of manner suggests that the way is separable from the material and thus may be followed in extension from material to material, that treatment is discernible across things treated." Milic interprets Buffon's aphorism anew, and Wellek reminds us that "the traits observable in one work (by an author) often permeate all his others." For Starobinski style "is the act of an individual," or more narrowly, "the fashion in which each autobiographer [or, presumably any writer] satisfies the conditions of the genre," though at the same time enjoying "the margin of liberty" left to him. And he illustrates his conception by dealing with style as manner of a genre, just as Sayce offers an analysis of the manner of an individual author and Zumthor that of the manner of an era.

Style as a heightened expressiveness—esthetic or emotive—a usage less frequent in Anglo-Saxon than in Continental stylistics is also evoked. This is the sense of Bally's "linguistic" (as opposed to literary) stylistics, as Guiraud and Wellek recall. And the influence of Riffaterre's important affective theories are rehearsed by several participants in papers and discussions. Ohmann too includes among the tasks of stylistics consideration of the "likely impact" of stylistic facts on the reader: what is involved is not only the discovery of stylistic facts, but "the weighing of their expressive import, and of their mimetic character; and the analysis of rhetorical effect."

As for style as a kind of cultural decorum, Todorov revives approvingly the division made in antiquity into low, middle, and elevated styles (though his reasoning is not sociological). Miss Hasan and Halliday reflect the interest of the British School in concepts like "register" and "style of discourse."[3] Halliday calls one of the functions in his triad "interpersonal," defining it as "the relationship that [the speaker] sets up between himself and the listener—in particular, the communication role that he adopts."

2. *How do style features emerge?* Though Enkvist feels that few people "would quarrel with the statement that style is one type of systematic language variation," and Starobinski argues that the deviation theory "offers us a system of revealing indices, of symptomatic traits" of autobiographic style, the papers and discussions reveal no general satisfaction with the idea that stylistic features are by definition *deviant* characteristics of texts. Much of the uneasiness has to do with the problem of establishing or even sensing a norm. Though Guiraud defends the necessity of recognizing the norm (since how else could "surprise" or "information" arise?), Barthes finds its identification with the current spoken language at once "excessive" and "insufficient," since on the one hand the spoken language is only one of several possible codes of stylistic reference, and on the other "the opposition of speech and writing has never been exploited to its ultimate end." For Zumthor, the only meaningful norm for medieval poetic texts is what is provided by that specific set of texts. Halliday and Todorov refer approvingly to Samuel Levin's important distinction between *qualitative* deviance (ungrammaticalness) and *quantitative* deviance (in the relative frequency in which normal features are chosen or avoided); the latter Halliday proposes to name "deflection." But Todorov observes that only one part of the problem is resolved if a more refined norm is assumed, for example the "whole of poetic (i.e. literary) language" or (in the discussion

of his paper) "the grammar of the language," since a deviant sentence cannot be an "automatic consequence of the grammar."

Why assume, for example, that the *difference* between two corpora entitles us to say that one represents the norm and the other the deviant? Halliday: "The text may be seen as 'this' in contrast with 'that,' with another poem or another novel; stylistic studies are essentially comparative in nature, and either may be taken as the point of departure." They both provide "egalitarian universes." Or, again: Is it not the case that "regularities," that is, precisely non-deviant linguistic elements in a text, seem often to be stylistic, whereas "many deviations . . . are not stylistically interesting"? Halliday recalls Dell Hymes' view that "style may not be deviation from but achievement of a norm." "Prominence" ("highlighting" or "foregrounding," as translations of the Czech term *aktualisace*) is relative to one's overall perspective and purpose "so that what is globally a departure may be locally a norm."

3. *Is linguistics sufficient to describe literary style? That is, Is stylistics merely a branch of linguistics?* The general opinion of the Symposium is "No." Hopefully that should relieve the fears of those (mostly Anglo-Saxon) scholars who worry about the "encroachment" of linguistics into literary studies. Doležel argues that descriptions and models of language are not particularly useful in accounting for literary stuctures, since text is an "autonomous semiotic structure" containing structures other than the linguistic. Wellek repeats an argument he has advanced several times before, namely that though stylistics bears a close relationship to linguistics, it is not possible simply to identify it with poetics or general theory of literature, since the latter includes additional areas "which elude a linguistic and stylistic approach"—for example, pantomime, plot, themes, motifs, and so on. Barthes points out extra-linguistic semantic structures or codes that operate in narrative texts: "actional, hermeneutic, semic, cultural, and symbolic."[4] For Miss Miles, style entails choices in content as well as in form: "Style chooses and discards matter as well as arranging it; it works in *invention* as well as in *disposition* and *elocution*." Sayce writes: "For literary studies style is a component of, and must be considered in relation to, a quite different system which is not strictly linguistic, which indeed transcends language as ordinarily understood: theme, plot, structure (in a wider sense) character, above all aesthetic significance . . ." According to Ullmann, "Stylistics is not a mere branch of linguistics but a parallel discipline which investigates the same phenomena from its own point of view." Levin argues that though the poetic conventions "comprise patterns or structures of language elements, the patterns or structures so constituted have no *linguistic* significance." And Halliday says "An adequate characterization of an author's style is much more than an inventory of linguistic highlights."

Whatever one feels about these views, one can hardly see them as representing a sinister attempt to reduce literary phenomena to the purely linguistic dimension. Still, it was widely urged—and even by the least "linguistic" of the stylisticians—that those things in literature *beyond* language may very well have their own codes or systems, and that the task of the literary student is to inquire into these as systematically as he can.

## NOTES

1. The proceedings of which appeared as *Style in Language* (New York, 1960), ed. by Thomas Sebeok.

2. There have been several recently published attempts to define the term. See, among others, Nils Erik Enkvist, "On Defining Style," in *Linguistics and Style*, ed. J. Spencer & M. Gregory (London, 1964), R. A. Sayce, "The Definition of the Term 'Style'," *Proceedings of the Third Congress of the International Comparative Literature Association* (The Hague, 1962), 156-66; and Seymour Chatman, "The Semantics of Style," *Social Science Information*, VI (1967), 77-99.

3. Elsewhere (M. A. K. Halliday, Agnes McIntosh, and Peter Strevens, *The Linguistic Sciences and Language Teaching*, Bloomington, Ind., 1964), "style of discourse" is introduced to refer "to the relations among the participants" (in communication) from temporary, "as when the participants are at a party," to permanent, "as between parents and offspring" (pp. 92-93).

4. See Barthes' S/Z (Paris, 1970) for an explanation of these terms.

# 1
## THEORY
## OF STYLE

# STYLE AND ITS IMAGE

### ROLAND BARTHES

PERMIT ME to start with a personal reference. For about twenty years I have been doing research on the language of literature without feeling completely comfortable in the role either of critic or of linguist. I should like to act on the authority of my ambiguous situation to deal with a concept which is mixed, which is at once metaphoric and theoretical. This is the concept of image. I don't think that scientific work can proceed without a certain image of its object (it is well known that there is nothing more resolutely metaphoric than the languages of mathematicians or geographers); nor do I believe that the intellectual image, heir of the ancient Pythagorean cosmogonies, at once spatial, musical, and abstract, can be divested of its theoretical import, that which preserves it from contingency, without being turned, in an exaggerated way, toward abstraction.

It is thus an image which I want to question. Or more exactly a vision: how do we *see* style? What is the image of style which troubles me, what is the one I long for?

To simplify the issue considerably, I would suggest that style (in the current sense of the word) has always been part of a binary system, or if one prefers, of a mythological paradigm of two terms; these terms have, of course, changed names and even reference through eras and schools. Let us take up two of these.

The first, the oldest (it still exists, and indeed is widespread in the teaching of literature) is that of Content and Form. As everyone knows, this dichotomy derives from the opposition in classical rhetoric between Res and Verba: Res (or the demonstrative materials of the discourse) depends on Inventio, or research into what one can say about a subject (Quæstio); on Verba depends Elocutio (or the transformation of these materials into a verbal form). This Elocutio is, roughly, our "style." The relationship of Content and Form is phenomenological: Form is taken to be the "appearance" or "dress" of Content, which is the "reality" or "substance" of Form. The metaphors applied to Form (style) are thus decorative: figures, colors, nuances. Or, in another way, the relationship between Form and Content was experienced as an expressive or alethic relationship: the critic (or commentator) was supposed to establish a just connection between Content (reality) and Form (appearance), between the message (as substance) and its medium (style); between these two concentric terms (one being *in* the other) there was presumed to be a warranted relationship. This warranty gave rise to a historical problem: can Form disguise Content, or must it be subjected to it (so that there cannot be a "coded" Form)? It was this debate which, over the centuries, opposed Aristotelian (then Jesuit) Rhetoric to Platonic (then Pascalian) Rhetoric. Despite changes in terminology, this is the same "vision" which persists in any treatment of text in terms of a *signifié* and a *signifiant*, the *signifié* being inevitably experienced (I speak here of a more or less assumed vision) as a secret which hides behind the *signifiant*.

The second opposition, a much more recent one, of a more scientific aspect and to a large extent a tributary of the Saussurian paradigm *Langue/Parole* (or Code/Message), is that of Norm and Deviation. Style is seen here as an exception (though coded) to a rule; it is the aberration (individual, yet institutional) from a current usage, a usage which is either colloquial (if one defines the norm in terms of the spoken language) or prosaic (if one opposes poetry as "the other thing"). Just as the opposition Content/Form implies a phenomenological vision, the opposition Norm/Deviation implies a vision which is eventually moral (under the guise of a logic of *endoxa*): there is a reduction from the systematic to the sociological (the code is what is statistically determined by the greatest number of users), and from the sociological to the normal, where social discourse begins. Literature is the domain of style, and because it is specifically that domain, it takes on a shamanic function, which Lévi-Strauss has well described in an introduction to one of Mauss's works.[1] Literature is the domain of the verbal anomaly in the sense that society fixes it, recognizes it, and assumes it in the act of honoring authors, in the same way that the ethnic group establishes the supernatural in the person of the witch-doctor (just as an abscess marks the boundary of a disease), in order to recapture it in the process of collective communication.

I should like to take these two visions as my point of departure, not to attack them but to complicate them.

Let us consider first of all the opposition of Content to Form, of *signifié* to *signifiant*. There is no doubt that it contains a certain irreducible grain of truth. The structural analysis of narrative,[2] in its present accomplishment and future promise, is based entirely on the conviction (and the practical proof) that one can transform a given text into a more schematic version, set it a metalanguage which is no longer the language of the original text, without essentially changing its narrative character. In order to enumerate the functions, to reconstitute the sequences or to distribute the agents (*actants*), in sum, in order to bring to light a narrative grammar which is no longer that of the vernacular of the text, it is essential to strip the stylistic (or, more generally, expressive or "elocutionary") film from an underlying structure of secondary (narrative) meanings, to which the stylistic features are irrelevant. One can vary these features without altering the structure. Thus Balzac's description of an old man as one who "conservait sur ses lèvres bleuâtres un rire fixe et arrêté, un rire implacable et goguenard comme celui d'une tête de mort,"[3] has exactly the same narrative (or more precisely semantic) function as any statement we might create which tells that the old man had something fantastic and funereal about him. (The *seme* is irreducible, since it is functionally necessary in the sequence of the story.) The error, however—and it is here that we need to modify our vision of Content and Form—would be to cease the stripping-off of style too soon. What this stripping-off reveals is not a content, a *signifié*, but another form, another *signifiant*, or if one prefers a more neutral term, another level, which is never the last, because the text is always articulated in terms of codes which themselves will never be exhausted. The *signifiés* are forms, as we know from Hjelmslev and even more clearly from the recent hypotheses of psychoanalysts, anthropologists, and philosophers. In an analysis of a story by Balzac,[4] I felt able to bring to light—without reference to style, with which I was not concerned, and while remaining within the boundaries of *signifié*—a play of five different codes: actional, hermeneutic, semic, cultural, and symbolic. The "facts" which the author (or more exactly the performer or "implied-author" of the text) extracts from these codes are juxtaposed, mixed, or superimposed within a given statement (a single sentence, for example, or more generally, a *lexie* or unit of reading) in such a way as to form an interwoven skein, a tissue, indeed, in the strict etymological sense, a *text*. Here is an example: the sculptor Sarrasine is the lover of a prima donna who, though he does not know it, is a eunuch; he abducts her, but the pretended songstress defends herself: "L'Italienne était armée d'un poignard.—Si tu approches, dit-elle, je serai forcée de te plonger cette arme dans le coeur."[5] Is there behind the expression a *signifié*? No, the sentence is an interweaving of several codes: a linguistic code (the French language), a rhetorical code (antonomasia, interpolation of an *inquit*, apostrophe), an actional code (the armed defense of the victim is a unit in the sequence "Abduction"), a hermeneutic code (the eunuch conceals his real sex by pretending to defend his virtue as a woman), and a symbolic code (the knife is a symbol of castration).

Therefore we can no longer see a text as a binary structure of Content and Form; the text is not double but multiple; within it there are only forms, or more exactly, the text in its entirety is only a multiplicity of forms without a content. We can say metaphorically that the literary text is a stereography: neither melody, nor harmony (or at least not unrelieved harmony), it is resolutely contrapuntal; it mixes voices in a volume, not in a line, not even a double line. Of course, there are among these voices (codes, systems, forms) certain ones which are particularly associated with the verbal substance, the verbal play (e.g. linguistics, rhetoric), but the distinctions between these are essentially historic, useful only for the literature of *signifié* (in general the only literature which has been studied). One need only think of certain modern texts to see that as the *signifié* (narrative, logical, symbolic, psychological) recedes more and more, it is no longer possible to oppose (even subtly) systems of Form and systems of Content. Style is a historic and not a universal concept which only has pertinence for historical works. Does it have, in the heart of this older literature, a definite function? I believe it does. The stylistic system, which is one system among others, has a function of naturalization or of familiarization or of domestication. The units of the codes of Content are in effect submitted to a rough pigeon-holing (action, character, and symbol are clearly distinguished, the march of truth is fragmented, retarded). Language, as sentence, period, and paragraph, superimposes on these discontinuous categories existing at the level of discourse an appearance of continuity. Because no matter how discontinuous language itself may appear, its structure is so well established in the experience of each man that he grasps discourse as a continuous reality: don't we speak of the "flux of speech"? What could be more familiar, more evident, more natural than a sentence as read? Style covers as with a tablecloth the semantic articulations of Content; by a metonymy it naturalizes the tale which is told, makes it innocent.

Let us turn now to the second opposition, that between Norm and Deviation, which is in effect that between Code and Message, since in this view style or literary effect is experienced as an aberrant message which "surprises" the code. Here again, as we proceed with the notion, we need to refine our vision rather than destroy it.

It is undeniable that features of style are drawn from a code, or at least from a systematic space (this distinction seems necessary if we wish to respect the possibility of a multi-code or even the existence of a *signifiant* whose space is ruled and yet infinite; that is, a paradigm which can never be completely filled out). Style is a distance, a difference; but in reference to what? The reference which is most frequently made, implicitly or explicitly, is to spoken ("current" or "normal") language. This idea seems to me at once excessive and insufficient: excessive because the stylistic codes of reference or difference are numerous, and the spoken language is always only one of these codes (to which there is no reason to grant special status as the incarnation of the fundamental code, the absolute norm); insufficient because, when one considers the matter closely, the opposition of speech and writing has never been completely clarified. A word on this latter point.

We all know that the object of linguistics, that which determines at once its province and limits, is the sentence (however difficult to define). Beyond the sentence there is no linguistics because that is the province of discourse, the combinatory rules of which differ from those of the *monemes*; but in discourse no linguistics is possible either because we cannot expect to find anything except syntagmas which are unformed, incomplete, "undeserving." Only the sentence, we feel, guarantees organization, structure, unity. Now internal language (the language of thought) is essentially a *subsentence* language; it can of course contain full sentences, but the normal rules of sentence-formation are not required for the success and fulfillment of the communication. We often speak without finishing our sentences. Listen to a conversation: note how many sentences have an incomplete or ambiguous structure, how many clauses are subordinated without reason or without being assigned to clear antecedents, how many subjects lack predicates, how many correlatives lack a partner, and so on, to the extent that it may be wrong to continue calling some of these "sentences," even "incomplete" or "ill-formed" ones. It would perhaps be better to speak in a more neutral fashion of syntagmas whose mode of assemblage remains to be described. If, however, we open a book, there is not one sentence whose completion is not marked by any number of features—structural, rhythmic, and punctuational.

Whence, rightfully, two autonomous linguistics: a linguistics of the syntagma and a linguistics of the sentence, a linguistics of the spoken word and a linguistics of the written. In taking this distinction to its ultimate conclusions, we would only be following the recommendations of philosophy, which today assigns different ontologies to speech and to writing. Philosophers tell us that it is a paradoxical error for linguistics to avoid dealing with written language (language in sentences) while at the same time asserting that the canonic form of language is speech, in respect to which, writing is only a "transcription."

We lack, clearly, a grammar of the written language. (But is this kind of grammar possible? Wouldn't the very notion of grammar be eliminated by such a division?) This deficiency requires a new classification of languages: there are sentence-languages, and then there are all the other kinds. The first are marked by a constraint, an obligatory rubric: the completion of the sentence. Style is evidently one of the written languages, and its generic feature (what connects it with the other written kinds but still does not distinguish it from them) is the requirement that it finish its sentences. By its finiteness, by its composition, the sentence is declared written, that is, in the process of becoming a literary object. The sentence is itself already a stylistic object: the absence of ink-blots by which it becomes itself is, in a way, the first criterion of style. That criterion can be clearly seen in two properly stylistic values: simplicity and strikingness. Both are effects of its nature, the one litotic, the other emphatic. If such a sentence of Claudel's as "La nuit est si calme qu'elle me paraît salée"[6] is at once simple and striking, it is because it ends with a necessary and sufficient fulfillment. This can be seen in relation to some historic facts: first, a certain gnomic inheritance attributed to written language (divinatory maxims, religious formulae, whose closure, typically sentential, assures a variety of meanings); then the humanist myth of the living phrase, the emanation of an organic model at once closed and generative (a myth which is explained in Longinus' *On the Sublime*); finally, attempts (though hardly very effective ones, since literature—even "subversive" literature—is so tied to the sentence), dictated by modernism, to explode the boundaries of the sentence (*Coup de dés* by Mallarmé, the hyperproliferated Proustian sentence, the destruction of the typographic sentence in modern poetry).

Thus, the sentence, in its closure and self-sufficiency, seems the fundamental goal of writing. From which many written codes arise (though these are not always clearly delineated): scholarly writing, academic writing, administrative writing, journalism, etc., each describable in terms of its audience, of its lexicon and syntactic protocols (inversions, figures, *clausulae*, all features marking the identity of a collective writing by their presence or absence). Among all these kinds of writing, and even before we speak of style in the individual sense in which we ordinarily take the word, there is *literary* language, a truly collective writing whose systematic features should be surveyed (and not merely its historical features, as has been done up till now). What, for example, is permitted in a literary text but not in an academic article? Inversions? *Clausulae?* Order of complements? Syntactic license? Archaisms? Figures? A certain lexicon? What is first necessary to grasp is not the idiolect of the author, but of the institution (literature).

That is not all. Literary writing must be placed, not only in reference to its closest neighbors, but also to its models. I understand by models not *sources* in the philological sense of the term (let us note in passing that the problem of sources has been posed almost exclusively at the level of content), but syntagmatic patterns, fragments typical of sentences, formulae if one likes, whose origins cannot be traced but which form a part of the collective memory of literature. To write is to let models come to one and to *transform* them, in the sense which this word has assumed in recent linguistics.

Let me point out three facts about this subject which are borrowed from recent experience. This first is a personal testimonial: though it was some time ago that I worked on a story of Balzac, I am often surprised to find myself even now carrying over into daily life Balzacian scraps of sentences and expressions which spring to mind from the text. This is evidence that I record life (it happens in my head) through formulae inherited from a previous style. Or more precisely: life is that which comes already constituted in literary language: even nascent writing is already consummated writing. The second fact is an example of external transformation. When Balzac writes "J'étais plongé dans l'une de ces rêveries profondes qui saisissent tout le monde, même un homme frivole, au sein des fêtes les plus tumultueuses,"[7] the sentence, if one excepts its personal trademark ("I was plunged"), is nothing more than the transformation of a proverb: *Amid tumultuous celebrations, profound reveries.* In other words, literary expression harks back, by transformation, to another syntactic structure: the primary content of the sentence is some other form (here the gnomic form), and the style is established by a work of transformation which is exercised not on some "idea" but on that form. The principal stereotypes (such as the proverb) from which literary language is generated remain to be discovered and analyzed. The third fact is an example of internal transformation which the author generates by his own formula: at a certain moment of his stay at Balbec, the Proustian narrator tries to engage the young elevator-boy at the Grand Hotel in conversation, but the boy does not respond to him, says Proust "soit étonnement de mes paroles, attention à son travail, souci de l'étiquette, dureté de son ouïe, respect du lieu, crainte du danger, paresse d'intelligence ou consigne du directeur."[8] The repetition of the same syntactic formula (a noun and its complements) is evidently a "turn." The style consists of 1) transforming a subordinate clause into a nominal phrase ("because he did not hear well" becomes "his hardness of hearing"); 2) repeating as many times as possible this transformational formula through different contents.

From these three precarious and almost impromptu remarks I would simply draw a working hypothesis: that of considering the stylistic features as transformations derived either from collective formulae (of unrecoverable origin, either literary or pre-literary), or, by a play of metaphor, from idiolectal forms. In both cases what would have to control the stylistic work is the search for models, of patterns: sentence structures, syntagmatic clichés, divisions and *clausulae* of sentences; and what would inspire such work is the conviction that style is essentially a citational process, a body of formulae, a memory (almost in the cybernetic sense of the word), a cultural and not an expressive inheritance. This permits one to identify the transformation to which one refers (and consequently the stylistic feature which one envisages): stylistic transformations certainly have some affinity with those of transformational grammar, but they differ in a fundamental point, where linguistics, inevitably implying a certain vision of language, becomes ideological. The stylistic "models" cannot be assimilated into "deep structures," universal forms issuing from a psychological logic. These models are only the depositaries of culture (even if they seem very old). They are repetitions, not essential elements; citations, not expressions; stereotypes, not archetypes.

[To come back to the vision of style which I spoke about at the beginning of this paper: in my opinion it must consist today of seeing style as one of a number of textual elements: a number of semantic levels (codes), the interweaving of which forms the text, and a number of citations which reside in that code which we call "style" and which I should prefer to call— at least as a first object of study—literary language. The problems of style can only be treated by reference to what I shall refer to as the "layeredness" (*feuilleté*) of the discourse. And to continue the alimentary metaphor, I will summarize these few remarks by saying that if up until now we have looked at the text as a species of fruit with a kernel (an apricot, for example), the flesh being the form and the pit being the content, it would be better to see it as an onion, a construction of layers (or levels, or systems) whose body contains, finally, no heart, no kernel, no secret, no irreducible principle, nothing except the infinity of its own envelopes—which envelop nothing other than the unity of its own surfaces.]

## NOTES

1. M. Mauss, *Sociologie et anthropologie* (Paris, 1950).
2. An issue of *Communications* (VIII, 1966) is entirely devoted to this topic, and includes definitions of terms like *function, actant*, etc.
3. ". . . kept a fixed and arrested smile on his bluish lips, a smile as implacable and mocking as that of a death's head."
4. The story is "Sarrasine"; see Roland Barthes, S/Z (Paris, 1970).
5. "The *Italienne* was armed with a dagger. 'If you come near,' she said, 'I will be forced to plunge this dagger into your heart.'"
6. "The night is so calm it seems salted" (from Paul Claudel, *Connaissance de l'Est* (Paris, 1900).
7. "I was plunged into one of those profound reveries which seize upon everyone, even frivolous men, in the midst of the most tumultuous celebrations."
8. ". . . whether from astonishment at my speaking, attention to his work, concern for etiquette, hardness of hearing, respect for the place, fear of danger, mental torpor or orders of the director."

## DISCUSSION OF BARTHES' PAPER

Barthes' final reduction of content to form raised some questions. It was argued that it is one thing to say that even the smallest details of a text have a structure, but quite another to say that that is all there is, that there is nothing *but* structure. Surely there must be such a thing as the subject of a literary work; that is, it is a meaningful thing to say (for example) that the subject of a story by Hemingway is the sensations of a man returned from the war who finds that even a trout-stream seems sinister to him. That is a subject, a choice among things in the world to write about that Hemingway has made, that is, a content—what Hemingway does with it is the form. How can one reduce the substantive or contentual choice to "form"? There must remain some pre-existent material which is irreducibly content or subject-matter. Barthes replied that for him "subject" was an illusory notion. There is no subject expressed by an author; subject is a level in the hierarchy of interpretation. It is in interpreting the work that the reader gives it a center, a principle, a content. For example, you could ascribe various subjects to Balzac's "Sarrasine":[1] you could say that it was the story of a sculptor who loves a eunuch disguised as a woman; or that it was an illustration of the dubious morality attending the fortunes of Parisians at the beginning of the nineteenth century, thus attaching it, as did Balzac himself, to a criticism of the society of the time; or that it was a case-study in castration, a psychoanalytic subject. Every résumé is already a coded transcription, a hierarchizing interpretation. But this is true precisely because the literary work does not possess a canonic subject, that is, it always contains many subjects; its life is transhistoric; it is indefinitely open to new interpretations.

Someone pointed out that it is necessary to distinguish between the Form/Content (*forme/fond*) dichotomy posited by philosophy and that posited by literary theory. In traditional philosophy, the image to express the opposition of *materia* and *forma* was likely to be drawn from sculpture, the concept of isomorphism being illustrated by the block of marble (*fond, materia*) which is nothing until it is shaped by the sculptor into a form (*forma*). Thus, for philosophy, form is all; content is nothing. In literature the emphasis is quite the reverse; the content (*fond*) is the message, the form, that is, the writing, the stylus and the wax tablet, are nothing—the medium vanishes once the communicative act has occurred. Barthes recalled that in philosophical perspectives on cultural history like Derrida's, too, style was seen as the product of the trace of stylus in wax tablet; the stylus *is* obviously only the instrument of the trace. But "trace" is ambiguous, because it can mean at once the utterance itself (Derrida opposes it to "voice") or the part that disappears, like the stylus. Thus one arrives at the image of texts as a kind of palimpsest, possessing a thickness of writings such that one only at times glimpses the writing underneath.

Barthes was asked whether in turning a text into a metatext he did not run the risk of omitting certain surface details of importance, details which are often stylistic. Does one avoid that by having recourse to a pluralism of levels? Barthes admitted that every metatext loses something of the original text. Indeed, criticism exists because something is lost in the text over the years. If a literature ever developed in which *everything* were lost, including the structure of the text, criticism would cease to exist. Thus, with the forms of modern experimental writing, in which structure and meaning are abandoned, criticism is difficult, if not impossible. A criticism of Lautréamont, for example, is probably not possible.

In connection with Barthes' discussion of norm and deviation, a participant pointed out that the basic concept derives from the institution of the law and the fact that rhetoric was originally ancillary to the law:[2] he who was to handle the language well needed to know the law. Norm meant *bon usage*. The sentence in a legal sense (the *sententia*) was a pronouncement; it summed up the lawsuit and made everything that had been said legal. Barthes agreed enthusiastically, finding that this provided a very important hypothesis for further work. He noted that it was customary to chastise anyone who could not finish his sentence for lack of education. As for the concept of norm itself, it was noted that there is a relatively simple way of judging the norm objectively; it is the traditional notion of *figure*. For a figure is by definition a deviation in respect to some norm. For example, in French the present tense is to be used for present time; when it is used thus, its use is the normal one. When the present tense is used to indicate the historical past or the immediate future, it becomes a deviation, hence stylistic. Barthes noted that the notion is ambiguous to the extent that we are only permitted to define a style in terms of its difference; but in respect to what is it different? He noted that his students were shocked by the idea that one should want to define the poetic as deviant; for them poetry is not a deviation from some code but constituted a separate code, one among others.

As for Barthes' plea for a grammar of written as well as of oral language, it was conceded that some linguists used to say that it was only the spoken language that mattered and that written language was merely an imperfect record of it. But that was not true of all linguistic schools; in Britain, for example, J. R. Firth always insisted that written language had a life of its own. Furthermore, linguistics in general has increasingly adopted this view; quite a few contemporary linguists hold that certain features in the written language are controlled by the medium.

It was proposed to Barthes that the one grammar, the traditional one with its subject and predicate, be called *predicative*, and that the other be called *locutive*; in the latter there would be no requirement for predicate or subject, the identificatory marks being purely prosodic. These are not equivalent to "written" vs. "spoken" grammar; rather, in the spoken language there is a greater frequency of locutive sentences than in the written, but that does not mean that only locutive sentences occur. Such sentences are only "incomplete" if one judges them, inappropriately, by the standard of the predicative grammar. But we can only judge these "incomplete" sentences in terms of a locutive grammar, which it is a pressing task to write. Barthes agreed.

Another participant argued that our view of the relative purity and completeness of the written sentence tends to be exaggerated. One should not assume that spoken language is somehow very different from written in that the ideal of completeness is irrelevant to it. Now that linguistics has taken a moral, even a puritanical, turn in refusing to deal with the messiness of speech—pushing it aside under some heading like "performance" and being willing only to touch the Platonic ideal of "competence"—it has fallen into the trap of refusing to recognize that many of the effects of our ideal sentences depend precisely on the messiness of performance. A good example is provided by nominalization—surely what interests us is *why* there is such nominalization (a feature not restricted to, but characteristic of, literary language). In English we cannot understand the effect or effectiveness of a nominal style except through an examination of its speech context, because it is in the spoken language that we see the reasons for preferring that over other structures. There are a number of potentialities of meaning in the spoken language that are open only to nouns and nominalizations, depending on intonation and related factors. For example, to make an element both thematic and informationally prominent in the sentence, you place it in first position and give it a separate intonation unit. But this is

permissible only with words having the structural function of nouns, i. e.,
nominals. We can change the emphasis in "Sir Christopher Wren built this
gazebo" by saying "This gazebo Sir Christopher Wren built," but we cannot say "Built Sir Christopher Wren this gazebo." To give prominence to
the verb we must convert it into nominal form—"Sir Christopher Wren's
building of this gazebo" or "What Sir Christopher Wren did was to build
this gazebo." Thus nominalization often has its motivation in speech."
Spoken language is not in any way the formless procession of untidy fragments that some linguists believe it to be. This is a myth that does a great
deal of harm, not the least to the study of literary language.

It was further noted that even the imputed absence of sentences in the
language of very young children is an illusion. In the evolution of the child's
language, there is a first phase in which the sentence has only a single term,
but it is marked as a sentence by the relaxing of tension through intonation.
There is a second phase in which two single-term sentences are synthesized
into one. In central aphasia, one can also observe a certain regression in
which only a single sentence remains, which is a cry, but which is marked
as a sentence by the intonation contour.

Another participant was reminded by Barthes' mention of proverbs of the
rhetorical figure of *enthymeme,* the imperfect syllogism. Barthes noted that
he had found many examples of enthymeme in "Sarrasine." The enthymeme may well be an important figure in literature. He was also reminded
that today we speak of literature more often as *oeuvre du désir* than as
*oeuvre de la pensée;* thought has been traditionally taken as, so to speak,
pure or nude; but can one consider desire as a motive force in literature to
be *mute?* Barthes thought not: one writes because one can never verbalize
what is desired except by treating its absence in symbolic terms.

Barthes was asked in what sense he took mathematics to be metaphorical.
He answered that he meant that mathematical language was metaphorical
when mathematicians talked about it, not when they practiced it, since of
course it is an algorithmic art, thus the opposite of metaphorical. But when
mathematicians are obliged, for pedagogic or other reasons, to talk about
mathematics, they often have recourse to metaphors, like "tree-structure,"
for example.

He was also asked to elaborate on his idea of style as a citational process.
Barthes answered that the idea of the work as a "citational space" is very
popular now in France—for example with the group *Tel Quel* and with
philosophers like Derrida. Writing is seen as a kind of hereditary process,
heredity without end, just as the whole world is seen as a system of codes
without end, each code forever connecting with another code. Whenever we
have to explain a message, we are obliged to go over to another code, which
in turn sends us to yet another code, and so on, in an infinite regress. This

is ultimately a metaphysical conception, coming down to the irreducible fact of the non-origin of origins, questioning the occidental idea that there are ultimate origins of a transcendent order.

Barthes was questioned about his "film" image—that there are a plurality of subcodes of signification, and that the most superficial one is style, which envelops the others like a film. Is it not true that each level has its own form? Barthes agreed that his image was not a good one, that "film" could open the door to many errors. What he was trying to convey was the notion of a layered sphericity, with its implication that what we say is only a mythic elaboration to satisfy our need for surface.

Finally, Barthes was reminded that in scholarly tradition, style was considered as an individualization, and that was natural in a culture in which the individual was constantly seeking his individuality. The tradition can be related to religious ideas of election developed by pietism and methodism in the eighteenth century. In this sense one could see stylistics as dealing with writers whose aim was to appropriate to their own purposes the universalizing powers of language. Thus we arrive at the paradox that it is precisely the literary institution that, like other institutions, prescribes individualization and style as the means of individualization. Barthes agreed, noting that we still live in a civilization in which propriety is evidenced by the signature, the sign of the proper name. Style too is a substitute for the proper name; literature is the institution which consists of attaching one's name to a verbal product.

### NOTES

1. See Roland Barthes, S/Z (Paris, 1970).
2. It was observed that the French expression *clause de style* means a weighty kind of expression with little content, but that for centuries the term *style* was a respectable legal term.

# IMMANENCE AND TRANSITIVITY
# OF STYLISTIC CRITERIA

PIERRE GUIRAUD

PRESENT-DAY STYLISTICS is divided into two large antagonistic tendencies or schools: traditional stylistics, originating with Bally, and a new stylistics, which is derived from Prague Structuralism by way of Jakobson. Both define style as the specific form of the text, but the first group looks for a source for its definition in a study of the stylistic properties of the code, while the second looks for it in a description of the internal structures of the message.

It is remarkable indeed that this disagreement, seemingly irreconcilable among the disciples, is far from being pronounced between the masters. Bally constantly pointed out the difference between his goal, the study of coded language, and the study of the particular style of the text, and it is not entirely his fault if he has not been generally understood or followed by his successors. At the most, he can only be blamed for not having outlined more clearly the practical and methodological implications of his theory. Jakobson, in turn, while approaching the problem textually, has always shown in theory as well as in practice that his "poetic" structures are derived from features of a system which would allow the construction of a grammar of poetry. It is clear that both men define style in terms of the code and in terms of the message. But neither has ever clearly pointed out this ambiguity.

However, Guillaume has called attention to it in his classic distinction between the "potential meaning" and the "effective meaning." Thus it is clear that there are characteristics of style not only in the very linguistic system but also in the effects of the system, that is, its realizations in discourse. It is clear, too, that a description of the values of the potential sign in language could not account for all the effects caused by its introduction into a text, but by the same token these effects could not be explained without reference to the values which form their basis.

The problem of whether to begin with the code, following Bally, or with the message, following Jakobson, is purely methodological. For example, regarding an archaism or an imperfect tense or a chiasmus, we can ask a rhetoric or a system of stylistics or a "grammar of poetry" what potential values are contained in these signs, in order to determine which are realized by the context; or, on the other hand, we can identify the nature of these realizations in order to explain them according to the values attached to the sign.

Unfortunately stylisticians have more often than not failed because they have neglected to maintain the distinction between the two levels of code and message. The traditionalists have frequently confused the effects of style with the properties of the system; and the structuralists in turn, in an understandable but unfortunate reaction, have considered as inherent properties of the structure of speech, values which have their origin in the system. We must now examine the postulates of this new or so-called "structuralist" stylistics.

The first postulate, upon which everyone agrees, without, however, drawing the same conclusions, is the "specificity of style": every stylistic feature is unique, based on a unique structure which allows it to create effects exclusively its own. The conclusion drawn by some stylisticians, notably R. L. Wagner, is that stylistics is impossible. One can imagine a criticism (but not a scientific system, a typology, a classification, a set of laws) which studies only individual, incommensurable features. Others—especially Jakobson, though not always—characterize the stylistician's task as purely descriptive. One simply explores the nature of internal structures—that is, the relations between signs at different levels—phonic, syntactic, lexical, metrical, etc.

The principal contribution of this new stylistics—and it is an important one—is the definition of new criteria of formalization: Jakobson's notion of "shifter," for example, or his distinction between metaphor and metonymy, or his definition of the poetic function as "the projection of the principle of equivalence from the axis of selection onto the axis of combination," from which derives Levin's theory of "coupling." Yet this purely descriptive analysis, although indispensable as a first step, has the disadvantage of providing no answer to important questions of interpretation. The new stylistics does not analyze the function of the structures which it describes, having rejected the traditional criteria of code or author which it considers external to the message and therefore stylistically irrelevant.

## THE CODE

One cannot define style without recourse to the code; no one has ever succeeded in doing so. For example, it has been justly observed that an archaism cannot be identified without reference to the context which determines
its effects. Nor can it be identified without reference to language, and the
word "archaism" implicitly refers the sign to the system and to values which
are evoked from outside the message. The mere introduction of the term
"metaphor" or "syntactic order," or whatever, similarly postulates a system
which defines "the normal meaning," "the normal order of words," and so
on. Every message is a collection of signs, and one cannot define or describe
signs without referring them implicitly to the system in which they occur.

Providing these assumptions are recognized, Bally's project of forming
an inventory of stylistic values which the language makes potential is not
only clearly justified but is the first condition and *sine qua non* of any
stylistic study.

## STATISTICS

When it rejects the study of the code, the new stylistics generally rejects
the statistical method, which at one time made so many promises, promises
which, to tell the truth, have not always been realized. As long as the
stylistic effect was generally thought of as a deviation, statistics was considered the most suitable science for identifying and describing it. I shall
not raise once more the objection made to the statisticians in the name of
a need to define deviation qualitatively. Clearly there can be two definitions, qualitative and quantitative, which pose two distinct types of problems; to confuse them or to think of them as irreconcilable is naïve.

But the real problem lies in the very notion of deviation. The adherents
of an immanent stylistics reject this notion because any deviation (quantitative or qualitative) can only be defined by reference to a norm which is
external to the text and hence subject to challenge. Their definition of style,
which excludes language, the qualitative norm, necessarily excludes any
possibility of a recourse to a quantitative norm. However, their discussion
would be pointless if they did not introduce the notion of "surprise" and
"information." This is especially the case of Riffaterre; he will excuse my
naming him so often, but one talks only about those whom one esteems,
and he has taken a polemical stance which invites discussion.

In brief, the "effect of style" produced on the reader would depend on
a "surprise," or on an "unfulfilled expectation" (or eventually on a fulfilled
expectation). Now how can surprise or expectation be defined if not in

terms of probability? And how can probability be defined if not in terms of statistics? And how can one evaluate, if not in reference to a series of events which are external and anterior to the message?

Clearly, reference to the code can only be rejected by substituting for it a criterion which exists only in relation to the code.

### THE AUTHOR

Even more than it rejects the idea of a common language, the new stylistics rejects that of a language proper to an author. The problem is complex, for it has been grafted onto the old quarrel between internal (linguistic) criticism and external (historical and biographical) criticism. Most stylisticians practice purely internal criticism (although the problem of how to do so is far from being resolved); but within this group a new disagreement pits those who believe that the essential nature of the message inheres in the language of the author against those who deny that proposition. Their argument is that the effect of style is an effect on the reader and as such depends only on him.

This is true to the extent that the reader deciphers the text by means of his own code and takes from it meanings and stylistic effects which are independent and sometimes very far from those the author might have put there, consciously or unconsciously. Each text "has the meaning which one attributes to it," and we know how much this meaning can vary among individuals and, still more, among milieus and eras. It is false, however, to the extent that common language is enriched by the impact of works. Each author has a personal language which his readers must learn. Each verse of Baudelaire implies previous readings, a whole linguistic, poetic, cultural experience of the work in its totality. The "gulf" of Baudelaire, the Baudelairian "sister" bring about specific *effects* which go beyond the context in which these words occur, and whose source lies in a "language" of Baudelaire, which must be learnt like German or slang.

Of course it is always possible, and even useful, in certain cases, to analyze the stylistic effects independently of any reference to the language of the author; but such reference is a means of deepening, enriching, and illuminating a reading which no stylistics can afford to neglect.

### THE READER

It remains for us to consider the response of the reader which, of course, is the cornerstone of Riffaterre's concept of stylistics. His is an approach which, in theory, seems indispensable and extremely profitable. That the value of a work is something created by its public is, furthermore, universally recognized. Indeed, it may be asked why stylistics hasn't made use of this criterion before. Its drawback, however, is the difficulty of defining the reader other than as an isolated individual whose judgment is thereby deprived of critical value. To avoid this result, Riffaterre has recourse to the notion of "average reader," a statistical entity which it seems very difficult to define in practice and of which—to my knowledge—Riffaterre has never given an example in his analyses. Riffaterre's brilliant studies, in fact, rely on "style effects" recorded by Riffaterre himself without collaboration or use of statistics. Thus, the method is lacking a foundation in its very inception. It is nonetheless true that it is rich in theoretical possibilities and that it could derive much that would be useful from the methods of inquiring into audience-effect now employed in the study of mass communication.

But in any case, the "reactions of the reader" take us outside the message and show again the uselessness of a stylistics which is purely formal and immanent to the text. Conceived as "specific form of the message," style is immanent to the latter; but the notion of message implies that of *sign* and thus necessarily of *code* (expression and content), which is external to the message; and code, in turn, cannot be defined except in terms of the linguistic experience of speakers (encoder and decoder).

But it is no less true that the text constitutes in itself an original linguistic experience which extends the limits of the code's use to the extent that it seems that certain privileged texts "imply their own codes." It is no less the case that this immanent encoding of the message is necessarily defined by reference to an external code from which it draws its meaning.

The debate which at present opposes a study of the stylistic values of the language (at once the common language and the language of the author or reader) to that of the stylistic effects which arise in discourse and the structure of the message rests on a fundamental distinction, but one whose two constitutive aspects cannot help being dissociated. The problem is how to keep them clearly distinct, how not to move, more or less unconsciously, from one level to another. Every approach is legitimate, even indispensable, provided one has a clear sense of one's intentions and methods, and provided these are unambiguously specified in the course of the analysis.

## DISCUSSION OF GUIRAUD'S PAPER

Guiraud's assertion of an opposition between the schools of Bally (style is a property of the code) and Jakobson (style is a property of the message) was strongly questioned. Far from Jakobson's being committed to the message, a statement of his was recalled to the effect that stylistic features could only be understood in terms of the code. Jakobson does not separate language and text in his analysis. Secondly, it was argued, the "two stylistics" are simply complements, the one being the practical application of the other. Style only exists at the level of language, not at that of text. The language contains a register or set of styles which each text can actualize differently, in its own way. Guiraud said that he saw no grounds for disagreement with these statements as long as one concurred that the language possesses only potential values (*valeurs*) while the actual effects (*effets*) occur at the level of message. But (was the reply) a complete theory of style should be able to predict the effects of style. It should be able to tell us what the effect of an archaism, for example, will be in a text. Guiraud answered that though the number of *valeurs* is limited and reducible to system, the number of effects in texts is immense. Prediction is only theoretically possible: to predict all of them would require an extremely complete and intricate generative grammar.

Guiraud was asked in what sense he was using the word "code." At one time he seemed to be using it in the sense of "norm." Do we mean by "code" something like "a system of stylistic effects which will find realization in the text"? Or is it the system of the *langue*? (The latter would take us back to the idea of deviation.) His response was that there is both a code of language and a code of style, that there are both linguistic *valeurs* and stylistic *valeurs*. As for the norm, he argued that it is not a system but merely the sum of the most frequent usages. The analysis of a system can only be qualitative; it becomes quantitative only at the level of usage.

One participant defended the task of pure description along with the need for statistical inquiry. He pointed out that the descriptions of literary texts generally available are inadequate and partial, and the latter in a particularly disturbing sense, the investigator typically describing the work of art in terms that argue some preconceived evaluation or thesis, rather than providing a reliable and complete guide upon which later students can build. But, Guiraud responded, description cannot help going *somewhere*; it leads you to expect something, an interpretation of some kind. Others agreed: the study of "Les Chats" by Jakobson and Lévi-Strauss did only half the job; no matter how extensive a description, it remains description unless it provides a basis for distinguishing facts that have stylistic relevance from those that do not. It was recalled that many dissertations at the Sorbonne have followed a standard formula of description, giving the reader the same feeling of "So what?" that Guiraud describes, instead of showing what was idiosyncratic in the style of the author under investigation.

The rest of the discussion concerned the role of the reader in relation to that of the author. It was generally agreed that it is the reader who is the crucial figure in the recovery of style and not the "author," in any nineteenth-century, psychological sense of the word. This attitude is essentially a modern return to the views of Aristotle and ancient rhetoric; for example, Aristotle's notions of pity and terror were descriptions of effect, not cause. It seems clear that it is a waste of time for us to concern ourselves about such questions as the incidence of intention in a work, or the proportion of conscious to unconscious material it contains.

But *who* is the reader? This question preoccupied the conferees for some time. It was agreed, for example, that even Riffaterre has renounced his notion of Average Reader for some Ideal or Super Reader who seems to be very much like the stylistician himself. Further, it is not fruitful for stylistics to investigate empirically the responses of a number of readers. What then should it do? One argument was that it should study the image of the reader contained in the text, on the assumption that each text entails such an image. For example, it can be shown that the *Portrait d'un inconnu* of Nathalie Sarraute is addressed to someone who has read Baudelaire; if one reads the book without knowing Baudelaire, one can only be described as an inadequate reader. (Doesn't this mean that the analysis of a text by someone who shares Baudelaire's culture will be different from one by someone who does not? Yes, said Guiraud, probably it will.) Thus, the image of the reader can be found in a detailed stylistic analysis of any literary work of art. Indeed, it was argued that the text *is* the reader, or more exactly that it is the "specific space" of the reader, the largest possible space since it includes all the readings possible. Because if it does not, we are back to an undesirable sociological study of the reactions of individual readers. For example, in Greek tragedy, each character speaks in a code which is incomprehensible to the others; therefore, the tragedy depends on a series of misunderstandings. But there is a "place" where the misunderstandings are understood—namely that occupied by the reader. In this sense, the author's role is one of creating ambiguities or polysemies, and it is the reader's task to comprehend this ambiguous "multicode." Guiraud agreed, but raised the question of exactly how this was done. He suggested that just as we refer to the *code* of the author (not his psychology or biography) when we say the "author," we should mean by "reader" the *code* of the reader. What happens is that the reader decodes a text by recovering the author's code; it is of course possible to read without knowing anything of the author's code, but that can hardly be accepted as successful reading. But (it was argued) when the critic speaks of a text, he means its "readability" (*lisibilité*); yet within the last 100 years we have had *textes limites* which raise the whole question of *lisibilité*, and thus that of the question of the relation of the reader or author to the text. This is clearly a little-studied area, and perhaps within this context the notion of style itself disappears. Can one speak of style in the work of Lautréamont, for example?

Another question concerned the relation of the reader and the text to the historical dimension. If it is the case that there is nothing in the text which cannot be explained by reference to the code of the language, perhaps it is history which links the message to the code (as Spitzer suggested); it is in this sense that the reader is important, for it is he who grasps and tries to assimilate the phenomena—not only in the synchronic but in the diachronic sense as well. Guiraud agreed (he had only omitted reference to Spitzer because of his desire to establish a very schematic opposition between the schools of Bally and Jakobson). But he noted that in this sense one should speak of the "reader" not as the mere consumer of the work but as one of the elements which create the code in which it is expressed, that is, the cultural group or society.

There was only one question specifically directed to Guiraud's discussion of the relation of author to stylistic effect. Shall such discussion be in any way concerned with causality? Or does Guiraud simply mean by *la langue d'auteur* that which is registered in the language of an era or a genre? Guiraud answered categorically that he could not accept the notion of author as stylistic cause, because it is the case that the author's message comes to the reader already encoded. Only the reader can decode it, and the reader's code (if he is successful) will be closely tied to that of the author. We learn to read *in* the code of Baudelaire, for example, although, of course, our own code must form the basis upon which we do so.

# STYLE AS STYLE

### JOSEPHINE MILES

THE VARIOUS PAPERS delivered at this conference focus either upon distinguishing elements and relations in a text or, more generally, upon the concept of style itself, with a concern for the relation of style to language, to value, and to other normative forces. Some discussion of the ways in which these two emphases are complementary may serve to suggest how much both are needed in any thorough discussion of style.

First, if we describe what is before us, what we perceive, as objectively and neutrally as possible, we start out with one of those thorough phonetic-syntactic-semantic-generic-social-thematic analyses of a poem that may give us more sheer data than we know how to use. We assume some basis for selection—say occurrence—and this enables us to bring to light some salient linguistic facts in the poem. It is interesting, for example, to note the steady co-occurrence, in alternate lines or stanzas, of plosive sounds with polysyllabic words with complex clausal structures and with a content of reference to a certain person in a tone of anger. We can then proceed to explain the reasons, linguistic, biographical, or artistic, for this co-occurrence; or we can attempt to estimate its extent, assess its effects, and so on.

A frequent danger lies in the fact that the principles for selection are not only established prior to thorough observation but are based on the reader's interest, with the result that the two elements of material and effect are immediately confused. To say, for instance, that the selection of doublets is an obvious feature of an author's style runs the risk of implying criteria of selection without exploring them. Why, and to whom, after all, is the feature "obvious"? Obviousness can arise not only from the nature of the text but from the nature of the reader; it could, for example, be the result of a strong sensitivity to a trait lacking or present in his own style or culture.

Many cautions have been made against giving excessive weight to co-occurrences, which, rather than being determined by aesthetic criteria, are simply made obtrusive by the particular set of linguistic or cultural conventions present behind the work. Brooks and Warren,[1] for example, have pointed out the danger of overrating the value of onomatopoeia in *s* sounds, or in the "murder of innumerable beeves," and Yvor Winters has dealt with the problem in the light of what he calls the fallacy of imitative form.[2]

On the other hand, without a basis for selection in personal interest or some externally derived concern for harmony, truth, and effect, as Professor Wellek warns, we can be submerged in a welter of data. Many years ago the aesthetician David Prall tried objectively to describe all the qualities and interqualities of one painting, and gave it up as an impossible job. The solution is, I think, simply to have and to state a criterion of selection, so that data and measure of data are kept separate, and interests of author not necessarily identified with interests of reader.

But to get at the identifying, the sufficient as well as the necessary features for the description of an individual literary text, a further basis of selection seems necessary, one that will separate identifying traits of interest not only from readers' interest but from other writers' interest, that is, from the common styles established by the language and culture and not just by the individual work. Rostrevor Hamilton's study[3] of the word *the* in English poetry is illuminating of *the* not just as an obvious word of the poetry and not just as a word of interest to him, but as a cultural vehicle of a kind of attitude, a weighted structure present in the language and made use of by certain specific poets to certain specific effect.

Such distinctions, based upon such extensions of interest from text to readers and to other texts, remind us why close study of the describable elements of text, however cautiously selected and correlated, does not provide the complete story of style. As manner in the treatment of matter, style chooses and discards matter as well as arranging it; it works within the category of *invention* as well as within those of *disposition* and *elocution*. Therefore we need to know not only disposition or arrangement of what materials, but also choice *from* what materials—the prior givens, the limits and potentialities of thought and attitude already weighting the available materials as well as the accustomed manners. The loaded materials and manners are met and confirmed or counteracted by the specific loadings of the specific artistic structure of the specific artistic work. A word weighted with a dull repetitive convention can be, for example, confined in that dull conventionality by the structure and sound of the line it is used in, or brightened by the shock of a new context; an alliterative pattern can be used inertly and neutrally, or comically, or with portentous grace. So we have the confluence in a literary text of ready-made forms and associations from the language, with those from the literature in general, and with those from specific genres of usage in particular, including the author's own; and all of these will be given the compacting force of an individual artistic entity in pattern and design.

It is at this point of individual entity that it is least possible to talk about style, unless with reference to the resources from which the work has been drawn. This poet's "way of writing," this poem's "way of writing" can be discerned chiefly by comparison and contrast, by relation to other works. The very concept of manner suggests that the way is separable from the material and thus may be followed in extension from material to material, that treatment is discernible across things treated. So if we are talking about a single work or entity we will probably not talk about its style, but as we relate it to other entities, and its elements to other elements, we necessarily do so.

Here we come back to the chief difference between the papers at this conference: some elect to consider certain features in a text in their extension and intension or interrelation, in order to be able to say that this work's or this author's or this genre's style can be characterized by certain describable elements—in other words, a partial intensive or necessary definition of their participation in a style. Others elect to consider the potentialities, the store of availabilities, or code, from which any text may be shaped; that is, an observation of what is not, as well as what is, drawn upon, and thus a sufficient as well as necessary definition, a setting apart of the entity as well as a focusing upon its central features.

Our own language structure gives us a clue as to how these two perspectives need to be related and interplayed. A dimension of reference often ignored at a time when connotativeness and figurativeness are considered is the dimension of the normative or intensive, where a word is used to label a good or bad example of a kind rather than just any example. Without any further modification except perhaps intonation, the word *cat* may vary its reference from "There's a cat," meaning animal, to "There's a cat," meaning woman, to "There's a *cat*," meaning a specially good example of either. A phrase that helpfully plays one of these meanings against the other is "out in the west where men are men." The necessary or extensive *men*, all we could call *men*, is made sufficient and intensive, implying what we would not. Such a linguistic usage, and I do not know whether it characterizes just English, or some, or all languages, makes for much cultural confusion in the discussion of any concept, including that of style. While we are assuming the normative, we may be suddenly dropped into the descriptive, as in H. H. Munro's use of the verb *go* in "She was a good cook as cooks go, and as cooks go, she went." When Professor Wellek says we must be careful to study not mere elements in style but the relation of all style to the fullest human values, he may be underplaying the point that it is exactly in mere elements that the values reside, that *cat* is both *a cat* and *the cat,* that eighteenth-century poetry is not only a collection of poems written in the eighteenth century, but a norm of poetry for some, of non-poetry for others. The relation of norm to non-norm, of poetry to non-poetry, for example, is not merely evaluative, not merely of good to bad, because for many speakers to exclude by definition is a prior sort of evaluation, and to be bad or to fail very different from not "really" representing a category at all. So, at least in English, evaluation is built into words as well as being a modification of them.

Some speak of style descriptively, noting and relating elements of styles; some normatively, trying to see its full reference to value. The two emphases can profitably come together, but probably not all in one way, for the reason that the basic relation differs from one philosophy to another. For formal idealism, I suppose the whole shape controls the parts. For organic idealism, I suppose the details emerge and develop from the germ or seed of the norm. For materialism, on the other hand, details build up to the norm. For much present-day existentialism, one vivid detail may establish the character of the whole. It is my thought that beyond all these, or implicit in them, is the concept of working back and forth between part and whole, with neither fully established, but always open to new effects from the other; so that ever new details may be seen to be relevant, and ever new relevances be discerned in constant interplay. In this sense, for style, every detail of usage is relevant; if we can show it to be so, so much the merrier. From plosives and fricatives to the frictions and explosions of mankind and the universe is a not impossible way, though never a way to be assumed. For the literary scholar the way is mediated twice, through the patterns of language as distinct from art and through the patterns of art as distinct from language, and thus through the two together.

We can explicitly relate certain linguistic features or codes to a writer's own style, just as we may set one text against another in a certain canon. It will be possible to speak descriptively of different stages or phases of an author's style and of the artistic principles relating them to other features of manner. It will also be possible to speak normatively, saying, for example, that such features show us certain qualities of coherence, consistency, relevance, and other evaluative criteria; or in the negative, that the writer has *no* style because he uses these features in such a muddled way that no clearly characterizing manner can be discerned.

The danger in either way lies in ignoring the grounds of artistic and linguistic relevance which make connection possible between the necessary and the sufficient, the descriptive and the normative aspects of reference. To assume that a describably dense sound structure makes for a highly valuable poem, that is, "necessarily establishes high poetic quality" would be as foolish as Professor Wellek makes it seem. On the other hand, it may not be foolish to say "I like dense sound structure so I am pretty sure to like this poem which has it," or, even more resoundingly, "For me a good poetic style requires a dense sound structure, so this style, which lacks it, is not really a good style; indeed, not really a style at all." It seems to me that we must allow for such common normative slides from descriptive characteristics, because they are easily and well made by certain philosophical procedures, notably the mechanist or existentialist in some forms. But the most philosophical, as most encompassing, of procedures is that which accepts the difference between, and thus the relation between, traits descriptive and traits normative, and so can relate not only specific message to specific code, and specific poem to specific school, and specific judgment to specific philosophy of values, but also, within any work itself, its own center to the periphery of its style; explaining its necessity and sufficiency, and the interplay between identity and possibility.

Style is what it is; what it is has deep involvement with what, linguistically, artistically, evaluatively, individually, it is not.

## NOTES

1. *Understanding Poetry* (New York, 1938).
2. *The Anatomy of Nonsense* (Norfolk, Conn., 1943).
3. *The Tell-Tale Article* (New York, 1950).

# THE PLACE OF STYLE
# IN THE STRUCTURE OF THE TEXT

### TZVETAN TODOROV

IN HIS BOOK *Le Problème du style*, Rémy de Gourmont wrote: "The point is not that there is science on the one hand and literature on the other; it is that there are brains which function well and brains which function badly . . . "[1] I do not presume to comment on the functioning of my own brain, but I believe, like Gourmont, that there is no reason to mistrust rigor, even if the object of our reflections is literature.

Stylistics is certainly the most rigorous division of literary studies; but in view of the level of rigor which one finds in general, the superlative does not mean much. The bibliographies of stylistics contain thousands of titles, there is no lack of observed facts; however, the polysemy of concepts, the imprecision of methods, the uncertainty about the very goal of this research hardly make for a prosperous discipline. Our efforts ought to be directed toward the elaboration of a general theory, toward the creation of a coherent and homogeneous framework within which individual stylistic studies could find a place. Therefore it is necessary to make our postulates and hypotheses explicit.

First of all, one must distinguish two possible attitudes toward the literary text (indeed toward any text; my examples are taken from literature only for convenience). In the first, the individual work is only a point of departure for the study of literature, of literary discourse. In the second, the work is the ultimate goal of a research which aims at description and thus interpretation. On the one hand, a study of virtual literary objects (literary "forms," as they used to be called); on the other, an effort to grasp the sense of the given work. The first activity—which I shall call *poetics*—is related clearly to science; the second depends on interpretation. Obviously no insurmountable wall separates the two; indeed, neither one nor the other is found in a pure state. To know literature, one always proceeds from concrete works. And interpretation can never remain absolutely fixed to a single text: to speak of one text creates another, thus causing us, whether we like it or not, to attenuate the originality of the first, to relate it to other texts, to generalize it. The only way of remaining absolutely faithful to a text is simply to repeat it, and even then the change of circumstances endangers the text's identity.

As a category of poetics, the concept of style obviously attaches to the first kind of activity. To become the object of a scholarly conference, style must have the status of a scientific object, and not that of something inimitable, unique, "special"—which would be, by definition, unnameable. But if it is such, we must distinguish at the outset two of the more current notions of style: style as coherence and style as deviation.

Style as coherence, that is as form, structure, totality, a unique and harmonious assemblage of several more general categories within the particular work—this conception can be found in America in the work of Cleanth Brooks; in Germany, in that of Wolfgang Kayser; in Russia, in that of Viktor Vinogradov.[2] There would be, in this view, as many styles as there are literary works. But, over and above objections which could be made against such a conception in the name of necessary generalization, it is hard to see why the use of the word "style" is preferable to "coherence," for example. This latter term, rather than being discarded, should be placed in another context, as we shall see later on.

Style as deviation, that is infraction, transgression of a norm—Spitzer in Germany and Pierre Guiraud in France[3] are the champions of this theory. The individual work is referred to the set of writing of an author, and this set is seen as a deviation from the norm constituted by the current language. This definition of style as idiosyncrasy has frequently been called into doubt, and still another argument can be adduced to support the existing grounds for dissent. The idea of an author as a homogeneous source of his texts, as an invariant behind the variables, a stable and primary essence looking out upon fugitive and derived appearances belongs to a philosophy which is no longer that of our time. To our way of thinking the text is written *through* the author much more than it is written *by* him.

The concept of style as deviation has developed recently into a modified form which escapes the criticism which has just been made: the first term of the comparison is changed and one no longer speaks of the language of a writer as deviation from a norm but from the whole of poetic language (this modification can already be found in the work of Mukařovský[4] in the thirties). But the second term of the relation can also be attacked, because there are only two possible ways of defining this norm:

1) One may identify the norm with everyday language, with all spoken

and written discourse. But then to characterize poetic language as a deviation from the norm is tautological: any homogeneous discourse will prove deviant, since the "norm" will be the agglomerate of all discourses and thus will not have the characteristics of any among them. It is unclear why we should speak of a norm; ordinary language is the meeting-place of a thousand norms and thus "normless" in the truest sense.

2) Or one may identify the norm with a particular type of discourse; thus Jean Cohen[5] compares the poems of the Symbolists of the nineteenth century to the prose of their scholarly contemporaries. There is, of course, a difference between the one and the other, but what permits us to consider one as the norm, the other as deviation? Furthermore, compared to a third type of discourse, for example, journalism, both are "deviant," but the deviation of poetic language would no longer be the same (thus one would characterize the style of Victor Hugo differently according to whether the basis of comparison were Flaubert or Gautier).

Having said this, we can consider certain useful distinctions which have resulted from work on deviation and which we owe above all to Samuel Levin:[6] that between quantitative deviation (deviation in frequency of occurrence) and qualitative deviation ("ungrammaticalness"); and also between deviations from a norm present in the text (i.e., "syntagmatic" deviation, which constitutes, for Riffaterre,[7] the object of stylistics) and deviations from a norm which is elsewhere (thus "paradigmatic").

If it is to become a theoretical discipline, stylistics must have styles, not style, as its object. It must make an inventory of the abstract categories of which any given text may be constituted. But in speaking of styles we risk introducing another confusion, so we must make another general digression.

A notion can be defined in two ways: either in terms of its internal organization or in terms of its functions. In the first case, one deals with a system of which this notion is the external limit; in the second, it is a constitutive element in another system. Let us take the notion "family": according to whether one describes it in terms of the elements which constitute it (man, woman, children, etc.), or of the role that it can play in a superior unit (e.g. the village), it will be assigned different definitions. Let us call the first type of definition structural and the second functional. We shall say that the structural description of linguistic facts is dependent on linguistics, their functional description on a (scarcely existent) linguistic anthropology. Let us note that there is no necessary correlation between the two domains—structural and functional.

We have not yet emerged from banalities; it seems, however, that stylistic studies has need of them. Unless one places oneself in a sociological or anthropological perspective, there is no reason to speak of scientific or journalistic style or whatever. These categories are perhaps justified; but, though popular, the hypothesis which postulates an isomorphism between the typology of styles given us by sociology and that given us by stylistics is ill-founded. Now it is this fact which presupposes the need for research into the internal characteristics of a style, whether scientific or literary or poetic (one looks in each case for the structural properties of the functional unit). As Juri Tynianov, one of the Russian Formalists, has already noted, "The existence of a fact as a *literary fact* depends on its differential quality, in other words, on its function. What is a 'literary fact' for one era will be a phenomenon of the everyday language for another, and vice versa, according to the literary system in which the fact occurs. Witness, for example, the literary character of memoirs and intimate journals in one literary system and their extra-literary character in another. . . ."[8] "Literature" is a functional (and sociological) notion; the object of stylistics should be constituted by structural notions.

Style is not coherence; nor is it deviation; nor a tracing made of this or that social stratum. But what is it then? I find the first useful occurrence of the term in the ancient division into low, middle, and elevated styles. Not because this division is satisfying in itself but because style is here conceived as an internal characteristic of a kind of discourse, and as an abstract category, not as a unique configuration of properties to be found in an individual work. Further, none of these three styles is seen as "deviant" in respect to any other, although each is, obviously, different from the others.

To define a concept, one must describe it in its relations with other, neighboring concepts, relations which are superordinate, parallel or subordinate. Let us begin by saying that no utterance can be deprived of its stylistic properties. Our job then is to define the image which we make of the utterance and the place occupied by style in its structure.

We shall distinguish three aspects in any utterance; let us call these verbal, syntactic, and semantic. The verbal aspect of a text is constituted by the concrete sentences which form it. The syntactic aspect involves the interrelations of the parts of the text. And the semantic aspect involves the global sense of the utterance, the themes which it evokes.

Let us consider an example. Nerval writes in *Aurélia*:

> "Eh quoi!" dis-je, "la terre pourrait mourir, et nous serions envahis par le néant?" "Le néant," dit-il, "n'existe pas dans le sens qu'on l'entend; mais la terre est elle-même un corps matériel dont la somme des esprits est l'âme. La matière ne peut pas plus périr que l'esprit, mais elle peut se modifier selon le bien et selon le mal. Notre passé et notre avenir sont solidaires. Nous vivons dans notre race, et notre race vit en nous."
>
> Cette idée me devint aussitôt sensible, et, comme si les murs de la salle se fussent ouverts sur des perspectives infinies, il me semblait voir

une chaîne non interrompue d'hommes et de femmes en qui j'étais et qui étaient moi-même; les costumes de tous les peuples, les images de tous les pays apparaissaient distinctement à la fois, comme si mes facultés d'attention s'étaient multipliées sans se confondre, par un phénomène d'espace analogue à celui du temps qui concentre un siècle d'action dans une minute de rêve.[9]

If we seek to characterize this passage, we need to note the presence of direct style (the exchange of remarks), the narration set in the first person, the presence of abstract terminology, certain comparisons and figures, etc. All these features derive from the verbal aspect of the text. If we want to study its syntactic aspect, we must inquire into the nature of the relation established between the different sentences. More precisely, the second part (narration) repeats the first (dialogue), but with an important difference: one passes from the abstract to the concrete. Finally, all the themes of the text belong to the semantic aspect, the principal theme being the relation between matter and spirit ("cette idée me devint aussitôt sensible").

Distinguishing these different aspects of the text amounts in no way to re-establishing the ancient dichotomy between form and content, or its recent avatar, *signifiant* and *signifié*. Each of these aspects is *signifiant* and *signifié* at the same time; each is integrated in a formal organization and each carries a meaning. So when Nerval writes "Il me semblait voir" ("I seemed to see . . .") or "comme si mes facultés" ("as if my faculties . . ."), he is not using a verbal device (modalization) which is the "form" for some kind of thematic content. The occurrence of this device here has a precise meaning; because of the modalization, the narrator can no longer be held responsible for the truth of his words; by the same token, the fundamental requirement of the fantastic *genre* is fulfilled, namely to set up in the reader's mind a hesitancy between the real and the illusory, the true and the imaginary. On the other hand, the presence of a theme like that of the relation between mind and body is in no way a sign of the direct and "informal" intervention of the author; one can demonstrate the existence of a formal distribution of themes into sets; the mind/body relationship is one of the constituents of a set which we could call "themes of perception."[10]

The verbal aspect is a larger category than that of style; it includes, in addition, everything which concerns "point of view" (or "vision"). The points of view may be grasped—only at times, not always—through stylistic properties. Thus, in this extract, narration in the first person and ambiguity in the point of view of the narrator have an immediate verbal reality. But one can equally characterize point of view by the degree to which the narrator penetrates the mind of the character, which degree of penetration cannot be conveyed by any stylistic process.

Once we have specified the place of style in the structure of the text, we must try to describe the inventory of categories which both presuppose and derive from any particular text. But to give a truly intelligible presentation of the different styles, one would need an elaborated model of the functioning of discourse, something which is not presently available. Thus I must be content with an ordered but rapid enumeration, which aims at only outlining the variety of problems posed by stylistics, and makes no pretentions to completeness. To introduce some kind of order, I shall use certain linguistic categories which seem applicable to the study of discourse; firstly, the opposition *utterance* (*énoncé*, thing said) vs. *speech act* (the act of uttering, *énonciation*); secondly, the tripartite division verbal-syntactic-semantic; and finally, the divisions which establish the dimensions of units: distinctive phonetic or semantic features up to the whole statement.

### CATEGORIES OF THE UTTERANCE

1) The phonetic or graphic characteristics of the utterance can be studied either within the limits of the morpheme or within the framework of the sentence or of the whole statement. We assume that the arrays of the distribution of phonemes or distinctive features are finite in number and lend themselves to typological study. Werner Winter has shown that one could characterize a text by the presence of (phonetic) words of one or more syllables.[11] At the level of the sentence, we can study rhythm and melody. The disposition of the text on the page is related to the same set of facts.

2) The study of style at the level of syntax will also take different forms according to whether one works within or beyond the limits of the sentence. Within the sentence one can follow the procedure advocated by Richard Ohmann,[12] in which the "portrait" of the sentence is constituted by its transformational history. Beyond the sentence, one can postulate the existence of three kinds of relations: logical (of implication, inclusion, etc.); temporal (of succession, in the manner in which the sentences of a logbook are followed); and "spatial," to the extent that relations of symmetry and contrast tie phrases together and thereby designate a textual space. The two paragraphs quoted from *Aurélia* have between them a relation of the spatial and logical type.

3) At the semantic level, the state of things is less clear. Let us propose three categories, none of which is ever present in a pure state nor, at the same time, ever completely absent. The lexicon is progressively penetrated by them.

a) *Representativeness*: At one extreme, we find sentences which stand alone as maxims, as eternal verities. In the extract from Nerval, the last proposition, "celui du temps qui concentre un siècle d'action dans une minute de rêve" is almost a maxim, without, however, having its form. At the other extreme are referential expressions evoking a material object ("les murs de la salle").

b) *"Figuredness"*: Since a figure is nothing more than the capacity of language to be perceived in itself, every expression is (virtually) a figure. The syntactic figures, like asyndeton, should be traceable in the transformational history of sentences. The semantic figures can be more or less intense ("une chaîne d'hommes," "les murs de la salle . . . ouverts," "nous vivons dans notre race," etc.). Anomalies of different sorts are only one means among others for rendering language perceptible.

c) *Connotation:* I call "connotative" any discourse which refers not only to its immediate object but also to a preceding discourse; thus, finally, every discourse is connotative (if it weren't, no one would understand it). Particular cases have been studied: for example, the parody with hidden polemic (by Tynianov[13]); what Bally[14] called the effect of evocation by milieu: here the discourse evoked is not a particular text but a series of texts, a discourse diffused and fragmented; the interpenetration of the words of the narrator and that of the character (frequent in Dostoevsky, as Bakhtin and Voloshinov have shown[15]).

### CATEGORIES OF THE SPEECH ACT

1) The description of a character's speech can be accomplished by reported discourse: *style direct, style indirect,* and *indirect libre* ("direct," "indirect," "indirect free"). This description customarily occupies an entire clause.[16]

2) The spatio-temporal situation of the protagonists in discourse is indicated most often (but not inevitably) by a morpheme: personal, demonstrative, and possessive pronouns, adverbs, endings of verbs and nouns. One can characterize a discourse marked by the presence of such elements as "personal," using the word in the sense which Benveniste has given it.[17]

3) The attitude of the speaker towards this discourse and/or its object may be grasped through semes (distinctive semantic features). Many cases may be distinguished:

a) The emotive style, categorized by linguists from Bally to Stankiewicz,[18] which is seen as the relation between speaker and object of discourse (its reference, which is not an extralinguistic category, but what the discourse evokes), the accent falling on the former;

b) the evaluative style, which also calls attention to the relation between speaker and object of discourse, with the accent now falling on the latter;

c) the modalizing style, which involves the speaker's appraisal of the truth value of the relation between the discourse and its object (context). We have seen examples of this in the text from Nerval: "il me semblait," "comme si," etc.

Many problems about this enumeration remain open, as much about each particular style as about the procedure as a whole. Let us mention only one. At what moment can one characterize a discourse as having a style which is, let us say, "emotive" or "personal"? Does the presence of a single "I" or of a single "ah" suffice? Can one rely on qualitative criteria as well as quantitative?

Every utterance will thus have a multitude of stylistic characteristics. But only a part of them will normally be "actualized." In other words, the structural description of a particular text will not consider a property stylistic if it cannot show that this property is found in relationship with others, at other levels, or, to put it in other terms, that it is meaningful.

Let us take another example, this time from William Beckford's *Vathek*. This text is told in the third person, by an impersonal narrator, whose relation to what he reports is continuously ambiguous. As he recounts, one after another, the events of the plot, his judgments intrude in the form of evaluative adjectives and adverbs. But these judgments—praise and blame— do not seem to issue from the same person. Thus in one place one reads "Le Calife, inspiré par les démons, se résolut au sacrifice *affreux*" ("The Calif, inspired by demons, nerved himself to this frightful sacrifice"), "il voyait que cela le conduirait à ses *abominables* fins" ("he saw that that would lead him to his abominable ends"); "Vathek l'examina avec une *perfide* avidité" ("Vathek examined it with perfidious avidity"); "On soupa gaiement sur la plateforme, encore noircie de *l'affreux* sacrifice" ("They ate gaily on the platform, still dark from the frightful sacrifice").

We conclude that the narrator, as a humane man, condemns the acts of his characters. But on the same pages we also read other kinds of evaluation. Thus when the negresses, the faithful slaves of Vathek, strangle his rescuers, they are characterized as "*aimables* personnes" ("loveable persons"); after having received a message from Eblis, Vathek "se laissa aller à la joie que lui inspiraient de si *bonnes* nouvelles, et but de nouveau" ("permitted himself the joy which such good news inspired in him, and drank anew"); after Carathis, mother of Vathek, has tortured her guests, strewing them with snakes and scorpions, we are told that "cette *bonne* Princesse avait en horreur l'oisiveté" ("this good princess had a horror of sloth"); or after a particularly revolting speech, "Lorsque Carathis eut finis ce *beau* discours . . ." ("When Carathis had finished this fine speech . . ."). The two positions are sometimes found squeezed into the same sentence: "Heureusement pour ces *misérables* créatures Carathis vint mettre le hola à une scène si *indé-cente*" ("Luckily for these miserable creatures, Carathis came to put a halt to so indecent a scene"): is it really the same person who characterizes the victims of Vathek as "misérables créatures" and yet their punishment as a "scène indécente"?

This is not, of course, an inconsistency, an "error" of Beckford's (as those who argue for "uniqueness in point of view" would suppose). These contradictory moral judgments cancel each other, indeed deride each other. We join the narrator in a world "beyond good and evil."

The relevance of this style-feature will be clear once it is related to another element in the text, for example, a thematic motif. This argument can be illustrated by one of the "nested" stories in the *Episodes* (a posthumous addition to *Vathek*). Homaiouna, a magician and the incarnation of virtue, decides to go among men to make them happy. But her attempts fail, one after another. A woman is imprisoned by her rival, a favorite of the sultan, and risks being sold to a slave-merchant. Homaiouna frees her; but her first action after being freed is to poison her rival. Has Homaiouna succeeded in doing good? Men seem too imperfect for "good" to make any sense in their world! Or as Homaiouna herself says: "on ne savait pas, lorsqu'on comptait faire ce bien, si ce n'était pas un mal" ("one didn't know, when one undertook some good action, whether it wasn't in fact an evil one"). Another time, she prepares to punish a husband who is too severe and too jealous of his wife. To assure herself that she is right, she touches the woman with a magic wand which induces absolute sincerity. The suspicions of the husband are found to be not only justified but even inadequate to the reality. Consequence: another death and another problem for Homaiouna. How to do good in a world full of such misleading appearances?

Thus, thematics and stylistics confirm each other, each being at once *signifiant* and *signifié* of the other; it is here that research into coherence finds its legitimate task. More generally, we see that there is no point in separating a "literary stylistics" from a "linguistic stylistics": one is only the application of the other.

This effort at a systematization of studies within the field of stylistics would have no value if it were to leave the impression of having attained a definitive result. And, since we have evoked Rémy de Gourmont to justify the direction chosen, let us borrow, to conclude, another sentence from the same work: "When one has attained the age of reason, it is as absurd to seek for the truth—and to find it—as it is to put one's shoes in the fireplace on Christmas Eve."[19]

## NOTES

1. "Il n'y a pas d'un côté la science, de l'autre, la littérature; il y a des cerveaux qui fonctionnent bien et des cerveaux qui fonctionnent mal. . . ."

2. Cleanth Brooks, *The Well-Wrought Urn* (New York, 1947); Wolfgang Kayser, *Das sprachliche Kunstwerk* (Bern, 1959); Viktor Vinogradov, *Stilistika. Teorija poeticheskoj rechi. Poetika* (Moscow, 1963).

3. Leo Spitzer, *Stilstudien* (Munich, 1961, second edition); Pierre Guiraud, *La Stylistique* (Paris, 1954).

4. Jan Mukařovsky, "Standard Language and Poetic Language," in *A Prague School Reader on Esthetics, Literary Structure, and Style* (Washington, 1964), 17-30.

5. Jean Cohen, *Structure du langage poétique* (Paris, 1966).

6. Samuel Levin, "Deviation—Statistical and Determinate—in Poetic Language," *Lingua*, XII (1963), 276-90; and "Internal and External Deviation in Poetry," *Word*, XXI (1965), 225-37.

7. Michael Riffaterre, "Stylistic Context," *Word*, XVI (1960), 207-18.

8. Juri Tynianov, "De l'évolution littéraire," in *Théorie de la littérature*, ed. by Tzvetan Todorov (Paris, 1965), 120-37.

9.
> "What!" I cried. "Do you mean the earth could die and we be hurled into oblivion?"
>
> "Oblivion," he answered, "does not exist in the sense it is understood, but the earth itself is a material body whose soul is the sum of the souls it contains. Matter can no more perish than mind, but it can be modified according to good and evil. Our past and future are intimately connected. We live in our race and our race lives in us."
>
> This idea immediately became clear to me. The walls of the room seemed to open onto infinite perspectives and I saw an uninterrupted chain of men and women, in whom I was and who were myself: the costumes of every nation, visions of every country, all appeared to me distinctly at the same time, as if my faculties of observation had been multiplied—and yet not muddled—by a phenomenon of space comparable to that of time, whereby a century of action is concentrated in a minute of dream.

Translation by Geoffrey Wagner, *Selected Writings of Gérard de Nerval* (New York, 1957), pp. 125-26.

10. See my *Introduction à la littérature fantastique* (Paris, 1970).

11. Werner Winter, "Styles as Dialects," in *Proceedings of the Ninth International Congress of Linguists* (Hague, 1964), 324-30.

12. Richard Ohmann, "Generative Grammar and the Concept of Literary Style," *Word*, XX (1964), 423-39.

13. Juri Tynianov, "Dostojevskij und Gogol (zur Theorie der Parodie)," in Jurij Striedter (ed.), *Texte der Russischen Formalisten* (Munich, 1969), 300-372.

14. Charles Bally, *Traité de stylistique française* (Paris, 1951).

15. M. M. Bakhtin, *Problemy Poetiki Dostojevskogo* (Moscow, 1963), and V.N. Voloshinov, *Marksizm i filsofija jazyka* (Leningrad, 1929); both reprinted in *Michigan Slavic Materials* 2 (Ann Arbor, 1963).

16. See my "Les Registres de la parole," *Journal de Psychologie*, III (1967), 265-78.

17. E. Benveniste, *Problèmes de linguistique générale* (Paris, 1966).

18. E. Stankiewicz, "Problems of Emotive Language," in *Approaches to Semiotics*, ed. by Th. A. Sebeok (Hague, 1964).

19. "Il est aussi absurde de chercher la vérité—et de la trouver—quand on a atteint l'âge de raison, que de mettre ses souliers dans le cheminée, la Nuit de Nöel."

# DISCUSSION OF TODOROV'S PAPER

Todorov's rejection of coherence as a definition of style was questioned. It was pointed out that no matter how haphazard an arrangement of sentences a text may be, one can always treat it as an organism, a unity, and can attribute some law of composition to it, though it is possible to agree with Todorov that finding an organic law or stylistic criterion or touchstone to cover all texts may be difficult. But as soon as one argues, as Todorov did, for relations of isomorphism, convergence or correlation between stylistic and thematic *données*, one is introducing something like a principle of coherence, a mutual reinforcement of features at different levels. That is implicit in observations like Todorov's that stylistic and thematic elements are at once *signifiant* and *signifié* of each other. The only thing that remains unpredictable—and which may be separated from stylistics—is the means by which this is done, that is, the realization of the coherence. Todorov replied that it seemed impossible to define style as coherence at the theoretic level, that coherence is only relevant at the level of particular text, that is, in applied stylistics, whether the coherence is one of repetition, isomorphism, contrast, or whatever. This is what he tried to show in his analysis of *Vathek*; it is only in the study of specific texts that the principle of internal relations emerges, not in theoretical discussions about style.

In the same connection, it was pointed out to Todorov that medieval texts reveal the existence of *registers*, of pre-established—one might even say prefabricated—coherence at the level of the expressive whole, a coherence which may be unpredictable in individual texts, but which is not totally unpredictable for the whole class. Might one not say the same thing about modern texts to a certain extent? Isn't that what is implied by terms like "coherence" and "subcode"? Doesn't there pre-exist a sort of inchoate coherence for many literary works? Todorov said that he preferred the term "genre" to "register" to designate such complex wholes. A genre is a norm consisting of a set of rules located at different levels. For example, the journalistic genre has its own rules, a selection or subcode taken from the language as a whole—one must be succinct, put the most important points first, avoid the lyric and the personal, etc. For him "genre" was the better term, provided one did not take it in its older sense; it should refer, rather, to those rules at different levels—theme, style, composition, and so on— which constitute a well-articulated set. Another participant noted that it might be useful to use the term "coherence" for works and "system" for style in general.

The next subject of discussion was that of deviance as a feature of style. It was agreed that present conceptions of norm were neither rational nor feasible for the reason mentioned by Todorov—namely that it was not at all clear how the norm was established. But might it not be possible to use (as a frame of reference at least) not statistics but the grammar of the language, an entity which exists, obviously, for different reasons than to account for deviation? If we assume that a grammar is designed to generate just the grammatical sentences of a language, then one can explain the fact of deviation by comparing the sentence containing the suspected deviation with the grammar, establishing the fact that the sentence would not be an automatic consequence of the grammar. Would that not be a satisfactory explanation of the deviation? Of course, one might argue that this simply pushes the question of deciding between normal and deviant sentences from one place to another, for we would have to decide in advance, in the construction of the grammar, between which sentences are normal and which deviant, so as to be sure that the grammar generated just normal sentences. But a reasonable answer to that objection is that there are independent reasons for devising the grammar in such a way that its output is just the set of normal sentences; for example, the rules of the grammar would have to be enormously complicated to make deviant sentences. And in that case you would either generate great numbers of classes of deviant sentences, far more than you wanted, to retain the generality of the rules, or else you would have to make a very complex and *ad hoc* set of rules to generate the small number of deviant sentences occurring in an individual text. Obviously neither alternative is desirable. If one argues that it is the task of a grammar not merely to generate well-formed sentences but also to give a characterization of deviant ones, one can account for the latter simply by noting the fact that certain transformations are blocked in the generation.

Furthermore, the conclusion from Todorov's observation that the attempt to characterize deviance and coherence is not possible because we don't have the theoretical means to do so, that we should turn in other directions (for example, look for particular styles in texts), is one to be avoided. If our means are inadequate to explain things we feel are important, we shouldn't simply give up and do something else. Rather we should build up our techniques so that we can account for things like deviance, because their reality and importance are greater than the things we can already comfortably do. Todorov acknowledged the possibility of using the grammar as the norm against which sentences may be recognized as deviant. He said that what he meant by rejecting the concept was that he did not believe it to be completely adequate to stylistic analysis. For example, as Halliday's paper shows, many linguistic elements which are not deviations are a part of style; on the other hand, there are many deviations in texts which are not stylistically interesting. What Todorov wished to suggest is that reliance on deviation is not the best possible strategy, not that it is an out-and-out error in method. The stylistician's task is to recognize that there are many choices which the author must exercise among the possibilities the language affords him, and that his text can best be described in terms of those choices.

Another participant who had struggled with the concept of deviance argued (as he had done in print) that the norm should be recognized as contextually related to the text, even though there was the danger of burying all the difficulties under the word "context." The norm must be somehow, functionally or socially, related to the text; we get an impression of a text by comparing it with something else. If the theory of low, middle, and high styles was successful for so many centuries, it must have been because it was significant to compare literary texts with such norms; this must have been the way in which literature, like society, was organized. As for the term "deviance" itself, one must recognize two types—quantitative, i.e., that something is deviant in the sense of being in a statistically unusual distribution, and qualitative, i.e., that something is deviant because it cannot be generated by the normal rules of the language. Todorov responded by arguing that if we define the norm as contextual (as, for example, Riffaterre does), we do not cover all the possible stylistic effects. There are some cases when the norm is not given in the context. Further, we do not always perceive the particular stylistic feature as a contrast. For instance, when we read the Beckford passage which appears in Todorov's paper we do not perceive as something extraordinary and deviant the fact that there are many evaluations or that there is direct discourse or that the narrative is in the third person. Specifying the person of a narrative is obviously important in a full stylistic description, but in what sense is it deviant? The participant answered that it is not deviant but rather part of the norm. For example, the first person would be normal for letter-writers; verbal person in this use is not a style-marker, that is, it is not a characteristic of the individual, but rather of the whole class of letter-writers.

As for the ancient trichotomy of high, middle, and low styles, as, for example, manifested in Virgil's *Aeneid, Georgics,* and *Bucolics,* it was suggested that these corresponded to three sociological statuses, and Todorov was asked whether one should retain sociological implications in modern stylistics as well. (But another participant denied that there existed such sociological implication in Virgil's work, pointing out that the application of the trichotomy was only a medieval extrapolation, a *figuration* in the proper sense of the word, which, ancient rhetoric tells us, is to be understood in terms of effects or impressions on the reader, effects of *movere, docere,* and *directare.*) Todorov said that he would not like to accept such sociological implications. He said that he had mentioned the three classical styles only as examples. Obviously he would not accept the present relevance of such a trichotomy. Even during the Middle Ages the definition was cast in the form of constraints: a certain vocabulary was prescribed for high style but proscribed for low style, and so on. Therefore it was possible to deduce a viable set of styles, although—since these were complex in nature—they might better be called genres.

It was pointed out that Todorov's strict separation of structure and function gave rise to another problem: isn't it necessary to study the relation between structure and, if not function, at least institution? The forms of speech correspond to institutions; the nature of the correspondence may be difficult, but one prejudges the case if he says that the institution cannot coincide with structure or that the coincidence is not pertinent. Among the variety of possible styles, there are some which have a simple relation to an institution—as, for example, the journalistic style has to the institution of the press. Literary style has a complex relation to the institution of literature from the moment that it denies that institution. Thus there are styles which are simply institutional (kinds of "writing" or *écriture*) and those which are *demoniac* in relation to their institution. This does not mean to say that the relation between style and institution is self-obvious, say "expressive" (in the sociological sense of the term), but that though complex, it can be studied. Further, one can often make predictions about language use if certain variables, including sociological ones, are known. We needn't talk about isomorphism, but certainly the concept of (sociolinguistic) register is relevant. Another participant noted that the "demoniac" could itself become institutional; for example, in a piece by Kafka, a tiger enters a temple and overturns a sacrificial bowl; after this happens several days running, the votaries come to accept it as an institution.

About his distinction among verbal, semantic, and syntactic components of a text, Todorov was asked why he included narrative point of view, with style, under the rubric "verbal." Todorov replied that he did so because both point of view (*"vision"* in recent French criticism) and style have to do with the manner of presenting a text; they are not features of composition or of theme but of presentation of theme. Linguistically, this opposition corresponds to that between *thing-uttered* (*énoncé*) and the *act of uttering* (*énonciation*). Point of view is the relation between the speaker and his utterance; speaker and utterance are more closely related to each other than either is to compositional devices or thematic structure.

Todorov was asked to explain the term "textual space," which he used in his discussion of intersentence relations. He responded by recalling that in the process of analyzing texts, he often observed that there seemed to be three kinds of relations. One was purely logical, for example, where one element of the discourse is to be interpreted as the cause or the effect of another. A second is temporal, where events simply succeed each other. The third he called "spatial" (perhaps without complete justification) because it entailed relations like similarity, contrast, gradation, antithesis, and so on; the sentences seem to have a relationship which is spatial or geometrical. This is implicit in the terms we use, which are spatial metaphors—"parallelism" for example. The spatial is the common mode of relating sentences in poetry, which often contains neither of the other two modes, temporal or logical. Rhyme and rhythm seem to be devices of spatial relation between sequences. It was observed that everyone could agree that there are two different levels, a linguistic stylistics and a literary stylistics, one analyzing forms and the other analyzing themes, but that it was unnecessary to equate these with the difference between code and message. In *both* cases—language and literature—there are both code and message; there is a linguistic code and a linguistic message, and a literary code and a literary message. Todorov replied that he did not accept the distinction; on the contrary, he believed that they are two complementary aspects of one and the same distinction, and that it is not necessary to oppose a stylistics of language and one of literature. There exists only a theoretical stylistics, which is an extension of linguistics and whose categories one can apply to particular texts in literature, journalism, science, or whatever.

The question was raised whether there were not two levels of the message—a linguistic one and a literary one—whose *signifiés* in turn became the signs of literature. For example, the cap of Charles Bovary could be seen as a sign within a code which corresponds to the novel *Madame Bovary*. Todorov agreed completely, noting that this formulation implies a giving up of the distinction between literary and linguistic stylistics; he reiterated his division into verbal, syntactic, and semantic aspects, reserving for the latter two all that is "literary," and for the first all that is "stylistic."

Concerning the discussion of *Vathek* it was noted that its French was written by an Englishman in England, not in Lausanne, so that there is a kind of ironic distance between content and expression which might be likened to that implicit in the notion "beyond good and evil." Todorov concurred, noting that there were correspondences to the ironic tales of Voltaire, an irony which takes a multiple form.

# 2
## STYLISTICS AND RELATED DISCIPLINES

# ON THE PLACE OF STYLE
# IN SOME LINGUISTIC THEORIES

## NILS ERIK ENKVIST

I DO NOT KNOW how many people would object to labelling style as a systemic variation of language. Fewer people, I presume, would quarrel with the statement that style is one type of systematic linguistic variation.

Simple and weak as such a statement may seem, it still brings with it a number of important corollaries. As a category of systematic linguistic variation, style is, and must be, a focus of linguistic investigation (which is of course not to say that everybody else except the linguist should keep out). And, to begin with, all students of linguistic variation must face two tasks: they must describe the variant language, either as an independent system in its own right or as a subsystem derivable by explicit rules from some known system; and they must make clear by whom, when, and where this particular variant is, or was, used.[1] The determination of these parameters of linguistic variance involves sociolinguistic considerations which cannot be bypassed in any full study of language varieties.

Further, as a full theory of language should carry the onus of accounting for different types of linguistic variation—regional dialects, social dialects, styles, registers, idiolects—and distinguish systematic, structurally significant variation from non-significant or random variation within each of these types, it can hardly avoid offering strategies on the hierarchization of language varieties. We should have at our disposal principles enabling us to decide which types and instances of variation are subordinate to others; in other words, we should know which systems are systems and which are subsystems. I have sometimes tried to illustrate the issue by comparing language to the contents of a huge container or tank, out of which texts emerge through a succession of filters. These filters impose constraints on the output and thus stand for rules. Some filters are grammatical: they pass grammatically well-formed structures while catching those not well formed. Others are dialectal, and so forth. In terms of such a model, the question of hierarchies can be translated into the selection and ordering of filters. In what order do the filters go? Are there special style filters, which perhaps even cluster together into a special stylistic section of the filter system? Or are the stylistic filters sandwiched between filters of other types—grammatical, dialectal, idiolectal, and the like? Or should style rather be regarded as a master programme governing the selection and ordering of filters, but having relatively few, or even no, filters of its own? Is a given style thus a subsystem of a language derivable from that language with the aid of a limited number of explicit processes: the frequency with which certain rules are used, and—for deviant texts—omission or suspension of rules, changes in the applicability (structural index) of rules, alterations in the structural changes indicated by rules, reordering of rules, and perhaps addition of new rules? If so, those describing styles are likely to profit from the recent studies in the methodology of historical syntax,[2] where a conceptual apparatus is emerging for the description of diachronic rule changes. Similar methods may well be adaptable to the comparison of related but different sets of rules in the description of stylistic variation.

Such crucial questions could be multiplied and rephrased. To what extent do their answers perhaps vary from one society and one language to the next? In other words: if linguistic varieties form a hierarchy, is there a universal pattern of such a hierarchy which can be stated within a general theory of language, or are these matters bound to individual languages and dialects to the extent that generalizations become meaningless or wrong?

These questions are likely to embarrass different people in very different degrees. Now linguistics is, proudly or notoriously, a theory-oriented discipline. In the manner of any scientist, the linguist is constantly looking for general, maximally powerful statements. He is hunting for the kind of underlying structures that explain features in whole dialects and languages, or even for linguistic universals that characterize all languages. This search for powerful statements is apt to abstract the linguist away from surface details in individual texts, and thus turns into an irritant in the relations between him and his literary colleagues. But the need for abstraction is not, as some irritated people tend to think, a new-fangled idea thought up by a few cliques of modern linguists. On the contrary, the principle has been the same throughout the history of language study. An excellent way of approaching the history of linguistics is to see where such underlying categories were sought from Plato to the present day. Yet generalizations such as the following are, at best, indications of major trends with many exceptions: as today, communication gaps have usually existed, for instance between avant-garde scholarship and classroom practice.

For many centuries, the quest resembled a pendulum swinging from philosophy and logic to the categories of Latin grammar, and back again. The early Greeks based grammar squarely on philosophy, whereas the later Greeks and the Romans as well as their mediaeval followers tended to rely more on formal distinctions on the surface of language. The scholastics and *modistae* went back to logic; the main currents of the Renaissance emphasized the forms of Latin. Scaliger, Sanctius, Descartes and the Port-Royalists have been said to mark another return to mentalism. When the emphasis came to lie on the history of languages, underlying structures were often defined with the aid of older, attested or reconstructed stages of language—witness for instance all the dialect studies grouping Modern English sounds under Old or Middle English ones. More recently, linguists have learned to group the bewildering variety of surface signals into functional units such as phonemes and morphemes: all features that do the same job belong in the same class. And today, many linguists are searching for deep semantic representations out of which surface structures can be derived through strict, explicit, and maximally economical rules. But, however different all these endeavours may seem, they have one common denominator: the search for underlying structures. What makes them different is the orientation of the search toward logic, the surface of Latin, linguistic history, function, or deep semantics.

In comparison and contrast, the philologist and the literary critic seem much more data-oriented and text-oriented. Both are, by definition, people with their noses in a text: the philologist's job is to study the language, content, and textual readings of a limited body of text in an old or otherwise strange language, whereas the literary critic's business is to correlate critical responses with specific stimuli in a text or corpus of texts. Thus the interests of philologists and literary critics readily tend to become particular rather than general; more accurately, their interest in the general is usually subordinate to, or a consequence of, their preoccupation with the particular. In the literary sphere, we have to go to the theorists to find an interest in abstraction comparable to that of the linguist.

I have spent a few minutes on these matters to sketch the background of today's situation. In brief, style and register are types of linguistic variation that linguists have tended to neglect. They have spent a great deal of time and effort on dialects, and the study of social strata in communities such as New York City has attracted a great deal of recent interest. Linguistic fieldwork has also compelled the field-worker to detailed observations of individual differences and of paralinguistic features, if only to rule them out as non-significant for his particular purpose and as unworthy of further, systematic analysis. But why has stylistic variation so often, and for so long, played the part of a linguistic Cinderella?

Apparently the answer should be sought in several circumstances rather than in just one. First of all, the very concept of "style" is notoriously slippery and difficult to codify into concrete terms that allow operational study. Then, stylistics leads the linguist into fields which he hesitates to enter. If style is defined as the aesthetic or emotive area of language, or even as a link between text and situation, the linguist will at once deplore the lack of firm and universally acceptable classifications of emotions, aesthetic responses or communication situations, feeling he has little or nothing to build on. Even in statistics, a linguist is venturing into not very congenial fields. And when studying written styles of languages with extensive cultural traditions, the linguist must cross another dangerous frontier—that between linguistics and literature—where he is exposed to barrages as well as to sniping. Finally, the so-called "organic" view of style—the insistence on the inseparable unity of content or meaning and surface form—may also have deterred linguists from the investigation of style. As I said, the linguist is looking for underlying patterns, and he may well be discouraged when the die-hard organicist tells him that the truth lies on the surface and that abstraction merely removes him from it.

## II

One way of approaching the question of the place of style in linguistic theory is simply to look at today's major linguistic theories and see what implications they possess for the study of style. The issue is somewhat confused by the fact that different people mean different things by the label "style." One man's style may be another man's register, and even a third man's poison. Nor does it follow that those linguistic theories that at first sight seem to ignore style are irrelevant to stylistics. All the same, if such a survey were attempted of some major linguistic movements—say, traditional grammar, structuralist-behaviourist linguistics, transformational linguistics, and British systems linguistics—I suppose its summary might read roughly as follows:

Traditional grammar was amorphous and flexible enough to swallow stylistic considerations practically *ad libitum*. In fact many of the rules of our old normative school grammars were stylistic rather than anything else: they advocated a selection of usage that was suitable for a definite set of situations and contexts. They were handbooks of approved linguistic manners, and thus of style. And as the border between grammar and rhetoric was left open, stylistic statements could seep in freely.

Structuralist grammars of the behaviourist variety were usually preoccupied with the shallow end of the linguistic pool, with phonemes, morphemes, morphological patterns, and the like. Their taxonomies of syntactic patterns were never exhaustive. Still, the emphasis on immanent categories emerging out of a text and on field work naturally made the structuralist at least conscious of the existence of styles. Even if the word "style" itself is conspicuously absent from Bloomfield's classic *Language*, many American structuralists have spoken and written about it. Zellig Harris, to take one prominent example, found the key to style in distribution: in single utterances or even discourses, usage tends to be consistent so that different styles do not co-occur.[3] And it is to Bernard Bloch that we owe the operationally concrete, fruitful, and suggestive definition of the style of a discourse as

> the message carried by the frequency distributions and transitional probabilities of its linguistic features, especially as they differ from those of the same features in the language as a whole.[4]

Kenneth Pike's interest in language as a subvariety of human behaviour made him provide a behaviourist frame for all linguistic patterns, including what I call style. Martin Joos's *Five Clocks*[5] still makes suggestive reading, and Archibald Hill is another of those who have written widely and incisively about linguistic approaches to literature. Still, in behaviorist structuralism, the study of style was on the whole a marginal, rather than a central, pursuit: style was not part of the hard core of theory.

In transformational linguistics, the basic theory itself has also avoided explicit discussions of style. Some transformationalists who dismiss instances of variation as stylistic seem to do so to imply that it is somebody else's job, not theirs, to discuss them in greater detail. Nor have statistical considerations, which have been so beneficial to stylistics, been accommodated into the core of transformational theory. It must, however, be emphasized at once that this does not mean that transformation grammar is irrelevant to stylistics. On the contrary: as Richard Ohmann and others have shown, it can be used to great advantage in stylolinguistic description, and it has a number of potentialities that we have hardly begun to exploit. Thus transformation grammar is a model which may ultimately yield a full and ordered inventory of the vastly complicated sequence of choices at the command of anybody who wishes to say something. If style is choice, then transformation grammar is, I take it, the grammatical model that so far most fully maps out the system and range of this choice. By giving substance to features that do not actually appear on the surface of a text, transformation grammar should be capable of analysing a figure such as ellipsis, for example, with increased rigour. And the semantic matrices of recent transformation grammar may contribute to the definition and study of metaphor, which has so far vexed many linguists. In fact, I am tempted to suggest that one of the arguments in favour of transformation grammar is its applicability to the study of a number of stylistic problems, even if it was designed for purposes other than the study of linguistic variation. I should perhaps also add that it is against the background of generative-transformational linguistics that my model of language as a tank plus a succession of filters assumes its full significance.

In British linguistics there has been a laudable concern with building style into linguistic theory, as we might expect of a school that acknowledges J. R. Firth as its stimulus. Terms such as "register" and "field," "mode" and "tenor of discourse" have given increasing precision to British discussion. Recent British work—notably Halliday's papers on transitivity and theme[6]—contains a number of concrete points very useful to the analyst of styles.

## III

Still, such a mechanical survey of what linguistic theorists do with or make of style is not likely to solve all the problems of those who wish to work with texts and not with theory. It may well be more relevant to try to find out how some different schools of linguists have answered some concrete problems that beset the analyst of styles.

To begin with, a student of style may well wish to rephrase our questions concerning the place of style in language in more style-centred terms. Is style a separate hierarchic level of language, implying that stylistics is the linguistics of this particular level and free to do whatever it likes as long as it does not unduly upset its neighbouring levels? Does stylistics perhaps rather consist of a set of separate compartments, one at each level of language? Or is it an autonomous discipline using linguistics as an ancillary, as a servant who may be chastised at will? These questions, of course, rephrase the questions I put in terms of filters a while ago. And all three views have had their advocates. Among those who have placed stylistics at a level of its own is Professor Galperin.[7] Among those who have found stylistic compartments at all levels of language is Professor Chatman, at least while operating with concepts such as phonostylistics, morphostylistics, and syntactostylistics.[8] In such frames, stylistics becomes a kind of "shadow linguistics" which, like a shadow cabinet, has its own ministers for every department. And if we reverse the roles of government and opposition, turn stylistics into the official government and linguistics into a shadow administration, we approach an autonomous stylistics which uses linguistics if it must. Too often, the political analogy has been only too apt: like any opposition, linguists have been consulted only in direst need.

But even here I am talking in abstractions. To be more concrete, I shall briefly mention two topical and specific problems by way of examples. First, what help can the student of style get from linguistics when discussing texts with a deviant linguistic structure? Secondly, what help can linguists give to those wishing to analyse connected texts and pay attention to units larger than the sentence? I have chosen to phrase the problems from the point of view of the student of the style of a given text; the point of view could, of course, be shifted to that of the theoretician.

## IV

First, then, the Problem of Deviance, familiar to readers of linguistic publications as the Problem of A Grief Ago or He Danced His Did. To introduce one common version of the problem—namely, the one connected with poetic deviance—I shall quote Sol Saporta from the *Style in Language* Conference:

> Now, it is in theory pointless to assert that linguistic methods may be applied to poetry, once we have defined poetry as a subclass of language. However, in practice, linguists have by and large operated on precisely the opposite assumption, namely, that a grammatical description need not accommodate poetic messages. Indeed, it has usually been implicit in most grammars that the occurrence of a particular sequence in poetry alone is sufficient grounds for classifying it as "ungrammatical" or in some way marginal. The danger of circularity is obvious. How do you know this sequence is ungrammatical? Because it occurs only in poetry. How do you know this is poetry? Because where else could you find such an ungrammatical sequence?[9]

Saporta's phrasing was here influenced by his interest in defining poetry by linguistic means. The same problem is important in the study of all styles that are characterized by true deviance (as opposed to styles marked by the more or less frequent use of different, but non-deviant, patterns).

In behaviourist linguistics, the Problem of Deviance was somewhat painful because it cut close to a major nerve of the basic method. The principle was that a corpus or text should be described inductively, only in terms of the text itself. Importing categories from the outside was forbidden. Now if Dylan Thomas and Cummings are included in the corpus, their grammar —including *a grief ago* and *he danced his did*—becomes part of the description, and thus non-deviant. If, on the contrary, Cummings and Thomas are excluded from the corpus of normal, non-deviant English and dealt with in a separate grammar, this latter grammar runs a risk of becoming a thing in itself without an automatic, firmly definable contact with the grammar of non-deviant texts. But this runs counter to our intuition: phrases such as *a grief ago* and *he danced his did* are not effective because of their structure as such. Their effect lies precisely in our registration and analysis of their deviance, in our comparison of their structure with the structure of non-deviant phrases. In other words: they belong to a subsystem rather than to a system of English.

Comparison, then, is necessary if we are to describe the essence of deviant structures. I should like to add that comparison is always the essence of all study of style: the very concept and feel and texture of style arise through comparison of the structure of the text we are studying with the structures of other texts. This is so, irrespective of whether these other texts are explicitly listed, tacitly remembered, or fictive in the sense of having been generated in one's imagination.

Granted that comparison is the basis of all stylistic effects, our next questions are: in studying deviance, what should we compare with what, and how? The very definition of deviance, of course, hinges upon the operational definition of ordinary, normal, grammatical, well-formed language, or whatever label we wish to give it, and thus unrolls the well-known problem of grammaticality. In practice at least, countless grammarians have cut through this Gordian knot by defining their corpus by contextual or socio-linguistic methods, by studying—perhaps by majority vote—the acceptability of doubtful constructions,[10] or even by preferring to consult themselves and nobody else as final arbiters of right and wrong. A reference to one's own idiolect is a very effective way of avoiding arguments about usage! And as soon as we have a grammar we can also define deviance if we agree to analyse the deviant text, not in the immanent terms of its own structure but in such terms as allow detailed comparison with non-deviant language.

Transformation grammar is the grammatical model which has most elaborated the concept of grammaticality and well-formedness, and which thus throws most light on deviance as well. It has in fact become possible to recognize levels of grammaticality, and thus of deviance, by finding out at what depth of the generative process a given construction deviates from normal. It seems to me that this opportunity provides the student of stylistic deviance with new weapons, and the first hints at results do in fact appear promising. Here, too, we may proceed in two ways. Either we derive the deviant text from an already existing grammar of non-deviant language, noting what rules we have to change in the process of derivation, or we write a complete new grammar for the deviant text and then proceed to compare the deviant grammar with the normal—always assuming that the two grammars are sufficiently akin to permit such comparison. These questions have been discussed by Samuel R. Levin, J. R. Thorne, and others, and I need not here repeat the points they have made.[11] It is, however, worth noting that if grammatical deviance is a stylistic device, and if the deviant language is a subsystem of the non-deviant language, style is likely to turn into a master programme directing the choice and form of rules rather than into a separate set of rules in one specific place of the generative rule sequence.

Lest somebody equate grammatical deviance with the type of deviance that must always exist if one style is to be different from another, I must note a further distinction. Grammatical deviance—the sort that produces *a grief ago* and *he danced his did*—involves an actual tinkering with the normal system of rules. This tinkering can be explained in terms of rule omission or suspension, rule change, or rule addition; I said more about this in the first section of my paper. Stylostatistical deviance, on the other hand, involves using the stock of available non-deviant rules in specific ways—for instance, using one rule very often and another very rarely or never. The latter type of deviance is, I take it, a ubiquitous characteristic of all styles, whereas only some styles—such as certain types of poetry—make use of deviant grammar. To what extent definitions of poetic language can build on deviance is another matter, for—alas—all deviant language is not poetry, just as all poetry is not deviant grammatically.

v

The student of style wishing to describe deviant patterns will thus do well to consult a linguist. What about those who find stylistic features not merely within single sentences, but in the way in which sentences are strung together into larger units and into discourse? What help and comfort can they draw from today's linguistics?

To introduce what I shall call the Problem of Discourse, I shall start with a very extreme kind of example:

> Granny died last night. I shall have lunch with him tomorrow. But it is useful as a demonstration of Swift's tendency to irregularity and as further evidence of his leaning to redundancy, even inserting lists within lists. In such discussions all possible ways in which the United Kingdom might be able to help bring peace have been covered. . . .

Mumbo-jumbo? Yes and no. This little fragment consists of a random string of sentences, each of which is well formed in itself. Most grammarians would therefore pass on the responsibility for saying what is wrong with this sentence string to somebody else. Each sentence—most grammarians would say—is all right, and this is where the grammarian's responsibility ends. But whose job is it, then, to show why such texts are deviant? Who is best equipped for this task? I should suggest that part of the responsibility at least should rest with the student of style.

In fact, and from a somewhat different angle, students of style have been conscious of the Problem of Discourse. I shall quote again:

The area of stylistics is here defined as that of characteristics which cannot be fully illustrated in a single sentence, or in separate sentences without considering relations between them. The definition here given is based on the commonly accepted belief that there is an area of study which describes items within sentences, and which stops with the border of the sentence. Such an area can be called by the term linguistics; the larger area of language study which is not bound by the limits of the sentence is here called the area of stylistics.[12]

Criticism, whatever else it does, must interpret works of literature. Theory concerns itself in part with the question, "what things legitimately bear on critical interpretation?" But beyond a doubt, interpretation begins with sentences. Whatever complex apprehension the critic develops of the whole work, that understanding arrives mundanely, sentence by sentence. . . . It is at the level of sentences, I would argue, that the distinction between form and content comes clear, and that the intuition of style has its formal equivalent. . . . [The] proper analysis of styles waits on a satisfactory analysis of sentences. Matters of rhetoric, such as emphasis and order, also promise to come clearer as we better understand internal relations in sentences. . . .[13]

It seems to me that there is a genuine difference in emphasis, if not in basic views, between Professor Hill and Professor Ohmann. Indeed both quotations are open to discussion. Professor Hill's definition of stylistics as linguistics beyond the sentence needs a supplement against two types of counter-example. First, some matters of grammar, such as pronominal reference, require going beyond the sentence without being, at least to my mind, stylistic: *My brother is eight. He/she/it/goes to school every day.* The opposite type of counterexample consists of stylistic features which can be spotted within a single sentence, without further context. I once heard a brilliant tourist guide say roughly this:

Peter the Great's bold venture was entirely successful, and his magnificent city, whose main drag the Nevsky Prospekt you are now traversing, quickly realized Peter's ambitions of opening a window towards the West.

Here, the phrase *main drag* is conspicuous within its own sentence, like brown shoes with black tie.

Professor Ohmann's emphasis on the sentence as a style carrier, is, of course, absolutely correct: sentence structure is a basic feature of style, and the way in which sentences are joined into coherent discourse can ultimately be described in terms of features within sentences. Even pauses can be ascribed to one sentence or another. I continue to wonder, however, whether discoursal intersentence phenomena could not be approached as such from the start. It might indeed be useful to have an apparatus for the direct description of the way in which sentences are strung into larger units, so that we need not perform a full analysis of every sentence in our text and wait for the intersentence features to emerge out of this laborious process. My own inclination would therefore be to attempt a synthesis of Hill and Ohmann: a large number of stylistic features are ultimately describable in terms of sentences and the comparison of sentences, but many intersentence devices may also possess stylistic relevance and should be decribed as such at once.

Comparison of random sentence strings such as the one I quoted a moment ago with samples of coherent discourse suggests that intersentence coherence is connected with a wide range of features that can be analysed and described in linguistic terms. Such features might very tentatively be grouped into three main areas: topic, focus, and linkage. Under *topic* I should put features pertaining to the main subject of the discoursal unit, the cohesion of the vocabulary, and the field of discourse. By *focussing* I mean the choice and marking of function for words and word groups in a clause and sentence; usually the most interesting focal devices are those marking certain items so that they come to occupy the centre of attention or are "foregrounded," to borrow a Prague School term. Focus is manifested, and positive focus marked, through a large number of phonological, syntactic, and lexical devices. Finally by *linkage* I mean the use of those phrases, conjunctions, pronouns, instances of concord and tense sequence, and the like, which form the surface layer of the formal marks linking each sentence to its discoursal environment.

If my argument is correct, in dealing with the Problem of Discourse, stylistics needs the support of an intersentence linguistics capable of dealing with features such as those I have roughly classified under topic, focus, and linkage. Actually the most recent linguistics has revealed considerable interest not only in focus and linkage but more generally in presuppositions, which include not only questions of truth value but also contextual and intersentence reference. There is little doubt that discourse linguistics is with us to stay.

This recent increase in interest in a "text linguistics" involving the study of units beyond the sentence can be traced to several origins. Traditional grammar, as well as traditional rhetoric, used to deal with phenomena such as definite and indefinite species, pronominal reference across sentence borders, conjunctions such as adversatives whose signalling of contrast or surprise only becomes clear through intersentence reference, and mood and tense sequence. In fact the frequent observation that grammar supposedly only dealt with phenomena within the sentence has been hallowed in the breach as well as in the observance. While many behaviourist grammarians were acutely conscious of the need to work with one problem at a time and therefore surrounded themselves with fences of their own making, the climate of behaviourist structuralism still fostered studies such as Kenneth Pike's *Language in Relation to a Unified Theory of the Structure of Human Behavior* and Zellig Harris's papers on discourse analysis, which applied the structuralist criteria of function and distribution to units beyond the sentence. Wilem Mathesius of Prague and his follower, Professor Firbas of Brno, have contributed to the study of functional sentence perspective, itself a valuable ingredient in discourse analysis. Transformationalists have noticed the need for intersentence features in the generation of even single sentences, and for dummies or formatives in order to distinguish between things mentioned and things new, and to embody other intersentence features needed on their tree diagrams. We may well get more of this if deep structure grows into a new deep semantics and if problems of presupposition go on increasing in topical interest. In Professor Halliday's recent work on transitivity and theme, for example, the discoursal component assumes its rightful place in an integrated discussion of English. This study is likely to open up a new area of style markers for qualitative and quantitative analysis, and it will bring linguistics closer to the study of literary structure, thematic development, and point of view, thus promoting contacts across one communication gap.[14] Then all that remains is the job of describing intersentence coherence in terms of sentence grammar. The second alternative involves building a special discourse grammar which explicitly describes or generates units beyond the sentence—say, paragraphs consisting of many sentences. The latter solution is, of course, enormously ambitious. It at once begs the question whether generating units larger than one sentence is the business of grammar proper or of some other area of linguistics such as semantics or a new linguistic logic or rhetoric. The latter might be free to use types of rules different from those of grammar, and its output would then become the input of the strictly grammatical part of the generative machine. The problem gains in poignancy at a time when deep structure is increasingly identified with, or changed into, a semantic generator related to logical predicate calculus.

The stylistic significance of the sentence as a unit, and of intersentence devices, is likely to vary from one style to the next. It is easy enough to recall styles in which the sentence division is unclear or ambiguous. If, for instance, a collector of folktales has recorded a text like

> . . . and then the girl entered her grandmother's house and then she saw her grandmother in bed with a shawl around her head and then

she went up to the old lady and then she said "Hello!" and then
Grandmother sat up and then . . .

we may be hard put to decide whether *and then* marks the beginnings of
new sentences, or whether the whole passage consists of one sentence made
up of many clauses joined through parataxis and polysyndeton. This poses
a caveat: in texts where the sentence division is ambiguous, obviously all
measurements of sentence attributes such as length or complexity will depend on the particular analysis adopted. In other words: there are texts in
which the most meaningful units of analysis are not necessarily sentences
at all, but either clauses or discourse units. I take it the paragraph is an example of a significant discourse unit in many types of writing. To repeat:
we shall thus do wisely to question the significance of the sentence as a
basis for all stylistic analysis.

VI

In sum, my argument runs roughly as follows. Though a full theory of language ought to deal explicitly with style, which is one type of systematic
linguistic variation, today's linguistic theories are hardly capable of offering
a full and explicit theory of style and a concomitant, uniform stylistic methodology to those practitioners who wish to analyse and describe the styles
of specific texts. On the other hand, an increasing number of linguistic
frames and methods are available for the study of a vast range of specific
types of stylistic problems. But, today, different problems are explained
differently within different linguistic theories. For example, the Problem of
Deviance seems, at the moment, best approachable through the degrees of
well-formedness of the transformationalists, whereas the Problem of Discourse has so far been more thoroughly dealt with by Professor Halliday's
systems of transitivity and, more particularly, of theme.

We should, of course, go on working toward and hoping for full linguistic
theories which also incorporate full theories of style. Meanwhile, however,
many tasks must be undertaken. And my final questions in a paper full of
questions are: Should we not define today's best approach to the linguistic
description of styles as an eclectic one? Should we not regard stylistics as a
subject free to pick and choose its linguistic methods from whatever quarters
seem most promising? Even if style as such occupies a very specific place in
the hierarchy of linguistic variation, we may legitimately go on regarding
stylistics as an autonomous, or at least eclectic, discipline until it is more
advantageous to do otherwise. But linguistics is an expanding science which
needs close watching, and all those interested in verbal styles will ignore
it at their own peril. One good setting for stylistic studies is an environment

where students of literature and style try to pinpoint stylistic stimuli in their texts, bring them to a friendly linguist, and succeed in eliciting new frames for their linguistic description if ready-made frames cannot be had at once. Whether the results are ultimately argued from stylistic effect to textual stimulus or from textual stimulus to stylistic effect is a matter of expediency, and need not reflect the order in which the work was conceived and carried out.

## NOTES

1. To what extent a linguist should be concerned with the effects of the use of language varieties is a question I shall here omit.

2. See Paul Kiparsky, "Linguistic Universals and Linguistic Change" in Emmon Bach and Robert T. Harms, eds., *Universals in Linguistic Theory* (New York, 1968).

3. *Structural Linguistics* (Chicago, 1960), pp. 10-11. On co-occurrence, see also Harris, "Co-occurrence and Transformation in Linguistic Structure," *Language*, 33 (1957), 283-340, also available in Jerry A. Fodor and Jerrold J. Katz, *The Structure of Language* (Englewood Cliffs, N.J., 1965), pp. 155-210.

4. In "Linguistic Structure and Linguistic Analysis," Archibald A. Hill, ed., *Report on the Fourth Annual Round Table Meeting on Linguistics and Language Teaching* (Washington, D.C., 1953), pp. 40 ff.

5. *The Five Clocks* was published by Indiana University Research Center in Anthropology, Folklore, and Linguistics, Publication 22, 1962, and also as Part V of the *International Journal of American Linguistics*, Vol. 28 No. 2.

6. In *Journal of Linguistics*, 3 (1967), 37-81 and 199-244; and 4 (1968), 179-216.

7. I. R. Galperin, "Javljaetsja li stilistika urovnem jazyka?" *Abstracts of Papers of the Xth Congress of Linguists* (Bucharest, 1967), p. 111, also in the Russian congress publication, *Problemy Jazykoznanija* (Moscow, 1967), pp. 198-202. Cf. also John Nist, "The Ontology of Style," *Linguistics*, 42 (1968), 44-47. The discussion is complicated by the fact that some linguists have used the word "level" to imply non-hierarchic levels or systems.

8. In "Stylistics: Quantitative and Qualitative," *Style*, 1 (1967), 29-43.

9. "The Application of Linguistics to the Study of Poetic Language," in *Style in Language*, ed. Thomas A. Sebeok (Cambridge, Mass., 1960), p. 84. See also Archibald A. Hill, "Some Further Thoughts on Grammaticality and Poetic Language," *Style*, 1 (1967), 81-91.

10. On acceptability, see Randolph Quirk and Jan Svartvik, *Investigating Linguistic Acceptability* (The Hague, 1966), and Dale Elliott, Stanley Legum, and Sandra Annear Thompson, "Syntactic Variation as Linguistic Data," in Robert I. Binnick *et al.*, eds., *Papers from the Fifth Regional Meeting of the Chicago Linguistic Society* (Chicago, 1969), pp. 52-59.

11. Samuel R. Levin, "Poetry and Grammaticalness," in Horace C. Lunt, ed., *Proceedings of the Ninth International Congress of Linguists* (The Hague, 1964), pp. 308-15, and J. P. Thorne, "Stylistics and Generative Grammars," *Journal of Linguistics*, 1 (1965), 49-59. Since this paper was written, there has

been a new round of debate on the Problem of Deviance. See William O. Hendricks, "Three Models for the Description of Poetry," *Journal of Linguistics*, 5 (1969), 1-22; Roger Fowler, "On the Interpretation of Nonsense Strings," *ibid*. 75-83; and J. P. Thorne, "Poetry, Stylistics and Imaginary Grammars," *ibid*. 147-50.

12. "A Program for the Definition of Literature," *University of Texas Studies in Literature and Language*, 1 (1959), here quoted from Hill's collected *Essays in Literary Analysis* (Austin, Texas, 1965), 69.

13. Richard Ohmann, "Literature as Sentences," *College English*, 1966, here quoted from the reprint in Seymour Chatman and Samuel R. Levin, eds., *Essays on the Language of Literature* (Boston, 1967), pp. 232, 233, and 238.

14. Harris, "Discourse Analysis," *Language*, 23 (1952), 1-30, reprinted in Fodor and Katz, *The Structure of Language*, pp. 355 ff.; and "Discourse Analysis: A Sample Text," *Language*, 28 (1957), 474-94. Jan Firbas, "From Comparative Word-Order Studies," *Brno Studies in English*, 4 (Praha, 1964), pp. 111-26, and "On the Interplay of Means of Functional Sentence Perspective," *Abstracts of Papers of the Xth Congress of Linguists*, pp. 94-95.

A general introduction to the intersentence approach is William O. Hendricks, "On the Notion 'Beyond the Sentence,'" *Linguistics*, 37 (1967), 12-51, which also deals with the connections between intersentence linguistics and narrative structure. Many relevant points appear *passim* in several recent conference volumes and papers, published and unpublished. See, for example, Karel Hausenblas, "On the Characterization and Classification of Discourses," *Travaux linguistiques de Prague*, 1 (1966), 67-83; K. E. Heidolph, "Kontextbeziehungen zwischen Sätzen in einer generativen Grammatik," *Kybernetik*, 3 (1966), 97-109; B. Drubig's unpublished M.A. thesis, "Kontextuelle Beziehungen zwischen Sätzen im Englischen" (Kiel, 1967); Gerhard Nickel, "Some Contextual Relations between Sentences in English," to appear in the *Acta of the Tenth International Congress of Linguists* held at Bucharest in 1967; Ruqaiya Hasan, *Grammatical Cohesion in Spoken and Written English* (Part One has appeared as Paper No. 7, "Programme in Linguistics and English Teaching," (London: University College and Longmans, Green and Co., 1968; Part Two is forthcoming in the same series); and the discussion between Harald Weinrich and others published in *Poetica*, 1 (1967), pp. 109 ff. Many relevant questions appear, implicitly or explicitly, in various works on stylostatistics, including those by Gustav Herdan. Several recent working papers on transformation grammar also touch on related problems. On the connection between intersentence analysis and literary structure, see *e.g.* Seymour Chatman, "New Ways of Analyzing Narrative Structure," *Language and Style*, 2 (1969), pp. 3-36. Another connection exists between focus and point of view: see *e.g.* John McH. Sinclair, "A Technique of Stylistic Description," *Language and Style*, 1 (1968), particularly pp. 223-24. Quite possibly shifts in point of view can be partly restated as shifts in focus, particularly subject focus: cf. Alain Renoir, "Point of View and Design for Terror," *Neuphilologische Mitteilungen*, 63 (1962), pp. 154-67, and Håkan Ringbom, *Studies in the Narrative Technique of Beowulf and Lawman's Brut*, Acta Academiae Aboensis, A, vol. 36 no. 2 (Abo, 1968). A classification of intersentence relations is available in Louis T. Milic, *Stylists on Style* (New York, 1969), Introduction.

# DISCUSSION OF ENKVIST'S PAPER

Enkvist's apparent acceptance of the possibility of establishing clear-cut boundaries between linguistics and stylistics was questioned; the boundaries, it was argued, are arbitrary, subtle, and vary in each specific case. Imagine (suggested the questioner) a machine which could generate brown birds that sing; those are the linguistic requirements, and any variety of singing brown bird would be acceptable, whether it were also carnivorous or herbivorous—these additional features would be "stylistic." But now imagine that we request from the machine a singing brown bird that is carnivorous—at that moment, "carnivorous" would become "linguistic," and cease being "stylistic." Enkvist's response was to recall that in some earlier work[1] he *had* made a clear-cut distinction between grammatical, stylistic, and pragmatic choices. And in fact the example of the brown bird illustrates one way of distinguishing between stylistically neutral features and style markers. In some contexts, a given feature may mark style; in other contexts, it need not.

Enkvist's esteem for the transformational-generative model of linguistics and for the search for abstractions that has always characterized linguistic inquiry as opposed to the search for particulars in texts that characterizes philology and literary criticism also came under discussion. What of the principle of parsimony? When you multiply principles isn't there a danger of ending up with as many of them as you have phenomena? Enkvist replied that the linguist is searching for a finite number of rules to explain an infinite number of phenomena. The questioner persisted: if only a *single* term seems to have an infinite or indefinite set of relations with the outside world, doesn't it seem unlikely that such a finite number of rules can be discovered? Enkvist felt that it could. The problem was to find the level of abstraction which was best suited to the study of a given feature.

The problem of deviation was raised in terms very similar to those used in the discussion of cognitive and expressive language in Ullmann's paper (see below): that is, the very opposition between norm and deviation was questioned and it was urged that we should not identify "'stylistic'" with "deviant." [Enkvist had not said that we should: indeed on p. 55 he points out that many deviations occur that we are not tempted to call stylistic—Ed.] The work of Richard Ohmann[2] was cited as an example of how we must develop techniques to analyze any sentence for stylistic purposes, not just deviant ones. Enkvist replied that he believed in a contextual norm (not to compare sonnets with laundry lists), and reiterated his distinction between statistical deviance (which every text contains) and the use of deviant language (a property of only certain texts such as poems in the modernist tradition).

Most of the discussion centered around the problem of the relation between linguistics and discourse or text analysis. For example, if the sentence was not the largest unit, what was? The paragraph? Enkvist said that he used the paragraph only as an example; he would leave the upper limit open. But it was generally agreed that the upper limit was not to be discovered in terms of size, but rather of function—it is the text which is the upper limit, and what one needs is a text-linguistics. (An example would be the use of a given grammatical feature to mark point of view throughout a whole fiction, for example the use of the *passé composé* instead of the historic past in Camus' *L'Étranger*.)

It was suggested that much of the dissatisfaction felt about defining stylistics, however, came from an overcommitment to the text at the expense of an independent general theory. That a limitation to intersentence analysis or to the concept of deviation or to that of choice is too narrowing seems clear; we should, rather, approach style the way a generative grammarian approaches questions of language, that is by first registering what our intuition about the style of a text is. Just as we say "This sentence is anomalous or ambiguous or constructionally homonymous," so we should look for the response that is stylistic in nature. That will determine in advance what we are looking at; we won't be troubled by the question "Is this really relevant?" This, of course, is the theory of Michael Riffaterre[3]—the response of the "Average Reader"—but the concept gives rise to another question: "How does your informant really know when something is 'stylistic'?" The only response demanded in linguistics is "Is it possible to say this?" ("Is this English, or whatever?"). But obviously the question "Is this stylistic?" is much more difficult, even ineffable; it gives rise to the informant's question "How do you mean, stylistic?" Riffaterre's answer is very antiseptic—not to ask such a question but simply to regard *any* response, whether evaluative or theoretical or moral or whatever, as the stylistic datum. One does not care so much about what is said as the fact that it has been said, that a stylistic device has been responded to. It was felt by another discussant that the content of that response—"this is unified, this is novel"—also bears consideration.

A final comment pointed out that the concept of choice as the crucial mechanism of style could be extended to the domain of content as well as form, that there is, indeed, a style of content. For example, that Hemingway elects to write about men of action—bullfighters, deep-sea fishermen, soldiers, big-game hunters—is as much a stylistic fact as his habit of writing in short, simple sentences, preferring the "dramatic" to the "interior monologue" point of view in narration, etc. Enkvist agreed, and suggested that as linguistics becomes more and more sophisticated in its capacity to deal with semantics, this aspect of style could be better accounted for.

## Notes

1. Nils Erik Enkvist, John Spencer, and Michael Gregory, *Linguistics and Style* (London, 1964).

2. Richard Ohmann, "Literature as Sentences," *College English*, XXVII (1966), 261-67, reprinted in Chatman and Levin, *Essays on the Language of Literature* (Boston, 1967).

3. Michael Riffaterre, "Criteria for Style Analysis" and "Stylistic Context," in *Word*, XV (1959), 154-74 and XVI (1960), 207-18, reprinted in Chatman and Levin, *op. cit.* pp. 412-30 and 323-36.

# STYLISTICS, POETICS, AND CRITICISM

### RENÉ WELLEK

THE QUESTION of the situation of stylistics among the various disciplines, its exact scope and its limits, has aroused considerable discussion. It seems to me, however, a mere logomachia to argue whether or not stylistics is an "independent" science, a view insisted on, for example, by Helmut Hatzfeld. "Independence" can never be total in such matters: clearly, stylistics studies language and thus must inevitably draw on linguistics, and if we assume that it includes the study of the style of verbal works of art, it is necessarily in contact with poetics or, as I prefer to call it, theory of literature. This term avoids the possibility of being restricted to verse as is often the case in English, and also any implication of prescriptive poetics. The close relationship of stylistics to linguistics needs no discussion: obviously the student of stylistics cannot get along without a knowledge of grammar in all it branches—phonetics and phonemics, morphology, syntax, lexicology of course, and hence the study of meaning, semantics.

Stylistics can, for our purposes, be divided into two fairly distinct disciplines: the study of style in all language pronouncements, and the study of style in works of imaginative literature. The first is represented by Charles Bally and his followers, and aims at an account of all devices serving a specific "expressive" end, securing emphasis or explicitness. It will draw for evidence on all language acts, oral ones or those preserved in print. Bally himself quotes examples also of individual styles and does not rigidly confine himself to collective usage. This type of study has been carried on since antiquity—since Aristotle, the Greek rhetoricians, and Quintilian—largely in the context of one language and often with prescriptive aims: to define and possibly to recommend or even to enforce "good style," mainly a middle style of exposition aiming at precision and clarity or an oratorical style bent on persuasion and emotional effect.

In more recent times attempts have been made to compare the styles of different languages, to construe something like a "comparative" stylistics, mainly of French, English, and German. Serious scholars such as Eduard Wechssler, Karl Vossler, Max Deutschbein, and even Leo Spitzer have often indulged in loose or arbitrary comparisons and jumped to conclusions on very little evidence. Thus Leo Spitzer considers what he calls "the *fait-accompli* construction in Spanish" "a linguistic reflection of Spanish Utopianism, of the Spanish *plus ultra* will," though in a postscript he himself quotes the same construction in German.[1] The writings of Benjamin Lee Whorf, who contrasted English with American Indian languages and was able to show that the "structure of a human being's language influences the manner in which he understands reality,"[2] have made a deeper impression on modern linguists, but I do not think we can really speak here of stylistics in any accepted sense when considering the problems raised by Whorf or, with a different philosophical background, by Ernst Cassirer's *Philosophy of Symbolic Forms*. These speculations lead rather to a study of our ways of construing and classifying the world: to a theory of knowledge, to epistemology, to comparative philosophy or *Weltanschauung* which uses linguistic evidence.

Finally there have been attempts to formulate "general" stylistics: to study the devices presumed to permeate all language pronouncements in whatever language. But I am not convinced that Herbert Seidler's *Allgemeine Stilistik* (1953) is a good beginning. He confines style to the expression of emotion, to the famous German *Gemüt*, draws almost exclusively on German examples, and rarely distinguishes clearly between style in any language function and in literary uses. Still, a general stylistics seems a legitimate task, however difficult it may be in practice.

Stylistics in all these senses: as study of a single language, as comparative, and as general stylistics, is, it seems to me, a part of linguistics. I do not see why one should object to this inclusion if one conceives of linguistics generously and widely. Stylistics in these senses laid claims to independence mainly because some schools of linguists voluntarily abandoned these problems. I remember Leonard Bloomfield bluntly telling me that he had no interest in stylistics or the study of poetic language, and there were theorists who considered the study of style merely a remote possibility.[3] But a vacuum has to be filled; whether we call the study of style in language a special branch of linguistics or an independent discipline, it will attract people who think about language and its uses.

The problem is very different as soon as we narrow our attention to a study of literary style, in the sense of style in imaginative literature, with an aesthetic function, particularly in poetry. We then raise the question of the nature of literature and the nature of aesthetic effect and response. And the study of style then has to come to grips with poetics and the theory of literature. I need not discuss all the various methods of such stylistic analysis. But some obvious divisions and choices may be mentioned. First, there is the analysis of a single work of art. It may proceed systematically, by elaborating something like a grammar of a work—an exhaustive description of its features working toward aesthetic ends or, more usually, by observing and isolating individual traits which can be contrasted or compared with the traits of non-aesthetic language or may be traced back to the mind of the author to account for their occurrence in genetic terms.

We might refer to such a book as Helmut Hatzfeld's *Don Quixote als Wortkunstwerk* (1927) as an example of a systematic analysis of a single work; we might point to the many recent writers who speak of "ungrammaticalness" or the "counter-grammar" of poetic texts, though I would agree with Edward Stankiewicz that "poetic language need not violate any rules of language and still remain what it is, that is, a highly patterned and organized mode of verbal expression."[4] I can barely allude to Spitzer's early papers, which try to trace stylistic features to the presumed mental dispositions of their authors: sometimes with psychoanalytical assumptions, as when he investigates the recurrence of such terms as "blood" and "wounds" in the writings of Henri Barbusse, or more often, with an interest in an underlying or implied philosophy, as when he shows that in Charles-Louis Phillipe the recurrent construction *à cause de* points to a personal fatalism.[5]

The analysis of a single work of art easily widens into the analysis of the total work of an author: the traits observable in one work permeate most often all his others. A style such as Thomas Carlyle's or Henry James' can be easily identified and described. Franz Dornseiff's *Pindars Stil* (1921), William K. Wimsatt's *Prose Style of Samuel Johnson* (1941), and Viktor Vinogradov's *Stil Pushkina* (1941) are fine examples of a systematic description of the style of a single writer. We can then go beyond the work of a single author and study a group of works, either in a specific genre or a specific period or in a historical sequence, in one national language or on an international scale. The combinations and permutations are numerous. Erich Auerbach in his *Mimesis* (1946) analyzes the style of passages selected from Western literature ranging from Homer to Proust always in order to use them as a springboard for comments on intellectual and social history, on the changing conceptions of reality and of the human condition. Stephen Ullmann's book on *Style in the French Novel* (1957) combines a selection of examples in historical order with theoretical reflections. Miss Josephine Miles, in many writings, has traced specific devices through the whole history of English poetry.[6] Morris W. Croll, in "The Baroque Style in English Prose" (1929), aims at characterizing a period style in English, while his other papers, "Attic Prose in the Seventeenth Century" and "Attic Prose: Lipsius, Montaigne, Bacon," trace a specific style in three languages.[7] These all seem to be legitimate topics and methods which have succeeded in what must be the aim of such studies: in the characterization of specific works, œuvres of a single author, or groups of works or genres or types by an analysis of their verbal style. I cannot see the justice of Louis T. Milic's objections to an attempt by James R. Sutherland to define Restoration prose.[8] The details of Sutherland's analysis may be wrong, but the enterprise is clearly defensible and even needed, as was the attempt to define and describe the style of Old Germanic poetry undertaken as long ago as 1875 by Richard Heinzel, or the study of German impressionism skillfully performed by Luise Thon.[9]

The claim has insistently been made that such stylistics replaces or rather pre-empts poetics and literary theory, that stylistics is simply poetics, or even, if we consider stylistics a branch of linguistics, that literary study is a part of linguistics. Roman Jakobson has put the claim forcefully, declaring that "since linguistics is the global science of verbal structure, poetics may be regarded as an integral part of linguistics."[10] Dámaso Alonso, with very different suppositions, declared in Poesía española that "Stylistics is the only 'science of literature.' "[11] But this seems to me a mistake. I would be the first to defend the enormous importance of linguistics for the study of literature: for a study of sound-patterns, inconceivable without the concept of the phoneme, for the study of rhythm and meter, for the study of vocabulary and syntax, and possibly even for the study of structures exceeding the limits of a sentence, as Samuel R. Levin has tried to demonstrate in his Linguistic Structures in Poetry (1962). Still, I fail to see how linguistic procedures can cope with the many features of a literary work which are not dependent on particular verbal formulations.

Let me grant immediately that all our thinking, certainly about literature, is done in language, and that a literary work of art is accessible only through its language. I found Roman Ingarden's phenomenological analysis in Das literarische Kunstwerk (1931) very helpful on this point. His concept of stratification allows one to recognize that a literary work of art has a basic sound-stratum out of which the units of meaning arise, while these in turn project a world of objects (not of course identical with objects in the real world) which have a status of their own and can be described independently of the linguistic stratum through which we have access to them. The general history of literature affords ample evidence for this view. Motifs, themes, images, symbols, plots, and compositional schemes, genre patterns, character and hero types, as well as qualities such as the tragic or the comic, the sublime or the grotesque, can be and have been discussed fruitfully with only little or no regard to their linguistic formulation. The mere fact that great poets and writers—Homer, Virgil, Dante, Shakespeare, Goethe, Tolstoy, and Dostoevsky—have exercised an enormous influence often in poor and loose translations which hardly convey even an inkling of the peculiarities of their verbal style should demonstrate the comparative independence of literature from language. To condemn research, the staple of literary scholarship, because it pays little or no attention to verbal texture means condemning the majority of serious literary studies. It is simply not true that only impressionistic appreciations or pronouncements of arbitrary opinions or subjective tastes are thus eliminated. All this seems to me a sufficient argument for the necessity of a poetics on an international scale, but one may strengthen it by adding that some of the problems raised in poetics are problems of general aesthetics (and not merely of literature) which elude a linguistic and stylistic approach. I might refer to pantomine, which can be a part of drama, or to the plot, themes, motifs, and images in the silent film, which are often comprehensible and aesthetically effective without recourse to subtitles. The film may, of course, draw on plots, themes, motifs, and images originally devised in literature. We are aware of the troubles and problems which arise with the filming of novels or dramas, but surely they prove that many devices and techniques of literature can be transferred into a non-linguistic medium. One may of course answer that neither drama nor film is literature. But the overlapping of such devices and procedures among the arts confirms the view that a literary work of art is not merely a "Wortkunstwerk" or "sprachliches Kunstwerk," to use the title of Wolfgang Kayser's well-known handbook.

One can write a history of narrative forms, as Robert Scholes and Robert Kellogg have done in *The Nature of Narrative* (1966), paying hardly any attention to the language of fiction; one can write a history of such themes or myths as that of Prometheus, as Raymond Trousson has done so impressively;[12] one can trace the image of the earthly paradise through many literatures, as Bartlett A. Giamatti has done recently;[13] or one can discuss the nature of tragedy or comedy without paying particular attention to the style of Sophocles or Shakespeare, Aristophanes or Molière. These seem to me truisms which are now being denied by the propagandists of the laudable cause of stylistics. It seems an oddly restrictive view of literary study to relegate these types to psychology or *Kulturgeschichte*. No doubt some of the questions involved are implicated in these neighboring disciplines. One cannot discuss the nature of tragedy without reference to religion and ritual, or isolate the history of fictional forms from such questions as the status of the teller of the tale or the composition of the audience addressed at a particular historical moment. I have always advocated a sharp focus for literary study on the work itself and have made a possibly oversharp distinction between "extrinsic" and "intrinsic" approaches to literature. Still, there are many genuinely literary problems that go beyond the analysis of style as language. They make up a vast body of knowledge which can be called poetics or literary theory. Such an international, supra-linguistic poetics or literary theory is, one should emphasize, an empirical science, concerned with a historical manifold which does not and cannot yield a system in the sense in which linguistic study leads to the construction of a system. The attempt of Northrop Frye, in his *Anatomy of Criticism* (1957), to devise such a system is *a priori* doomed to fail, however ingeniously contrived his scheme of modes, symbols, genres, and myths may be. "A scheme or system which would interpret all literary phenomena as limited internal relations and combinations cannot exist," says Hugo Friedrich, rejecting similar ambitions of the new French structuralism.[14]

I am aware that the term "style" has been used in a sense which goes beyond the conception of style as language, particularly in the movement that is called *Stilforschung* and has profoundly influenced Italian and Spanish developments. For instance, the late Ulrich Leo argued that anything that makes the "how" (instead of the "what") of a work of art is style—not only the linguistic expression but also the structure as totality, the characters, the situations, and even the plot or the action.[15] Style is identical with form or simply with the work itself. This view is substantially that of Benedetto Croce, though Croce, reasoning consistently from his rigidly monistic outlook, could decide that style is simply synonymous with form or expression and hence a superfluous term.[16]

In this concept of stylistics, the term "style," as transferred from its original meaning related to a writing *stylus* and applied to architecture and sculpture, returned to literary studies. J. J. Winckelmann, in his *Geschichte der Kunst im Altertum* (1764) seems to have been the first to describe the different stages of the style of Greek art. In ways which are not entirely clear the terms "Gothic," "Renaissance," "Baroque," "Rococo," and the like were established in art history and thence transferred to literature. I have brought out this in detail in my study of the history of the term "Baroque,"[17] and the same could be done with the other terms modeled on art history. The influence of Heinrich Wölfflin's *Kunstgeschichtliche Grundbegriffe* (1915) on literary studies has been particularly strong in Germany. But it is sufficient to refer to books such as Wylie Sypher's *Four Stages of Renaissance Style* (1955) and his *Rococo to Cubism* (1960) or to Roy Daniells' *Milton, Mannerism and Baroque* (1963) to see that this use is still very common and successful, as it appeals to our sense of the unity of the arts, of a unified time-spirit, and the unitary development of the arts, however tenuous some of the analogies and parallels may be if looked at with a critical eye. The linguistic concept of style is here abandoned almost completely. I shall not attempt to discuss questions raised by this use of the term, as I have tried to criticize it before, possibly with excessive skepticism.[18]

In all these discriminations I have assumed that stylistics and poetics are strictly descriptive disciplines aiming at the observation, classification, and characterization either of verbal style or of the verbal devices used in literature. This certainly is the ideal of our scientific age: objectivity, reticence as to value judgment, and abstention from criticism is the dominant mood. Sol Saporta has assured us that "terms like *value, aesthetic purpose, etc.*" are not available to linguists.[19] The proliferation of quantitative methods in the study of style, whether statistical or based on computer research, are sufficient evidence. I, for one, am not disposed to dismiss these methods, though I doubt their adequacy for some problems or refuse to consider them the only panacea. Quantitative relations establish only dependent functions, more or less necessary concomitants in the totality of a work of art, but cannot define its central meaning, its historical, social and generally human import. Other scholars too, even some who could be suspected of an aversion to quantification, have rejected all concern for value judgment. Thus Northrop Frye, in the "Polemical Introduction" to his highly influential *Anatomy of Criticism* (1957), argued that "the study of literature can never be founded on value judgments" and that "criticism should show a steady advance toward undiscriminating catholicity."[20] Ulrich Leo, who comes from a totally different background, refers, almost with horror, to the danger that "evaluation" might "creep" into his method of stylistic study.[21] Examples of this kind could be easily multiplied. But I believe, however, that the idea of emptying the study of literature, on whatever level, of criticism in the sense of evaluation and judgment is doomed to failure. The mere fact that we select certain texts out of millions for investigation is a critical judgment, even though it may be inherited and accepted without examination. The selection has been accomplished by preceding acts of judgment on the part of readers, critics, and even professors. The study of any work of art is impossible without our constantly choosing the traits we are to discuss, the angle from which we are to approach it. We weigh, discriminate, compare, portion out, and single out at every step.

Neither can the practice of ranking be avoided. I understand the dissatisfaction with rankings on a single scale and can sympathize with the ridicule that T. S. Eliot and, borrowing his figure, Northrop Frye have poured on the imaginary stock exchange of literature. "That wealthy investor T. S. Eliot, after dumping Milton on the market, is now buying him again; Donne has probably reached his peak and will begin to taper off; Tennyson may be in for a slight flutter but the Shelley stocks are still bearish."[22] We may indeed balk at the crudity of some pronouncements about first-rank and second-rank writers, about "good," "better," and "best." Nevertheless, it is an illusion to think that we can shirk the problem of what we may call the "canon" of literature. Its historical development has been traced by Ernst Robert Curtius in the main European literatures.[23] In an attempt to refute the historical relativism of such a great scholar as the late Erich Auerbach, I myself have argued that "there is a wide agreement on the great classics: the main canon of literature."[24] There is the irrefutable distinction between really great art and very bad art: between, say, the "Ode on a Grecian Urn" and a poem in a provincial newspaper, between Tolstoy's *Anna Karenina* and a story in *True Romances*. Relativists always shirk the issue of thoroughly bad poetry. Even Northrop Frye has to admit that "Milton is a more rewarding and suggestive poet to work with than Blackmore," and Frye makes frequent value judgments. In the same book, he calls Aristophanes' *Birds* his "greatest play" and Robert Burton's *Anatomy of Melancholy* "the greatest Mennipean satire in English before Swift."[25]

A work of art is not an assemblage of neutral facts or traits but is, by its very nature, an object charged with values. These values do not merely sit on or "inhere" in structures, as the Husserlian phenomenology of Roman Ingarden concludes. The very fact that I recognize a certain structure as a work of art already implies a judgment of value. Literary description and evaluation are inseparable: evaluation not only grows out of description but is presupposed and implied in the very act of cognition itself. Recently E. D. Hirsch, Jr., in his paper "Literary Evaluation as Knowledge" has accepted my view of knowledge and value, though he had earlier disagreed with me about interpretation, and he has shown how closely this view agrees with Kant's. Value judgments, to use his words, "necessarily subsist in the relationship between meanings and these correlative subjective stances."[26]

Thus we must face the question whether style or any particular style or stylistic device can be considered a criterion of aesthetic value. It can hardly be so considered if we take style in isolation from the totality of a work of art. Descriptions of style have traditionally been governed by criteria of effective communication: clarity, vivacity, persuasiveness, etc.—all ultimately rhetorical categories, which cannot by themselves establish the artistic merit of a specific text; in a specific context, vagueness, obscurity, illogicality, and even monotony may contribute to aesthetic value. Nor can the occurrence of a specific stylistic trait do so; hyperbole may be tragic or pathetic, grotesque or comic, yet completely ineffective artistically. A dense sound texture does not necessarily establish high poetic quality. Poe's "Raven" has been rightly listed as a prime example of "vulgarity in literature."[27] Its intricate rhyme-scheme and sound-patterns do not make it a good poem. There are plenty of virtuoso performances in all possible metrical and stanzaic forms in many languages which have only slight aesthetic merit. Nor can a specific choice of vocabulary, figuration, grammatical correspondences, or sentence structure constitute aesthetic merit. I admire the ingenuity with which Roman Jakobson and Claude Lévi-Strauss have analyzed Baudelaire's sonnet "Les Chats."[28] They have demonstrated the parallelisms, correspondences, reiterations, and contrasts convincingly, but I fail to see that they have or could have established anything about the aesthetic value of the poem. I agree with Michael Riffaterre's view that "no grammatical analysis of a poem can give us more than the grammar of the poem."[29] Jakobson himself showed long ago that the supposedly indispensable criterion of poetry: "metaphoricness," can, on occasion, be dispensed with or can be replaced by metonymic relations, grammatical echoes, and contrasts.[30] Pushkin's "Ja vas ljubil" is Jakobson's example of an imageless poem, and I may add Wordsworth's "We Are Seven" or Robert Bridges' "I love all beauteous things. I seek and adore them," poems to which it would be impossible to deny aesthetic merit. This type of poetry could be called "poetry of statement," a term first used by Mark Van Doren in defense of Dryden's verse.[31] One could, however, argue that all poetry is metaphorical merely by being poetry, language, and *mimesis*, not life, a view propounded eloquently in the Epilogue to William K. Wimsatt and Cleanth Brooks' *Literary Criticism: A Short History*. But this seems to me a very different use of the term "metaphor": the whole work is seen as such. "Metaphor is a substantive—or mock-substantive—universal."[32]

No grounds of total evaluation can, I conclude, be established by linguistic or stylistic analysis as such, though an intricate sound texture, a closely knit grammatical structure, or a dense web of effective metaphors may contribute to the total aesthetic value of a work of art. A *fortiori*, no genetic criterion can establish aesthetic value. Leo Spitzer's perceptive recognition of an author's psychological traits observable in his stylistic quirks does not and cannot establish the aesthetic value of these works. On the contrary, one feels that Leo Spitzer has often overrated authors of ephemeral merit such as Charles-Louis Phillipe or Jules Romains because he has been able to establish such links between mind and word. Similarly, Jakobson overrates poems which lend themselves to an analysis of their sound patterns or grammatical organization or which simply experiment with language, with the result that the perspective on much modern poetry seems distorted. Actually, a very special taste for poetry playing with language is exalted at the expense of the great tradition. Futurism is consistently preferred to Symbolism.

We have to become literary critics to see the function of style within a totality which inevitably will appeal to extra-linguistic and extra-stylistic values, to the harmony and coherence of a work of art, to its relation to reality, to its insight into the meaning of life, and hence to its social and generally human import. Thus we cannot ignore the meaning given the word "style" by Goethe in his first paper after his return from Italy, "Einfache Nachahmung, Manier, Stil" (1788). "Imitation," he says, is the lowest stage of art, "manner" arises when the artist expresses himself, "style" is above objective imitation and subjective manner. It "rests on the deepest foundation of knowledge, on the essence of things, so far as we are able to know it in visible and palpable forms." It is the term to designate "the highest stage which art has ever reached and will ever reach."[33] Style in this sense is identical with great art. It is a critical concept, a criterion of evaluation.

## NOTES

1. "Die *fait-accompli* Darstellung im Spanischen" in *Stilstudien* (Munich, 1928), Vol. I, 258-94. Quotation on p. 289.

2. *Language, Thought, and Reality*, ed. John B. Carroll (Cambridge, Mass., 1956), p. 23.

3. E.g., George L. Trager and Henry Lee Smith, *An Outline of English Structure* (Norman, Oklahoma, 1951), pp. 86ff.

4. "Linguistics and the Study of Poetic Language" in *Style in Language*, ed. Thomas E. Sebeok (Boston, Mass., 1960), p. 70.

5. *Studien zu Henri Barbusse* (Bonn, 1920) and "Pseudo-objektive Motivierung bei Charles-Louis Phillipe" in *Stilstudien, loc. cit.*, Vol. 2, 166-207.

6. E.g., *Eras and Modes in English Poetry* (Berkeley, Cal., 1964) and *The Continuity of Poetic Language* (New York, 1965).

7. Now collected in *Style, Rhetoric and Rhythm* (Princeton, N.J. 1966).

8. "Against the Typology of Styles," in *Essays on the Language of Literature*, ed. Seymour Chatman and Samuel R. Levin (Boston, Mass., 1967), pp. 442-50.

9. *Über den Stil der altgermanischen Poesie* (Strassburg, 1875); *Die Sprache des deutschen Impressionismus* (Munich, 1928).

10. *Style in Language, loc. cit.*, p. 350.

11. Madrid, 1950, p. 429. "La Estílistica será la única 'Ciencia de la literatura.'" I am aware that Don Dámaso Alonso uses the term "stylistics" in a very wide sense. See his protest in *The Critical Moment: Essays on the Nature of Literature* (London, 1964), p. 149.

12. *Le Thème de Prométhée dans la littérature européenne*, 2 vols. (Geneva, 1964) and his defense *Les Etudes de thèmes: Essai de méthodologie* (Paris, 1965).

13. *The Earthly Paradise and the Renaissance Epic* (Princeton, N.J. 1966).

14. "Strukturalismus und Struktur in literaturwissenschaftlicher Hinsicht" in *Europäische Aufklärung, Herbert Dieckmann zum 60. Geburtstag* (Munich, 1967), p. 81: "Ein Schema oder System, das alle Erscheinungen der Literatur als begrenzte interne Relationen und Kombinationen auffassen wollte, kann es nicht geben."

15. *Stilforschung und dichterische Einheit* (Munich, 1966), p. 30.

16. *Estetica*, 8th ed. (Bari, 1945), p. 79.

17. 1946. Reprinted in *Concepts of Criticism* (New Haven, Conn., 1963) with a Postscript 1962 containing some additions and corrections.

18. See the chapter "Literature and the Other Arts" in *Theory of Literature* (New York, 1949).

19. *Style in Language, loc. cit.*, p. 83.

20. Princeton, N.J., 1957, pp. 20, 25.

21. *Loc. cit.*, p. 22.

22. Cf. T. S. Eliot, "What Is Minor Poetry?" (1944) in *On Poetry and Poets* (London, 1957), pp. 48-9; and Frye's *Anatomy of Criticism, loc. cit.*, p. 18.

23. *Europäische Literatur und lateinisches Mittelalter* (Bern, 1948), especially pp. 267ff.

24. "Literary Theory, Criticism and History" (1959) reprinted in *Concepts of Criticism, loc. cit.*, pp. 18-9.

25. *Anatomy of Criticism, loc. cit.*, pp. 25, 44, 311.

26. In *Criticism*, ed. L. S. Dembo (Madison, Wis., 1968), pp. 45-57.

27. Aldous Huxley, *Vulgarity in Literature: Digressions from a Theme* (London, 1930).

28. In *L'Homme*, 2 (1962), 5-21.

29. "Describing Poetic Structures: Two Approaches to Baudelaire's 'Les Chats' " in *Yale French Studies*, 36-37 (1966), 213.

30. "The Metaphoric and Metonymic Poles" in *Fundamentals of Language* (The Hague, 1956), pp. 76-82.

31. *John Dryden: A Study of His Poetry* (New York, 1946), p. 67. First published in 1920.

32. New York, 1957, p. 750.

33. *Sämtliche Werke*, Jubiläumsausgabe, ed. Eduard von der Hellen (Stuttgart, 1903), Vol. 33, 57. "So ruht der Stil auf den tiefsten Grundfesten der Erkenntnis, auf dem Wesen der Dinge, insofern es uns erlaubt ist, es in sichtbaren und greiflichen Gestalten zu erkennen." P. 59: "um den höchsten Grad zu bezeichnen, welchen die Kunst je erreicht hat und je erreichen kann."

# DISCUSSION OF WELLEK'S PAPER

The first speaker agreed completely with Wellek and spoke of the real danger that linguistics—though it had produced useful results—might become imperialistic in literary studies. Another participant observed that natural language is only one of many systems of communication—all of which are only metaphorically "languages"; though Wellek had referred to pantomime as the least linguistic part of theater, recent theoreticians have shown pantomime to be a language, though obviously this is a different use of the term "language." Wellek agreed that "language" has been used in reference to mathematics, gestures, signs, etc., and that of course there did exist the field of semiotics or semiology. But he had meant "language" in the conventional sense in his paper.

Another participant agreed that the literary work transcended style and language, and that our views must necessarily differ according to whether we are concerned with style as part of language or as part of literature. This is an important if subtle difference: our whole perspective changes accordingly. But he wondered whether it might not be preferable to make two distinct oppositions, namely between linguistics and poetics on the one hand, and between description and theory on the other. In poetics one deals with real, individual works, not, as in linguistics, with all possible sentences that can be generated. We work with a text, not with a set of generative rules. In the second dichotomy, we may divide poetics into the development of general theory as opposed to the description of particular texts. It is always possible for a linguist to write as a critic, to be interested in the poetic structure of a given work and not in the language at large. Indeed, he may be concerned with features in that text that are not of the sort to be found in any linguistic treatise. But that may also reflect an accidental lack in the development of linguistics, semantics, or rhetoric. Wellek replied that he was not sure one could draw the distinction between description and theory so sharply. Any description must benefit from a firm basis in theory; one has to generalize, one has to rely on a knowledge of syntax, and so on, in order to be able to describe features. He recalled Spitzer's philological circle, the going back and forth between theory and practice. Nobody reads with an empty mind; we all have preconceptions. We start with a general idea of the author, then look for further details which may or may not be confirmed by further intensive study.

# RHETORICAL CHOICE AND
# STYLISTIC OPTION:
## The Conscious and Unconscious Poles

### LOUIS T. MILIC

THE QUESTION I propose to take up may be simply stated: How much conscious control does the writer have over his style? It is my contention that no stylistic analysis can properly take place unless this question is answered in some way, if only to be dismissed, which is itself a kind of answer. The kind of answer given to this question determines the nature of the model of the stylistic process which the theoretician or analyst of style has constructed and on which his work is based. The traditional answer, provided by not propounding the question, implies a condition of total consciousness or control by the writer. Yet this traditional view embodies within it another view which contradicts it: that the style in some sense is the image of the man. Though many writers on the subject have expressed themselves about this theory of the reflection of the personality by the style, the unlikely claimant for the honor of having given it a permanent form is the great French academician and naturalist, Buffon.

Much has been said about Buffon's famous aphorism, usually rendered as "The style is the man." It is usually interpreted to mean that the style of a work reflects the personality of its author. To be more precise—since *reflects* is a metaphor, both conventional and misleading—the specific linguistic forms of a text and their arrangement in some sense duplicate the traits of the author's personality, which is the aggregate of idiosyncrasies and peculiarities which differentiate him from other men. Ideally, if this hypothesis existed in a fully worked-out form, each trait of personality would be represented by a linguistic equivalent. Actually, the hypothesis is never realized except in impressionistic metaphors such as *economical,*

77

*flabby, muscular, pedantic, masculine,* which seem vaguely appropriate to the description of both style and personality but actually say almost nothing about either.

The personality-style paradigm has an ancient lineage (Seneca and Montaigne, for example) and passes current in a variety of forms in every sort of critical statement which juxtaposes the writer, as a historical person, with the aspect of his writing which is supposed to betray his individuality. For the benefit of those who have been seduced by Buffon's aphorism without understanding it, a number of scholars have furnished the necessary correction, i.e., that what Buffon actually said was quite different and in fact almost the opposite of what is usually understood. As Lane Cooper, for example, points out,

> Buffon's thought is perfectly clear: whereas the subject-matter of a scientific treatise, say, is external to the man, and would exist whether the man existed or not, the style, or the order in which the man arranges his thoughts on the subject-matter, springs from the man himself; the style is so much of the man as exists in the ordering of his thoughts.[1]

The facts are always there and belong to Nature, but the presentation, the style, is not natural but human or artificial. The style constitutes the enduring value of any work—though Buffon was obviously thinking of natural history rather than of non-narrative prose in general.

In an interesting earlier work on the Cartesian aesthetic, Emile Krantz explains Buffon's views on style and composition as deriving from Descartes' emphasis on the general and the abstract:

> Le *Discours sur le style* représente, à notre avis, le développement suprême de la doctrine classique. Avec Buffon, la tendance à l'universel se perd dans la poursuite de la généralité; et la recherche de la simplicité va jusqu'à retirer de l'éloquence tous les elements sensibles, à lui interdire toutes les ressources qu'elle était l'art de puiser dans la passion, dans l'imagination, dans le coeur, pour la réduire à n'être plus que le "style" c'est-à-dire l'expression pure et simple de la pensée par un minimum de termes impersonnels.[2]

In his correction of the usual view of Buffon's aphorism, Krantz redefines its key terms (*style* and *homme*) in such a way as to wipe out any possible interest on Buffon's part in human individuality or originality. His revision of the aphorism takes the form: "Le *style*—mais le style *général*—c'est l'*homme*—mais l'*homme essentiel et abstrait*."[3] In these terms, there is no danger of misinterpreting Buffon, but there is also no interest in what is left of the aphorism. If this is what Buffon intended, and if he had couched the statement in the form Krantz gives it, it is doubtful whether anyone would ever have cited it. There is a question, however, whether Krantz was not carried away by his thesis and did not distort Buffon's ideas in the process. Although Buffon's *Discours sur le style* (its usual title) is readily obtainable and often mentioned, it is probably seldom read, and its contents are rarely cited except from secondary sources. A short summary may thus be appropriate.

Real eloquence, says Buffon, is not merely a knack or gift of words. Style arises from the proper ordering of one's thoughts. Emphasis on ornaments and devices of style reveals that a writer's ideas are thin or disorderly. Style is concerned with thought, not with the manipulation of words. Writers mainly concerned with words cannot have style, merely its shadow. Writing well thus requires a full knowledge of the subject and a clear sense of the interrelation of one's ideas. To write well is to think, to feel, and to express well. Because tone is merely the agreement of the style with the subject, it cannot be forced but must arise spontaneously from the nature of the subject. Only well-written works will descend to posterity, since facts and discoveries are separable and can be passed from one to another. Such things are not man's work. The style, however, is a man's own. It cannot be subtracted from the work. But a good style is such only by virtue of the truths it presents.

The essential problem in this argument—if it can be called that—concerns the individual contribution of the writer. Krantz concludes that Buffon as a confirmed Cartesian could not have intended to give any credit for merit of style to its human uniqueness, its originality or individuality. Actually, such a belief would not require a Cartesian orientation: a mere dedication to the Platonic notion of perfection would suffice. And Buffon's reference to style as a good, an absolute, something that can be present or absent from a work, confirms this. But the notion of style as an achievable perfection raises a question which Buffon does not answer. If the stylistic merit of a composition lies in its proper ordering of ideas, is that order an inevitable one that must be discovered, as the sculptor searches for the statue in the block of marble? Or is it an order that he imposes on the refractory materials of thought according to his own unique vision of the world? In the former case, discovering the inevitable order confers no credit on the finder, and having style is merely finding the key to a puzzle. In the latter case, which is doubtless what Buffon intended, the individual contribution is inescapable. Having ideas about facts and ordering them well, finding appropriate expression for them, is not a general human achievement. It is an individual one—the triumph of the individual writer, of the personality.

If this conclusion is accurate, Buffon was forced, despite his own beliefs about the process of composition, into a position he would have found repugnant if it had been explicit. The ultimate extreme of the belief that a writer's personality determines the quiddity of his style is surely the case in which the writer can exert no control over the style at all, all of it being determined by habits, associations, and conditioning. At the other pole is the belief that the writer can consciously control and artistically shape every detail of his utterance. The evident underlying contradictions in Buffon's argument perhaps reflect the curious circumstance that some truth lies at both of these poles. Obviously, if he chooses to do so, the writer can weigh every word before he commits himself to it; and he can, moreover, alter at will any word that he has set down, so that he may be said, in a sense, to have complete power over his language. Yet at the same time he cannot choose any word that is not part of his vocabulary or any form that is not included in his own repertory of syntactical resources. He cannot, that is, exceed his idiolect. Every writer—everyone who has ever set pen to paper—knows how mysteriously the words do flow on some occasions and refuse to on others. And yet the theory of style and the applications of theory (with the exception of attribution problems) have proceeded as if the process of composition and therefore the stylistic performance were a fully conscious process.

What is the evidence for the unconscious nature of the process of composition? Or, what sort of evidence is available for the hypothesis that a substantial part of the language-generating behavior of the writer is not conscious and deliberate but unconscious, determined, and habitual? One might suppose, from the lack of interest that this question has elicited, that not much could be said for the hypothesis. Yet the evidence for it is considerable.

The most immediately available support for it is derived from introspection or from the observation of our own behavior while writing. Every writer has had to deal with the problem of "finding the right words." According to one model of the stylistic process, this could be restated as finding suitable linguistic equivalents for the wordless thoughts or ideas in the mind. According to another model, it could be taken to mean generating the appropriate linguistic forms (including ideas) which the mind scans as they are produced and either accepts or rejects as appropriate, where *appropriate* does not mean in conformity with some wordless notion. The process as experienced by any writer consists of constant false starts, revisions, deletions, modifications, and occasionally total frustration by the inability to generate a set of forms which the scanner will accept. The conclusion is inevitable that the process of generating the forms is not under total control, although it seems evident that conscious mental participation is present, but in the role of critic not of artist. It is perhaps in the confusion of these two functions of the process of composition that the difficulty lies.

The speed at which language strings are generated is another consideration that suggests the important contribution of unconscious processes in composition. The average speed of written composition is perhaps twenty-five words a minute, not including the pauses that arise between sentences and the longer ones between paragraphs. The speed of oral output is probably ten times greater. Although many writers find themselves slowed by the physical necessity of tracing the letters when writing, this sense of being delayed by the medium is seldom evident when speaking. Still, whether speaking or writing, there is hardly any capability (while engaged in the process rather than reflecting about it after it has been completed) of paying attention simultaneously to the semantic and syntactic components. That is to say, the writer or speaker intent on the succession of semantic items (meanings) he is producing cannot spare any mind to a conscious examination of the syntactic structures in which those meanings are presented. If he allows himself to be distracted from the semantic stream, he at once loses his control, being forced to stop in order to avoid producing substantive nonsense or ungrammatical structures. It does not seem possible, for example, to decide *in medias res* that a given bit of information will be put into the form of a relative clause or an infinitive phrase without losing track of meaning. The meanings, including specifically lexical choices, seem to require most of the available attention. If they are properly sequenced and articulated, the grammar seems to take care of itself. To say this is surely to say that the grammar is generated by a faculty largely unconscious.

When the writer, having completed some tract of writing (a paragraph, a page, or a treatise), sets about to revise it, he seems to bring into play the same processes as in the writing itself but in a different order. He scans the words until he finds something to arrest him, an ambiguity, an infelicity, or some deviation in the sequencing of larger clusters of meanings. If he is revising, he allows the language-generating mechanism to operate again, substituting as much of the new forms for the old ones as necessary, subsequently making the grammatical adjustments required by the intrusion of the new forms into the body of the old ones. Curiously, though, many writers find revision intolerably difficult or inconvenient, preferring to strike out unsatisfactory sentences and generate new ones. At least one advantage of this procedure is that it precludes the necessity of adjustments and makes it possible to avoid unintended emphases, as by the repetition of words. The degree to which the writer is dominated by the writing is suggested by the frequency with which he finds it necessary to discard, throw away, and start again, as if there were some satisfaction in the clean slate or as if the previously-generated language imposed intolerable constraints on his freedom, as in fact it does within sentences on the syntactic level and beyond this, at the rhetorical level. The verdict of those who have studied the revisions performed by writers on their own works has generally been that the revised results do not repay the effort expended. Extant holograph manuscripts reveal that changes tend to occur in a very narrow range and that what is gained in one place is lost in another.[4] In terms of the effect produced, such changes are frequently self-cancelling or self-defeating. Yet they are of interest as revealing the lack of freedom available to the writer, who seems imprisoned by his idiolect on the outer circumference and by what he has already written at closer range. Part of this lack of freedom is unquestionably due to the chain of syntactic-semantic implications built up by a succession of the units of the sentence, a condition best explained by the work of the information theorists. The nature of the linguistic code forces certain choices on the writer which imply later decisions and ultimately (say at the end of the sentence) eliminate nearly all free choice. But it is not only the nature of language that so determines the writer, but the nature of the language in him, the nature of his language generator, if those two can be distinguished. Doubtless the nature of language is in a very specific way related to the nature of the apparatus that produces it.

The nature of the constraints which operate within the writer to keep his style uniform and stable is unknown, but that they exist is certain. To say that it is his idiolect is merely to substitute one name for another. The difficulty encountered when a writer tries to alter his style, however, testifies to the power and tenacity of these constraints.[5]

Obviously, writers can modify their styles: Carlyle apparently did so, though the specific nature of the changes, apart from the obvious lexical ones, has not been thoroughly investigated. By analogy, one could describe the process as similar to that of altering one's handwriting. It is possible to do it, but it is slow work and, when efficiency or speed is required, one tends to fall back on one's habitual pattern. With considerable effort one might succeed in writing in a manner which emphasized one particular aspect of one's style (e.g., parallelism) always within the confines of one's idiolect, but it would be difficult to adapt such a mode to the transmission of a general set of meanings rather than the specific ones best conveyed by the particular device. To truly write in the style of Hemingway would probably require one to convey Hemingway's meanings. Parodists, no matter how astute, cannot keep themselves out of their parodies, as Mr. Sayce has observed of Marcel Proust's brilliant take-off of Flaubert in "L'Affaire Lemoine."[6]

Proust's parodies go deeper than those of common parodists. Proust had remarked, for instance, Flaubert's use of tenses as truly distinctive. Most parodists, however, limit themselves to the most obvious superficial features of style and make burlesque use of the writer's traditional subject matter. Hemingway's parodists (E. B. White, Wolcott Gibbs, Max Shulman) fail to get beyond subject matter. The obvious explanation is not only that such parodies are easy to contrive and to recognize but also that the Hemingway frame will only fit around his canvases.

When writers come to describe their own styles, the gap between consciousness and its alternative is most dramatically made clear. Swift spent much effort fulminating against monosyllables, contractions, and such words as *mob* and *banter*, while proclaiming the virtues of simplicity and short sentences. Yet he did not practice his own preachings. This is partly explained as the fate of every purist, whose theories cannot withstand the strain of dealing with the constant linguistic necessity. One can no more avoid monosyllables than words containing the letter o. Moreover, one cannot censor these matters while intent on the process of composition. But the main issue is the inability of the writer to describe what he is actually doing stylistically. He may be able to discourse sensibly of his narrative practice, of his theory of the novel, as Henry James has done. But when he talks about his style or his ideals of style, the writer is on shaky ground because he does not know what he does. First, he does not have the vocabulary to describe it, not being a grammarian or a stylistician. But more important, he has, it seems, very little awareness of what mechanism or process is involved in the stylistic decisions he is constantly required to make. A writer may write confessionally as Maugham does in *The Summing-Up* or cleverly, like E. B. White in the last chapter of *The Elements of Style*. But it is useless because the problem eludes him. He tells us only what he wants us to think his style is—not what it actually is. Perhaps the most perceptive intuition recently voiced by an author describing his own style was Hemingway's remark "In stating as fully as I could how things really were, it was often very difficult and I wrote awkwardly and the awkwardness is what they called my style."[7] The acuity lies in the recognition by this author that his most subtle but most frequent deviation from the norm lay in a direction he properly called *awkwardness*, a phraseology grammatical but not idiomatic, one which would indicate that a struggle with the medium was taking place, the sort of thing that authors generally try to revise out of their writings. Hemingway is an interesting exhibit also because the marked decline in his work during the later part of his career (a decline which made some of his last work read like self-parody) may be traced to some extent to his willingly trying to write in the way that his early critics said he did. The features of style they noticed were the ones that so glaringly denatured *Across the River and Into the Trees* and even *The Old Man and the Sea*.

From the professional to the novice is a very large step but no different in kind. The student of composition, like the professional writer, does not know what he is doing when he composes. And the teacher of composition seems helpless to tell him. It is hardly necessary to rehearse the endless cycle of attempts to find the new formula which will enable us to teach undergraduates how to write. Everything fails because the nature of the process is still unclear, despite studies of language acquisition and development. Everything that succeeds has an uncanny resemblance to the prescriptions of Quintilian, to whom most of what is known was familiar. One cannot teach an eighteen-year-old student to write instantly because the process takes a dozen years and must be begun much earlier. European students learn not because they follow the French or the German system, but because they follow the only system, namely, allowing writing to become a habitual process. Paul Roberts once said that anyone who had put a million words on paper had no writing problem. This is an exaggeration but only of detail. The best instruction in writing is practice with words: reading, writing, and the whole paraphernalia of epitome, imitation, translation recommended by Roger Ascham in his *Scholemaster*, which was far from original when it was written. What all these indications point to is the large and perhaps dominant contribution of unconscious process to the production of language and, by implication, to the formation of individual style.

Speculative though these indications may be, they derive from the experience of writers and square with the observations of those, too numerous and diverse to mention, who have recorded their sensations about the mysteries of the process. As different a pair of writers as Bertrand Russell and Henry Miller have described their writing fit in ways reminiscent of Rousseau on the way to Dijon with his prize-winning first discourse. To be sure, the testimony of writers is always suspect, especially since vanity inclines them to subscribe to the myth that the god speaks through them and the Romantic tradition has renewed the notion of poetic inspiration. A more substantial testimony, however, may be found in the work of those who have tried to attribute literary works of uncertain authorship to their proper authors. The two best-known cases of recent date, the work of Ellegård on the *Junius* letters and of Mosteller and Wallace on the *Federalist* papers, both relied on statistics and computers for objectivity and reliability.[8] Both of these studies were based on the assumption that the style of an author has a consistency due to the habitual nature of the writing process and that this consistency can be detected, measured, and used to determine consanguinity between an unknown and a set of authenticated texts.

Both studies by different routes arrived at the conclusion that the habitual aspects of composition are more distinctly manifested at the minor syntactic level, as in the use of function words and their distributional parameters. In other words, the style is most consistent at those levels where the unconsciousness is the greatest.

Evidently this implies that writers are more conscious of some aspects of the writing process than of others, which is the point that this argument has been leading up to. I have arbitrarily distinguished between two levels of consciousness, although it is obvious that there must be a gradation and an overlap. Still, for the sake of a precision in the model which is not in the reality, I distinguish between decisions made unconsciously while the language-generating mechanism is proceeding as *stylistic options* and decisions made consciously while the mechanism is at rest as *rhetorical choices*. I am well aware how artificial this distinction must seem, expressed in these terms, yet there is no gainsaying that it corresponds to the reality in some sense. The correspondence can be illustrated by recourse to examples at the extremes of the process. For instance, no writer consciously determines the *average* length of his sentences, though he may well decide that a given sentence is too long or too short. The same is true for any of the other parameters of distribution that have been statistically investigated by Yule, Herdan, Ellegård, Mosteller and Wallace, Fucks, Williams, and Morton and his associates. The constituents of these parameters are the large numbers of stylistic options taken as the stream of words is produced. Because a writer does not know what these recondite measures are he can take no conscious steps to control them. But even if he took the trouble to discover what his entropy or K factor value was, it is doubtful that he could do much to affect them because these are incidental second-order abstractions of his primary decisions. These primary decisions involve the necessary syntactic consequences of certain semantic choices as well as the available stylistic options, such as the alternative forms of noun modification, the placement of adverbials, the construction of verb groups. These are some of the stylistic options determined by habit which form a pattern that constitutes one aspect of a writer's style. Incidentally, it seems unlikely that the speed of language production could be maintained if these habitual options were not so determined, if every decision at these low levels were conscious and free.

The conscious decisions which I have called *rhetorical choice* are made not as a part of language generation but of the process I have called scanning, that is, evaluation of what has been generated. In this category I would include significant lexical choices, word order for emphasis, the kinds of sentence arrangements which are subsumed under some of the rhetorical figures (anaphora, chiasmus, homoioteleuton), and the logical ordering of the parts of the discourse. It would be convenient if the distinction could be made so that stylistic options were below the sentence level and rhetorical choices above, but the facts are otherwise. Stylistic options do indeed generally take place below the sentence level, usually in the design of constructions, but rhetorical choices can be made anywhere because any aspect of the text may be consciously scrutinized at will.

One implication of this model is that stylistic options will maintain a greater consistency in a writer's work than rhetorical choices, provided that they are not determined by the context, as, for instance, the frequency of personal pronouns is affected by the fact that a text is an autobiographical narrative. This consistency should manifest itself broadly over a wide range of his work in various genres, always allowing for the possible dynamic effect of chronology. Inversely, it is probable that those items that show consistency could be classified as stylistic options as these have been defined here. Rhetorical choices, consciously selected for the production of effects appropriate to various works, would reveal no such consistency. It is doubtful whether numerical values for such devices can have much usefulness.

A difficulty with this distinction arises when what appears to be a rhetorical choice becomes habitual and then serves as a stylistic option. As Mr. Wimsatt observed, Johnson's devotion to parallelism and antithesis became a habit (a bad habit, I believe he called it). In effect, one must suppose that the specific language forms which produce parallel antithetic clauses arose first to his mind and were generated even when the semantic component was mismatched with it. Similarly, Swift's use of lists, series, and catalogues must have once been a rhetorical choice but became a habitual option. Lists are found almost everywhere in his writing, sometimes where there is no possible artistic justification either for the presence of a list or for the order in which the items appear. It would not be difficult to develop a specious hypothesis to account for the ubiquity of the lists and their randomness by recourse to Swift's increasing disorientation in his later years or other aspects of mind associated with his eventual lunacy. The frequent doublets that Lannering found in Addison's prose have a similar explanation. Lannering tried to account for the pleonastic doublets of nouns he found to be so frequent in Addison by reference to the concept of *copia verborum* and Addison's desire to diffuse the strength of his writings, to avoid the "energetick" style. The explanation seems unnecessary. Whatever may have been responsible for Addison's original use of doublets it seems probable that it became a habit.[9]

That rhetorical choices may become stylistic options, and that the part of language generation which I have called stylistic option comes from the least degree of consciousness that our minds are capable of while engaged

in linguistic activity does not deny that normal linguistic activity is creative and innovative. New sentences are constantly being produced, as
Chomsky has frequently announced.[10] But some parts of these sentences
are not new, at least in syntactic structure. It is these familiar structures
which are repeated and which impress themselves on the reader as constituting the style of the writer. The stylistic options taken together are the
style of the writer and represent the primary field of inquiry for the analyst
of style.

By suggesting that the analysis of style be more concerned with the
writer's unconscious machinery, I am not suggesting anything really new,
for the studies of individual style that are most commonly admired are in
fact, for the most part, investigations of stylistic options. Where I differ
from most investigators is in the conviction that they have erroneously
treated all decisions constituting style as conscious rhetorical choices, representing the realization of artistic intentions, or that they have mingled together habitual and artistic characteristics. Without for a moment denying
the possibility that some part of a writer's style is conscious artistry or
craftsmanship, I am convinced that most writers, even some of the greatest,
knew very little about what they were doing when they wrote and had
much less conscious control over the final product than is commonly supposed. The writer's typical feeling about his work is dissatisfaction, at least
one reason for which is that he could not sufficiently govern its form.

When we study a writer's style, we are studying a man writing as well as
an artist at work. Because he is an artist he has perhaps a more highly
marked individuality, at least in the intellectual and emotional spheres.
Consequently, it ought to be of interest to us how that individuality expresses itself without conscious effort in his work. We ought, that is, to attempt to determine how he has stamped the human contribution on the
facts, as Buffon said.

## Notes

1. *Theories of Style* (New York, 1907), p. 179.
2. *Essai sur l'esthétique de Descartes: Rapports de la doctrine cartésienne
avec la littérature classique française au XVII siècle* (Paris, 1898, 2nd ed.), p. 342.
("The *Treatise on Style* represents, in my opinion, the ultimate development of
classical doctrine. In Buffon's conception, universality becomes lost in generality.
The search for simplicity goes so far as to deprive eloquence of all sensuous in-
gredients, and to deny it all the resources deriving from passion and imagination, so that it becomes merely style, that is, the pure expression of thought by
means of a minimum of impersonal terms.")
3. *Ibid.*, p. 359. ("Style—that is, general style—is the man—that is, the essential
and abstract man.")

4. Wallace Hildick's interesting *Word for Word: A Study of Authors' Altera-tions* (London, 1965) shows how often the revised wording is cancelled in favor of the original.

5. An illuminating example is found in the changes that take place when a writer quotes from memory. He tends to distort the original into conformity with his own stylistic tendencies. Dr. Johnson quoting Jacob Tonson's remarks about Addison, "He had thoughts of getting that lady from his first being rec-ommended into that family," renders it: "He formed the design of getting that lady from the time when he was first recommended into the family," *Lives of the Poets*, ed. G. B. Hill (Oxford, 1905), II, 110. Johnson prefers specific finite verb constructions to the vaguer and more awkward, but also more flexible, verb idiom and participle phrase.

6. R. A. Sayce, *Style in French Prose* (Oxford, 1958), pp. 147-48.

7. A. E. Hotchner, "Hemingway Talks to American Youth," *This Week* (Oct. 18, 1959), p. 11.

8. Alvar Ellegård, *A Statistical Method for Determining Authorship: The Junius Letters, 1769-1772* (Goteborg, 1962); Frederick Mosteller and David L. Wallace, *Inference and Disputed Authorship: The Federalist* (Reading, Mass., 1964).

9. The observations cited may be found in W. K. Wimsatt, *The Prose Style of Samuel Johnson* (New Haven, Conn., 1941), Louis T. Milic, *A Quantitative Approach to the Style of Jonathan Swift* (The Hague, 1967), and Jan Lanner-ing, *Studies in the Prose Style of Joseph Addison* (Upsala, 1951), *passim*.

10. Noam Chomsky, *Language and Mind* (New York, 1968), p. 10, where this carefully hedged statement appears: "the normal use of language is innova-tive, in the sense that much of what we say in the course of normal language use is entirely new, not a repetition of anything that we have heard before and not even similar in pattern—in any useful sense of the terms 'similar' and 'pattern'— to sentences or discourse that we have heard in the past." This statement is shortly followed by the claim, in figurative terms, that the number of sentence patterns in English exceeds 220 billion. It should be noted that *pattern* need not be limited to *sentence pattern*.

# DISCUSSION OF MILIC'S PAPER

It was noted that the distinction between conscious rhetorical choice and less conscious stylistic option raises the question of "consciousness," which linguists have fought shy of because of its difficulty. Linguistics would be

a great deal easier if we could start out from something like logic and rhetoric, if, in generative terms, we could have a logic machine with some kind
of output which would go through a rhetoric machine, whose output is input to a grammar machine. The distinction between conscious and unconscious implies the possibility of breaking the process up into steps. But how
is that to be done and what are the ultimate criteria for doing it? Milic responded that the distinction is not very clear-cut; the unconscious options
are in the smaller syntactic choices and the rhetorical choices are in the
larger ones. This is not saying a great deal theoretically. The things that are
consistent throughout an author's canon are the things that he does not
have conscious interest in or control over. In other words, if you study the
whole of an author's work, you will find that he uses chiasmus only in certain formal contexts, whereas he uses initial adverbial constructions in a
steady percentage of all his sentences. The first is rhetorical choice, the second stylistic option. Milic would have recourse to intuition to help locate
those things which the writer is least conscious of.

Milic was asked if he had said that rhetorical choices are structurally related to the work, while stylistic options are an over-all feature of all the
writings of the author. He said that he had, though there is an area where
that which is required by the work becomes habitual.

On the question of "consciousness," it was suggested that between the
poles of consciousness and unconsciousness there is a wide field of human
behavior, with all its nuances. Can we expect to have a typology of human
behavior to determine degrees of consciousness? There is a typical behavior
which has its own degree of consciousness, i.e., teleological behavior. If you
want to hang a picture, your consciousness is on the nail, not on the hammer, though you are not absolutely unconscious of the hammer; it is attended with a kind of secondary consciousness, and the nail is secondary to
the picture. But we have to recognize the instrumental character of language; normally there is no full consciousness of the linguistic instrument,
but in case the instrument does not work, our full consciousness falls on
the language rather than on what we aim to do with it. Therefore, we have
to recognize that there is a special form of semi-consciousness typical of
final processes, and one of these processes is the normal linguistic act when
there is no special finality reflected on the process itself; this would be typical of artistic, that is, for our purposes, literary behavior. Milic replied that
in the image of hanging a picture, there are both conscious and unconscious decisions; the decision about what picture to hang is artistic and
conscious (involving principles of design, etc.), while the muscular effort
to hang the picture and to hit the nail rather than one's thumb is unconscious to a large degree. The middle stage—some semi-conscious process—
is at work somewhere in the production of linguistic strings, but it is un-

certain where to place it or how to define it. But Milic thought that two bits of information might be relevant: 1) When one is sleepy, one often can produce words, but they don't seem to have much interrelationship; 2) In the writing of schizophrenics, there are small-scale patterns which do not come together to make ordered sets of meanings. The linguistic process is working, but it is not dominated by consciousness.

It was suggested that the problems that were being discussed arose from a confusion about the definition of style. Is style a form of thought or a form of writing? It was argued that style should be defined as a form of thought, and *écriture* ("writing") as the linguistic expression. When Buffon says *le style, c'est l'homme*, he means that style is the form of a man's thought. Nineteenth-century writers like Rémy de Gourmont agree. Although we find great differences of style among individual writers, there is also a great similarity of writing (*écriture*). So what Milic must be talking about is writing; for which "automatic" (*automatisée*) is a better term than "unconscious." There are writings of genre, class, schools; though style may be the man, writing certainly is not. Milic found himself in agreement with much of this argument. He stated that he had not stressed sufficiently that the unconscious components formed only a part of style; he would be perfectly happy to call the unconscious base one thing and the conscious artistic effects something else. He did not support the view that the personality is reflected in the style; there is no way to tell whether this is so or not, because personality theory is not yet sufficiently developed to let us do so. What he insisted on was that, though it is true indeed that two authors may have a similar "dialect" because they both wrote at the same time and in the same genre, each possesses an absolute, demonstrable uniqueness. No writer can write like any other, especially no great writer. If our instruments are sensitive enough, the characteristics of any writer must diverge from every other. Whether we say that the uniqueness of these characteristics reflects something in his personality or merely that the characteristics are associated with him is another question.

On the question of collecting data, Milic was asked if it were not true that it is impossible to collect meaningful data without some kind of theory, even if that theory is implicit or unconscious. As long as there is at least one reader, the collector himself, doesn't the thrust of his personality and interests entail a theory about what is to be collected? Milic acknowledged that the analyst is a reader and to that extent formulates the categories; this, of course, implies something about what is likely to be of interest to him. But that does not mean that he needs to impose the categories to find what he is looking for; he can rather permit them to elicit from the text the kind of data that may lead to conclusions. It is quite possible that a large investigation would not lead to any conclusions. But that might be a good thing; at least it would be clear that there were no preconceptions.

A participant wondered whether it was necessary to make the distinction between conscious and unconscious at all. Whenever one does so, one seems to be departing from an immanent consideration of the work, from the problem of analyzing stylistic effects, in order to speculate about the act of creation, an issue which, in the last analysis, is imponderable. One cannot equate "unknown" with "unconscious," because what is unknown may some day be known. The antithesis between rhetorical choice and stylistic option is misleading because it implies that all conscious choices are in the direction of efficacy, because "rhetoric" implies a more efficient communication with the reader, and the choices that we are interested in do not necessarily seem to be of that sort. Further, if one insists upon the distinction, there is clearly a need for a middle term. Granted that sentence length is unconscious, while the use of zeugma is conscious—what about the choice between a relative clause and a participial phrase: is it really unconscious? Of course the writer does not formulate the term in his mind, he does not say to himself "I am now electing to use a participle instead of a relative clause"; but still it is a choice which he makes, one which the possibilities of the language offer him. And in that sense, you cannot call it totally unconscious. It seems that the distinction conscious/unconscious is not fruitful for this particular decision, that it is an idle speculation whether an author was conscious of electing a certain feature; all that matters is that he did do so, and that the feature is more or less useful and meaningful in the work. Thus it is not only difficult, but finally unnecessary to define and use the concept of consciousness in stylistics. Milic responded that he had erected the dichotomy for convenience and clarity, and that conscious and unconscious are to be taken as two poles—that in most cases, one must speak of a greater or lesser degree of consciousness. The use of a relative clause, which is clearly a large-scale device, may be more conscious than the placement of a middle adverb in a verb cluster. That doesn't mean that every decision to use a relative clause is one that the writer is aware of. (We are limited to the terms available to us.) He said that he was willing to agree that there is no way of telling whether a given choice is one or the other, except by reference to its size or its ability to fit into an artistic structure. He took as an example a recent study of Milton's use of past participles,[1] in which it is argued that Milton was imposing his theology on the reader, in a subliminal way, by means of the past participle without agent, but in which the implicit agent was God. But it may only have been that past participles came readily to Milton, that it was a structure that he was "programmed" to use. Though the consequence was that it made his task of organizing the religious beliefs of the reader easier, it is not necessarily something he intended. The question is what is the importance of that distinction; the article argues that it is an artistic effect, but maybe it is not. If we are trying to establish a picture of Milton's artistic intentions or his artistic achievement, it is probably worthwhile to distinguish the use or non-use of this kind of device in the sense that it is important to establish anything in literary criticism by stylistic means. As for the statement that not everything that goes on in the writer's mind is unconscious, Milic argued that he had only said that *some* things were unconscious. Perhaps we will eventually know what goes on in his mind; it is at least as interesting to know how the writer's mind works as it is to know how its effects work on the reader. We are interested in literature—to some extent, at least—because it is a human production, and we are interested in all parts of the process.

It was noted that though the distinction between *stylistic* and *rhetorical* is useful, the fact that the word "choice" (or "option") is associated with both obscures a certain difference that obtains between them. While it is correct to talk about choices where there is a conscious mode of language use, it does not seem useful to talk about unconscious choice. Where there is such unconscious use of language, there is an implication that the author's mind is in some sense pre-set—and if that is true, it does not seem useful to talk about his ability to make choices. Of course, we could draw a distinction between habitual and unconscious, which Milic seems to use synonymously, in the sense that the habitual mode is predetermined by training and use, whereas the unconscious mode is predetermined by psychological factors. Whatever the author is doing, the habitual mode manifests itself as a patterning or global effect throughout the text, whereas the unconscious choices would be isolated instances. Milic said that he had intentionally used "option" in connection with style, to avoid the sense that the choice is willed, although he acknowledged that he should have perhaps used the terms "stylistic program," in the sense that the word has in computer technology. He accepted the suggestion that a useful distinction might be made between habitual and unconscious.

Milic was reminded that there is a certain ambiguity in the word "unconscious." It can mean either to be unaware of something by personal or social habit, or to be unaware of it by repressing it (in the Freudian sense). Someone might suffer an emotional crisis of sorts as a response to a practical situation—say the request of a friend to lend him a large sum of money. But a moral man would react immediately by giving the money; we can speak of a moral "ethos" in that "unconscious" reaction. It is really the ethos that we are concerned with in stylistics; it is from this that choices emerge and "branch." Milic pointed out that he was not, of course, referring to the mechanism of repression, and that he intentionally used the term "unconscious" rather than "subconscious" to avoid Freudian implications.

In defense of Milic's thesis, it was argued that though it is proper to ask whether we need the concept of unconsciousness, whether it adds anything to what we would know without it, Milic was offering an explanatory hypothesis that helped make sense of quite a variety of data, not only what happens in the manuscript revisions of authors, but also how difficult it is to teach eighteen-year-olds to write. This is the function of an explanatory rubric—to make sense of a cluster of diverse facts. It might not help us to interpret a style or understand a literary work in the particular way that a stylistic critic wants it to and yet still be valuable as a hypothesis. Further, it seems a corroboration of Milic's argument that period-styles, like parodies, seem to be built on very superficial characteristics, that there continue to be enormous stylistic differences between, say, Johnson and Gibbon as soon as one goes beneath the kind of parallelism which may be superficially imposed and learned as an artifice, in short as soon as one goes down to deep structure. Apparently, a writer may acquire the characteristics of a period-style, but they tend to be the more superficial ones, and his own unconscious work will go on undisturbed. Milic agreed.

One participant was surprised to hear Milic say that there was no work on unconscious stylistics—all the early work of Spitzer was concerned with that, as, for instance, his article on the style of Charles-Louis Phillipe, in which he showed that the use of *à cause de* is indicative of a certain *Weltanschauung* of Phillipe. Or the essay on the style of Diderot. There is a lot of work, some of it psychoanalytical, on the identification of conscious and unconscious features in the styles of many writers. Milic said that he was aware of Spitzer's work, but that he had not brought it up because that work was primarily concerned with finding the physiognomy of the author in the style, whereas he was interested primarily in the association between the characteristics which are unconsciously produced; he believes that there is now no efficient method for bringing the two together.

It was noted that Milic had said that conscious rhetorical choice will sometimes lapse into stylistic option or routine (e.g., Johnson's parallelism). But the reverse can happen too; for example, Dryden's early prose (as in the first edition of the "Essay of Dramatic Poesy") uses the preposition at the end of relative clauses in final position in sentences, something that we are still taught is careless (". . . the ideas which I swear by"). Archbishop Tillotson, a classically trained stylist, told Dryden that this was not the thing to do, and Dryden went through the essay and changed all those constructions in the revised edition. The first instance might be called an unconscious stylistic option, but surely Dryden was conscious when he revised all those sentences. In general there is much more of an interplay between these things than has been suggested, and what is chiefly interesting is the case where the two merge, the effect or meaning, that is, which involves both of them.

## Note

1. Seymour Chatman, "Milton's Participial Style," *PMLA*, LXXXIII (1968), 1386-99.

# TOWARD A STRUCTURAL THEORY
# OF CONTENT IN PROSE FICTION

## LUBOMÍR DOLEŽEL

THE DEVELOPMENT of stylistics has benefited enormously from the contributions of modern structural linguistics to its theory and techniques of descriptive analysis. However, to make stylistics a division of linguistics would be to limit its scope, goals, and methods unnecessarily and undesirably. Modern Western linguistics, as represented by the "schools" of de Saussure, Bloomfield, and Chomsky, has been primarily concerned with the study of language (*langue*), while the study of texts (*parole*) has received only lip service.[1] Stylistics, in its double capacity as theory of "productive" potentials and of verbal "products," is focused almost uniquely on texts and text structures.

The main weakness of linguistically oriented stylistics is its derivation of descriptions (and models) of the text structures from descriptions (and models) of language. This approach does not take into account the fact that the text is an autonomous semiotic structure; its properties can be explained only partly (and, even at that, only on the lower levels of organization) by a theory of language. It can be assumed, therefore, that the structure of the text sign can best be accounted for by a special text theory, conceived as a branch of the general theory of signs (semiotics).[2] The framework of general semiotics makes it possible to establish the relationships between text theory and language theory, as well as between text theory and theory of non-verbal messages. An autonomous text theory will then serve as the basis for a stylistics which is primarily concerned with the variety of texts "produced" in one and the same language.

One of the essential properties of text structure—and one which no linguistic theory is able to account for fully—is the organization of textual units in a temporal sequence. Text is a function of time, and its sequential "growth," by symmetry, parallelism, gradation, contrast, "coupling," etc., represents the time dimension of the text structure. A second essential property of the text structure which clearly transcends the current competence of linguistics is its content dimension.

The notion of content has been important to various theories of text and specifically of literary texts. The dichotomy of form and content has been considered crucial (either in a positive or a negative sense) to any system of literary criticism. In this paper, an attempt will be made to formulate the first steps toward a structural (i.e., immanent) theory of text content; current empirical notions will be taken into account as far as possible, but the main emphasis will be on a systematic approach to the theory.

### SYSTEM OF A MOTIF THEORY

The special problem of content theory which will be approached in this paper concerns that type of literary text which is commonly called prose fiction (narrative prose). There are two main reasons for my concern with this text type: 1. Though a work of prose fiction, like a poem, is a text, i.e., a verbal "product," it has been commonly felt that an interpretation of prose fiction is insufficient if it is limited to verbal structure of form and meaning and neglects the structures of content (although this kind of analysis often seems quite satisfactory in the case of poetry). I shall assume that any theory of prose fiction is inadequate which does not account for the structures of content. 2. Many scholars have attempted a description of content structures in narrative prose. Their results furnish a reliable starting point for a systematic theory of content in fiction. In this paper, a tribute to these efforts can be paid only in a very brief enumeration: the German "rhetoric" school (Scuffert, von Fleschenberg, Dibelius) with their works on "composition"; the Russian Formalist school (Shklovskij, Tomashevskij) with their system of plot-construction analysis; the morphological folklorists and anthropologists (Propp, Lévi-Strauss); the Czech school of structural literary theory (Mukařovský, Vodička) with their studies in "thematic" analysis.[3] Whatever merits this paper may have are mainly due to the inspiration of these outstanding predecessors.

As in other theoretical systems, the best starting point for developing a structural theory of content in fiction is to define the elementary unit. Earlier studies have already specified this unit and given it the name of *motif*. According to Tomashevskij, whose account of motifs and their classification is the most systematic, motif is "the minimal dissection of the thematic material." "Each sentence," wrote Tomashevskij, "contains a motif of its own." He gives the following examples: "Evening came," "Raskolnikov killed the old woman," "The hero died," "A letter was received."[4]

Propp, who undertook a systematic investigation of motifs in the Russian fairy-tale, arrived at a small number of general *motif functions* common to the whole corpus of fairy-tale texts, such as: "The hero leaves home," "The villain is defeated," "The hero returns."

Tomashevskij's and Propp's examples indicate that the segment of text which a motif can represent is variable. A motif of the type "A letter was received" can be identical in wording as an actual bit of the text, whereas one like "Raskolnikov killed the old woman" summarizes a large portion of the text of *Crime and Punishment*, and these exact words do not occur in the text. This important observation leads us to the conclusion that a distinction between the actual wording of the text and the general metalingual expression of a motif is fundamental for a theory of motifs. Let us call the actual segment from the text a *motif texture* and any metalingual representation of a motif a *motif paraphrase*.

It is obvious that texture expresses the stylistic variety of the motif (reflecting both idiosyncrasies and supraindividual stereotypes); while, on the contrary, paraphrase expresses the motif as a content invariant. I would like to illustrate this distinction with an example borrowed from Jan Mukařovský. Mukařovský pointed out that romantic poets were fond of expressing certain human acts in such a way as to make a human organ (ear, eye, voice, heart) the grammatical subject of the sentence.[5] Instead of "The prisoner looked out the small window," the romantic poet is likely to say "The prisoner's eye peered out the small window." In our terminology, the first sentence is the motif paraphrase, the second one its texture.

As already indicated, the distinction between texture and paraphrase makes possible a study of individual and supraindividual manipulations of motifs. These manipulations include not only stylization, but also the ways of introducing motifs into the narrative text. Tomashevskij pointed out that motifs can be introduced either in characters' speech (dialogue, monologue) or in narrative ("author's speech"). The manner of introduction is reflected in the motif texture, but it is irrelevant for the motif as content invariant; therefore, it does not find expression in the motif paraphrase.

On the basis of the distinction between motif texture and motif paraphrase some crucial notions of the motif theory can be defined. Motifs are *identical* if they are expressed by the same texture and the same paraphrase. Motifs are *equivalent* if they are expressed by the same paraphrase but differ in their texture. Motifs are *similar in texture* if they are different in the paraphrase but identical in a certain segment of their texture.

Let us now proceed one step further in the development of our system. It is assumed that to each sentence of the motif paraphrase a general formula can be assigned; in its form this formula expresses the type of the motif. In this stage of the development of our system, the set of motif formulas will not be arrived at by induction, but rather will be considered to be given *a priori*.

In order to make our task easier and our explanation simpler, we will limit ourselves in the further discussion to one type of motif only, the so-called *dynamic motifs*. It will be assumed that dynamic motifs correspond to one of the following abstract formulas:

    1. A performed an action affecting B;

    2. A performed an action;

    3. A was affected by an action;

where A and B are characters (dramatis personae) or groups of characters in the story.[6]

The formula of dynamic motifs consists of three basic terms—agent (Ag.), action (Act.), and patient (Pat.), agent or patient being deletable. The basic formula expresses either three-member motifs of the type "The hero killed the dragon" (Ag.-Act.-Pat.), or two-member motifs of the types "The hero returned" (Ag.-Act.), and "The villain was defeated" (Pat.-Act.). Any of the three basic terms can be expanded by one or more modifiers (Mod.): "The older brother went to the south" (Mod./Ag.-Act./Mod.).

The assignment of motif formulas and the distinction of the basic and modifying terms in the formula lead to a further specification of relations between dynamic motifs. A motif is *negative* if the term of action is negative. A motif is *contrary* if the term of action is antonymous to the term of action of an equivalent motif: "The hero left home. The hero returned home." Motifs are *variants* if their paraphrases are identical in basic terms but differ in modifiers: "The first *pig built* a house of straw. The second *pig built* a house of twigs. The third *pig built* a house of bricks." Motifs are *similar* if their paraphrase expressions of the term of action are identical: "A dragon *carried off* the king's daughter." "A witch *carried off* a boy."[7]

So far we have been concerned only with forms of motif expression (texture, paraphrase, formula) and with the basic relationships between dynamic motifs (identity, equivalence, variance, similarity). A second component of the motif theory must account for the temporal sequence of motifs and for their clustering into higher units. In this context, I consider it important to deal briefly with the notions of motif configuration, scene composition, and plot construction.

*Motif configuration* will be defined as a sequence of two or more motifs displaying a certain order, as, for example, when the motifs of the sequence belong to one of the above-defined classes. Thus, for example, the three motif variants given above in "The Three Little Pigs" form a configuration of gradation. It is important to note in this connection that the study of motif configurations can profit greatly from the study of "poetic devices" conducted by structural poetics. Shklovskij, who first attempted a systematic study of motif configurations, has already pointed to a homomorphism existing between configurations of motifs in narrative prose and configurations of sounds in poetry.[8] It can be further assumed that this homomorphism extends also to grammatical configurations; these have been studied by Roman Jakobson.[9] Thus, a theory of motifs can be expected to provide further evidence for the assumption that in various forms of literature there exist homomorphic patterns operating on units of different "material" or different text levels.

Before attempting a definition of scene composition, the notion of scene has to be introduced into our system. *Scene* is an aggregate of dynamic motifs presenting certain constituent features. These features can be of various kinds, such as a certain place of action (setting), a certain time-span of action, a group of acting characters, etc. Purely formal features can also constitute a scene, for example, the way of introducing the motifs (dialogue scene, narrative scene, "letter" scene, etc.). I find it advisable to characterize the notion of scene in this general form for the time being; only a detailed study of the variety of motif aggregates can lead to further specification and elaboration of the notion.

A sequence of scenes displaying a certain pattern of order will be called a *scene composition*. It is obvious that scene composition is analogous to motif configuration. The pattern of scene composition, again, inheres in the equivalence or similarity of scenes in the sequence. However, in the present framework, the notion of equivalence of scenes cannot be defined in a formal way.[10]

The most general term of the theory of dynamic motifs is that of *plot construction*. It was precisely by differentiating the notion of *plot* (*sjužet*) from that of *action* (*fabula*) that the theory of fiction of the Russian school was successful.[11] Since we have introduced the elementary plot units —dynamic motifs—our concept of plot construction can be outlined without reference to the notion of action. *Plot construction* is the superstructure of all sequential structures which can be described in the sequence of dynamic motifs of a particular narrative text. Thus, it is a synthesizing concept, integrating motif configurations, scene composition and other sequential structures of dynamic motifs which are not discussed in this paper, especially the structure of narrative time.

### EXAMPLE OF MOTIF ANALYSIS

In order to demonstrate my system, I shall offer a token motif analysis, using the text of Ernest Hemingway's short story "The Killers" as its sub-

ject-matter. The story is rather well suited for analysis of this kind; it
manipulates the motifs in such a sophisticated and patterned way that it
could almost be called "a poem of motifs."

A basic and easily discernible feature of "The Killers" is its symmetrical
scene composition. Three scenes, established in terms of setting, are arranged in a symmetrical pattern: At Henry's/At Ole Anderson's/At Henry's.
Nick's return to Henry's lunch-room in the third scene makes the symmetrical pattern a cycle. Nothing has happened, seemingly; the action returns to where it started. There is only one new motif introduced in the
third scene—Nick Adams leaves town. But this motif is apparently a functional joint linking "The Killers" with the other stories of the Nick Adams
cycle.

Symmetry of scene composition is, however, only one manifestation of
the overall symmetrical pattern of motif structure in "The Killers." A
more sophisticated symmetry is to be found in the motif configurations of
the second scene. It consists of several layers: the core of the scene—Nick's
meeting with Ole Anderson—is framed by two corresponding sequences of
motifs, the sequence of Nick's walk and that of his meeting with Mrs. Bell.
Moreover, the core of the scene has an internal symmetry provided by the
sequence of motifs of Nick's entry and departure. The "tiered" symmetry
of motif sequences in the second scene can be represented as follows:

NICK'S WALK
*Nick's meeting with Mrs. Bell*
Nick's entry
Nick's meeting with Ole Anderson
Nick's departure
*Nick's meeting with Mrs. Bell*
NICK'S WALK.

The symmetry of the motifs in the sequence of Nick's walk is "mirror-
imaged": they have the order A-B at the beginning of the scene, but B-A at
the end: "Nick walked up the street beside the car-tracks and turned at the
next arc-light down a side street": "Nick walked up the dark street to
the corner under the arc-light, and then along the car-tracks to Henry's
eating house."

The symmetrical motif configurations are, of course, materialized by repeating equivalent or similar motifs. However, as in the case of symmetry,
*motif repetition* has a much more general currency in Hemingway's narrative style: it is one of its essential and most typical qualities. This quality
has been already pointed out by critics.[12] Our system of motif analysis

however makes possible a systematic study of motif repetition; it enables us not only to describe the repetition patterns but also to reveal specific ways in which these patterns are implemented and functionally employed. It is important to note that a simple repetition of identical motifs is not typical of Hemingway; rather, his motif repetitions are based on the relations of equivalence, similarity, contrariety, etc. This means that repeated motifs display a rich variety in texture. It is this game of repetition and variation which, in my opinion, constitutes one of the brilliant effects of Hemingway's style.

The appendix to this paper presents a tentative transcription of the second scene of "The Killers" in sentences of motif paraphrase, grouping motifs into classes as defined in the first part of the paper. The investigation of the motif classes vividly confirms our statement about Hemingway's specific motif repetitions.

Another interesting result can be reached by assigning frequencies of occurrence to the particular motif classes of the scene core:

| A | 2 | G | 1 |
|---|---|---|---|
| B | 2 | H | 1 |
| C | 4 | I | 1 |
| D | 7 | J | 1 |
| E | 2 | K | 1 |
| F | 4 | | |

It is apparent that motifs C, D, and F represent leitmotifs of the scene. Class D is set up (with the exception of motif #19) by the motifs "Ole Anderson looked at the wall" and "Ole Anderson did not look at Nick." The importance of this leitmotif is emphasized by the fact that it is repeated three times in the same texture, although elsewhere Hemingway is careful to differentiate equivalent motifs by means of minor details in the texture (compare "Ole Anderson said nothing" and "[Ole Anderson] did not say anything"). The repetition of two identical motifs can also be found in class F ("There ain't anything to do"). The leitmotifs "Ole Anderson was lying in bed," "Ole Anderson looked at the wall," and "Ole Anderson did nothing" form a repetitive pattern which governs the content structure of the scene.

Another group of motifs which is highly relevant to the content structure of the scene is formed by action terms similar in texture; the texture of this term contains modal expressions of the type "I cannot," "I do not want to." These motifs express Ole Anderson's desperate immobility.[13] They are joined by a set of negative motifs (more than one-half of all

Ole Anderson's motifs are negative) to create an explicit and emphatic expression of Ole's passive submission to the power of "fate."

If we also consider the motifs of the first and third scene, we note a clear distinction of characters in the story: on the one hand, a passive group—the victim and onlookers, Ole, George, Sam; on the other hand, the active "professionals"—Al and Max. In between stands Nick Adams, powerless against the killers' game, but attempting at least the humane act of warning Ole Anderson; however Nick is ineffectual against the fateful menace. In the end, he decides to leave town. His last action however, brings him close to the passivity of George and Sam, who do not want "to hear" and "to think" about "it."

Here, apparently, a structural analysis of motifs of "The Killers" should stop. A "metastructural" interpretation of the story could take over. Any frontier of structural analysis is, however, little more than a convention. The two stages of literary study—structural analysis and metastructural interpretation—necessarily overlap. It is to be emphasized, however, that structural analysis is a necessary precondition of any consistent critical interpretation, which otherwise is nothing more than ingenious speculation.[14]

### GENERAL FRAMEWORK

It has already been pointed out that a text theory which does not account for structures of content cannot be considered adequate. Most theories of literary texts have taken content into account. Their approach, however, is usually "external": content is interpreted in terms of psychology, sociology, metaphysics, ethics, etc. Typical of these "extratextual" approaches are the interpretations of characters (dramatis personae) so common in criticism of fiction. In psychologically oriented interpretations, characters are representatives of certain mental types; in sociological interpretations, they are treated as members of a certain class or social group at a certain moment of social history; in metaphysical interpretation, they are images of a certain "human condition"; in ethical interpretations, they are representatives of a certain morality (or immorality), etc.

Our understanding of literature requires an immanent (structural) theory of content, but such a theory cannot be systematically formulated at this moment. What I shall attempt here is no more than a sketch of one possible approach.

A point of departure is provided by the usual assumption that any semiotic structure has two indispensable dimensions, that of expression and that of meaning. Without going into a detailed discussion of the relationship between these, I would like to emphasize one aspect of the relationship which, in my opinion, is most important for the theory of content. It is the principle called by P. L. Garvin "the form-meaning covariance": "When linguistic form varies" with respect to the linguistic sign, writes Garvin, "linguistic meaning almost always varies with it, and conversely." Garvin also takes into account the possibility of synonymy and homonymy, designated by Karcevski as a "dualisme assymétrique du signe linguistique."[15] These are "exceptions to the generality of the form-meaning covariance." The existence of synonymy makes a semantic paraphrasing possible, i.e., such a reformulation of the original text as will preserve meaning as invariant.[16]

By introducing the dimension of content into the model of the text structure, we will be able to account for the fact that some referential qualities of texts survive even a more substantial paraphrasing than suggested by Garvin. We know that some referential qualities remain invariant even when the text is transposed into another sign system; for example, by translation or conversion from the literary to the film medium. These transformations are feasible only because of the existence of referential invariants.

Thus, our basic assumption is that text content is a set of referential invariants which survive a substantial (suprasemantic) paraphrasing of the original text expression. Text content can be defined as the aggregate of meaning associated with a text paraphrase which is referentially equivalent to the original text; in other words, the original text expression and its content paraphrase denote the same referent.

The concepts of semantic (synonymic) paraphrase and content paraphrase define the relationship between the dimensions of text meaning and text content. The limit of synonymy marks off semantic invariants from content invariants. This demarcation outlines, at least theoretically, the scope of the theory of content as well as the semantic theories of literary texts like that conceived by Wimsatt and Beardsley.[17]

There is, however, another empirical fact which should be accounted for by a systematic theory of text content. I have in mind the common assumption that content is a certain *condensation* of the original meaning of text. Content, apparently, is an aspect of text structure which enables us to grasp and to store the complexity and totality of text meaning in a condensed and simplified manner. In incorporating the notion of condensation into the structural theory of content, we are, however, obliged to recognize that content can be defined on various levels of condensation. In other words, the text content can be expressed by content paraphrases of various degrees of condensation. This assumption corresponds to the common practice of content analysis which has used such terms as "detailed" or "brief" content.

Summarizing, we can represent the relationships between the dimensions of the text structure in the following scheme:

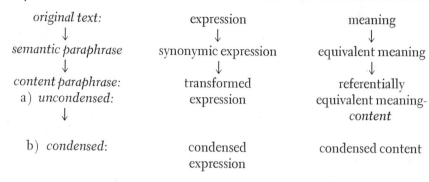

The first task of content analysis is to derive a content paraphrase. In order to avoid difficulties of "referential equivalence," the operation will be defined as a set of explicit and controlled rewrite instructions which lead from the original text wording to the content paraphrase. Thus conceived, content paraphrasing shows a certain analogy with the operations of automatic abstracting in the theory of information retrieval. At the same time, there is an essential difference: whereas automatic abstracting aims at a paraphrase which would reveal the text content itself, a structural theory of content is interested in a paraphrase which would reveal its structure. For a structural theory of content, any content paraphrase which destroyed the text's inherent content structure would be illegitimate.

The operation of content paraphrasing should consist of the following basic steps:

1. A transformation of the sentences of the original text into a limited number of simple sentence structures. This step is analogous to the derivation of sentences in transformational grammar; however, it proceeds in the opposite direction: from the "derived" sentences of the original text to the "kernel" sentences of the paraphrase.[18]

It can be assumed that some standardized transformational rules of transformational grammar could be utilized in this step (for example, the transformation of non-verbal into verbal sentences). However, many additional transformational rules will be needed to achieve the specific goals of content paraphrasing. It is quite likely that these rules will apply only to a certain type of text. Thus, for example, content paraphrasing of narrative texts will require specific rules dealing with various forms of dialogue.[19]

2. An assignment of the terms of kernel sentences to their abstract equivalence classes. In other words, referentially equivalent terms are to be rewritten as the same abstract class term. This is the critical point in the paraphrasing procedure. Because no satisfactory criterion of the referential equivalence is known, we are entirely dependent on trial and error.

It is obvious that referential equivalence must occur first in the context of a concrete text.[20] It is, however, conceivable that the limits of a single text could be transcended and equivalence classes could be found for a type of texts. As a matter of fact, it was probably for this purpose that Vladimir Propp developed his theory of "functions."

As a result of the application of the two operations, the original text should be rewritten in a sequence of kernel sentences consisting of abstract equivalence class terms. It is assumed that this sequence will represent the desired non-condensed content paraphrase. I am convinced that this paraphrase permits a viable study of content structures.

3. Finally, a condensation, leading to a condensed paraphrase. These operations will be variable, depending on the degree of condensation required and perhaps also on the nature of the text. In general, this step can be formulated as a search for key sentences relevant to the content structure of the given degree of condensation. Experience suggests two ways of arriving at key sentences: a) synthesizing two or more sentences of the non-condensed paraphrase into one condensed sentence; b) indexing key sentences by using a certain formal or semantic criterion of relevance.[21]   (chatman)

This brief sketch of content paraphrasing provides a tentative theoretical framework for particular investigations. While such a theoretical framework indicates the general direction of the study of content, real progress can be expected only by concentrating on individual text types. It was with this expectation that my token analysis of motifs in prose fiction was undertaken.

Let me return briefly to the fundamental results of that analysis and evaluate them from the viewpoint of my general framework. The analysis was based on a non-condensed content paraphrase. The notions of motif texture and motif paraphrase correspond to the general notions of "original expression" and "non-condensed content paraphrase." The distinction between the sentences of the original expression and those of paraphrase enabled me to define some basic relationships between my content units— the motifs—and to define the fundamental motif classes. Investigating the content paraphrase, I concentrated on one type of sentence only, that corresponding to the formulas of dynamic motifs. This means that my token study did not proceed in the direction of paraphrase condensation, but in that of classifying sentences of the uncondensed paraphrase.

On this basis I set up a system of analysis of dynamic motifs, or, in other words, a partial system of plot-construction analysis. A complete and systematic analysis of the non-condensed content paraphrase of the narrative text type is conceivable along these lines. It would require, of course, additional sets of motif formulas for the identification of the remaining non-dynamic motif types (for example, the so-called "static" motifs). If we accept the plausible assumption that the set of motif types in a narrative text is limited, then there is no obstacle to the development of a systematic method of analysis of the narrative text type. Once a system of structural content analysis is set up for one type of literary text, the content theory of other text types (poetry, drama, essays, etc.), as well as a general theory of text content, might be developed along similar lines.

A structural theory of content would represent a major contribution to a systematic and, to a certain degree, formalized theory of literature and literary styles. Of course, many arguments against such a theory of literature are in wide circulation; many literary critics are skeptical about it. The apprehension that a systematic and formalized theory of literature would "destroy" the aesthetic qualities of the literary object is a prejudice arising from a misconception of the aims and purport of theoretical study. Still, there are important reasons for accepting various forms of "non-formalized" literary criticism. A formalized literary theory is only one way of studying literature; it requires both a specific goal and a specific audience. It does not preclude the use of other ways of talking about literature for other purposes and to other types of audience.

## NOTES

1. For L. Bloomfield, text was just a unit of corpus used for arriving at a description of the abstract language system (see S. R. Levin, "*Langue* and *Parole* in American Linguistics," *Foundations of Language*, I (1965), 86ff.). The consequences of this approach for stylistics were catastrophic: "The linguist . . . studies the language of all persons alike; the individual features in which the language of a great writer differs from the ordinary speech of his time and place interest the linguist no more than do the individual features of any other person's speech, and much less than do the features that are common to all speakers" (L. Bloomfield, *Language*, New York, 1933, p. 22). The Chomskian attitude to this problem is typified by this quotation: "In the widest sense, linguistics is concerned with both language and speech. But scientific understanding of speech can be gained only on the basis of extensive knowledge about language. For this reason, linguists have traditionally narrowed the scope of their investigations to the study of language proper" (J. J. Katz and P. M. Postal, *An Integrated Theory of Linguistic Description*, Cambridge, Mass., 1964, p. ix). It is characteristic that Katz and Postal even repeat de Saussure's misleading comparison of language with a symphony and of speech with a symphony performance.
2. Cf. M. Bense, *Theorie der Texte* (Cologne, 1962).
3. See especially B. Seuffert, "Beobachtungen über dichterische Komposition," GRM, I (1909); O. Schlissel von Fleschenberg, *Novellenkomposition in E. T. A. Hoffmanns "Elixieren des Teufels"* (Halle a.S., 1910); W. Dibelius, *Englische Romankunst. Die Technik des englischen Romans im achtzehnten und zu Anfang des neunzehnten Jahrhunderts* (Berlin, 1910); V. Shklovskij, *O teorii prozy* (Moscow, 1925); B. Tomashevskij, *Teorija literatury (Poetika)* (Leningrad, 1925); V. Propp, *Morfologija skazki* (Leningrad, 1928), English translation: *Morphology of the Folktale* (Bloomington, Ind., 1958), ed. by

S. Pirkova-Jakobson; C. Lévi-Strauss, *Anthropologie structurale* (Paris, 1958);
J. Mukařovský, *Kapitoly z české poetiky* (Praha, 1948), Vols. I-III; F. Vodička,
*Počátky krásné prózy novočeské* (Praha, 1948).

4. B. Tomashevskij, *op. cit.*, p. 137.

5. J. Mukařovský, *op. cit.*, Vol. III, p. 162ff.

6. Tomashevskij characterizes dynamic motifs by their function; that is,
they "change the situation." The opposite are static motifs: "descriptions of nature, place, environment, characters, their personality, etc." (*op. cit.*, pp. 139-
40). Tomashevskij's "dynamic motifs" correspond to "cardinal functions" in the
R. Barthes-S. Chatman system. Chatman defines a formal feature of these
motifs: "Functions . . . are always reducible to the noncopulative verb,
which can generally be replaced by *do*" (S. Chatman, "New Ways of Analyzing
Narrative Structure with an Example from Joyce's *Dubliners*," *Language and
Style*, II (1968), 22).

7. The relationship of similarity is defined with respect to the term of action
only; in this stage of the theory, it would make no sense with respect to the
terms of characters.

8. Shklovskij, *Svjaz' prijemov sjužetosloženija s obščimi prijemami stilja*, in
*O teorii prozy* (Moscow, 1925).

9. See especially *Linguistics and Poetics*, in T. Sebeok, ed., *Style in Language*
(New York, 1960) and "Grammatical Parallelism and its Russian Facet," *Language*, XLII (1966).

10. The distinction between "scene" as a simple temporal sequence of motifs
and "scene-composition" corresponds to the differentiation of "disposition" and
"composition" introduced in the German "rhetoric" school.

11. "Action (*fabula*) is the ensemble of mutually connected events which
are conveyed in a literary work. Action can be described pragmatically, in the
natural chronological and causal order, independently from their order and introduction in the literary work. The opposite of action is plot (*sjužet*): the same
events, but in their distribution, in that order in which information about the
events is given in the literary work" (*op. cit.*, p. 137). In later editions of his
book Tomashevskij gave a more elaborate description of the relationship between action and plot, without modifying the opposition itself.

12. Cf.: "His [Hemingway's] deepest trust was placed in cumulative effect
of ostensibly simple, carefully selective statements, with occasional reiteration of
key phrases for thematic emphasis" (C. Baker, *Hemingway The Writer as
Artist*, Princeton, N.J., 1952, p. 118).

13. Ole Anderson's passivity is the more striking because it is contrasted with
several characterization motifs emphasizing his physical strength: he was "a
heavyweight prizefighter," a "big man," "too long for the bed."

14. Any interpretation should take into account as many aspects of the story
structure as possible. This is not the case, I feel, with the one-sided interpretation of "The Killers" as "Nick's story" (Cleanth Brooks and Robert Penn Warren, *Understanding Fiction*, 2nd ed., New York, p. 305). The role of one character and his motifs is strongly emphasized and the relationships to other motif
lines neglected. The authors of *Understanding Fiction* are so eager to find arguments in favor of their interpretation that they ascribe to Nick a dialogue with
gangsters (about movies) which in fact belongs to George.

15. S. Karcevskij, *Travaux du Cercle linguistique de Prague*, I (1929), pp.
88-93.

16. P. L. Garvin, J. Brewer, and M. Mathiot, *Predication-Typing: A Pilot Study in Semantic Analysis*, Language Monograph No. 27 (Supplement to *Language*, June 1967), p. 1.

17. W. K. Wimsatt, *The Prose Style of Samuel Johnson* (New Haven, Conn., 1963); M. Beardsley, *Aesthetics* (New York, 1958); the summary of the argument in S. Chatman, "The Semantics of Style," *Social Science Information*, VI (1967), 77-99.

18. A similar procedure of "kernelization" was suggested by Z. S. Harris for the purposes of information processing in "Linguistic Transformations for Information Retrieval," in *Proceedings of the International Conference on Scientific Information* (Washington, D.C., 1959), Vol. II, pp. 937-50.

19. The procedure applied in our token analysis presupposes, for example, a special transformation of the "question-answer" dialogue: (Nick:) "Couldn't you get out of town?" "No," Ole Anderson said. ⟶ Ole Anderson couldn't get out of town ⟶ (deleting modality) Ole Anderson did not get out of town.

20. Thus, for example, in the text of "The Killers," the expression "two men" (in the sentence "Two men came in") is equivalent to the expression "Al and Max"; outside the context of "The Killers," this equivalence is, of course, invalid.

21. A Czech information engineer, J. Valach, has suggested a procedure of indexing key sentences on the basis of a suprasyntactic graph (in *Kybernetické modelování*, Prague, 1966). M. Mathiot has suggested an ingenious distributional procedure for determining key sentences in an Andamanese myth ("Cognitive Analysis of a Myth," unpublished manuscript). It is, however, very difficult to accept the idea that the abstract structure of an Andamanese myth can be established on the basis of distributional properties of English (through an English translation). S. Chatman's distinction between "kernels" and "catalysts" (within the class of "functions") points in the same direction: "Only the kernels are essential to the causal network [of the story] . . . Catalysts are always deletable" (*op. cit.*, p. 14).

## Appendix

### I. Sequence of Motifs in the Second Scene of "The Killers"

*N . . . Nick Adams   O . . . Ole Anderson   B . . . Mrs. Bell*

| | | |
|---|---|---|
| 1. | N walked up the street beside the car-tracks. | a |
| 2. | N turned at the arc-light down a side street. | b |
| | | |
| 3. | N walked up the two steps. | c |
| 4. | N pushed the bell. | d |
| 5. | B came to the door. | e |
| 6. | N followed B. | f |
| 7. | B knocked on the door. | g |
| | | |
| 8. | N opened the door. | A |
| 9. | N went into the room. | B |
| 10. | O was lying on the bed with all his clothes on. | C′ |
| 11. | O was lying with his head on two pillows. | C′ |
| 12. | O did not look at N. | D̄′ |
| | | |
| 13. | O said nothing. | Ē |
| 14. | O looked at the wall. | D |
| 15. | O said nothing. | Ē |
| 16. | O did nothing about it. | F̄′ |
| 17. | O did not know what the men were like. | Ḡ |
| 18. | O looked at the wall. | D |
| 19. | N looked at O. | D″ |
| 20. | O was lying on the bed. | C |
| 21. | N did not go to the police. | H̄ |
| 22. | N did nothing. | F̄″ |
| 23. | O rolled over toward the wall. | I |
| 24. | O did not get out of town. | J̄ |
| 25. | O looked at the wall. | D |
| 26. | O did nothing. | F̄ |
| 27. | O did not fix it up. | K̄ |
| 28. | O did nothing. | F̄ |
| | | |
| 29. | O did not look at N. | D̄′ |
| 30. | N went out. | B̄ |
| 31. | O was lying on the bed with all his clothes on. | C′ |
| 32. | O looked at the wall. | D |
| 33. | N shut the door. | Ā |
| | | |
| 34. | N and B stood inside the street door. | h |
| | | |
| 35. | N walked up the dark street to the corner under the arc-light. | b |
| 36. | N walked along the car tracks to Henry's. | a |

II. MOTIF CLASSES OF THE SCENE CORE

1. Equivalence classes:

| | |
|---|---|
| A: | N opened the door. |
| contrary $\overline{\overline{A}}$: | N shut the door. |
| | |
| B: | N went into the room. |
| contrary $\overline{\overline{B}}$: | N went out. |
| | |
| C: | O was lying on the bed. |
| variants C′: | O was lying on his bed with all his clothes on. |
| | O was lying with his head on two pillows. |
| | |
| D: | O looked at the wall. |
| neg. variant $\overline{D}′$: | O did not look at N. |
| similar D″: | N looked at O. |
| | |
| E—negative $\overline{E}$: | O said nothing. |
| | |
| F—negative $\overline{F}$: | O did nothing. |
| neg. variant F′: | O did nothing about it. |
| neg. similar $\overline{F}″$: | N did nothing. |

2. Similar in texture:

    #16: "There *isn't anything I can* do about it."
    #24: *"Couldn't you* get out of town?" "No."
    #27: *"Couldn't you* fix it up?" "No."

    #17: "*I don't want* to know what they were like."
    #21: *"Don't you want* me to go and see the police?" "No."

3. Identical motifs:

    #14: Ole Anderson looked at the wall.
    #18: He looked at the wall.
    #25: He looked at the wall.

    #26: "There ain't anything to do."
    #28: "There ain't anything to do."

# PHILOLOGY:
## Factualness and History

### KARL D. UITTI

OUR MID-TWENTIETH CENTURY'S FASCINATION with literature as "language" is nowhere more evident than in the increasing number of symposia, anthologies, monographs, and journals devoted to questions of style and poetics. The nature of this fascination can be fairly accurately gauged by the very wide variety of topics, approaches, values, and concerns voiced in the different publications. At the very moment when, once again, the primacy of literature is seriously threatened by other forms of discourse—the specialized prose of the social sciences has come to challenge literature on its own ground (even in schools and colleges), for example, the novel is being pressured by a kind of neo-naturalist sociological case-history or anthropological survey[1]—many of the most vigorous of today's scholars and critics agree only that literary works may be most profitably approached as structures of (linguistic) signs.[2] Of course, what is intended by the different approaches is hardly uniform. On the surface, at any rate, the aesthetic position defended by René Wellek[3] hardly resembles the sociological orientation favored by Roland Barthes; the latter, moreover, has little in common with the kind of sociology favored by the late Lucien Goldmann.

Paradoxically, the linguistic bent of much recent literary study, reflecting as it does our age's general infatuation with signs, systems, and images, must be attributed in part to an earlier generation's rejection of older, more traditional techniques of dealing with the language of literature. Years of modernist erosion and of built-in changes of fashion within our terminological frameworks have virtually done away with the kind of analysis to which young students were introduced in the established Freshman Composition courses and *classes de rhétorique*. Concomitantly, the first modernist reconciliation of "linguistics" and "literary study"—what during the nineteenth century went by the name of classical, and especially modern, philology—has also been swept away in the same recent trends. The gaps left by the demise of rhetoric may be eventually attributed to attacks by thinkers like Condillac, whereas the more recent decline of what critics still often label "old-fashioned philology" seems to be closely linked to the anti-historicism of structural linguistics and certain social sciences as well as of recent schools of literary criticism (e.g., the New Critics).[4] In short, the contemporary discovery of the "language" of literature partially compensates for the losses incurred when enthusiasm for historical philology waned. And, analogously, linguists who show interest in literary structures are perhaps making up for earlier rejections of written, or what was often deprecatingly called "secondary," discourse. However, all losses have not yet been recouped. The analytic finesse and sympathy one willingly associates with the best kinds of philological research has hardly been adequately replaced by today's theoretical rigor.

Our present-day interest in literary signs is highly problematic, as is our concern for sign workings in general, including, to be sure, the different kinds of "linguistics" current today. Similarly, to say the least, the kind of discourse-in-the-culture that literature is does not always benefit from analytic approaches that propose specifically to deny the value of that status. Given these facts, and given, one hopes, the passing by now of any polemical or disciplinary urgency with respect to the real or imaginary dangers of philology, it might well be worth our while to reopen dispassionately the case for a rejuvenated philological analysis. After all, the study of literature as a humane and meaningful branch of traditional learning has had an old and sometimes venerable history. The very fact of its traditionalism ought to be taken into account, for not only does traditionalism suggest continuity, but it implies flexibility as well. One should therefore ask: How might recent developments in linguistics, the social sciences, philosophy, and other sign-oriented disciplines encourage one to restate cogently certain values and techniques usually associated with philology? And conversely, what might a renovated philology have to offer related disciplines within the spectrum of what our French friends call the *sciences humaines*?[5]

### FACTUALNESS

The factual permeates all levels of philological activity. That is, the existentially irreducible contact of text and reader, with all the dialogic implications of such contact, constitutes the essential philological experience, and has done so since time immemorial. In the long run philology has always been more vulnerable to attack on grounds of lack of rigor rather than, quite trivially, on grounds of "dullness" or of excessive formalism.[6] Indispensable to the proper achievement of philological goals has been, as well, the *de facto* recognition of the text's autonomy: its nature being, then, what it is made to serve as tempered by how the reader circumscribes it and accepts its limitations. The text controls the ways in which it is studied in a far more concrete manner than a "language" governs the fashion in which its phenomena are, as the saying goes, "accounted for." Similarly, the philologist-linguist (e.g., Meyer-Lübke, A. Thomas, and especially L. Foulet) is in more intimate and experiential contact with the language—French, English, Greek—he studies than his more abstract-minded structuralist colleague.

Few theorists have understood the importance of dialogue in the philological confrontation between textual or linguistic phenomena and reader or scholar.[7] Surely this has been the case, because in nineteenth-century Europe the cultural assumptions shared by most philologists were remarkably homogeneous. Texts and languages were studied by and large from within the analyst's culture; consequently, "exotic" cultures were often subject to prejudiced views.[8] After World War I, however, when the philological disciplines began their decline, these common assumptions no longer held so securely as previously. Disagreements became a matter of principle, e.g., between idealists and positivists in Romance studies, and, analogously, between linguistic historians and descriptive structuralists, whose ties with anthropologists were far more intimate than those they held with students of literature. Theory came into vogue, a kind of "objective mediation" designed to circumvent bias and prejudice. Thus, Saussure's *Cours* (1916) constitutes a body of coherent theory that seeks to displace the looser tactical assumptions which reigned at least up to the Neogrammarians, if not beyond; after all, Meyer-Lübke and Diez have more in common with one another than either does with Saussure. It is interesting to see how the *Cours* attempts to cope cogently with the fact of dialogue. As reported by Bally and Sechehaye, Saussure subsumes dialogue into something he labels the *circuit de la parole*, or "speech circuit," that includes speaker and interlocutor, "concept" and "acoustic image." But this depiction of dialogue serves only to enable Saussure to free himself from the "individual act" and, in subsequent pages, to take on what he calls the "social fact" of language, that which is shared by speaker and interlocutor: *langue* or "code." The systematic code is what, in essence, makes such dialogue possible; its study is Saussure's concern. There is little that is truly factual in Saussure's "social fact." Others will refine Saussure's speech circuit, e.g., the Gestaltist Karl Bühler and, more recently, Roman Jakobson in his breakdown of language into six factors and functions. All six of these are operative in most speech situations but when, say, in a given instance the articulation focuses on the message itself, its predominant function is poetic, whereas when the context

is stressed, then the function is especially contextual. The effect is somewhat contrapuntal. This breakdown and its concomitant notion of set provide a framework for incorporating poetic analysis into a general linguistic
and semiotic theory, but, simultaneously, the text, or "message," as "poetic
object," retains an essentially independent character, amenable to methodologically determined approaches that tend to minimize the *fact* of dialogue.
Very typically, Jakobson equates "investigator of literature" and "linguist,"
claiming that the term "literary critic" would mislabel the student of poetic
operations as seriously as "grammatical (or lexical) critic" would misrepre-
sent the linguist.[9]

Unless, however, some loopholes in either linguistic or literary analysis are
left, allowing one to deal relevantly with the experiential fact of confrontation beween text (and/or author) and reader, the reality of language or of
the poetic experience will be necessarily shunted aside, and, quite possibly,
other kinds of understanding themselves vitiated. We do not have to stress
here the dangers of abstraction present in the exclusive practice of many
varieties of structuralism current these days. Conversely, one can no longer
afford to dismiss the structuralist belief in the autonomy or "inwardness" of
poetic discourse, i.e., the structuralists' association of " 'literature' with discourse that calls attention to the ways general grammatical possibilities are
worked out in combination" (LLT, 258). Blanket condemnation of
this view on grounds of its potentially exclusive aesthetic orientation simply
misrepresents the case. Nor, for that matter, does this view necessarily lead
to a monolithic, "monumentalist" interpretation of poetic discourse. On
the contrary, only by positing the autonomy of the poetic text can one hope
to reach eventually a sense of its ramifications in the world. These, as we
shall see, are not gratuitous but depend upon the text's organization, and
this organiaztion, finally, may not be penetrated except by the active participation of the reader: the "dialogue" must take place.

In ordinary vocal communication the interlocutor "creates" what he
hears; without this re-creation the message goes nowhere. Similarly, certain
literary texts demand a more intense, or more creative, effort to be understood. And this *difficulté vaincue* in turn modulates the value of one's understanding. It is theoretically possible to so downplay the activities involved
in this process of creation/re-creation that, in analysing the text, an illusion
of objectivity, or at least of greater abstraction, is achieved. (Nevertheless,
curiously, one familiar with Lévi-Strauss' writings will recognize his characteristic playfulness even in the highly "objective" study he and Jakobson
dedicated to Baudelaire's "Les Chats.") But that remains only an illusion,
unless the real subject of one's remarks is other than the text, in which case
the text as pretext is successful to the degree that it is obliterated by higher
considerations.

Let me illustrate some of these points with reference to a specific text. The Old French version of the *Song of Roland* contained in the Oxford MS Digby 23 (*ca.* 1170) was in all likelihood composed toward the end of the eleventh century. It tells the familiar story of Charlemagne's expedition to Spain, Ganelon's betrayal of Roland and the twelve peers, the massacre of the French rear-guard at Roncevaux where Roland dies victorious, Charles' return to avenge his losses, and finally the trial, judgment, and execution of Ganelon. In Joseph Bédier's edition the poem is divided into 291 assonanced *laisses*, i.e., irregular stanzas, ranging from less than ten lines to one that has over thirty-five; most have between ten and twenty lines. These *laisses* are themselves made up of ten-syllable verses with a caesura after the fourth syllable (the epic *décasyllabe*). The poem, like other *chansons de geste*, was meant to be sung from memory by a professional performer, either a poet (*trouvère*) or an entertainer (*jongleur*), accompanied on a stringed instrument called a *vielle*. Performances were usually held before large audiences, frequently outdoors in public squares or in castle halls and grounds. The audiences were presumably made up of people from all walks of life, representing the most varied levels of sophistication, taste, and literary intelligence.

It goes without saying that the poem as represented by the Oxford text was designed to be experienced by its audiences in a wide variety of ways and with varying degrees of intensity. That is, the basic narrative line is rendered loudly and clearly; a bumpkin standing at the outer fringes of the crowd and listening, let us say, with divided attention could hardly fail to grasp the essential sequence of events and even, as we shall see, certain "high points" or episodes of concentration. Repetitions, reprises, interventions by the narrator—all these clarify the happenings. In this the *Song of Roland* resembles any run-of-the-mill *chanson de geste*. It differs from most other Old French epics, however, in that the constraints built into the kind of diffusion it was constructed for are transformed uniformly into highly effective poetic resources. In short, the *Roland* turns its rhetorical framework—the very basis of the kind of dialogue I have spoken of here—into a source of poetic value.

The *laisse similaire* is one device that helps assure everyone's getting the point. An important event may be recounted several times in various consecutive *laisses* (or in more or less interrupted series). Moreover the degree of autonomy of each *laisse* prompts one to affirm that the poem as a whole must be seen as reverberating upon the *laisses* at least as much as the *laisse* upon the poem, that, in fact, this "mutual reverberation" constitutes a significant feature of the work's poetic rhythm. Hearing out the *laisse* is comparable to understanding a lyric poem in terms of the *recueil* into which it is inserted. The *laisses similaires* behave adverbially, so to speak, with respect to the movement of the narrative. For those in the audience willing and able to make the necessary creative effort, then, the modulations provided by the *laisses similaires* and the analogous repetitions deepen and thicken the kind of fiction making up the *Song of Roland*. An event is almost never merely repeated in a *laisse similaire*; it is restated and modulated. The narrator intervenes with a commentary, a throwback recalls a previous scene. Thus Roland's fiancée, Aude, does not wish to survive her betrothed; as soon as she hears the terrible news of his death, she too dies (*laisse* CCLXVIII). Her death is taken up in the following *laisse* as well; the narrator states: "Alde la bel' *est a sa fin alee*" (3723). This recalls directly Roland's death, as told in the marvelous *laisse* CLXXVI: "Juntes ses mains *est alet a sa fin*" (2392). The parallelism is evident in the common italicized expression. As one reflects further, the interpolation of Aude's death integrates itself even more completely into the fabric of the poem. The episode intervenes sequentially just after the narrator has announced that Ganelon's trial is about to begin (*laisse* CCLXVII), and, as we recall, Ganelon comes close to being let off, since only Thierry's successful taking up of Pinabel's challenge allows Charles to proceed with the traitor's judgment and execution. Aude's death reminds us poignantly of Roland's sacrifice—she is figuratively a part, and therefore a symbol, of that sacrifice—and she brings to mind once again the enormity of Ganelon's betrayal. Heartbreaking in its own right, then, Aude's story plays off upon the sequence of episodes which comprise the poem at the same time that it transcends such juxtaposition for those in the audience who remember accurately the articulation of Roland's death. Nothing is irreparably lost if one does not "recreate" the connection; but to do so makes the poem much richer. Meanwhile, thanks to the recapitulation given in *laisse* CCLXIX, the most remote listener cannot fail to know of Aude's death.

Integral to philological reconstruction are, of course, the establishment of texts, the glossing and explanation of recalcitrant terms and phrases, the elucidation of literary devices prevalent at the time of composition and perhaps less familiar today, and so on; but no less a part of such reconstruction is the active participation of the critic in the text's workings. He must be an "audience." Indeed, participation of this kind must accompany all other aspects of the philologist's activity, and, I suspect, the judgments involved cannot be postponed until after the text has been set down and glossed. Rather, the process of judgment and the rest occur simultaneously. We have had a glimpse of the type of poetic operations characteristic of the Oxford *Roland*; a deeper look confirms the validity of our findings.

The most central event in the poem is perhaps Roland's death. It takes place over a number of *laisses* that culminate slightly past the half-way point of the poem in *laisse* CLXXVI (vv. 2375-96). One's "re-creation" of this event, however, involves an in-depth reconstruction that lends itself, precisely, to the fictional thickening of the poem. In a sense one gets out of the reading what one puts into it. The event—it is virtually a theme—of Roland's death is first suggested, of course, by the epic legend itself. As with all epic poetry, the legend must be viewed as a "component" of the poem, though its structural role is never susceptible of precise delimitation. But the opposition that eventually leads to this death is first articulated within the poem's confines when, in *laisse* XIV, Roland tells Charles: "Ja mar crerez Marsilie!" (v. 196), and, in the following *laisse*, Ganelon takes up the same term in response to Roland: "Ja mar crerez bricun!" (220). The fact of parallelism-in-opposition carries the burden of meaning here; it must be experienced as such to do so. Premonitions of disaster accompany Ganelon's dropping Charles' glove; and, of course, Ganelon's plot with Blancandrin (*laisse* XXIX) and later with Marsile (XLIff.) confirms these premonitions. The poem comments upon these events to come; thus, in *laisse* LV, after Roland has given the sign to break camp and the four hundred thousand Franks prepare to leave for their country, we hear: "Deus! quel dulur que li Franceis nel sevent! AOI" (716). The narrator intervenes with the legend. Charles' dream follows immediately: Ganelon wrenches Charles' lance away from him, he is attacked by an unnamed animal and a leopard, but a furious hound defends him. The next day, when Ganelon nominates Roland to lead the rear-guard, Charles, forebodingly, accuses him of *mortel rage*. In *laisse* LXVI the refrain "Halt sunt li pui e li val tenebrus" occurs for the first time and, in *laisse* LXVIII, Charles cannot hold back his tears; the French weep for Roland and the peers: "Guenes li fels en ad fait traïsun" (844). The connection between what we know (from the legend as well as from the poem), what will happen, and what Charles and the Franks fear is explicitly stated; also the relationship of Roland's death and Ganelon's treason is reaffirmed. But once Roland's death has been, so to speak, fully established and articulated in a kind of implacable conditional time, it is once again narrationally modulated. *Laisse* LXIX introduces Marsile's nephew Aelroth, an "anti-Roland," who asks of his uncle a boon: "le colp de Rollant" (866). If Roland's death by betrayal is certain, so is, as well, his victory, for we know that Aelroth will not defeat Roland; the poem deliberately capitalizes on our knowledge.

Before the battle is joined, then, Roland's death is effectively linked to both Ganelon's treason and the Frankish victory. The battle itself, with its dichotomy of Christians and Saracens, its polarization (and reconciliation) of Roland the *preux* and Olivier the *sage*, not to mention the contrastive setting of high mountains and deep valleys, plays on these connections. But, curiously, as it does so, the battle gives a spiritual meaning to Roland's death.

The process, clearly, is one of dovetailing; the narrative rhythm exploits the high degree of autonomy of the *laisses*. But we go from the suggestive plays of Ganelon's "Ja mar crerez bricun" in *laisse* XV and the more intense opposition of the type expressed in the above-quoted *laisses* LXVIII and LXIX to the amazingly high-powered and marvelously rich series of *laisses* in which the French are cut down, almost one by one. The betrayal literally takes effect as the field is strewn with the French dead. In a kind of metonymic way Roland "dies" too, as the military organism of which he is a part—and which also includes us—is slowly destroyed during the pagan onslaughts. The *douze pairs* are no more. Meanwhile, however, by a kind of epic *tour de force*, Roland takes the place of his dead companions. He is progressively glorified while, through the death of his *cumpainz*, he is in fact diminished. Note that the very setting of Roncevaux becomes a stage, with real funereal props, for his death and epiphany. The immediate "cause" of his death—his terrible sounding of the oliphant—occurs in *laisse* CXXXIII, this process of glorification in diminishment having begun some time before; but he does not actually give up the ghost until about six hundred lines later. Meanwhile, Olivier dies, and, last of all the peers, Archbishop Turpin, who, in *laisse* CLXII, blesses the dead and, just before dying himself, helps Roland in *laisse* CLXV. It is certainly no accident that the last to precede Roland in death was his priest. By the time Roland's soul is carried off to Paradise, the personal, political, and, indeed, cosmic implications of his death are clarified. However, at no time are these implications expressly stated; they derive from the juxtapositions of the *laisses* as we understand them.

The technique of dovetailing carries with it—built in as it were—both visible and potential confusions of time and space. Chronologies are disturbed, indeed made light of, as are the locations of actions and their consequences. Similarly, clusters of fact and modifications adhering to given events tend to comprise different orders of reality; naturalistic detail readily combines with the supernatural, or with dreams and even narrative interpolations. Perspectives are blurred, often blended, at times, seemingly, quite gratuitously—much more so, even, than in the *Life of Saint Alexis* (ca. 1050). Such blending has probably prompted most judgments (stemming from a nineteenth-century obsession with neat evolutionary patterns?) that describe the poem as technically "naïve," "simple," "artless," or "popular." This is surely why Rychner equated the degree of autonomy of the *laisses* with "lyrical tendencies" and with "lack of respect" for the narrative. However, if, indeed, the constraints of oral diffusion favored the organization of the poem into highly autonomous *laisses*, it nonetheless follows from what we have observed that this organization does not necessarily imply lack of sophistication. Not only is it "respected," the narrative line of the *Song of Roland* is structurally quite sound. In fact, its very security encourages the kinds of modulations I have described. If temporal sequences other than the logic starting with Ganelon's betrayal and culminating in his trial and execution are, in fact, disturbed, it must be for deliberate cause. Normal sequential chronologies are simply less important than the authentic temporality of the poem: *ævum*, of course, and what might be called the "concrete" time of events—a time possessing its own relational logic. Thus, Roland's death takes place in a diachrony that presumably extends back through legendary material to a point earlier than that actually marked by the poem (the moment of some blood feud?). Its synchrony encompasses, if not the whole poem, at least the Roncevaux episode. As an event, it exists in relation to other "events." These relationships, as we have seen, constitute an important segment of the fictional texture (as well as "texturing") of the poem.

A work of history, conceived, like the *Roland*, in the framework of eternity and, so to speak, related directly to its audience can consequently better convey the higher integrity of concrete events than, one suspects, many a modern novel. By requiring and utilizing our participation in the work's reconstruction, the poem succeeds in conferring upon what happens a kind of authenticity or "reality" that pierces through all its many conventions and constraints. What at first glance may look like confusion turns out to be, in most cases in the Oxford text, a more adequate order, that is, a form perfectly suited to value and to structural possibilities. It is hard to explain why *laisse* CLXXVI is so sublime a poem.[10] No matter how carefully one has followed the work up to that point, one is nevertheless captivated by it. Perhaps this is so because the centrality of the *event* of Roland's death in the architecture of the poem has been architecturally focused on *laisse* CLXXVI; it is the point of concentration.[11] Everything I have mentioned so far becomes once again pertinent. For the last time it is asserted that Roland is lying beneath a pine tree, his face is turned toward Spain, he remembers his past life—all these things are repetitions, including the fact that he must confess and that he does so. His prayer is an even more beautiful restatement of the prayer given in CLXXV (in point of fact, it is the "same" prayer, but here, quite literally, "related" somewhat differently). Once again he is visited by angels. However, the last line is entirely new; it justifies and, narrationally, makes sense of all the rest: "L'anme del cunte portent en pareïs" (2396). The whole *Chanson de Roland* lies latent in this *laisse* which, when it is sung, brings back to us the entire "event" of Roland's death and, of course, its justification, what it leads up to: Roland's salvation and, by extension, the impact of his exemplum upon us. The poem operates upon the *laisse* as fully as the *laisse* functions within the poem.

*Laisse* and poem partake of the same epic "binary impulse" elsewhere illustrated in the *Song of Roland*.[12] Here as elsewhere there are grounds for stressing the high degree of fusion and unity that characterize the relationships operative in the work. A sense of this fusion and unity, I think, is forthcoming from our preceding remarks. Were we to pursue still further our "experience" of the poem, we should be in an even better position to speak of its order and structure. But far more important from the viewpoint of the present article, one can see the relevance of what we have attempted for, say, a more comprehensive study of the Old French narrative, of the epic in general, or, for that matter, of possibly universal narrative patterns. How the *Song of Roland* functions is of undeniable importance to these broader questions. Thus, to take up the problem of the Old French narrative, we might observe that the *Roland* is fictionally considerably more complex than the *Life of Saint Alexis*.[13] In the *Roland* historicity is less a means than an indispensable goal of the fiction, whereas, in the *Alexis*, without the illusion of historicity the hagiographic values would not have been adequately conveyed. The *Alexis* is thus more obviously didactic. In the *Roland* the "collaboration" of poetry and value is so close, so tightly knit, that one's attention is channelled constantly and evenly from the one to the other. By focusing on poetic constructs the audience is led into a more profound understanding of that meaning and its ramifications; conversely, when one refers properly to the meaning, the poetic techniques employed are illuminated. Yet the *Song of Roland*—a bit like the *Alexis*—remains epic, not novelistic; literature serves the myth. Structural ironies that one must associate with certain later romances—e.g., Chrétien de Troyes, the *Tristan Folies*—are startlingly absent from the *Roland*. In Chrétien's *Yvain*, for example, one's primary loyalty is shifted from what is told to the telling; this fact modulates the truth of what is told.[14]

Let me stress that the disjointed facts themselves are far less significant than what I have called here, for lack of a better term, "factualness." Only by experiencing—not merely "observing"—the text, and with great care, can the philologist formulate the reconstruction that underlies both his analysis of the text and the broader considerations he may wish to make. Just the dialogue must be active, so these broader considerations must be firmly rooted in the reality of the confrontation. Critical discrimination is consequently every bit as much a part of philological activity as it is said to be of less "scientific" approaches. The value of the facts one pays heed to must, however, be determined by the results achieved. A kind of relevance enters into play here that is at least analogous to the relevance claimed by certain phonologists or ethnologists.

### HISTORY

By definition, dialogic confrontation is historical. It is based on a here-and-now, a specificity that, at times, seems to belie its apparent timelessness. Just as the *Song of Roland*, in its relationship to its audience, expresses a certain historicity upon which its meaning depends, so the philologist, by preserving the historicity of his relationship to his subject-matter, contributes directly to the relevance of his undertaking with respect to that poem and other such works. In this way philological activity departs most markedly from the abstract timelessness of the purest structuralist analysis: "Synchrony" and "diachrony" were designed, in fact, to eliminate "history."

Among the founders of contemporary structuralism only Edward Sapir, with his notion of "drift," actually worked a view of history into his relatively systematic conception of linguistic phenomena. "Drift" enabled him to posit the leveling of *who:whom→who* within an English variety of general Indo-European movement, namely the convergence in English of case reduction, the tendency to fixed position in the sentence, and a preference for "the invariable word."[15] "Drift" exists in a becoming; it is the reconciliation in process of linguistic facts with such tendencies. Though not entirely unabstract, it nevertheless respects the historicity of phenomena. Not surprisingly, then, Sapir also suggested conditions under which the relationship of language and culture might be more adequately viewed. But in so doing his work points symptomatically to some of the confusions still current today. This relationship, he insisted, is not "intrinsic," i.e., correlations between, on the one hand, linguistic structure and, on the other, either race or culture are simply not demonstrable. Or, to put it another way, only when "it can be shown that culture has an innate form, a series of contours, quite apart from subject-matter of any description whatsoever, we have something in culture that may serve as a term of comparison with and possibly a means of relating it to language. But until such purely formal patterns of culture are discovered and laid bare, we shall do well to hold the drifts of language and of culture to be non-comparable and unrelated processes." Consequently, to the degree that "language" is "structure," i.e., out of history, or until such time as culture may be described structurally, it will not do, methodologically, to seek terms of comparison. This much said, however, Sapir did proceed to show relationships, almost inadvertently: "Culture may be defined as *what* a society does and thinks [and] language is a particular *how* of thought." Thus, though the "latent content of all languages is the same . . . it is the manifest form that is never twice the same." And, finally: "It goes without saying that the mere content of language is intimately related to culture." Sapir is explicit: "In the sense that the vocabulary of a language more or less faithfully reflects the culture whose purpose it serves it is perfectly true that the *history of language* and the *history of culture* [italics mine] move along parallel lines." (He goes on to deny the "interest" of this phenomenon to "the linguist," but, in my opinion at least, his methodological grounds for so doing are today no longer convincing.) We might read Sapir, so to speak, backwards, and conclude that to the extent that matters of history are at issue, the relationship of language and culture is pertinent.

Recent work on linguistic change by the late Uriel Weinreich (with Labov and Herzog) seems to suggest that that, precisely, is the case. Their above-mentioned study (see fn. 7) outlines a theory of historical change in which the "composition" of the speech community—e.g., degree and direction of social mobility, etc.—plays an important and isolable role. Cultural patterns in contemporary New York City society—e.g., the influence of childhood peer groups—seems to determine modes of grammatical stylization that eventually congeal into standard usage. Linguistic choice exploits a multitude of expressive, cultural, social, and grammatical conditions. What has often been called creativity (as well as eventual linguistic change over time) lies in the exercise of such choice. The possibilities of choice lie latent in the body of linguistic structure which, in a sense, may be better conceived as a kind of conglomerate of structures, as something more concrete at any rate than the generalized idiolect posited in much structuralist theory. We may, I think, identify such concreteness with historicity, with the dimension of real usage, something observable most readily in recorded discourse: written texts and the like. Creations thus lead us to a deeper understanding of creativity.

On the level, then, of dialogue, that is, by considering discourse at least partly in terms of one's active participation in its workings and by focusing upon its historicity, one copes primarily with its form, to be sure, but also one deals necessarily with its ramifications in the world of reality, as well as with the relationships of the form to relevant social, cultural, and psychological values. Philological activity is ideally *ad hoc*; therein lies its general interest and, paradoxically, its scientific validity. Its bias, quite clearly, is humanist. Again, the theoretical looseness must be put to good use; the results, including whatever feedback accrues to the stricter, more rigid ways of doing things, can be evaluated only with respect to how much or how well understanding has been furthered.

For the sake of illustration, I should like to paraphrase once again a brief section of a study that Yakov Malkiel and I recently devoted to the Old French suffix *-ois*.[16] We concentrated upon the facetious and playful uses of *-ois*, a usage strikingly analogous to contemporary American *-ese*, as in *academ-ese, journal-ese, sociolog-ese*. On the one hand, the suffix indicated, in addition to nationality and provenience, types of language or jargon and behavior, and, on the other, as is the case with *-ese*, the degree of detachability of *-ois* was quite high. Of course this was true for Old French suffixation in general, but it was particularly true, up through the sixteenth century, of *-ois*. Here an Old French trait is preserved through the period of *français fluent*, dying out only when the values generally subsumed under the broad heading of seventeenth-century classicism replace the less circumscribed boisterousness of the old farces and of Rabelais. (It is hard to tell how alive *-ois* was in popular speech; its preservation by Rabelais is no doubt largely due to literary, even poetic, concerns for which, as we shall see, ample justification was forthcoming from the French literary tradition.)

After examining in considerable detail the formal and semantic evolution of *-ois* as well as its extraordinary fortune in Old and Middle French, we found that the several uses of this suffix illustrate an isolable process which, in turn, seems to clarify and to exemplify a fundamental aspect of suffixal derivation in French (up to the seventeenth century). The process may be described as essentially a mutual "contamination" of semantic contents and grammatical formations—a contamination governed by metonymic tendencies in the history of the French vocabulary. In the Romance languages suffixes of this sort tend to straddle grammar and lexicon. By "metonymic tendencies" we understood semantic relations based on contiguity that seem to underlie the formal processes of suffixation in general; the latter "realize" functionally and economically these relations in a virtually paradigmatic way, and, in so doing, they receive a semantico-grammatical value that sets them apart from other types of forms.

So much, then, for the general background to our study. What I wish to stress here is the nature of our documentation—our confrontation with the material. Obviously, we perused with great care the available dictionaries, the previously established repertories (like that of H. Lewicka[17]) and the relevant Old French texts. Few of these were more rewarding than the following thirteenth-century lines by Rutebeuf:

> Aillors covient lor penssers voise,
> Quar dui *tornois*,
> Trois paresis, cinq *vienois*
> Ne pueent pas fere un *borgois*
> D'un nu despris.[18]

Rutebeuf not only exploits the possibilities contained in the *-ois* forms; his poem creates these possibilities and invites us to re-create them after him. Thus the playfulness and detachability of the suffix are worked into the construct as is the fact that, in Old French usage, *-ois* served to indicate the provenience of coins—e.g., *tornois* "money from Tours," *vienois* "money from Vienne," *borgois* "money from Bourges" (hence the pun on *bourgeois* and the irony of the *nu despris* never quite "adding up" to the proper sum).

The text is unusually dense and demanding. It is the series itself—i.e., the principle of such a series—that is juxtaposed both lexically and syntagmatically against the opposition *borgois:nu despris*. Also both rhyme and rhythm reinforce the series; they converge upon and strengthen the opposition:juxtaposition of *borgois:nu despris*. Note the play of *Trois paresis* against its counterpart-in-the-poem *D'un nu despris* (four syllables apiece, the contrast and parallelism of *trois* and *un*, the sound effects of *paresis:despris*).[19] The process unfolds itself and works. The sophistication of the poetic concept becomes apparent *in* or *through* the reading. (Similarly, as we noted in our study, the proliferation of semantic categories like *-ois* 'provenience→coin' alongside 'facetious language,' etc., will contribute to the eventual fragmentation of this suffix, and to its final weakening within the general decline of suffixation in French. It fell of its own weight.) Clearly, Rutebeuf's poem documents the true vitality and the complexity of a linguistic fact in Old French, but, I repeat, the documentation depends on the reader's active understanding. One would get nowhere by merely recording and classifying *-ois* forms in Rutebeuf's work.

The kind of examination I have just hinted at is surely pertinent to the study of Rutebeuf's style and his poetics. One can find no better—nor more concrete—example of his playfully bitter irony or, for that matter, of his brilliant craftsmanship. And we could quite naturally go on to discuss the kind of ambivalence that seems to prevail in his highly intellectual lyric. Rutebeuf builds on oppositions—special kinds of antitheses—which retain their original terms at the same time that these terms influence one another in quite provocative ways. In short, this stanza offers a fine example of Rutebeuf's putting stylistic means (available within the rules and conventions of literary Old French as well as within the confines of lyric diction) to relevant poetic use. And yet, despite the nuanced sense of these means provided by our "reading" of Rutebeuf, we have not had to flounder about in sterile attempts at exhaustive catalogues of stylistic possibilities. It is possible and indeed desirable to avoid the abstract: we need but to restrict our purview to relations involving relevant historical fact. By establishing these relations, the study itself gives them form and pertinence, and, in turn, they help deepen our understanding of literary Old French, of Rutebeuf's poetry, and to some extent, one hopes, of language and poetry in general.

Reliance on concrete readings does not necessarily block the path to higher generalizations. The *style:poetic* antinomy may be developed further. Thus, to continue very briefly the Rutebeuf commentary, our initial remarks could easily lead to a more thorough investigation of suffixation as a device in the Old French lyric. Note the wordplay on *-oier* in these lines from "La Mort Rutebeuf":

> Lessier m'estuet le *rimoier,*
> Quar je me doi moult esmaier
> Quant tenu l'ai si longuement.
> Bien me doit le cuer *lermoier,*
> C'onques ne me poi *amoier*
> A Dieu servir parfetement,
> Ainz ai mis mon entendement
> En geu et en esbatement,
> Qu'ainz ne daignai nés *saumoier,*
> Se por moi n'est au Jugement
> Cele ou Diex prist aombrement,
> Mau marchié pris au *paumoier.*[20]

Forms in *-oi(i)er*—a highly creative verbal suffix in Old French—lent themselves to lyric invention, signifying, along with sheer inventiveness, a kind of personalized activity, and frequently straddling the limits of activity, appearance, and behavior. They often served to signal, and thereby characterize, the kind of discourse in which they were employed. Certain verbs in *-oi(i)er* came to be identified with poetic diction of a courtly, elegant type. The Chastelain de Couci uses *cointoier* "warble [like a nightingale]," *foloier* "play the fool, behave foolishly," *guerroier* "attack, torment [metaphorically]," *maistroier* "rule, torment," *raverdoier,* "turn green [*reverdir*]" (*tens qui raverdoie* "Spring"); these terms fit perfectly into the ambiance of the courtly love rhetoric and its sometimes stately, but often precious and sentimental diction. Rutebeuf's verses utilize the preciosity inherent in the *-oier* suffix—the verb *rimoier* sets the reader off on the right track. But irony once again supplants courtly *tendresse* as *-oier* forms are played off deliberately against the heavy *-[e]ment* constructions. The contrast in the rhyme position is remarkable; it is based entirely on suffixal opposition, i.e., two quite separate categories of word-formation that nevertheless result in ambiguously similar verbal nouns and nominal verbs (*entendement; le rimoier* vs. its near homonym *lermoier*). The considerable pathos of Rutebeuf's text is a function, exactly, of this ambiguity and irony. It would indeed be difficult to overrate the expressive capabilities of Old French suffixal formation.

Use of constructions of the type we have examined ought to be interpreted with respect to the kinds of poetic diction favored by *trouvères* like the Chastelain de Couci and Rutebeuf. The inventiveness built into these forms was certainly ready-made for the special language forged by the twelfth-century courtly poets and maintained—sometimes ironically—by their successors.[21] A similar playfulness underlies the popular and wide-spread suffixation we find in the later farces as well as in the verbal sprees of Rabelais. A kind of "figurativeness," a potential poetry, lies close to the surface in the *-ois* and *-oi(i)er* words (as well as in other Old French forms, half "composed," half "derived," that rely on suffixal putting together). Since these words naturally invited certain liberties—a purposefully wide range of meanings—they might well provide an easier access than most to the mysteries of Old and Middle French poetic stylization.

The elaboration of poetic diction, that is, of conventions, generic and other constraints, of formulas, constitutes a process in which, to use Sapir's terms, "what a society does and thinks" and the "how of thought" intersect. Or, in other words, what I have described as suffixation is deeply rooted in the medieval and early Renaissance reality of France as that reality is available to us. Analogously, the popularity, in certain kinds of narrative diction, e.g., the epics and saints' lives, of mixed temporality, of apparently casual switching from present to preterite and imperfect, suggests a formalized manner of viewing time that no longer prevailed, say, in the nineteenth century. The subsequent decline of suffixal freedom in French and the rise, in eighteenth- and nineteenth-century narrative fiction, of rather strict temporal sequence can hardly be without relevance to the cultural historian, nor should these phenomena be unfamiliar to the student of the French language. Certainly such changes in fashion have much to do with which linguistic resources will be exploited in usage and, with due regard to drift, which new resources will develop, and how. One suspects that linguists—concerned as they are with the patterns and modalities of linguistic structure—cannot be indifferent to these matters. Sapir's "manifest form" is quite pertinent to structure after all.

As Sapir once put it, "All grammars leak." More optimistic concerning the eventual comprehensiveness of his science, Bloomfield allowed that material not fitting into the proper grammatical description of a language could be handled by the lexicon; "linguistic" were opposed to "lexical" meanings, though he added "we must remember only that the meanings cannot be defined in terms of our science."[22] Structuralisms usually base their methodological claims on pretensions to completeness, i.e., on analytic adequacy. But to date—and, in fact, the debate is age-old, with roots in antiquity and the Middle Ages—no "scientific," or "philosophical," or "general" grammar has really ever accounted for the complexity of linguistic phenomena, not even on its own terms. When Bloomfield states that "Poetic metaphor is largely an outgrowth of the transferred uses of ordinary speech,"[23] inferring, presumably, that it should be "explained" that way, poetic metaphor is not adequately clarified. Certainly Rutebeuf made use of *-ois* forms already present in Old French speech—though, let us admit, the ontological status of "Old French speech" is not all that secure—but the purely verbal intricacy of his poetic construct requires our full attention and collaboration to be grasped. And, I contend, only through work along similar lines with other poetic texts will we ever come to a satisfactory understanding of Old French suffixation. Here we have clearly a linguistic process that is intimately connected with operations more traditionally defined as "grammatical" as well as with figurational tendencies—metonymic, especially—the latter perhaps requiring patterns of literary usage and diction as well as correlation with features of the French drift.

But in linguistic matters, the philologist's concentration upon truly factual phenomena causes his interests to overlap with those of his more systematic colleague, the descriptive linguist. The philological perspective offers a closer, more sympathetic contact between the material "analyzed" and the techniques of analysis; the former is more perfectly respected in its integrity than is possible in other analytic approaches, which tend to reformulate the material in terms of methodology. (To be sure, such reformulations are designed expressly in order to provide more economical and wider coverage of the material.) One is tempted to describe philology as a more "humane"—or humanistic—science whereas, naturally, descriptive linguists are fond of stressing their ties with the mathematical and exact sciences. Because of the ways the philologist's resources are brought to bear upon his material—and the very choice of the material constitutes, clearly, a "resource"—and because nothing precludes his using whatever he deems best to handle the problem at hand, the different kinds of philological analysis offer potentially valuable testing-grounds for new theoretical hypotheses. One might conceive of a study, for example, that would combine matters of linguistic form and what Sapir called "formal patterns of culture." (In a sense a good deal of Lévi-Strauss' *Tristes tropiques*[24] hints at such possibilities: his "ethnology" is close to my "philology.") Meanwhile, in poetic analysis, the informed readings that underlie authentic philological soundings would do much, I think, to eliminate the trivial impressionism that tends to vitiate so many style studies today. Still more important, however, philological factualness implies a kind of built-in respect for the entity of the poetic text. Freedom to handle simultaneously literary works and linguistic principles in fashions I have suggested may well provide the surest insights into general poetic creativity, insights based, as we have observed, on real and complex creations. Conversely, the categories of linguistic analysis—e.g., the dialogue underpinning the speech circuit—provide a framework that shapes what might otherwise be merely amorphous "readings."

Speaking more generally, however, the characteristic historicity of philological approaches—whatever specific forms they may take—suggests that
they offer a context in which our contemporary fascination with sign patterning might once again be reconciled with some of the traditional values
associated with literary study. After all, the reading remains a reading.
When it is recognized as such, the chances are slimmer that what makes
the text literary will be somehow subverted to other, possibly extraneous
ends. If a discourse is worth preserving and if knowledge of a literary canon
is considered a vital part of one's spiritual and intellectual heritage, then
precisely does the properly structured dialogue of text and reader become
a precious instrument of authentic cultural conservation and transmission.
Our reading helps "preserve" the *Song of Roland* in terms that respect the
poem as well as our interest in poetic operations. Let me once again stress
the flexibility of these values. Though continuous, the canon stands for
works that have been successfully transmitted; it is by no means an un-
changing body of texts established in some arbitrary fashion.

The acts, or the phenomena, of discourse *per se* involve most intimately
the philologist, whether the issue be a Baroque poem, an Old Spanish word
cluster, or, to borrow an example from Lucien Foulet, the disappearance of
the Old French preterite. Though he may—and frequently does—adopt
what Bloomfield called the "methods and results . . . of natural science,"[25] his material claims the lion's share of his attention. By understanding and by communicating his comprehension of these acts of discourse,
he expects to widen our grasp of human signs. This too is traditional
and points to a unity of purpose. After all, Bloomfield dreamed "that
the study of language might help us toward the understanding and control
of human events." Whether we still believe in the "control of human
events" may be a moot point. Ultimately, however, our study of signs is
conceived so as to cast a still brighter light on our "events."

## NOTES

1. These pressures have had curious side-effects. The generic distinctions tend
to blur as novelistic devices are utilized by our social scientists. Thus, in its
maiden issue, a new journal, *Novel: A Forum on Fiction* (1967), 92ff., re-
viewed Oscar Lewis' *La Vida* (1966) as "recent fiction." Interestingly, as par-
tisans of increased quantification in sociology and anthropology gain more
ground, one might expect greater tensions to evolve between the mathematicians
and the more literary social scientists.
2. The literary "work of art . . . is a structure of linguistic signs," according to René Wellek, *A History of Modern Criticism: 1750-1950*, II (New
Haven, Conn., 1955), p. 165. This post-Prague School view may be contrasted
with the earlier attitude of one of this century's greatest students of literary

devices and workings, Edmond Faral, who examined the question of literary techniques as understood by the twelfth and thirteenth centuries in *Les Arts poétiques du XII<sup>e</sup> et du XIII<sup>e</sup> siècle* (Paris, 1924 [repr. 1962]). In defending the study of "style," Faral wrote: "C'est une matière qui, dans les textes, se prête à un examen aussi scientifique que les phénomènes linguistiques et grammaticaux et qui, jusqu'ici, a été trop négligé" (xii). ["This material lends itself to as scientific an examination as linguistic and grammatical phenomena do, but, up to this point, it has been too often neglected."]

3. See, in addition to Wellek's statements in *Theory of Literature* (New York, 1949), those in *Style in Language* (1960), pp. 408-19.

4. An extremely difficult problem in intellectual history suggests itself at this point, namely, the possible relationship between, on the one hand, the anti-historicism and pro-structuralism shared by so many contemporary critics and scholars and, on the other hand, dominant intellectual and literary modes during the period 1890-1914 (when, of course, Saussure flourished). No definition of structural relationships has as yet superseded Mallarmé's: "Comparses, il le faut! car dans l'idéale peinture de la scène tout se meut *selon une réciprocité symbolique des types entre eux ou relativement à une figure seule*" (italics Mallarmé's), in "Hamlet," *Crayonné au théâtre; Œuvres complètes*, Pléiade (Paris, 1945), p. 301. ["O walk-ons, it must be so! for in the ideal painting of the stage everything moves according to a symbolic reciprocity of the types with respect to one another or with respect to a single figure."] One might also quote the critic, Camille Mauclair: "Tout est réciprocité, allusion et allégorie, dans la vie et dans l'art. Celui qui posséderait la faculté de saisir immédiatement toutes les analogies, celui-là serait l'artiste immortel, et du même coup le psychologue par excellence"—quoted by A. G. Lehmann, *The Symbolist Aesthetic in France, 1885-1895* (Oxford, 1950), p. 210. ["All is reciprocity, allusion and allegory, in life and in art. He who would have the capacity of grasping immediately all the analogies would be the immortal artist and, by the same token, the psychologist *par excellence*."] Symbolist "idealism," with its anti-evolutionary prejudice and its debt to Schopenhauer, shows many affinities with the temper of mind prevailing in structuralist circles today. Obviously, many of the great forebears of contemporary thought were themselves formed in the late years of the nineteenth century and the beginning of the twentieth: Saussure, Trubetzkoy, Jakobson, not to mention certain influential psychologists, anthropologists, and sociologists. If I may be permitted a personal note, I should like to record that a recent student of mine at Princeton, James A. Boon, '68, wrote a very commendable senior thesis on Lévi-Strauss as a participant in the Symbolist "literary tradition"; his findings were quite interesting. The widespread popularity these days of a *symboliste attardé* like Borges, attests, it seems to me, to similar affinities between Symbolist values and certain aspects of the contemporary temper. These issues certainly bear further looking into.

5. For the sake of convenience, my bias here is academic, though the boundaries between academic, para-academic, and extra-academic critical investigation are becoming less and less discernible. I shall have occasion in these pages to refer to certain of my publications. The following abbreviations stand for: LLT = *Linguistics and Literary Theory* (Englewood Cliffs, N.J., 1969); "Remarques" = "Remarques sur la linguistique historique," *Romanische Forschungen*, LXXXI (1969), 1-21; "LD" = "Literary Discourse: Some Definitions and Approaches," to appear in *Patterns of Literary Style: Yearbook of Comparative*

*Criticism*, ed. Joseph Strelka, published by the Pennsylvania State University Press.

6. Thus, the medieval grammarians known as Modistæ attacked the validity of Priscian's *Institutiones* on the grounds that he did not provide sufficiently rational causes for the phenomena he described. Similarly, the eighteenth-century philosophical grammarians—e.g., Thomas—criticized Vaugelas' theoretical looseness. See *LLT*, p. 53; also, É. Gilson, *La Philosophie au Moyen-Âge*, 3rd ed. (Paris, 1947), p. 404, and F. Brunot, *Histoire de la langue française des origines à 1900*, VI, No. 2, by A. François (Paris, 1932), especially the chapter entitled "La Grammaire et les grammairiens."

7. A singularly important exception: U. Weinreich, W. Labov, and M. I. Herzog, "Empirical Foundations for a Theory of Language Change," in *Directions for Historical Linguistics, A Symposium*, eds. W. P. Lehmann and Y. Malkiel (Texas, 1968). For a summary, see my "Remarques," and discussion below.

8. One recalls Lévi-Strauss' rejection of Lévy-Bruhl's theory of a "primitive," "pre-logical" mentality—a theory reflecting views of history, or rather, views set in an historical context; here are the titles of Lévy-Bruhl's major works: *Les Fonctions mentales dans les sociétés inférieures* (Paris, 1910; this is the work, I believe, translated into English by Lévy-Bruhl's authorized translator as: *How Natives Think* [London, 1926]; *La Mentalité primitive* (Paris, 1922; Eng. tr. 1923); *L'Âme primitive* (Paris, 1927; Eng. tr. 1928). Just as many Symbolist writers were bored with the "dreary determinism" spouted by their Naturalist counterparts, so were early "structuralists" appalled by remarks like the following made by culture-conscious linguists (for the most part historians): "[Swahili is] a language which, through its Arabic relations, has a hold on revealed religion, and even on European thought while, through its negro structure, it is exactly fitted to serve as an interpreter of that religion and those thoughts to men who have not yet even heard of their existence," in the Preface (1870) to E. Steere, *A Handbook of the Swahili Language as Spoken at Zanzibar*, 7th ed. (revised by A. C. Madan) (London, 1906), p. iv.

9. I take it that though Jakobson means to incorporate poetics into general semiotics, he does not intend to exclude other possibilities. What is not clear, however, is whether he would be willing to concede "scientific" status to any of these other possibilities.

10. Here is the *laisse* in question:

```
2375    Li quens Rollant se jut desuz un pin;
        Envers Espaigne en ad turnet sun vis.
        De plusurs choses a remembrer li prist,
        De tantes teres cum li bers cunquist,
        De dulce France, des humes de sun lign,
2380    De Carlemagne, sun seignor, kil nurrit;
        Ne poet muer n'en plurt e ne suspirt.
        Mais lui meïsme ne volt mettre en ubli,
        Cleimet sa culpe, si priet Deu mercit:
        "Veire Patene, ki unkes ne mentis,
2385    Seint Lazaron de mort resurrexis
        E Daniel des leons guaresis,
        Guaris de mei l'anme de tuz perilz
        Pur les pecchez que en ma vie fis!"
        Sun destre guant a Deu en puroffrit.
```

2390        Seint Gabriel de sa main l'ad pris.
            Desur sun bras teneit le chef enclin;
            Juntes ses mains est alet a sa fin.
            Deus tramist sun angle Cherubin
            E seint Michel del Peril;
2395        Ensembl'od els sent Gabriel i vint.
            L'anme del cunte portent en pareïs.

In literal English:

> "Count Roland lay down under a pine-tree;
> Toward Spain he has turned his face.
> He began to remember many things:
> The many lands he, the brave man, has conquered,
> Sweet France, the men of his lineage,
> Charlemagne, his lord, who raised him;
> He cannot restrain himself from weeping
>       and sighing about all these.
> But he does not wish to neglect his own well-being;
> He confesses his sin and implores God's mercy:
> "True Father, who never didst lie,
> Who hast resurrected Lazarus from death
> And saved Daniel from the lions,
> Keep my soul free from all dangers,
> For the sins that I have committed in my lifetime!"
> He offered God his right glove.
> Saint Gabriel has taken it from his hand.
> He rests his head, bowed, on his arm;
> With his hands clasped together he has gone to his end.
> God sent his angel Cherubin
> And Saint Michael of the Peril;
> Together with them came Saint Gabriel.
> They carry the count's soul up into Paradise."

11. I should like here to call attention to F. Farnham's "Romanesque Design in the *Chanson de Roland*," *RPh*, XVIII (1964), 143-64. Mrs. Farnham writes convincingly of the structural and spiritual kinship of the *Roland* and Romanesque stylization. Her arguments are quite pertinent to my remarks.

12. The point requires more extensive development, but, for the moment, let me cite a few parallels-in-opposition among the characters: Charles:Thierry (vs. Ganelon:Pinabel and, of course, Thierry:Pinabel); Charles:Balignant; Roland:Oliver (in the Roncevaux episode) as *preux* and *sage*. Even the landscape at Roncevaux reflects this binary quality, with its high mountains and deep valleys, etc.

13. See *RPh*, XX (1967), 263-95.

14. See *RPh*, XXII (1969), 471-83.

15. Edward Sapir, *Language* (New York, 1921), Chapter VII.

16. "L'Ancien français *gab-ois, ir-ois, jargon-ois* et leurs contreparties dans l'anglais d'Amérique," *RLiR*, XXXII (1968), 126-74. (A number of paragraphs here have been taken from "Remarques" and "LD.")

17. *La Langue et le style du théâtre comique français des XVe et XVIe siècles* (Warsaw-Paris, 1960).

18. "La Griesche d'Esté," ed. Faral and Bastin, I (1959), 529. In English:

> "Their thoughts must be directed elsewhere,
>      For two Tours francs,
> Three Parisian francs, five coins from Vienne
> Cannot make a *borgois* ["coin from Bourges," "bourgeois"]
>      Out of a naked good-for-nothing."

19. Note here a relevant passage from the "Thèses" of the Cercle Linguistique de Prague (1929): "Tous les plans d'un système linguistique, qui n'ont dans le langage de communication qu'un rôle de service, prennent, dans le langage poétique, des valeurs autonomes plus ou moins considérables" (18). Thus rhyme, which "est étroitement liée . . . avec la syntaxe (éléments de celle-ci qui sont mis en relief et posés en face l'un de l'autre dans la rime) ainsi qu'avec le lexique (importance des mots mis en relief par la rime, et leur degré de parenté sémantique)" (19). ["All levels of a linguistic system that, in the language of communication, have but a service role, take on, in poetic language, more or less considerable autonomous values . . . is closely linked . . . to syntax (elements of the latter which are placed in relief and placed opposite one another in rhyme) as well as to the lexicon (the importance of words placed in relief by rhyme, and their degree of semantic kinship)."]

20. Faral-Bastin, I, 575. In English:

> "I must give up rhyming,
> For I must be much concerned,
> So long have I kept at it.
> My heart must weep,
> Since never am I able to apply myself
> To serve God perfectly,
> But rather have I given over my intentions
> To gaming and fun,
> Without even condescending to write psalms.
> If, on Judgment Day, on my behalf there does not appear
> The Lady in whom God took shelter ["was incarnate"],
> I shall get a raw deal when the bargain is struck
> ["the palms are clapped"]."

21. It would be more accurate to state that irony constituted from the beginning an important ingredient in courtly poetry. On the narrative side one need only recall the example of Chrétien de Troyes (see P. Haidu, *Aesthetic Distance in Chrétien de Troyes: Irony and Comedy in* Cligès *and* Perceval [Geneva, 1968] and, say, the two "Folies Tristan." The lyric poet, Conon de Béthune, exploits a kind of built-in ambivalence throughout his work, especially in his well-known "Moult me semont Amors," with its rhymes in *-oise, -ois,* and, finally, a questioning *-er* and an angry *-age.* Later poets will use the ironic mood in different ways.

22. *Language* (New York, 1933), p. 167.
23. *Ibid.,* p. 443.
24. (Paris, 1955).
25. Bloomfield, *op. cit.,* p. 509.

# STYLISTICS AND SEMANTICS

## STEPHEN ULLMANN

OPINIONS DIFFER as to what constitutes the essence of style. Some would agree with Proust that style is to the writer what colour is to the painter: it is a matter not of technique, but of a highly personal mode of vision.[1] Others would regard style as the product of conscious or unconscious choices, on the lines of a formula found in a well known textbook: "two utterances in the same language which convey appoximately the same information, but which are different in their linguistic structure, can be said to differ in style."[2] A third group would consider deviation from a "contextually related norm" as fundamental to the concept of style;[3] some of these critics would merely note and interpret deviations, whereas others would try to state them in statistical terms. A recent article on the subject suggests that a complex factor which may be described as "general purport" lies at the root of style.[4] Perhaps the most neutral of all definitions is the one which equates style with *"expressiveness"* as distinct from cognitive meaning. Valéry had already advocated a study of "The expressive and suggestive devices which have been invented to enhance the power and penetration of speech,"[5] and a Latin American critic has tried to define this factor in purely negative terms, by arguing that "stylistics is the study of what is extra-logical in language."[6]

However different these various approaches may seem to be—and some are really complementary rather than mutually exclusive—they have one thing in common: they all assume the existence of some feature or features which are peculiar to style and distinguish it from language. It follows that stylistics is not a mere branch of linguistics but a parallel discipline which investigates the same phenomena from its own point of view. This would suggest a certain isomorphism between the two sciences: to each main division of linguistics there is likely to correspond a stylistic sector. If, for the sake of simplicity, one adopts the transformational-generative model which distinguishes between three components of grammar, phonology, semantics, and syntax,[7] then stylistics will show the same three-level structure. In other models of linguistics, semantics will appear as a subdivision of the study of lexis; elsewhere, the two will be assigned to different levels,[8] etc. The present paper is not concerned with the place of semantics in the genneral model, but with its inner structure within linguistics and stylistics. Moreover, it will be confined to lexical semantics, the study of word-meanings. Needless to say, important semantic problems do arise both below and above the word level; these problems, however, and their stylistic ramifications, fall outside the scope of this essay. Within this linguistic framework, I shall try to identify the "expressive" values which certain semantic features can acquire: those elements which colour the cognitive meaning of a word, deepen its effect, or strengthen its impact.

During the last twenty years or so, the broad outlines of a theory of semantics have begun to emerge; these have now to be reconsidered in the light of recent work on the structure of the vocabulary. Accordingly, there seem to be two main divisions in this branch of linguistics: one is concerned with the semantic structure of individual words ("micro-semantics"), the other with semantic relations between words ("macro-semantics").

## SEMANTIC STRUCTURE OF INDIVIDUAL WORDS

Saussure's analysis of the linguistic sign as the combination of a *signifiant* and a *signifié*,[9] which was under a cloud for some time, has recently been vindicated, and further refined, by structural semantics.[10] It also provides a convenient framework for the classification of semantic phenomena. I shall use the simpler terminology which I have suggested elsewhere: "name" for the *signifiant* of a word, "sense" for its *signifié*.[11] We shall have to distinguish between two kinds of semantic situations: simple ones, in which one name is connected with one sense, and complex ones, where one name is attached to several senses.

### SIMPLE SEMANTIC SITUATIONS

In this area, semantic research has concentrated on three problems, each of which has significant stylistic corollaries: the "motivation" of the name, the vagueness of the sense, and the overtones which may arise around either the name or the sense or both.

*Motivated and unmotivated (transparent and opaque) words*
Since the age-old debate between the naturalist and the conventionalist view of meaning was reopened thirty years ago,[12] some vital aspects of the problem have been clarified. It has been found, for example, that words can be motivated in three different ways: phonetically, morphologically and semantically. Each of these processes can have powerful stylistic implications.

*Phonetic motivation.*    Here there are two possibilities: the phonetic structure of a word may imitate some sound or noise (primary onomatopoeia), or it may evoke some non-acoustic experience (secondary onomatopoeia), as in the closing lines of Mallarmé's "Le vierge, le vivace et le bel aujourd'hui," where the concentration of /i/ sounds, reinforced by the rhyme scheme of the whole sonnet, suggests whiteness, coldness, purity, and other associations:

> Il s'immobilise au songe froid de mépris
> Que vêt parmi l'exil inutile le Cygne.
> ["It comes to a stop in the cold scornful dream
> in which the Swan wraps itself in useless exile."]

Onomatopoeia, sound symbolism, phonaesthetic effects and kindred phenomena are part of the very fabric of poetry, and although a recent monograph[13] has uttered a salutary warning against auto-suggestion and fanciful speculations, this remains one of the most active areas of stylistic study. It also forms the connecting link between two major divisions of stylistics: the phonological[14] and the semantic component.

*Morphological motivation.*    The existence of morphologically transparent compounds and derivatives is stylistically relevant mainly because of the emotive (pejorative, facetious, etc.) connotations of some of these processes: these can best be handled in the section on overtones. It also happens that formations which had become opaque are "revitalized" by being placed in a suitable collocation which will restore their transparency and enhance their expressiveness, as in these lines by T. S. Eliot where the word "revision" is rejuvenated:

> And time yet for a hundred indecisions,
> And for a hundred visions and revisions.[15]

*Semantic motivation.*    All words based on a metaphor, metonymy, or some allied figure are motivated by the similarity or other connexion which exists between the literal and the transferred meaning. "Channel" in the sense of "a narrow band of sound frequencies wide enough for one-way communication" is a motivated word because of the similarity between this meaning and "channel" in the sense of "a natural or artificial course for running water."[16] This simple and trivial semantic fact has far-reaching consequences for style: it underlies *imagery* in all its countless manifestations. The supreme importance of imagery, and more particularly of metaphor and its explicit variety, simile, has been proclaimed by many writers and thinkers. Aristotle had already declared in the *Poetics:* "The greatest thing by far is to have a command of metaphor. This alone cannot be imparted to another: it is the mark of genius."[17] Some extravagant claims have been put forward on behalf of imagery: Mallarmé has spoken of the "absolute power" of metaphor; André Breton has compared certain images to an earthquake;[18] Proust has actually suggested that "metaphor alone can give a kind of eternity to style,"[19] and Ezra Pound once stated that "it is better to present one Image in a lifetime than to produce voluminous works."[20] Even if one discounts some of the more inflated claims, there are at least three very good reasons for metaphor to be regarded as a factor of fundamental importance in style. Firstly, by combining two elements—a "tenor" and a "vehicle," a *comparé* and a *comparant*—metaphor (and simile) produce a kind of double vision in which both terms illuminate each other. In Dr. Johnson's words, "as to metaphorical expression, that is a great excellence in style, when it is used with propriety, for it gives you two ideas for one."[21] A modern philosopher has expressed the same idea in these terms: "The fact that a sign can intend one thing without ceasing to intend another, that, indeed, the very condition of its being an *expressive* sign for the second is that it is also a sign for the first, is precisely what makes language an instrument of knowing."[22]

Secondly, a really memorable image does not merely state an obvious similarity, but discovers a hidden analogy between two seemingly disparate phenomena; it works, as Wordsworth said,

> By observation of affinities
> In objects where no brotherhood exists
> To passive minds.[23]

Modern writers attach particular importance to this aspect of metaphor. In André Breton's view, for example, "to compare two objects, as remote from one another in character as possible, or by any other method put them together in a sudden and striking fashion, this remains the highest task to which poetry can aspire."[24] A quotation from Baudelaire will illustrate the two points made by Breton, the remoteness of the two "objects" from each other, and the striking way in which they are juxtaposed. When Baudelaire writes in one of his "Spleen" poems:

> Je suis un cimetière abhorré de la lune,
> Où *comme des remords* se traînent de longs *vers*
> Qui s'acharnent toujours sur mes morts les plus chers[25]
> ["I am a graveyard abhorred by the Moon,
> in which long worms crawl like Remorses,
> always battening on those dead whom I hold most dear"
> Francis Scarfe's translation],

the "angle"[26] of the image in the second line is very wide: a comparison between two phenomena as different as remorse and gnawing and crawling worms is quite unusual but nonetheless convincing. The formal structure of the simile is equally unusual: rather than comparing an abstract tenor to a concrete vehicle ("remorse is like worms"), which is the normal procedure, Baudelaire inverts the two terms and assimilates a painfully concrete and repellent physical experience to an abstract mental process.

The third factor which explains the extraordinary importance of metaphor in style is the freedom of choice which exists in this area. The grammatical choices which a writer can make are as a rule severely limited: he can choose from among only a few—sometimes no more than two—alternative expressions which are equally well formed and have roughly the same cognitive meaning. In the lexical field, we sometimes have more synonyms to choose from, but even here the scope for choice is very restricted. The only sphere where we can choose with virtually unlimited freedom is imagery, and in particular, simile and metaphor: any tenor may be compared to any vehicle as long as there is the remotest resemblance or analogy between them. In fact, the writer may find this experience of absolute freedom somewhat frightening; to quote André Breton again:

> The image alone gives me, by its unexpectedness and suddenness, a full sense of potential liberation, and this liberation is so complete that it frightens me.[27]

The semantic motivation of words can be restored in the same way as their morphological transparency. Even where the original image has been completely forgotten, an attempt can be made to re-create it: thus Valéry re-establishes the link between the concrete meaning of Latin *scrupulus*, "small sharp or pointed stone," and the modern sense of *scruple* by inventing the collocation "un ruisseau *scrupuleux*" ("a scrupulous brook").[28] Elsewhere, a faded image is revitalized by being placed in a suitable context.

Thus Ionesco, like Camus before him, remotivates the various transferred senses of the verb *"exécuter"* when he makes a doctor say in one of his plays: *"Exécuter*, Majesté, non pas assassiner. J'obéissais aux ordres. J'étais un simple instrument, un *exécutant* plutôt qu'un *exécuteur*, et je le faisais euthanasiquement." ["Execute, your Majesty, not assassinate. I obey orders. I was a simple instrument, an executor rather than an executioner, and I did it by euthanasia."].[29] There is an obvious connection at this point between semantic motivation and ambiguity.

*Vagueness*
Vagueness in meaning is a condition due to a variety of factors: the "generic" nature of our words which usually stand for class-concepts and in which individual differences are inevitably neglected; inconsistencies, looseness, and contextual shifts in the way we use language; absence of clear boundaries between the things we talk about; lack of familiarity with these things, and fumbling or muddled thinking in general. Such vagueness will be a serious disadvantage in all situations where clarity and precision are essential and where concepts have to be sharply delimited. Even poets have denounced vagueness as one of the major shortcomings of language. T. S. Eliot has spoken of the "intolerable wrestle with words and meanings," and more specifically of:

> . . . a raid on the inarticulate
> With shabby equipment always deteriorating
> In the general mess of imprecision of feeling[30]

and Dylan Thomas has complained:

> Were vaguenesses enough and the sweet lies plenty,
> The hollow words could bear all suffering
> And cure me of ills.[31]

There are, however, many situations where vague, tentative, or suggestive language is preferable to precise formulation. Wittgenstein has an interesting simile about what he calls "concepts with blurred edges": "Is a blurred concept a concept at all?—Is an indistinct photograph a picture of a person at all? Is it even always an advantage to replace an indistinct picture by a sharp one? Isn't the indistinct one often exactly what we need?"[32] Many poets would agree with Wittgenstein. Vagueness was, in fact, one of the basic principles of the Symbolist aesthetic. Verlaine embodied it in the programme outlined in his *Art poétique*:

> Il faut aussi que tu n'ailles point
> Choisir tes mots sans quelque méprise:
> Rien de plus cher que la chanson grise
> Où l'Indécis au Précis se joint.
> ["It is also essential that you should not
> always choose the right word:
> Nothing is more precious than the grey song
> where vagueness and precision meet."]

Mallarmé put the same idea in a lighter vein in the short poem, "Toute l'âme résumée":

> Le sens trop précis rature
> Ta vague littérature.
> ["Too precise a meaning will erase
> your vague literature."]

Gide has given a specific example of this attitude. Speaking of his early literary experiments, he writes:

> J'affectionnais en ce temps les mots qui laissent à l'imagination pleine licence, tels qu'*incertain, infini, indicible*. . . . Les mots de ce genre, qui abondent dans la langue allemande, lui donnaient à mes yeux un caractère particulièrement poétique. Je ne compris que beaucoup plus tard que le caractère propre de la langue française est de tendre à la précision.[33] ["At that time I was fond of words which give free scope to the imagination, such as 'uncertain,' 'infinite,' 'unutterable' . . . Words of that kind, which abound in the German language, gave it in my view a particularly poetic character. I understood only much later that it is the nature of French to tend towards precision."]

In this way, vagueness of meaning can become an important source of stylistic effect, of those "inventions suggestives" of which Valéry spoke, in a passage already quoted.

### Overtones

It has often been suggested that there exists a fundamental distinction between two uses of language, one referential and cognitive, the other emotive. This dichotomy—the theory of the Great Divide, as it has been called —is clearly oversimplified and even misleading: as a recent critic has pointed out, " 'emotive,' or 'affective,' is being used as a catch-all term to refer to a number of quite distinct factors,"[34] some of which have very little to do with "emotions" in the ordinary sense of the term. Some scholars have therefore devised a more delicate set of distinctions to handle these complex and elusive phenomena: one recent contribution would distinguish as many as nine different aspects of meaning.[35] From the semantic and stylistic point of view, it is preferable to discard the term "emotive" altogether and to speak, more neutrally, of "connotations" or "overtones": some of these will be directly related to emotional attitudes, whereas others will be merely "expressive" in the broader sense defined at the beginning of this paper. As far as meaning is concerned, such overtones would seem to fall into three groups: those generated by the name, those connected with the sense, and a third type which involves the word as a whole and depends on what is nowadays called "register."

(1) *Overtones connected with the name.* Quite apart from the onomato-poeic values discussed in a previous section, the phonetic—acoustic as well as articulatory—structure of a word may give rise to pleasant or unpleasant aesthetic overtones. These are particularly noticeable in elements which are on the fringe of organized language: foreign words, neologisms, proper names. A passage in Boileau's *Art poétique* is significant in this respect:

> La Fable offre à l'esprit mille agrémens divers
> Là tous les noms heureux semblent nés pour les vers,
> Ulysse, Agamemnon, Oreste, Idomenée,
> Helene, Menelas, Paris, Hector, Enée . . .
> D'un seul nom quelquefois le son dur ou bizarre
> Rend un Poëme entier, ou burlesque ou barbare.
> ["Mythology offers a thousand diverse pleasures to the mind.
> There all the happy names seem born for the verse:
> Ulysses, Agamemnon, Orestes, Idomeneus,
> Helen, Menelaus, Paris, Hector, Aeneas . . .
> Sometimes the hard or bizarre sound of a single name
> renders a whole poem ludicrous or barbarous." (Pléiade ed., p. 174)]

One is reminded of the famous line in *Phèdre*: "La fille de Minos et de Pasiphaé," where mythological associations of fateful heredity are reinforced by the purely aesthetic effect of the names. In ordinary words, where form and sense are indissolubly interlinked and automatically recall one another, such overtones are less common. An interesting example is the theory of sound values evolved by Dante in *De Vulgari Eloquentia*. Dante borrows images from textiles to explain his reactions to words: "amore" or "donna" are "pexa," like "fine velvet with its full but evenly and smoothly combed-out pile"; "terra" is "hirsutum," having "the more abundant and less smoothly finished nap of a high-grade wool"; "corpo" is "reburrum," "sug-gesting the somewhat excessive shagginess of fustian."[36]

(2) *Overtones connected with the sense.* There is a whole gamut of these, ranging from particular to general effects. Some overtones are con-

fined to one special context or situation. Others are fairly constant but limited to the language of a single person. As opposed to these idiosyncratic overtones, there are more general ones which arise around the fashionable slogans and key-words of a particular period: they are extremely widespread while they last but are usually short-lived. Terms like "confrontation," "escalation," "integration," "apartheid," "permissive," "psychedelic" are enjoying such a vogue at the present time. Even more general are the permanent emotive overtones which certain words develop in a particular community, such as *rex* in ancient Rome: "pulso Tarquinio nomen regis audire non poterat (populus Romanus)," says Cicero in *De Re Publica*.[37] Finally, there are terms whose actual meaning contains an element of evaluation: "gawky," "grumpy," "slouch," "squawk," "mawkish" and many others fall into this category. The fact that some at least of these words are also onomatopoeic adds to their expressive force.

Overtones of meaning can also result from certain processes of word-formation. Here belong such cases of "emotive derivation" as the Italian "poveretto," "poverino" and "poveraccio," where the diminutive or pejorative suffix modifies not only the denotation but the connotation of the word. Portmanteau terms coined by such writers as Laforgue, Lewis Carroll or Joyce are also rich in expressive overtones, whereas some of Gerard Manley Hopkins's compounds ("lovely-dumb," "feel-of-primrose hands," "fresh-firecoal chestnut-falls")[38] are not only striking in their novelty and their unusual appearance but also achieve an extraordinary effect of density.

(3) *Overtones associated with particular registers.* Words, like other linguistic elements, have the ability to evoke those "registers" to which they normally belong. Hence the term "evocative value", sometimes employed to denote these overtones. A register has been defined as "a variety of a language distinguished according to use,"[39] and these registers have been classified according to three important criteria: field, mode, and tenor of discourse.[40] "Field" of discourse refers to "the area of operation" of linguistic activity, and this criterion yields such registers as personal relations, politics, or the various technical languages. "Mode" denotes the medium of linguistic activity, with spoken versus written language as the fundamental distinction. The "tenor" of discourse is determined by relations between the participants. The basic dichotomy here is between "colloquial" and "polite" (or "formal") language. It has been suggested that this criterion, rather than yielding distinct registers, "is best treated as a cline," with such categories as "casual," "intimate," and "deferential" appearing at various points. In addition to these three dimensions, evocative overtones can also arise from linguistic differences in space (regional, dialectal, foreign elements) or in time (archaisms, neologisms), those between the speech of the two sexes, and various other factors. Local colour and a multiplicity of other

stylistic effects can be derived from the existence of registers and the innumerable overtones associated with them.

Each language also possesses some special devices for heightening the overtones of words. While the resulting effect will be semantic, the devices themselves may be phonological, lexical, or grammatical. A classic example of such a phonological device is the so-called "emotive accent" in French, which tends to fall on the first syllable of words beginning with a consonant ("C'est *fo*rmidable!") and on the second syllable of those with an initial vowel ("Tu es in*to*lérable!"). At the lexical level, we have such hyperbolical expressions as "awfully," "terrific," "tremendous," etc., whose cognitive meaning has been radically modified by emotive use. In grammar, word-order may help to strengthen semantic overtones: the anteposition of the adjective in French provides a very clear example. When Baudelaire wrote, in the opening lines of the sonnet "Correspondances":

> La Nature est un temple où de *vivants* piliers
> Laissent parfois sortir de *confuses* paroles
> ["Nature is a temple, in which living pillars
> sometimes utter a babel of words"
>                     Francis Scarfe's translation],

he could have placed the two adjectives after their nouns: the sense would have been the same, but the overtones, the emphasis, and emotive impact would have been different. This can of course develop into an affectation, as in the case of the Proustian character who "trouvait raffiné de dire . . . au lieu de 'mes sentiments *distingués*' 'mes *distingués* sentiments.' "[41]

It will have been noticed that the whole division of semantics dealing with overtones of meaning lies astride the boundary between linguistics and stylistics and could be regarded as a kind of condominium of the two disciplines.

### COMPLEX SEMANTIC SITUATIONS

In complex semantic situations, where more than one sense is connected with the same name, the ambiguity which results is often exploited for stylistic purposes. These purely semantic ambiguities, as distinct from those due to grammatical (morphological or syntactic) factors, have two cardinal types: polysemy (several senses of a single word) and homonymy (several words identical in form). The latter type has three subdivisions: homographs (words spelt alike but pronounced differently), homophones (words spelt differently but pronounced alike), and homonyms in the strict sense (words both written and pronounced in the same way).[42] The basic dichotomy between polysemy and homonymy, which is sometimes overlooked by writers on the subject, is a linguistic reality which every lexicographer has to take into account. There is, however, no clear-cut frontier between the two, and although modern semantics has suggested a number of criteria for the interpretation of borderline cases,[43] the unity of many words remains doubtful, and dictionaries tend to solve these problems in a purely arbitrary fashion. Etymological considerations are, of course, entirely irrelevant to the synchronic interpretation of an ambiguous form: the fact that *port* "harbour" and *port* wine both derive ultimately from Latin *portus*—the first directly, the second through the Portuguese place-name *Oporto*—does not in any way affect the fact that in present-day English the two words are unrelated homonyms.

The distinction between polysemy and homonymy is fully applicable to stylistic uses of ambiguity, ranging from the humble—and often excruciating —efforts of the punster to the most sublime examples of Shakespearean word-play. Both types have two further subdivisions according to whether the ambiguity is implicit or explicit. Explicitness can be achieved in two ways: by repeating the same form with a different meaning, or by making some explanatory comment; in certain cases, the two methods are combined. These criteria yield a system of six types of semantic ambiguity used as a device of style.

## Polysemy

*Implicit.*   The extreme form of implicitness is found in those cases where the title of a book is itself ambiguous. Since there is no immediate context or situation to help the reader, he may not even notice the pun until it begins to emerge from the text. Such a title is for instance that of Robbe-Grillet's novel, *La Jalousie*, where the word means both "jealousy" and "screen, Venetian blind." A little less cryptic are those cases of *double entendre* which are clarified by the context or situation in which they occur; but even here, the reader may not immediately grasp the full implications. A sinister pun of this type is found in the last act of Racine's *Bajazet* when Roxane says to her rival, speaking of the man they both love:

> Loin de vous séparer, je prétends aujourd'hui
> Par des *noeuds* éternels vous unir avec lui
> ["Far from separating you, I intend today
> to unite you to him with eternal bonds"],

a cruel play on the physical and metaphorical meaning of *noeuds*, "knots" and "bonds of marriage."

*Explicit.*    The polysemy may be made explicit by *repetition*, as in *Paradise Lost*, Book III, 11.214-15, where Milton uses the adjective *mortal* twice, first in the sense "subject to death," then in the meaning "deadly":

> Which of ye will be *mortal* to redeem
> Man's *mortal* crime, and just the unjust to save?

(It may be noted that the same adjective had been used, in a slightly different sense, at the very beginning of the poem:

> Of man's first disobedience, and the fruit
> Of that forbidden tree, whose *mortal* taste
> Brought death into the world  . . .)

or by *explanatory comment*: a pun on the double meaning of the verb *to eat*, in the ordinary sense and in the expression *to eat one's words*, occurs in *Much Ado About Nothing*, Act IV, scene 1, where Benedick gives a witty twist to a question by Beatrice:

> BEATRICE:    Will you not *eat* your word?
> BENEDICK:    With no sauce that can be devised to it.


## Homonymy

*Implicit.*    A subtle critic has suggested that there is a homonymic pun in the title of Michel Butor's novel, *Passage de Milan*. This is the name of an imaginary street in Paris, which one would naturally connect with the Italian city; it is, however, possible that *milan* in the sense of "kite" is also relevant. The fact that the bird of prey is mentioned twice in the story lends colour to this interpretation, especially as one of these passages appears quite early in the book: "Dans le haut de l'air, ailes déployées, si ce n'est un avion, c'est un *milan*." ["High up in the air, wings spread, if it is not a plane, it is a kite."] This will make the reader wonder, even at this early stage, about the full meaning and symbolic implications of the title.[44]

*Explicit.*
*Repetition*: there is a pun on the two meanings of "hail" in *Love's Labour's Lost*, Act V, scene 2:

> KING:    All *hail*, sweet madam, and fair time of day!
> PRINCESS:    'Fair' in 'all *hail*' is foul, as I conceive.

*Explanatory comment*: in Hervé Bazin's novel, *Lève-toi et marche*, the narrator, an invalid girl who suffers from an incurable disease but whose intellectual vitality is unimpaired, plays on the two senses of *caillette*, "frivolous person, flirt," and "petrel," and adds a descriptive touch which does not merely explain the pun but develops it into an image: "la téléphoniste, cette *caillette* à bec pourpre" ["the telephone operator, this *caillette* with a purple beak"]. The homonyms mentioned so far were purely lexical: the two forms involved were identical in their ordinary phonetic structure. A different type of semantic homonymy is also exploited by writers: that brought about by syntactic factors. An interesting example is found in *La Jalousie* where the self-effacing narrator, who tells the story without ever referring explicitly to himself, writes: "Sa phrase se termine par 'savoir *la prendre*' ou 'savoir *l'apprendre*,' sans qu'il soit possible de déterminer avec certitude de qui il s'agit, ou de quoi." ["His sentence ends with 'to know how to take it or her' or 'to know how to learn it,' and one cannot be sure whom or what it is about."]

It is clear from this small selection of examples that semantic ambiguity is often more than a mere witticism: it can help to underline important ideas or implications, portray a character, or play its part in the general structure of the work.

## SEMANTIC RELATIONS BETWEEN WORDS

One of the most promising approaches to structural semantics at the present time is concerned with the relations in which words may stand to each other. A recent textbook goes so far as to define the "sense" of a term as "its place in a system of relationships which it contracts with other words in the vocabulary."[45] This may be a somewhat misleading use of the term "sense," but there can be no doubt about the importance of these semantic relations. Those investigated so far include synonymy, incompatibility (*blue —yellow*), subordination (*oak—tree*), antonymy and allied structures.[46] These relations can be further analysed in the light of the distinction between "paradigmatic" and "syntagmatic" connexions. According to a recent definition, a unit "enters into *paradigmatic* relations with all the units which can also occur in the same context," and "into *syntagmatic* relations with the other units of the same level with which it occurs and which constitute its context."[47] As Saussure put it, syntagmatic relations work *in praesentia*, paradigmatic ones *in absentia*.[48]

### PARADIGMATIC RELATIONS

A paradigmatic relationship which is of crucial importance to stylistics is *synonymy*. Choice between synonyms—or quasi-synonyms—is often dictated by considerations which have nothing to do with cognitive meaning.

Various attempts have been made to classify the criteria which determine these choices. A recent suggestion is that we should distinguish between "complete" synonymy ("equivalence of both cognitive and emotive sense"), and "total" synonymy (words "interchangeable in all contexts"). There would thus be four possible combinations: "(1) complete and total; (2) complete, but not total; (3) incomplete, but total; (4) incomplete, and not total."[49] A more "delicate" scheme put forward thirty years ago[50] comprises nine categories:

(1) One term is more general than another: *refuse—reject*.
(2) One term is more intense than another: *repudiate—refuse*.
(3) One term is more emotive than another: *reject—decline*.
(4) One term may imply moral approbation or censure: *thrifty—economical*.
(5) One term is more professional than another: *decease—death*.
(6) One term is more literary than another: *passing—death*.
(7) One term is more colloquial than another: *turn down—refuse*.
(8) One term is more local or dialectal than another: Scots *flesher—butcher*.
(9) One of the synonyms belongs to child-talk: *daddy—father*.

It is worth noting that all but one or two of these criteria are connected with emotive overtones, differences of register, and other stylistic factors. An even more complex scheme, put forward at a symposium on semantics held in Mainz in December 1966,[51] distinguishes between as many as twenty-five criteria.

The position is further complicated by the fact that we may have to choose, not between two or more synonyms, but between a direct and a *periphrastic* expression. As Pascal said, there are situations where we have to call Paris Paris, and others where we have to call it "the capital of France." Periphrasis was a popular figure in traditional rhetoric, and although the Romantics tried to avoid it, it can be the source of valuable stylistic effects. I have already mentioned the famous line from *Phèdre*, "la fille de Minos et de Pasiphaé," with the wide vistas of mythology and heredity which the names open up. The same play (Act I, scene 3) provides a striking example of the contrast between periphrasis and direct statement:

PHÈDRE: J'aime . . . À ce nom fatal, je tremble, je frissonne.
         J'aime . . .
OENONE:                  Qui?
PHÈDRE:                            Tu connais ce fils de l'Amazone,
         Ce prince si longtemps par moi-même opprimé?
OENONE: Hippolyte! Grands Dieux!
PHÈDRE:                                C'est toi qui l'as nommé!

[PHÈDRE:   I love . . . At the mention of that fatal name I tremble, I
shudder. I love . . .
OENONE:              Whom?
PHÈDRE:                          You know the son of the Amazon,
that prince so long oppressed by me?
OENONE:   Hippolyte! Great Gods!
PHÈDRE:                        It's you who have named him.]

As a perceptive critic has said, "the effect may be compared to that of a sword drawn from its sheath."[52]

## SYNTAGMATIC RELATIONS

As this last example shows, terms which are in a paradigmatic relationship to each other may sometimes be combined, and a syntagmatic connexion may thus arise between them. *Collocation of synonyms* is a very common stylistic device. It often has an emotional motivation: we may give vent to our indignation, anger, excitement, or other strong feelings by piling synonyms on each other. Thus, when we first meet Hamlet, he speaks to his mother of "all forms, moods, shapes of grief, That can denote me truly"; a little later, when he is on his own, his repressed feelings reveal themselves by accumulations of synonyms or words with closely similar meanings:

> O, that this too too solid flesh would melt,
> Thaw, and resolve itself into a dew! . . .
> How weary, stale, flat, and unprofitable,
> Seem to me all the uses of this world!

Synonyms can also be collocated for emphasis or contrast, to describe one's groping for the *mot juste*, and for other purposes.

Combinations of *antonymous* and incompatible terms are also a frequent device underlying some well known rhetorical figures such as antithesis: "*Rentre* dans le néant dont je t'ai fait *sortir*" ["Go back to the obscurity from which I brought you out," Racine, *Bajazet*, Act II, scene 1]; 'Hier la *grande armée*, et maintenant *troupeau*" ["Yesterday the Grand Army, and today a herd," Hugo, "L'Expiation"].

The purely semantic antithesis may be reinforced by a contrast of tenses: "Que je le *hais*; enfin, Seigneur, que je *l'aimai*" ["That I hate him; indeed, Lord, that I loved him," Racine, *Andromaque*, Act IV, scene 3].

In another traditional figure, the "oxymoron," two contradictory terms are combined, often in an adjectival phrase. Thus Racine revitalizes the hackneyed comparison between love and a fire when he makes Phèdre say: "Et dérober au jour une *flamme* si *noire*" ["And hide from the day a flame so black," Act I, scene 3].

To the poetic imagination even the sun can appear as black: Nerval speaks of "le *Soleil noir* de la Mélancolie" ["The black Sun of Melancholy," "El Desdichado"] and Hugo of "*ces noirs soleils* pestiférés" ["these plague-stricken black suns," *La Légende des siècles*, "Inferi"], and Baudelaire explicitly notes the incongruity: "Je la (*viz.*, a woman) comparerais à un *soleil noir*, si l'on pouvait concevoir un astre noir versant la lumière et le bonheur" ["I would compare her to a black sun, if one could conceive a black star pouring down light and happiness," *Le Spleen de Paris*, XXXVI: "Le Désir de peindre."].[53]

Yet another time-honoured rhetorical device, *repetition*, is based on syntagmatic relations between words. Even one repetition may be sufficient to produce an impression of monotony, as in "L'Expiation":

> Après la *plaine blanche*, une autre *plaine blanche* . . .
> Pour cette *immense* armée un *immense* linceul

> ["After the white plain, another white plain . . .
> For this immense army an immense shroud"],

with the recurrent verb *il neigeait* providing the keynote of the whole scene. Elsewhere, simple repetition serves to express strong feelings, as in Racine's *Iphigénie*, Act V, scene 4, where lexical and grammatical devices combine to depict Clytemnestre's despair at the impending sacrifice of her daughter:

> Les *vents*, les mêmes *vents*, si longtemps accusés,
> Ne te couvriront pas de ses vaisseaux brisés?
> *Et toi*, Soleil, *et toi*, qui dans cette contrée,
> Reconnais l'héritier et le vrai fils d'Atrée . . .

> ["The winds, the very winds, so long decried,
> will they not cover you with his broken vessels?
> And you, Sun, and you, who in this country
> recognise the true son and heir of Atreus . . ."]

There are also more complex patterns, as in this sentence from *Candide*:

> il me VENDIT à un autre marchand qui me REVENDIT à *Tripoli*; de *Tripoli* je fus REVENDUE à *Alexandrie*; d'*Alexandrie*, REVENDUE à *Smyrne*; de *Smyrne* à Constantinople [". . . he sold me to another merchant who in turn sold me in Tripoli; from Tripoli I was taken to

be resold in Alexandria; from Alexandria I was taken to be resold in Smyrna; from Smyrna to Constantinople"].[54]

In another passage from the same novel, repetition is combined with "chiasmus" to evoke the melancholy and mechanical procession of exiled Turkish dignitaries and their successors who are ultimately doomed to the same fate:

> On voyait souvent passer . . . des bateaux chargés d'effendis, de bachas, de cadis, qu'on envoyait en exil . . . , on voyait venir d'AUTRES cadis, d'AUTRES bachas, d'AUTRES effendis, qui prenaient la place des expulsés, et qui étaient expulsés à leur tour ["One could often see passing . . . boats loaded with effendis, pashas, cadis who were being sent into exile . . . and one could see other cadis, other pashas, other effendis who came to take the place of those expelled and who would themselves be expelled in turn"].[55]

In one sentence in Voltaire's Dictionnaire philosophique, the verb assassiner appears fifteen times.[56] In Proust, Charlus's litany over his dead friends, in which the word mort occurs six times, is followed by the comment:

> Et chaque fois, ce mot 'mort' semblait tomber sur ces défunts comme une pelletée de terre plus lourde, lancée par un fossoyeur qui tenait à les river plus profondément à la tombe ["And each time, that word 'dead' seemed to fall on the deceased like a heavier shovelful of earth, thrown by a grave-digger who was anxious to rivet them more tightly to their tombs"].[57]

With these syntagmatic relations between words, we have arrived at the boundary between semantics and syntax. Connexions between these two branches of linguistics have aroused a great deal of interest in recent years,[58] and the problem has obvious implications for stylistic studies. It should also be noted that our entire analysis has been confined to synchronic aspects of semantics and their stylistic ramifications. Naturally, all these semantic phenomena are subject to change, and these changes may have direct or indirect stylistic repercussions, so that each of the divisions and subdivisions we have discussed will have a diachronic dimension.

Two general impressions emerge from this rapid survey of relations between semantics and stylistics. Firstly, the initial assumption of some kind of isomorphism between the two disciplines has been fully confirmed by our analysis: each major sector of semantics has a stylistic counterpart, even though in some cases the latter may be of limited importance. Secondly, there is a considerable amount of overlapping between the two studies: in certain areas (e.g. onomatopoeia, imagery, overtones, and registers, etc.), semantic and stylistic factors are inextricably interwoven and can hardly be treated in separate compartments. One wonders whether this degree of interpenetration is peculiar to semantics and whether relations between linguistics and stylistics at other levels are quite as intimate and all-pervasive.

## NOTES

1. "Le style pour l'écrivain, aussi bien que la couleur pour le peintre, est une question non de technique mais de vision" (*Le Temps retrouvé: À la Recherche du temps perdu*, Pléiade ed., Vol. III, p. 895).

2. C. F. Hockett, *A Course in Modern Linguistics* (New York, 1958), p. 556. This idea is developed in B. Dupriez, *L'Étude des styles* (Paris, 1969).

3. N. E. Enkvist, "On Defining Style," in N. E. Enkvist, J. Spencer, M. J. Gregory, *Linguistics and Style* (London, 1964), p. 28. Cf. now Karl Uitti, *Linguistics and Literary Theory* (Englewood Cliffs, N.J., 1969) pp. 211 ff.

4. S. Chatman, "The Semantics of Style," *Social Science Information*, VI (1967), pp. 77-99.

5. *Introduction à la poétique*, pp. 12 ff., quoted by R. A. Sayce, *Style in French Prose* (Oxford, 1953), p. 7: "les inventions expressives et suggestives qui ont été faites pour accroître le pouvoir et la pénétration de la parole."

6. R. Fernández Retamar, *Idea de la estilística* (Havana, 1958), p. 11.

7. See, for example, Noam Chomsky, *Language and Mind* (New York, 1968), pp. 49 ff.

8. As in the stratificational model; cf. S. M. Lamb, *Outline of Stratificational Grammar* (Washington, D.C., 1966).

9. Or "expression" and "content" in glossematic terminology.

10. See, for example, A. J. Greimas, *Sémantique structurale* (Paris, 1966), p. 10.

11. Cf. my *Semantics: An Introduction to the Science of Meaning* (Oxford, 1962), p. 57.

12. On the history of this controversial issue since Saussure, cf. R. Engler, "Théorie et critique d'un principe saussurien: l'arbitraire du signe," *Cahiers Ferdinand de Saussure*, XIX (1962), pp. 5-66.

13. P. Delbouille, *Poésie et sonorités. La Critique contemporaine devant le pouvoir suggestif des sons* (Paris, 1961).

14. Or "phonostylistics," as it has been called; cf. N. S. Troubetzkoy, *Principes de phonologie* (Paris, 1949), pp. 16-29.

15. "The Love Song of J. Alfred Prufrock." Cf. M. Schlauch, *The Gift of Tongues*, subsequently renamed *The Gift of Language* (London, 1943), pp. 247 ff.

16. These definitions are taken from *Longmans English Larousse* (London, 1968).

17. Cf. C. Day Lewis, *The Poetic Image* (London, 1947), p. 17.

18. On the quotations from Mallarmé and Breton, see G. Antoine, "Pour

une méthode d'analyse stylistique des images," in *Langue et littérature. Actes du VIIIᵉ Congrès de la Fédération Internationale des Langues et Littératures Modernes* (Paris, 1961), pp. 151-62.

19. "À propos du 'style' de Flaubert," *Nouvelle revue française*, XIV, 1 (1920), 72-90.

20. Quoted by C. Day Lewis, *op. cit.*, p. 25.

21. Cf. I. A. Richards, *The Philosophy of Rhetoric* (New York-London, 1936), p. 93.

22. W. M. Urban, *Language and Reality* (London, 1939), pp. 112 ff. Cf. recently G. Genette, *Figures* (Paris, 1966), pp. 218 ff.

23. Quoted by C. Day Lewis, *op. cit.*, p. 36.

24. "Comparer deux objets aussi éloignés que possible l'un de l'autre, ou, par toute autre méthode, les mettre en présence d'une manière brusque et saisissante, demeure la tâche la plus haute à laquelle la poésie puisse prétendre" (*Les Vases communicants*, Paris, 1955 ed., p. 148; the English translation is by I. A. Richards, *op. cit.*, p. 123).

25. Pléiade ed., p. 69.

26. On this concept see R. A. Sayce, *Style in French Prose* (Oxford, 1953), pp. 62 f. Cf. also H. Weinrich, "Semantik der kühnen Metapher," *Deutsche Vierteljahrsschrift für Literaturwissenschaft und Geistesgeschichte*, XXXVII (1963), 325-44.

27. Quoted by Antoine, *loc. cit.*: "Seule l'image, en ce qu'elle a d'imprévu et de soudain, me donne la mesure de la libération possible et cette libération est si complète qu'elle m'effraye."

28. Quoted by M. Wandruszka, "Etymologie und Philosophie," *Etymologica. W. v. Wartburg zum 70.Geburtstag* (Tübingen, 1958), pp. 857-71.

29. *Le Roi se meurt*, quoted by Th. Buch, "Ionesco et notre réalité," *Recueil commémoratif du xᵉ anniversaire de la Faculté de Philosophie et Lettres* (Publications de l'Université Lovanium de Kinshasa, Paris-Louvain, 1968), pp. 81-107.

30. "Four Quartets: East Coker." The quotations from Eliot and Thomas are taken from R. Quirk, *The Use of English*, London, 1962, pp. 231 ff.

31. "Out of the Sighs."

32. *Philosophical Investigations* (Oxford, 1953), p. 34.

33. *Si le grain ne meurt*, 37th ed. (Paris, 1928), p. 246.

34. J. Lyons, *Introduction to Theoretical Linguistics* (Cambridge University Press, 1968), p. 449.

35. W. K. Frankena in Chapters 5 and 6 of P. Henle (ed.), *Language, Thought, and Culture* (Ann Arbor, Mich., 1958).

36. See A. Ewert, "Dante's Theory of Diction," *MHRA, Annual Bulletin of the Modern Humanities Research Association*, no. 31 (1959), 15-30.

37. Quoted by Lewis and Short, *s.v. rex.*

38. From the poems, "The Habit of Perfection" and "Pied Beauty."

39. M. A. K. Halliday, A. McIntosh, P. Strevens, *The Linguistic Sciences and Language Teaching* (London, 1964), pp. 87 and 90 ff. On the role of registers in stylistics, see D. Crystal and D. Davy, *Investigating English Style* (London, 1969) and G. N. Leech, *A Linguistic Guide to English Poetry* (London, 1969).

40. *The Linguistic Sciences and Language Teaching*, from which the definitions which follow are taken, distinguishes between "field," "mode," and "style."

J. Spencer and M. J. Gregory, "An Approach to the Study of Style" (*Linguistics and Style*, p. 87, n.) suggest "tenor" instead of "style."

41. *Contre Sainte-Beuve* (Paris, 1954), p. 235.

42. See, on somewhat different lines, K. Heger, "Homographie, Homonymie und Polysemie," *Zeitschrift für Romanische Philologie*, LXXIX (1963), 471-91.

43. Cf. my book, *Language and Style* (Oxford, 1964), pp. 32ff. See also J. McH. Sinclair, "Beginning the Study of Lexis," *In Memory of J. R. Firth* (London, 1966), p. 425. In his monograph, *Explorations in Semantic Theory* (*Current Trends in Linguistics*, ed. T. A. Sebeok, Vol. III (The Hague/Paris, 1966), p. 402, the late Uriel Weinreich criticized the semantic theory of Katz and Fodor for its failure to "discriminate between fortuitous homonymy and lexicologically interesting polysemy"; cf. J. J. Katz's reply in "Recent Issues in Semantic Theory," *Foundations of Language*, III (1967), 148ff. Cf. also D. Bolinger, "The Atomization of Meaning," *Language*, XLI (1965), 562.

44. See L. Spitzer, "Quelques aspects de la technique des romans de Michel Butor," *Archivum Linguisticum*, XIV (1962), 65, n. 1.

45. Lyons, *op. cit.*, p. 427.

46. See *ibid.*, Ch. 10, developing the ideas put forward by the same author in *Structural Semantics. An Analysis of Part of the Vocabulary of Plato* (Publications of the Philological Society, XX, Oxford, 1963).

47. Lyons, *Introduction to Theoretical Linguistics*, p. 73.

48. *Cours de linguistique générale*, 4th ed. (Paris, 1949), p. 171.

49. Lyons, *Introduction to Theoretical Linguistics*, p. 448.

50. W. E. Collinson, "Comparative Synonymics: Some Principles and Illustrations," *Transactions of the Philological Society* (1939), 61ff.

51. K. Baldinger, "La Synonymie—problèmes sémantiques et stylistiques," *Probleme der Semantik*, ed. W. Th. Elwert, *Zeitschrift für französische Sprache und Literatur*, Beiheft, Neue Folge, Heft 1 (Wiesbaden, 1968), pp. 46ff.

52. R. A. Sayce, "Racine's Style: Periphrasis and Direct Statement," *The French Mind. Studies in Honour of Gustave Rudler* (Oxford, 1952), p. 80.

53. See Antoine, *loc. cit.*, p. 161. Cf. H. Tuzet, *Revue des Sciences Humaines*, fasc. 88 (1957), 479-502.

54. Ed. O. R. Taylor, 13th impr. (Oxford, 1965), p. 26.

55. *Ibid.*, p. 83.

56. See J. R. Monty, *Étude sur le style polémique de Voltaire: le "Dictionnaire philosophique"* (*Studies on Voltaire and the Eighteenth Century*, vol. XLIV, Geneva, 1966), pp. 64ff.

57. *Le Temps retrouvé*, p. 862.

58. Cf. e.g. Chomsky, *Aspects of the Theory of Syntax* (Cambridge, Mass., 1965), pp. 148ff., and Weinreich, *op. cit.*, pp. 467ff. See also recently G. N. Leech, *Towards a Semantic Description of English* (London, 1969).

# DISCUSSION OF ULLMANN'S PAPER

This was the first paper to be presented at the symposium, and it proved a good one to start with, since it raised at the outset old but crucial questions about how to define style. Ullmann's argument that style contains features "peculiar to itself" and distinct from those of language, and hence that stylistics is not a mere branch of linguistics, was approved in at least one quarter, as a reaction against the tendency to think of "style" as a mere aggregate of language features. But his equation of stylistics with the "expressive use of language" ran into opposition. It was argued, for example, that though he spoke in principle of isomorphism, and hence the similarity between stylistics and linguistics, the general tendency of his paper was to fortify the dichotomy; that not only the expressive but the cognitive too is stylistic, for example, the fact that one elects to write in a purely referential manner is itself a matter of considerable stylistic import; and, finally, that if expressive means "connotative," it must be a part of language just as much as it is of style. Roland Barthes' *Le Dégre zéro de l'écriture*[1] was cited as evidence that the absence of all expressiveness itself is a powerful stylistic marker. There was further the suggestion that the analyst's basic question is "What is the underlying disposition of linguistic resources as they are found in a given text?" and that such a question does not require us to take over ready-made functions from other disciplines.

Ullmann responded by questioning the sense in which "linguistic" was being used; obviously, he felt style is "linguistic" to the extent that we are not talking about the style of architecture or cricket, and thus that non-cognitive as well as cognitive elements must be expressed "linguistically." But as regards the subject matter of these fields, linguistics accents cognitive elements and stylistics non-cognitive elements. But, he continued, every statement inevitably has a modicum of both intellectual and emotive content; this is a question of dosage (or *cline* in Halliday's term); for example, the *-ino* in *poverino*—though predominantly expressive—does have a cognitive sense, namely "little."

Ullmann agreed with those who disliked the term "expressive" (a dissatisfaction he expresses in the paper itself), but he said he didn't know a better one for a lot of elements that have only a negative thing in common, namely that they are not merely informational. (Not only "expressive" was objected to as a term but "cognitive" as well: it was suggested that "ideational" or "experiential" might be better.) Still, there was the sense that the question was more than terminological, that even the purely cognitive inevitably manifests stylistic features as well.

In response to Ullmann's view that an isomorphism exists between linguistics and stylistics, it was noted that we have a three-part division in linguistics only because, on empirical grounds, that has proved best for describing languages; but if need be, a fourth part could easily be introduced if it should prove useful to do so. Further, there doesn't seem to be any particular reason why stylistics should follow the same organization as linguistics—that question can only be answered when we decide whether stylistics is to be a theory of something, and if so, what sort of thing that something is. One notion worth thinking about is that stylistic theory is a theory about a reader, or more specifically about his intuitions or perceptions.

As for Ullmann's discussion of a "semantic motivation," the discussion was principally about metaphor, first taking a terminological direction. Richards' distinction of "tenor" and "vehicle" was both attacked as unedifying ("subject" and "object" being offered as alternatives), and defended on the grounds that metaphor does not cite the thing being referred to and the referring thing separately but both at the same time. Ullmann agreed that it was difficult to keep straight which term was which and that one could wish for more immediately transparent terms. He said he envied the French critics their terms *comparant* and *comparé*.

The importance of other figures was urged too. For example, it was held that metonymy was a fundamental principle in modern art; that it formed the basis of psychoanalysis; that if one were to pursue powerful metaphors —like those of Gaston Bachelard—[2] one would often find their ultimate basis to be metonymic. Catachresis, too, the *abusio* of ancient rhetoric, was brought up as even more *passionant* than metaphor. Two other problems concerning metaphor could only be touched upon for lack of time: whether the comparison of metaphor is of words only or of things stood for by the words (Ullmann thought it was the thing); and how to account for metaphors in which there is simply no other word than the vehicle (*comparant*) to refer to the object, e.g. the arms of a chair—these are metaphors of the language, not of style.

Ullmann had to admit that stylistics could not be expected to account for the semantic dimension of literature with a zero semantic component—dada, surrealism, Gertrude Stein.

It was pointed out—and Ullmann agreed completely—that "polysemy" was an inadequate term to characterize the connotative power of a word like *caillette*. The connotative spectrum in such cases has something infinite about it: the reverberations are almost endless, and the "stylized" word becomes profoundly symbolic. This seems even truer if the word is rare, or unpredictable in the context.

What Ullmann called "overtones" and his depiction of the mechanisms of choice were subjected to the same kinds of questioning as his basic dichotomy of cognitive vs. expressive language: in other words, could one really hope to separate a "purely" linguistic from a "purely" stylistic function? The notion of choice, it was argued, cannot be limited to stylistics, since language too is constantly a matter of choice: one chooses words in a string and the range of choice distinctly narrows as the end of the string is approached. But then it is difficult to conceive of two separate choices at such junctures—one linguistic and the other stylistic. But what is the mechanism for distinguishing the two: for example, in *pover-ino*, how do we know that *pover-* is a cognitive and *-ino* a stylistic choice? This is in addition to the objections reported above, that the neutral form, in this case *poveretto*, was just as "stylistic" as the other. Isn't it, in short, impossible to conceive of terms *without* overtones? Ullmann responded that he was untroubled by the idea that choice is complex, that it consists of several components, and he reminded the group that he had not said that *-ino* was devoid of cognitive content, but simply that "emotional" overtones make it preferable in certain cases to *poveretto*. Thus there seemed to be agreement on the "shuttling back and forth" effect between cognitive and expressive, linguistic and stylistic in linguistic choice, and at least one participant felt "much heartened" by the direction Ullmann's paper took as symptomatic of the general drift of recent work in linguistics and stylistics.

## NOTES

1. (Paris, 1953), now in English translation.
2. In books like the *L'Eau et les rêves, L'Air et les songes, La Terre et les rêveries de la volonté*, and *La Psychanalyse du feu*.

# 3
# STYLE FEATURES

# THE FUNCTIONS OF VOCAL STYLE

## IVAN FÓNAGY

THE ANALYSIS OF X-RAYS of emotive speech have produced some paradoxical results. It has been discovered that in Hungarian the most closed vowel, /i/, is often more open than /e/, the vowel of middle aperture: notably, in the distraught affirmation *igen* ("yes!") /i/ is slightly more open than the vowel /e/ in *én* /e:n/ said with hatred.

According to the evidence of facial cinematography, Hungarian or French actresses pronounce /i/ with rounded lips when they mimic a young mother who says tenderly *igy* ("like that") or *mais si* ("yes, indeed") to her child.[1]

However, subjects who heard the films believed they heard an "i," despite the labialization, which ordinarily transforms [i] into [y], apparently on the basis of context and situation. Though the speakers deformed the habitual pronunciation of these vowels, their auditors, in decoding the phonological component of the message, re-established the intended phonemes, interpreting the distortion as an expressive manner of pronouncing the phoneme. In the decoding, the sound is broken up into two elements:

[y]→/i/ + expression of tenderness
[e]→/i/ + expression of indifference
[i]→/e/ + expression of hatred

Now these two components of the concrete sound, these two *endo-* and *ectosemantic* messages, to use the terms of Meyer-Eppler,[2] are different in nature: a) the phoneme /i/ is a *fragment* of an arbitrary *signifiant*; the tender pout which distorts the habitual pronunciation is a *sign* in itself, a motivated sign; b) the phoneme is transmitted by digital encoding, the second element, the buccal gesture, by analogical encoding; c) the second element presupposes the existence of the first, the buccal gesture is grafted onto the phoneme; the phoneme is independent and directly representable by a graphic sign conveying no other message; d) this explains in part that the first component is perceived as a substance, the second, which is no less substantial than the first, as a "manner of pronouncing," even if the two elements do not coincide in time and the expressive gesture occupies another segment in the spoken chain, as, for example, the French sentence /il la ʔɛ / ("He hates her"). The glottal stop /ɛ/ will not be perceived as a sound. It will be invalidated as such and integrated into the following vowel lending it a certain "hardness."[3]

I use the term "phonetic gesture."[4] In the case of the labialization of the vowel /i/→[y] there is clearly a pout—[me sy] *mais si!*—which in turn can be considered as preparation for a kiss. The glottal stop appears in many unrelated languages, figuring neither as phoneme nor as contextual variant, but as an expression of anger, hatred, or a firm attitude. Tomographic traces show that a strong glottal constriction accompanies the expression of hatred.[5]

What is the relation between aggression and the contraction of the glottal sphincter? Darwin considered the emotions to be the residue of certain ancestral activities: fear represents flight, anger represents combat.[6] Strong muscular contraction is an essential element in preparation for combat, in combat itself.

The glottal stop is constituted by a specific muscular contraction, a contraction which results in a complete closure at the glottal level. The metaphor of "strangled voice" seems to contain the germ of an explanation. "Strangling" foreshadows homicide. Here we have an action which, according to the magical conception of the world, should suffice in itself to eliminate one's adversary.

We must also consider the primary function of the glottal sphincter—to prevent harmful corpuscles from entering the lungs. The cough is only a glottal closure which, under high subglottal pressure, serves to eliminate these corpuscles. By extension, by biological transfer, this reflex appears as a sort of rejection, a refusal of food, of the environment, of existence itself. It has inspired the laryngologist and phonetician Gutzman to create the term *Unlusteinsatz* ("attack of displeasure"). The second and equally important role played by the glottal closure is the exertion of strong pressure on the diaphragm, indirectly on the intestines. This double biological function of glottal stops is the basis of hysterical asthmas which have as origin an anal cathexis of the glottal sphincters (observed by E. Weiss[7] and other psychoanalysts). The glottal stop (or hiatus) is considered by grammarians to be particularly "hard" or unpleasant.[8] The biological functions of glottal occlusion, and the transfer of the anal libido to the glottal level seems associated with the "hard attack" of anger and hatred.

As Thomas Mann wrote, "The mouth is a tool which is more closely connected with and which conforms more closely to infernal powers than do the eyes."[9] Thus one explains that a particularly open pronunciation of a vowel is often declared vulgar, while a too closed pronunciation is felt to be "delicate" or "mincing." Henri Estienne sees in the Parisian preference for a closed /e/ over [ɛ] and [wɛ] a desire not to open the mouth in an indecent fashion.[10] In the fifties, the opened lips were *de rigueur* in the photobehavior of models. In the more recent fashion, the lips are severely closed, and it is the legs which are brutally separated. The study of neurotic symptoms and of dreams has taught us that a faint resemblance or a certain functional analogy are sufficient for an unconscious identification of one sexual organ with another.[11]

It is no coincidence, for example, that it is the phallic period during which children learn to master the rolled [r], a sound which presupposes a strong erection of the tongue. It seems as if we could take literally the metaphor of the English phonetician T. H. Pear which characterizes the non-apical pronunciation of /r/ as an "emasculation."[12]

Elise Richter has described the habit of a certain doctor of pronouncing /r/ with strong rolling when he addressed inferiors.[13] The rolling became weaker according to the social status of his clients, vanishing completely in the presence of the Queen of Serbia. The technique of a priest in a thirteenth-century tale who pronounced *Barraban* with a strongly rolled /r/ to impress his sleepy congregation could scarcely fulfill this function if it were not considered by the archaic ego as a phallic menace. It is the same gesture that we encounter in the form of an erect menacing finger. (This explains, in part, the taboos in several languages which simultaneously proscribe words for the tongue, the fingers, and the hand.[14]) This apical *r* is significantly more frequent in aggressive and erotic poems than in idyllic poems by the same authors.[15]

Whether or not we accept the psychoanalytic interpretation of articulation, the *viva voce* presupposes a double encoding. The choice of phoneme is followed by a choice of concrete sound to represent the phoneme. The mimetic movements of the organs of phonation graft a second message onto the original one being transmitted by the sequence of phonemes. It seems preferable to assign to the second encoding a place outside the grammar. It is useful to locate the second act of encoding in a "distorting" component which contains as many levels as the grammar but which operates according to essentially different rules. At the phonetic level apparently three principles are operative:

1) The voluntary reproduction of vocal symptoms of a certain bodily state signals the presence of emotions associated with that state. For ex-

ample, the contraction of muscles of the pharynx which accompanies the act of vomiting can signal nausea, disgust, scorn.[16]

2) The organs of speech can represent other animate or inanimate objects with which they are associated by resemblance or functional analogy. For example, the tongue can represent arm, finger, penis, and thereby the displacement of the tongue, frontwards and upwards, can emulate a similar movement of these organs.

3) To different degrees of intensity of sonorous expression correspond different degrees of semantic intensity: for example, different degrees of intensity of accent, different degrees of emphatic lengthening of phonemes reflect more or less strong emotions.

According to the model proposed, all phonemes must pass through the "distorting" component: this merely states again the fact that all articulated sounds are expressive. Non-distortion is not necessarily less expressive than distortion—it simply expresses something else. Our model, therefore, permits two interpretations of a "neutral" sound: non-distortion and double distortion (in opposed senses).

That these preconscious stylistic messages are effectively "received" and decoded by one's interlocutor is reflected in spontaneous reactions, verbal or otherwise. In the course of my short military career, I was able to observe a seizure of anger elicited by a laryngeal gesture, or more exactly by the lack of such a gesture. One of the young recruits was supposed to produce military commands, among others *Hátra arc!* ("Half-turn!"). Shouting in what he assumed to be a correct manner, he was astonished to find himself cursed out by the sergeant, who repeated the same command, but with a vigorous glottal stop between the two vowels. The sergeant behaved as if he knew that the glottal stop is a laryngeal gesture to which anal-sadistic cathexis lends a very authoritarian character. All he cared about, of course, was that the command when uttered with a glottal stop set off immediate and precise reactions, and he felt vaguely that the recruit's pronunciation showed a relaxed attitude that clashed violently with the rigors of military discipline. His angry metaphors—he accused the recruit of flabbiness, characterized his attitude as soft, effeminate—were based on a preconscious but exact analysis of the articulatory gesture and a decoding of the unconscious message. The metaphors with which grammar, rhetoric, and modern phonetics swarm—"clear" or "acute" vowels, "hard" or "soft" consonants, a "virile" or "effeminate," a "vulgar" or "effete" articulation— indicate in the majority of cases a complicity, a kind of perfect *entente* between interlocutors, who seem to know everything which they give the appearance of not knowing.[17]

To come back to our model: each sound which issues forth in modified form from the "Distorting Component" will be recorded by a Memory which is coupled at once with the "Distorter" and with the Grammar. This is what allows the rules of the Grammar to be radically changed by distortions which have become frequent and typical. It is also what explains the fact that the linguistic code changes independently of the will of the persons who use it.[18]

In daily language phonetic style is often called "accent" or "intonation." This may be explained and justified by the fact that secondary stylistic messages are more important on the *prosodic level*. It is almost an open field in languages which do not have distinctive tone. Communication by arbitrary pitch-patterns occupies a relatively small place. Emotive intonation can be considered as a kind of indirect gesticulation in which the laryngeal mimicry is projected into the sound-space. Changes in fundamental frequency are perceived as a spatial movement, as a change of height. (The Hungarian term *hanglejtés* means literally "sound-dance.") Although integrated within the linguistic system, intonational forms preserve their gestural character, their motivation, their transparence—to use the plastic term of Ullmann.[19] This motivation is more or less masked by differences between prosodic systems, for example, the principle of oxytony in French vs. the accent on the first syllable in other languages, like Hungarian, a contrast which necessarily influences the intonation of the sentence. The same tendency, the same transformation-rule will yield different results according to the different neutral intonation-patterns of the input.[20]

The intonations of certain complex attitudes seem to be equally motivated. One could cite ironic intonation as an example, on the basis of research that has been done on synthesized Hungarian sentences.

The expression of irony presupposes three phases, at least in Hungarian and probably also in English, German, and French:[21]

1) a first phase characterized by "chest-voice," a strong constriction of the laryngeal sphincter, "creak," a very low pitch with intervals reduced to quarter-tones, a fairly straight melodic line, a relaxed labial articulation, the corners of the lips slightly lowered;

2) a second phase characterized by "head-voice," reduction of global intensity, rise in pitch towards a very high note ($250$ $H_2$ for the voice of a man), tense articulation, palatalization, that is to say displacement of tongue forwards and upwards, resulting in a clearer and sharper voice, pharyngeal contraction;

3) a third phase in which the voice returns to the chest, with compressed attack, renewed "creak," the pitch returned to the former level and immobilized, the tongue moved this time backwards (these tongue movements have been clearly visible in radiographic films).

In these three phases the velum is more or less lowered, lending a nasal timbre to the sentence.

Thus we have a drama in three acts. The changes of tension in the tragedy are physically present in the changes of muscular tension. What meaning can be derived from this pantomime?

1) In the protasis of the drama the pharyngeal constriction is a sign of rejection; it regularly accompanies the expression of hatred. This "strangled voice" could even contain an allusion to homicide. The low register and chest-voice indicate virility, force. Moses calls it an "ultra-paternal" tone.[22] The "creak" is a sinister growling, in whose slow delivery and immobility of tone there is something menacing, something that suggests a wild animal crouching in order to pounce upon its victim. The delabialization and the lowered corners of lips express general scorn and disgust. The *protasis* of our drama is thus dominated completely by despite, hatred, menace.

2) The second phase, or *epitasis* of the drama, is marked by sudden change: the head-voice, raised pitch, reduced intensity, and palatalization seem to reflect an affectionate, feminine, infantile attitude. This gentleness is partially belied by clearly aggressive elements like muscular tension and pharyngeal constriction. These antagonistic attitudes create a certain dramatic tension which prepares for the *dénouement*.

3) And this is not delayed. The *catastrophe* is marked by a brusque return to aggression. The mask of sweetness is torn off. The interlocutor, seemingly carried toward the glorious heights, falls suddenly from the clouds, sees himself cast into the abyss where he must meet face to face the diabolical speaker who lies in wait.

The ironic tone, the expressive modification of neutral intonation, is thus a *dramatic performance* in three acts which accompany and differentiate the primary message of the sentence. And intonation is only one voice in the chorus of simultaneous messages which make up speech.


### INDIVIDUATION

Can one reduce phonological style to a series of expressive gestures, to a sensible distortion of articulation, accentuation, and intonation, from normal utterance, to the expressive manipulation of the sound object?

By this restriction one would seem to be excluding what has always been considered (from Seneca to Granger[23]) the basic function of style, namely *individuation*.

In previous studies,[24] I have tried to reduce the function of individuation to the expressive function, to consider individual style as a *permanent message*.

A vocal tic may be interpreted as a gesture by the auditor who meets for the first time the person having the tic. A tendency to displace the accent from the first to the second and third syllables will be judged, according to the verbal and objective context, as an expression of strong emotion, as a strong inhibition or simply as a putting of things into strong relief. If this de-accentuation or pluri-accentuation persists, the word-highlighting hypothesis is the first to go, then that of the sentence, then that of strong emotion or momentary inhibition. One ends by assuming nothing more than a simple idiosyncrasy, that is, by not hearing the feature any longer. The pulmonary and glottal gesture is deprived of significance through too frequent occurrence. This paradox arises out of the physiology and psychology of perception: at all levels of perception, one reacts more and more feebly to a given stimulus. The simplest and most effective way of camouflaging a message is to communicate it *ad infinitum.*

Here are two "individual voices,"[25] two series of suppressed pulmonary and glottal gestures. The very fact of delivery, the continuous flow of the speech itself seems in the first voice to reflect a feverish excitement (joyful or anguished). However, it is only the expression of a quasi-permanent, individual attitude.

In the second voice, the violent contractions of expiratory muscles and the simultaneous spasms of the glottal sphincter seem to reflect strong inner conflict. In reality, we are listening to the voice of a lecturer who is in the process of explaining—without emotion or emphasis—a passage from Georg Lukács. This vocal expression reveals his character and does not refer to the present situation.

The metaphor of "expression of individuality" implicitly takes a position: that of assuming *individuality as a content* which is communicated like any other message. The psychotherapist and the orthoëpist will lend attentive ears to "permanent" vocal messages and will try to get back to their sources, to the source of the permanent excitement which is reflected in the feminine voice on our tape, and of the lack of pauses in her relation of events. He will look for the permanent conflict behind the violent simultaneous innervation of groups of antagonistic muscles in the voice of our lecturer, a repression of everything that wells up from below. There is probably something even deeper, indicating an *urethral cathexis* in the flow of the girl's inarticulate speech and an *anal-sadistic cathexis* with violent contraction of the abdominal muscles and glottal sphincter, the vocal constipation, the retention of speech, the tearing of sentences to pieces through irregular accents in that of the lecturer. The metaphors of phonetic terminology seem to corroborate this interpretation. Thus the terms *stress, Druckakzent,* Hungarian *nyomaték* ("pressure") refer to the action of pressing. Latin *ictus,* the Russian word *udarenie* "blow" highlight the aggressive side of the dynamic accent.

The expression of a momentary attitude is sometimes transformed into a permanent message—that is, into an individual trait—under our very eyes.

I have described elsewhere[26] an extreme case, the phono-pathological behavior of a five-year-old boy who was traumatized by a brutal threat of castration. The boy developed a temporary agrophobia and at the same time
gave up the apical [r] that he had already acquired. Such faults in lingual
articulation, such quasi-permanent symptoms are—according to the evidence of the orthoëpists—much more frequent in boys than in girls of the
same age.[27]

The individual message is masked by its constancy. The word "mask"
might also express the set or "frozen" character of individual style. There
is an obvious contradiction between the dynamism of style and the rigidity
which one ordinarily associates with the idea of "form." I think that it
would be wrong to wish to resolve this contradiction at any price. Individual style is dynamic insofar as the unconscious content displayed at the
surface is concerned. This expressive movement is perpetuated by the repetition compulsion.[28] Its very rigidity—W. Reich uses the term "armor"[29]—
probably has an important function. By its constancy, individual style preserves the equlibrium of the ego, maintaining a balance between antagonistic forces (the needs of the id, the opposed needs of the superego). One
could even say that style contributes broadly to the formation of the ego.
Style is the "skin" or husk of the ego; it belongs to it and at the same time
girdles it like a belt. It protects it against overpowering forces from the outside and destructive impulses from within, from the id, the archaic kernel
of the ego. The moral consolidation of the individual by style has a biological analogy in the formation of the epithelial tissue whose function is
to defend the cell against external excitations and to prevent its dissolution.

In extreme cases individuation can create the verbal wall which separates
the schizophrenic from his environment. (But the schizophrenic poets
manage to surmount even these obstacles.)

### EVOCATION

Individuation in language is the basis of a third function of phonological
style. Charles Bally has distinguished two different processes which are capable of lending an affective character to speech: "natural" and "evocative."[30]
One can evoke a person by imitating (instinctively or voluntarily) his fashion of speaking, that is, by adopting a certain number of phonic, lexical,
and syntactic peculiarities of the idiolect; and one can evoke a social milieu
by using variants which are particularly frequent in the language of that
milieu.

Individual articulation, which is by definition "deviant" (in relation to
the norm), and above all the prosodic features constituting personal "accent" are highly contagious. This contagion is due in part to the attraction

exercised by the pre-conscious or unconscious message of the individual phonological gesture, but also to that exercised by the personality or milieu from which the trait is borrowed. The metaphor of "attraction" can be replaced by more direct terms. Markuszevicz has given us an extreme example of phonological evocation.[31] A young girl experienced a very grave loss: her cat died. She was inconsolable for several days. Suddenly she recovered her gaiety. But she also started going on all fours, meowing, purring, and refusing to eat at table. She no longer spoke about the cat, it was the cat who spoke through her, who lived in her.

The phonetic borrowings of adults do not differ essentially from this one made from animal language. The open or secret motive is always to identify with a person or group. This identification is interpreted at the unconscious level as an "incorporation," a taking of the other into the body. Thus the preponderant role played by oral behavior, language, in these identifications. Cannibalism is only a more direct oral (but non-verbal) realization of this same impulse to identify. The verbal "incorporation" is based on the principle of *pars pro toto*.

The developed ego, having adopted the reality principle,[32] regards the naïve efforts of the archaic self of others with an ironic smile, a bit like the rifleman in Schiller's *Wallenstein* who observes to the sergeant that he has done a good imitation of the voice and tics of his superior.

> Wie er sich räuspert und wie er spuckt
> Das habt Ihr ihm glücklich abgeguckt.[33]

The developed ego generally closes its eyes to the "incorporating" urges of the archaic ego, seeing only a means of lending a certain timbre to the voice.

The poet, more conscious of stylistic processes, knowingly evokes the voice of another poet, by rhythm, melody, rhymes and sometimes even by timbre (by a certain deviation in the mean frequency distribution of phonemes). It is by this means that Mallarmé in "Un Tombeau" ("An Epitaph") evokes the stylistic profile of Verlaine by the structure and simplicity of the verse. Verlaine in turn evokes, in the "Ballade de la vie en rouge," another Parisian poet who saw *la vie en rouge*, François Villon (imitated by many other poets, for example by Vitezslav Nazval in a series of *ballades*). Villon used the same means to evoke the good old days in his "Ballade en vieil langage françois." The change of tone, the features of imitative prosody, are particularly striking in *pastiches* and literary caricatures. One could study the changes in melody and rhythmic patterns in the verbal caricatures of the Hungarian humorist Frigyes Karinthy and relate the variations among prosodic peculiarities to the styles of the imitated authors. What distinguishes a vocal imitation from its original is its condensation and exaggeration of individual peculiarities.[34]

The literary counterpart of the evocation of milieu is the evocation of genres, of Barthes' "writings" (*écritures*).[35] The comic epic, *Le Lutrin* (*The Music-stand*) of Boileau, for example, presents, through certain lexical and syntactic particularities, the solemn tone—the raised norm, the slow melodic movement—of the classical epic. On the other hand, the melodic level is more heightened, the movement more lively in the poems of the *Fêtes galantes* in which Verlaine evokes the literary intonation of the eighteenth century than in his poems preceding or following the *Fêtes*.

In part, these spectacular effects of phonological evocation, these urges to identify, play a major role in the process of phonetic change by favoring certain phonetic variants instead of others.[36]

The unconscious desire to "incorporate" is the basis of all language learning, which renders the task difficult every time the instructor is distasteful to us or we feel hostility toward the community which speaks that language. The relations between learning a language and oral "incorporation" appear above all in the course of acquiring one's native language.

### PLAYING WITH SOUNDS

A chapter in classical rhetoric treats of the sound figures, the *metaplasms*. This chapter could be enriched by studies of recursiveness in phonemes and distinctive features.[37] Let us take an example from Mallarmé's "Ses purs ongles":

> ce lac dur // pur éclat   (a y/y a//l k r r k e)
> ["This hard lake,/ Pure glitter"]

The regular recurrence of certain vowels and consonants, and above all, the more or less complete reversal of the order of that recurrence obviously differs from recurrences in everyday language.

It would be a gratuitous deviation from common usage to exclude metrical structure, that is, the stylization of sound-expression, from the concept of vocal style. So it is necessary to enlarge this concept in such a way that it comprehends on the one hand occasional or permanent phonetic gestures, that is "expressive style," and on the other, playful sound-repetitions, the quasi-regular recurrence of phonic elements, that is "autistic style."[38]

Repetition plays an essential role in verbal orchestration. It is completed by another force: the tendency to introduce within sentences and verses tensions which must ultimately be resolved.

The intonation of a sentence is a model of tension and relief. The height of the voice (the frequency of vocal cord vibration) is a function of sub-glottal pressure and of the tension of the vocal cords and thereby an indicator of these two tensions. The poet often plays cleverly on this instrument, controlling, regulating from a distance, by the structure of his verses, the physiological tensions of the speech organs of the reader. The solution of a tension is always joyful, and probably inherent to pleasure.[39] These tendencies—independent of communicational requirements—are deeply rooted in the earliest phase of mental and verbal development, in babbling, which is entirely dominated by the principles of pleasure and repetition. At this autistic (narcissistic) stage, the ego hardly yet formed, hardly emerged from its surroundings, the need for communication is not, or only barely, felt. It is content to recreate a pleasant situation, to reduce tension by means of hallucination.

How does the infant leave this imaginary paradise and enter the real world, a world less perfect, but one offering real gratification to its desires? How is autistic play transformed into communication?

Phonostylistics can offer us certain indications:

> Barangoló borongó
> ki bamba bún borong
> borzongó bús bolyongó
> baráttalan bolond
> > (Babits,
> > *Szomoru Verses*)

These lines of the Hungarian poet M. Babits seem to retreat directly to the babbling-stage. The playfulness of the alliterations is obvious. At the same time, according to the results of experiments made with Hungarian readers, within this given context—this "Sad Poem" (the title of Babit's poem)—constant recourse to the voiced stop suggested mainly two images: nine readers out of twenty heard a bell sounding or saw a solitary bell-tower, while six others were reminded of the mournful sound of funeral drums.

There is a transitional area between autistic play and communication, wherein there is still redundance, but redundance of a certain kind. The recurrence of the liquid /l/ and the labial nasal /m/ seems to lend to the verse an expression quite different from that lent by the recurrence of the consonants /k/, /t/, and /r/. This ancient subjective impression can be corroborated in two ways—by the analysis of correlations between the content of the poems and the frequency-distribution of the phonemes, or by synthetically generating experimental poems. For example, when we systematically varied poems in "pseudo-Hungarian" by multiplying or diminishing the relative frequency of "hard" and "soft" consonants, it seemed that large numbers of /k/ and /t/ and /r/ suggested a martial subject.[40]

The play of resolving tensions also can be put to an expressive use. Different degrees of melodic tension faithfully reflect differences in psychic tension or different physical and moral attitudes. Certain periods of Hugo impose on the reader a forced respiration called "clavicular," a society posture, the attitude of a field marshal. When he speaks to a child, however, Hugo changes attitude and the tension in the sentences attenuates considerably. But then he can forget his role and the perspective of the child whom he is supposed to be addressing by suddenly assuming a historic and cosmic role, an attitude of naïve pride, swelling the reader's breast by a period of thirty-four verses.[41] The mean length of sentences addressed to the child is 4.7 words. The philosophical period contains 315 words.

These examples show that autistic musical play is easily transformed—in the social context—into *expressive play*. Similarly, the narcissistic babbling of the infant or the angry cries by which he tries directly to reduce internal tension will be interpreted as signals by those around him. Realizing this, the child will reproduce the same vocal gestures to obtain the same results, thus resolving the tension by a real gratification of his desires. The expressive phonational gestures—pulmonary, glottal, or buccal—seem thus to recall narcissistic phonational play. These movements had originally the sole aim of reducing tension in an immediate way: they were literally *ex-pressive*—but then became *expressive* in the transferred sense of the term. As expressive gestures, they are half-way between real actions and the arbitrary signs with which they are integrated.

### THE PLACE OF PHONETIC STYLE IN VERBAL COMMUNICATION

In a manuscript of a hundred pages, which naturally cannot be presented on this occasion, I have tried to work upwards into the higher levels of language and verbal style, up to the literary work, to see what forms are taken by the tendencies we have met at the phonetic level. There is a certain parallelism between the symptomatic distortion of phonemes and the expressive rearrangement of monemes, between the symbolic gesticulation of phonational organs and the symbolic manipulation of the spoken sentence conceived of as a series of cubes.[42] I believe that there is a strong analogy between phonetic substitution (distortion) and transfer of the *signifiant*, the lexical and grammatical tropes. To see the full flowering of autistic tendencies in style (repetitions and mechanisms of tension and relaxation), it is necessary to go beyond the level of the sentence. Despite the great variety of orchestration in literary works, it seems that all the figures of thought depend on two principal tendencies—that of recurrence, and that of the creation of tension—and of their mixture. These two tendencies in turn probably depend on two forces whose interplay determines all human activity: 1) in the play of tension and release is manifested the vital—that is, sexual—principle; 2) metrical organization of expression and content reveals the presence of the death instinct.[43]

To conclude, I should like to respond to a question of a pragmatic sort which necessarily arises when one associates phonological style with mental regression, with the archaic ego, with babbling. Are phonological style and, more broadly, verbal style to be considered regressions, lapses?

This conclusion would contradict the high value we instinctively place on stylistic features in literature.

And this intuition seems to me clearly justified. Verbal style is a precious accomplishment which integrates, with linguistic—that is grammatical and conscious—communication, psychic elements which would otherwise remain unexpressed; and which transforms autistic play into verbal message. This is a voluntary, transient regression, a well-organized "descent into Hell" which permits the liberation and expression of repressed emotions and fantasies. Phonological style—and other processes like the expressive arrangement of monemes—permit, further, access to preverbal, non-communicable mental contents.[44] This regression is dynamic in two senses of the word—it liberates latent energies and it directs language toward action. Style "acts out" its content, and this involves a real activity for verbal concepts. This realization presupposes a transposition, the drama must be played out in the microcosm of glottis, pharynx, buccal and nasal cavities— a considerable reduction of dimension and intensity. The unconscious, however, is scarcely aware of changes of dimension; the phonetic gesturing satisfies our "thirst for concrete reality."[45]

To gain access to preverbal mental contents, style must descend to the sources of human language; it must recreate the history of the language. It is by means of style that language is constantly reborn and acquires a plasticity unknown to other systems of communication.

It is to verbal syle that we are indebted for poetry, an art which is distinguished from other verbal expression by its form rather than its substance. The poet could never dispense with style. What distinguishes poetic sincerity from the ordinary kind is that to be sincere in daily life, it is enough simply not to lie. The poet, on the other hand, must express, by the same language that everybody uses, something that he does not know, and that expression would be impossible if there did not exist the second language offered to him by verbal style.

Style seems to play a role no less important than that of dreams in the equilibrium of the human psyche.

# NOTES

1. Ivan Fónagy, "Hörbare Mimik," *Phonetica*, XVI (1967), 23-35; "La Mimétique buccale. Aspect radiologique de la vive voix," *Travaux de l'Institut de Linguistique et de Phonétique de l'Université de Paris*, I (1971), forthcoming.

2. W. Meyer-Eppler, *Informationstheorie* (Berlin-Heidelberg, New York, 1969), p. 3.

3. Ivan Fónagy, "L'Information du style verbale," *Linguistics*, IV (1964), 19-47.

4. The notion of articulation as gesture was already postulated in the "physei" or "naturalist" theory of verbal signs. The first reference may be found in Plato's *Cratylus*. The principle of imitative harmony (sound-painting in poetry) presupposes a gestural character of phonation, but does not depend directly on the "physei" theory. Denys of Halicarnassus (eighth century A.D.), an advocate of the theory of sound-imitation, accepted implicitly, for example, the principle of the arbitrary character of signs. He felt, however, that the poet establishes—by his choice and grouping of words—a natural harmony between the sense of verse and its sound-expression. The supreme task of the poet would be—according to Mallarmé ("Crise des vers," *Oeuvres complètes*, Paris, 1945, p. 364)—to re-establish the supposed harmony of the "ancestral language." Poets and aestheticians speak, above all, of the relations between sound and meaning. André Spire broke with this tradition when he made tactile and kinetic sensations the primary ones (*Plaisir poétique et plaisir musculaire*, Paris, 1949). There are relatively few phoneticians or linguists who have ventured into this (ill-reputed) domain. For important efforts, instrumental research, statistical analyses, critical studies, we are indebted to the following: Otto Jespersen, *Language* (London, 1922), Edward Sapir, "A Study of Phonetic Symbolism," *Journal of Experimental Psychology*, XII (1929), 225-39, R. Paget, *Human Speech* (New York, 1930), T. H. Pear, *Voice and Personality* (London, 1931), Maurice Grammont, *Traité de phonétique* (Paris, 1939), pp. 377-424, *Le vers français* (Paris, 1947), *Essai de psychologie linguistique: Style et poésie* (Paris, 1950), Pierre Guiraud, *Langage et versification d'après l'oeuvre de Paul Valéry* (Paris, 1953), M. Chastaing, "Le Symbolisme des voyelles," *Journal de Psychologie normale et pathologique*, LV (1958). Cf also Ivan Fónagy, "Über die Eigenart des sprachlichen Zeichens," *Lingua*, VI (1956), 67-88, and Ivan Fónagy, "Der Ausdruck als Inhalt," *Mathematik und Dichtung* (Stuttgart, 1965), 243-74.

5. Ivan Fónagy, "Mimetik auf glottaler Ebene," *Phonetica*, VIII (1962), 309-20.

6. Charles Darwin, *The Expression of Emotions in Man and Animals* (London, 1872); G. W. Crile, *The Origin and Nature of the Emotions* (Philadelphia and London, 1915).

7. Ed. Weiss, "Psychoanalyse eines Falles von nervösem Asthma," in *Internationale Zeitschrift für Psychoanalyse*, VIII (1922).

8. Ivan Fónagy, *Die Metaphern in der Phonetik* (The Hague, 1963), pp. 24ff.

9. *Josef in Ägypten* (Vienna, 1956), p. 425.

10. *Deux dialogues* (Paris, 1885), II, 252.

11. Sandor Ferenczi, *Bausteine zur Psychoanalyse* (Leipzig-Vienna-Zurich, 1927-39), I. 15, 62, 104.

12. T. H. Pear, *Voice and Personality* (London, 1931).

13. In "Das psychische Geschehen und die Artikulation," *Archives néerland-aises de phonétique expérimentale*, XIII.

14. W. Havers, *Neuere Literatur zum Sprachtaber* (Vienna, 1946), pp. 6off.

15. Ivan Fónagy, *The Phonetics of Poetic Language* (in Hungarian with a summary in German, Budapest, 1959), and "Communication in Poetry," *Word*, XVII (1961), 194-218.

16. F. Trojan, *Der Ausdruck der Sprechstimme* (Vienna-Düsseldorf, 1952).

17. Fónagy, *Die Metaphern* . . . , op. cit.

18. Ivan Fónagy, *Variation und Lautwandel: Phonologentagung* (Vienna, 1967), pp. 59-60. E. Stankiewicz, "Problems of Emotive Language," *Approaches to Semiotics* (The Hague, 1964), 239-64, has tried in a very well-documented study to systematize the expressive variants. These variants belong to *langue*. The rules which govern expressive deformation are probably universal.

19. Stephen Ullmann, *Semantics* (Oxford, 1967), pp. 82ff.

20. Ivan Fónagy, "Über die Eigenart . . ." *op. cit.*

21. Ivan Fónagy and K. Magdics, "Emotional Patterns in Speech and Music," *Zeitschrift für Phonetik*, XVI (1963), 293-326.

22. P. J. Moses, *The Voice of Neurosis* (New York, 1954).

23. G. Granger, *Essai d'une philosophie du style* (Paris, 1968).

24. "L'information du style verbal," *op. cit.*, and "Der Ausdruck als Inhalt," in *Mathematik und Dichtung* (Stuttgart, 1965), 243-74.

25. [At this point a tape recording was played at the conference.]

26. "Les Bases pulsionnelles de la phonation," *Revue française de psychanalyse*, XXXIV (1970), 101-36.

27. S. M. Stinchfield, *Speech Disorders* (London, 1933), p. 306.

28. Sigmund Freud, *Gesammelte Werke* (London, 1940-1951), XIII, 17.

29. *Characteranalyse* (Vienna, 1933), p. 169.

30. *Traité de stylistique française* (Heidelberg-Paris, 1921), I, 140-202 and I, 203-49.

31. "Beitrag zum autistischen Denken bei Kindern," *Internationale Zeitschrift für Psychoanalyse*, VI (1920).

32. Freud, *op. cit.*, XI, pp. 370ff.

33. "You have observed with great accuracy how he clears his throat and spits."

34. Edward Sievers, *Rhythmischmelodiesche Studien* (Heidelberg, 1912) succeeded on several occasions in attributing a text or certain parts of one to a given author on the basis of prosodic patterns. According to Sievers the Middle High German poets scarcely ever altered their melodic patterns. A strophe added later to a poem by Spervogel the Elder contrasts with the authentic part, for example, by its relatively higher voice.

35. Roland Barthes, *Le Degré zero de l'écriture* (Paris, 1954).

36. R. Reichenstein, "Etude des variations sociales et géographiques des faits linguistiques," *Word*, XVI (1960), 55-59; W. Labov, "The Social Motivation of a Sound Change," *Word*, XIX (1963), 273-309 and *The Social Stratification of English in New York City* (Washington, D.C., 1966); Fónagy, *Variation* . . . *op. cit.*

37. Cf. K. Knauer, "Die Analyse von Feinstrukturen," *Mathematik und Dichtung* (Munich, 1965), pp. 193-210.

38. Cf. Fónagy, "Der Ausdruck . . ." *op. cit.*

39. Freud, *Gesammelte Werke* XIII, pp. 68ff.

40. Fónagy, "Communication . . ." *op. cit.*

41. [A recorded tape.]

42. Fónagy, "L'Information . . ." *op. cit.* The term moneme—"minimal significant unit, the set including *lexemes* and *morphemes*"—is taken from André Martinet, *Éléments de linguistique générale* (Paris, 1967), pp. 15ff.

43. Freud, *op. cit.*, XIII. pp. 3-69.

44. *Ibid.*, X. pp. 299ff.

45. Karl Bühler, "L'Onomatopée et la fonction du langage," *Journale de Psychologie*, XXX (1933), 101-19.

## DISCUSSION OF FÓNAGY'S PAPER

Fónagy was questioned about his suggestion that the expressive code of phonetic gestures had something absolute and universal about it. Surely the gestures which accompany speech are relative to a system. In a Japanese film, for example, though we Westerners may assume from their gestures that a woman and a man are fighting, the subtitles may indicate that they are making love. So it is impossible to ascribe values to body movements without reference to the system to which they belong. Similarly, how can one speak of the expressive value of a glottal stop in a given language when it is a phoneme? Would Fónagy say that such a language is more aggressive than one which does not contain the glottal stop as phoneme? This would seem to lead to a kind of linguistic racism. Should one go back to archaic philosophy of language and believe (as is stated in certain medieval manuscripts) that the letters "r" and "k" are bad? The participant also found himself far from accepting the psychoanalytic analyses of Fónagy. Could one really say that the French lost their virility when they lost their apical /r/? Or that when fear strangles the vocal sphincter it opens the anal sphincter by way of compensation? Surely the effects of emotions are not organ-specific, but rather entail general intensity, that is, the closed phonemes become more closed, the open more open, and so on. Fónagy said that he had not intended to suggest that the output of expressive distortion was the same in different languages. He meant rather that the transformational *processes* were. For example, happy surprise is reflected in French and in Hungarian by different intonation curves: a final rise in French as opposed to a final fall in Hungarian. But Hungarian subjects, pronouncing and listening to a given sentence, will have the impression of hearing an ascending melody. It *is* ascending in comparison with the intonation of the emotionally unmarked sentence. By following, through each centi-second, the deviation between the two, we obtain a differential curve. It is this differential which is marked by a final rise and thus resembles the differential curve of analogous French sentences. The outputs are different since the inputs of neutral sentences, Hungarian and French, are different; but the transformation-function in both cases is essentially the same. What is important to consider is not the absolute but the relative contour. In the interpretation of phonetic gestures, too, the principle of relativity must always be respected. The guttural /r/ was particularly frequent in the aristocratic milieu of the old Austro-Hungarian monarchy, and the regular army officers were recruited above all from among the nobility. That is why the guttural /r/ acquired so "noble" and favorable a coloring. The value of a variant depends in part on the phonetic gesture and in part on its distribution in the social network. As for psychoanalysis, Fónagy sustained his thesis that phonetic regression in children's speech, for example the loss of the apical /r/, implies, as a general rule, the negative effects of the oedipus complex. However, he would agree that one can never pass from the level of the individual to that of the group without absurd results. At the social level, there are other laws which control behavior and which must be correlated with those operating at the individual level. But as far as individual psychology is concerned, Fónagy accepted the insights of psychoanalysis quite literally and without the slightest grain of salt.

Another participant expressed interest in the notion of the interpretation of oral delivery in which the listener formed hypotheses about what was deviant, and hence individual, on the basis of certain traditional norms of emphasis. He cited some studies of Irving Goffman on the use of body language to support what cannot be wholly expressed by the linguistic system, and wondered, too, whether this might not serve as a model for the interpretation of written style. In the latter, an hypothesis is also made about the forms of emphasis one can expect in this or that genre or type of communication. Those features that go counter to the expectation are then interpreted as individual deviations. We may try to integrate these into our conception of the speaker's personality structure, and yet we are generally dissatisfied with that kind of explanation. If the instances of deviation are too thickly strewn in his speech or written style, we may conclude that he is a very strange person, or even insane, even though we understand every item in the linguistic stream. These individual deviations, of course, also play a part in general linguistic change through history. In connection with the attribution of "irony" by subjects to one of Fonagy's tape-recorded sentences, the participant asked whether the word "irony" came freely to them or whether it was presented as one of a series of epithets that might be applied. If the latter were the case, it seems that there would be an element of predetermination. Fónagy replied that the voice that was played was not human but synthesized, although, of course, the synthesis was based on natural human voices, recorded in conversation or theatrical performance. The aim of the experiment was to determine which were the prosodic factors that lent an ironic (or whatever) emotive value to the sentence. The sentence which he had just played during the presentation of his paper had received the highest vote for irony. As for the rest of the question, Fónagy said that it was obvious that changes of accent and other distortions of the message cannot pass a certain limit without making the message simply incomprehensible. Further, it was not merely a question of the quantity of distortion, but above all of its quality. The amount of distortion is very high in the poems of Mallarmé, for example, yet a reconstruction of the primary message is nevertheless possible.

Another participant observed that there was implicit in such discussion the classical principles of protasis and apodosis. Without restricting the definition to sentences containing a subordinate clause, these two terms were applicable to both melody and syntax. They suggest a return to an equilibrium, like a kind of question that contains its own answer. The melody, for example, contains a rise and then a descent—it does not require any response by the listener. Therefore it is situated at a literary level; it is a kind of babbling with no implications of social interchange. The phenomenon can be found in the pronunciation of the Suisses Romanes, for example: one hears housewives saying "J'ai fait ma confiture; j'ai fait ma confiture" ("I made my jam; I made my jam"), the first with a rising pitch and the second with a descending. Thus, there is a return to the equilibrium which takes place without the intervention of an interlocutor. Similarly, it was in the vocalism of the natural cry that Rousseau found the origin of language. Thus he proposed an evolutionary theory in which the spoken word was the heir of the expressive gesture. Thus, to him, the musical voice was a privileged form of expression, since it had closer ties with the primitive state. Consonantism, or what Rousseau called "articulation," developed in the language of action.

# THE CONVENTIONS OF POETRY

### SAMUEL R. LEVIN

A POEM is an aesthetic object composed of language. This is to say implicitly that it is also a cognitive object, since the primary function of language is to communicate information. A poem thus comprises at least the cognitive and the aesthetic dimensions of language. And in this context the conventions are unique. For unlike the other language features of poetry, which function either cognitively or in some combination of the cognitive and aesthetic dimensions, it can be shown for the conventions—rhyme, meter, etc.—that the function they perform is a purely aesthetic one.[1] The fact that the conventions function in this way poses a problem—especially for those who approach the study of poetry from the side of linguistics. For if we assume that linguistics is concerned to analyze the cognitive dimension of language or, more precisely in the present context, that it is not designed to explicate its aesthetic function, then the essential fact about the conventions is that, even though they comprise patterns or structures of language elements, the patterns or structures so constituted have no *linguistic* significance. Another way to put this is to say that a structure has linguistic significance if it figures in a grammatical or phonological rule, and that the structures entered into by the conventional features figure in no such rule.[2] The conventions therefore have to be singled out and isolated from the general linguistic analysis. They must be approached from the traditional point of view which sees them primarily as artistic, not as linguistic devices. Proceeding otherwise will result in a leveling of "poetic" features and ordinary linguistic structures, in which case the specifically poetic nature of these features will escape analysis. For it is a corollary of the conventional status of a feature that linguistic analysis will fail to explain its poetic significance.

Conventional features may be defined as those which an author puts himself under an obligation to observe (or at least to consider) by the mere act of engaging to write a poem. These features do not remain constant through time, nor are they identical in all the poems of a given period. Despite the fact that they change and vary, however, they are, in some form or another, always present. And in whatever form they exist they provide the first, outer definition of poetry. When one is uncertain whether a given work is or is not poetry, it is usually because it is not clear that the work in question observes the conventions of poetry. The descriptions "poetic prose" and "prosaic poetry" are usually accorded to works that incorporate, respectively, more or less of the conventional features than is typical of what is taken as the putative genre.

Among the conventional features of English poetry are meter, rhyme, alliteration, enjambement, and caesura. That features like meter and rhyme perform a special function in poetry has long been recognized; the very designation "convention" bears witness to this fact. The significance of the function performed by the conventions has been variously assessed. In some treatments of the problem, the function is said to be one of decoration or embellishment. Others point to the organizing, unifying function of the conventions. Still others discuss the interaction of the conventions with linguistic characteristics of the poem and claim that this interaction imparts a certain complexity to the whole. If we conceive of a poem as an aesthetic object composed of language, then these various assessments have important ramifications. On the view of the conventions as decoration, their having any cognitive meaning is largely precluded, but they can be held to induce an aesthetic response, one that is rather superficial, however, induced as it is by a mere overlay or addition of features. If we look to the organizing, unifying function of the conventions, this function cannot be said to have any cognitive import, but the aesthetic effect produced by the conventions on this approach is a deeper and more integral one. Finally, if we consider the interaction of the conventional features with other linguistic characteristics of the poem, the resulting complexity partakes of the cognitive dimension, and it is also possible to speak of an aesthetic effect of a larger, more global order. Most recent treatments of the subject have taken the latter approach, justifying it on the basis of the proportionately greater richness a poem displays when it is analyzed in this way.[3] While I agree that ultimately criticism should strive to integrate ever more closely the various factors that interact in a poem, I believe that there are good reasons for analyzing the conventions at the outset in isolation from other parts of the poem. There is, first of all, the linguistic argument which I have already mentioned.[4] But beyond that, it seems to me that in the commitment to analyze a poem globally some important functions of the conventions can easily be slighted. There are important aesthetic functions, which the conventions perform independently of the cognitive meanings expressed by the linguistic elements with which they co-occur. I will thus examine the subject in terms of the second of the three approaches described above: I will consider the conventions in their function of organizing and unifying the poetry in which they occur. I claim of course that this function is responsible for part of the aesthetic effect induced by poetry. When the conventions are adequately evaluated in this function, it will be possible to discuss, as part of a larger synthesis, their interaction with the cognitive dimension of poetry.

METER

Meter is an abstract schema of periodicity.[5] In whatever form it appears— as syllabic, quantitative, accentual, or accentual-syllabic—it is not a linguistic phenomenon. Which is not to say that the attempt may not be made to describe it linguistically. If it is so described, however, it ceases to be meter. In the simplest case, that of pure syllabic meter, a linguistic analysis could provide a count and description of the syllables in any specimen of poetry. But since any stretch of language will consist of syllables, no poetic significance would attach to that description. For syllabism to count as meter some regularly recurring number of syllables must be signalled. This regularity can be indicated on the printed page by the line, in an oral reading by a pause corresponding to the end of the line or by a special accent or intonation on the last syllable of the line. Only in some such way can the periodicity that marks pure syllabic meter be ascertained. But none of the features mentioned above has any significance in a linguistic description: the line is a purely typographic device of poetry; similarly, the vocal features mentioned above are all non-significant from the linguistic point of view. Thus, the pauses have no necessary linguistic significance since syntactic boundaries of various kinds, ranging all the way from syntactically trivial morpheme boundaries to sentence-endings, occur at line-end. In the same way, the factitious accents and intonations may remain constant in the face of widely varying rhythmic requirements at the end of the line. The most important fact, however, is that the unit marked off by these means, say, a decasyllable, is for linguistic purposes, an irrelevant unit. The inference to be drawn from all this is that pure syllabic meter is a poetic convention.

With quantitative meter the situation is somewhat different. Unlike pure syllabic meter, where there is no line-internal opposition between elements to make up a metrical unit, the metrical unit being really the line (or, with caesura, the half-line), quantitative meter introduces such an internal opposition, the elements consisting of long and short syllables. Thus, in addition to the line, it is customary in quantitative meter to speak also of the

foot as a metrical unit. Where in syllabic meter the abstract schema is defined on the line (say, one consisting of ten syllables), and where it is thus
the line-ends (defined in some manner) that make it possible to speak of
a periodicity at all, in quantitative meter there is in addition to length of
the line also a regular alternation of long and short syllables within it. Now
length of syllables is, of course, a linguistic phenomenon and so can be described linguistically. The regular alternation of long and short syllables,
however, is not a structure of linguistic significance. The import of this
regularity can be explained only against the background of poetry as a literary genre. Against this background it has a significance. Which is to say
that quantitative meter is a convention.

Accentual (strong stress) meter substitutes stress for length as the dynamic of the metrical opposition. The metrical unit consists of an unspecified number of unaccented syllables grouped around a syllable bearing the
stress. The number of unaccented syllables in any given line may vary, but
the number of stressed syllables is fixed—frequently, as in Old English poetry, at four (or five, with secondary stresses). The statement just made is
a fair description of accentual verse as it is presented on the printed page.
But any language in which stress plays a distinctive linguistic role will *normally* dispose its unaccented and stressed syllables in just this way. So a description of these elements cannot by itself define the meter. In Old English (and Germanic) accentual verse, alliteration obviously plays an important role in this connection. The larger metrical span in Old English is
no doubt signalled by the second stress in the second half-line, the first
stress being indicated by its occurrence on the alliterating syllable. The individual metrical units perhaps asserted themselves as such in virtue of a
hearer's knowledge of the stress sequences permitted in poetry—something
on the order of Sievers' inventory of Types. Naturally, certain details are
needed to fill out this account. The important fact, however, is that the
type of regularity evinced by accentual meter is not a feature of linguistic
significance. The same argument holds for accentual-syllabic (syllabotonic)
meter where, in addition to the fixed number of stresses, there is the added
regularity of fixed syllable-spans within the feet.

When poetry is read aloud, another set of dynamic features co-occurs
with the convention of meter, namely the suprasegmental features of
stress,[6] pitch, intonation contours, and junctures. The actual relationship
between these two sets of features is a complicated problem which raises
many questions. The subject has been treated extensively in many standard
discussions of meter, and I will not go into it here in any detail. What is
clear is that in a performance the abstract schema is somehow inherent in
sentences (or lines) which display the full range of suprasegmental features
found in the ordinary language. Meter in poetry is realized in language

which carries its own freight of dynamics. What emerges in a performance is thus sometimes referred to as the rhythm of the poem, as opposed to its meter. But the relation between the two, meter and rhythm, is not to be conceived as that of token to type.[7] The rhythm is more than simply a realization of the meter; it is an amalgam of the meter and the particular suprasegmental features required by the sentences of the poem. Now, since the suprasegmental features have as a primary function the delimitation of syntactic units, it is possible to give a linguistic description of the poem's dynamics at this level. This is not, however, at the level of meter—that would be an abstraction—but at that of the stresses and intonations which the language of the poem exacts just because it is language. Of course, in a sensitive reading of a poem the stresses and intonations will be modified as they are submitted to the demands that the meter makes, so that even the application of linguistic methods to this level is not straightforward. But be that as it may, the fact that meter is a convention is not affected.

### THE LINE

In order to discuss the significance of caesura and enjambement, it is first necessary to say a few words about the line as an element of poetry. Obviously, the line has typographical identity. To this typographical identity there may correspond a factitious pause.[8] Which determines which is a question of the perspective between visual and oral readings of poetry. Except possibly in free verse, however, the typographical groupings (and the concomitant pauses) are not random; some organizing principle must thus be at work behind them. This is the principle of meter.[9] At times the meter is such that its line-defining function is self-evident. In the Greek hexameter, for example, the sixth foot, and only the sixth foot, consists of a trochee. The fact that this last foot is scanned long (*syllaba anceps*), so that the foot counts as a spondee, does not compromise the demarcative function since phonetically the foot comprises a long and a short syllable and is registered as such. When this phonetic fact is seen in its larger framework, as regularly recurring, we see that the line is defined metrically. An even clearer case may be seen in the Greek Choliambic (the so-called "lame" trimeter), in which five iambs are regularly followed by a spondee, the end of the line thus being signalled by a succession of three long syllables.[10]

In cases like those described above, the meter defines the line both for the poet and the hearer. In other types of verse, however, the meter may define the line for the poet but some other feature must perform that function for the hearer (we disregard the typography at this point). In fact, most meters are not in themselves transparent over the larger span; they provide no recurrent distinctive metrical configuration to mark off the end of the line. In such meters the feature that functions to signal the end of the line is usually some sort of sound-euphony—rhyme or assonance.[11] Thus in the Old French *chanson de geste* the decasyllabic line is defined by assonance or in some cases by full rhyme. Throughout an entire *laisse* the end of the line is signalled by the same assonance or rhyme. In the heroic couplet and *terza rima* rhyme performs a similar function, although less directly, since the rhymes define the patterns they form only retrospectively. In some meters, finally—and blank verse is a weighty example—none of these factors operate to define the line for the hearer. Moreover, syntax cannot be invoked for this purpose, because of caesura and enjambement. No doubt, statistical preponderances and an awareness of the tradition contribute to a sense of line-identity, but in general the line in blank verse would seem to be ill-defined for the hearer.[12] Although the preceding account is oversimplified in many respects, the fact that emerges seems to be clear: When the line is defined for the hearer it is defined by conventional features of poetry and is thus itself a convention; it has no linguistic relevance. Moreover, once constituted, the line enjoys an autonomous status in poetry. It consists of a unit of length, with a beginning and an end. As such a unit, and in coordination with the various other elements of poetry, it raises the expectation of progress through its length and arrest or pause at its end. It is this expectation that is played against by what is ordinarily called caesura and enjambement.

### ENJAMBEMENT

That enjambement is a poetic convention would seem to follow from the fact that it would make no sense to speak of enjambement in prose. From this it would also appear that enjambement is not a linguistically significant phenomenon. But although it is clear that enjambement is a poetic convention, the customary definitions of it tend to obscure that fact. Enjambement is usually defined as a syntactic running-over of the line.[13] Sometimes a phrase is added to the effect that the running-over takes place without a pause at line-end.[14] Now it seems to me that however we choose to define enjambement, the important event taking place at the end of the line is not the syntactic running-over, but a pause—even though this pause need not be expressed acoustically (see, however footnote 8). Since the running-over is enjoined by the syntax, to describe enjambement as this running-over is simply to make a rather commonplace observation. Unless the end of the line had a function beyond that of typographic terminus, it would hardly be worth our while to characterize enjambement. This is thus to say that the standard definitions of enjambement describe a rather trivial property. But in those cases where we speak of enjambement something quite untrivial is going on. It is common in this connection to speak of a tension or interplay between two opposing forces.[15] And this interplay is, of course, between the onward movement demanded by the syntax and the sense of completion signalled by the line-end; the opposition, in other words, between a linguistic and a conventional fact. Since the syntactic process is self-evident, whereas the mark of completion—a conceptual or acoustic pause—is not, I would think that the latter is the significant fact to be described. To express this somewhat differently, what is important is not so much what the syntax is doing at the end of the line—this is surely obvious—but what the line-end is doing in the middle of the syntax. The difficulty with the term "enjambement" stems from the fact that, although it is generally understood as pertaining to a metrical or rhythmic phenomenon, it is defined in essentially linguistic terms. To overcome this difficulty, it seems to me that "enjambement" should either be used to describe the metrical pause, or it should be retained as a description of the syntactic overflowing, but a new term, say "counter-enjambement," be introduced to describe the pause. This discussion of definitions is prompted, of course, by a desire to range enjambement along with the other conventions. If we understand by enjambement the pause occasioned by the line-end, then, since that pause has no linguistic justification or status, enjambement is clearly a convention.

Furthermore, this view of enjambement explains certain facts in respect to which the ordinary view is quite inconsistent. Consider the following: The linguistic unit enjambed may range from a word to a sentence. Thus, the enjambed unit may consist of (a) two morphemes (of a word), (b) two words (of a phrase), (c) two phrases (of a clause), (d) two clauses (of a sentence).[16] All of these units are regulated by purely linguistic conditions as to their flow, in such a manner that junctural features increase in force from (a) to (d), as, for example, in the following:

(a)           Rags and prayers down the knee-
        Deep hillocks and loud on the numbed lakes,
                    (Thomas, "A Winter's Tale")
(b)     But I was well
        Upon my way to sleep before it fell
                    (Frost, "After Apple-Picking")
(c)     The whiskey on your breath
        Could make a small boy dizzy;
                    (Roethke, "My Papa's Waltz")
(d)     So when small humours gather to a gout,
        The doctor fancies he has driv'n them out.
                    (Pope, "Essay on Man")

Now it is a curious fact that, as has been remarked by Fowler, the smaller the grammatical unit involved, the greater seems to be its resistance to being enjambed.[17] This fact is curious because, from the linguistic point of view, we should expect just the reverse—we should expect the elements of (a), where there is a strong grammatical bonding and a weak juncture or none at all, to flow into each other much more readily than the elements of (d), where the grammatical bonding is weaker and there is strong juncture. If, however, we look at enjambement in terms of the conceptual or actual metrical pause at the end of the line, the results described above are the expected ones; such a pause between the elements of a word is unnatural and harsh. Then, as the enjambed unit increases in grammatical size, the opposition between the pause and the linguistic properties of bonding and juncture is successively down-graded, until when we come to clauses it is completely neutralized by the syntactic juncture and loses most of its effect. The staple types of enjambement in English poetry are therefore (b) and (c), where the tension set up is neither too turbid nor too flaccid.

## CAESURA

In English prosody the caesura is usually defined as a syntactic break occurring inside (usually near the middle of) the line. Cf. the following definition: "A rhetorical and extrametrical pause or phrasal break within the poetic line."[18] As was argued for enjambement, definitions of this kind point to an obvious fact—they do not explain, for example, why such a break occurring in the middle of the line should produce an effect any different from one occurring at the end of it. Looked at in this way caesura would be a convention only in virtue of its occurring within the poetic line. Given the line as an autonomous unit, however, then, just as its end occasions a pause, so its length exacts a forward movement. The line exerts a pressure for completion, upon which the syntactic break obtrudes. In rhyming verse the impulse to move forward is augmented by the anticipation of hearing the rhyme at the end of the line. In unrhymed verse it is the line itself that imposes the demand for continuation.[19]

Caesura, looked at in this way, is thus not the syntactic pause—it is rather the progress of the meter through the line. It is only on this conception of caesura that certain metrical facts can be explained. The pause breaks into and interrupts the syntactic flow of the line. If we use the notion of caesura to characterize the break, we are left with nothing to explain how it is that the meter itself is not interrupted but continues to progress across and through the break. In fact, regarding caesura as a syntactic break throws into jeopardy one of meter's most important aspects, namely, the tension developed between the abstract metrical scheme and the natural language dynamics. In lines that are metrically regular across the syntactic division, it makes little difference what we take the nature of caesura to be. But consider the following lines (from Yeats' "Hound Voice"):

> Our voices carry; and though slumber-bound . . . (l. 5)
>
> And yet gave tongue. "Hound Voices" were they all (l. 9).

These lines are iambic pentameter, as is the poem from which they come. In order for the metrical promotion of *and* to be effected in (1), it is necessary for the meter to be projected across the syntactic pause. The same projection of the meter is necessary in order that *Hound* in (2) be metrically demoted. Without this projection *and* and *Hound* would simply take their natural linguistic stresses and there would be nothing to explain the sense of rhythmic interaction that occurs at those points in the line. Thus, if caesura is regarded as the syntactic pause or break, nothing is left to explain the required sense of metrical impulsion across that break. If, on the other hand, we regard caesura as the metrical progress through the line, then it becomes understandable why a syllable occurring after a syntactic pause should be metrically affected.

As with enjambement earlier, caesura is thus regarded as a metrical and not a linguistic fact. Since the language of the poem is given independently —since the syntax asserts itself in any case—caesura and enjambement as here defined become available as terms to oppose to the action of the syntax in the line, and in this way account for a certain type of metrical tension. As the metrical tension usually spoken of involves the interaction of a conventional and a linguistic feature, namely, between the abstract metrical pattern and the natural language stresses, so the tension here described similarly involves such an interaction—between the conventions of enjambement and caesura and the natural language syntax.

## RHYME

*Prima facie,* rhyme is an acoustic fact. From the linguistic point of view it is a trivial phonetic fact. In a pair like *roam/foam,* the rhyme is made by repetition of the phonetic element *-oam* and has no grammatical or semantic value. (Rhymes like *make/take,* in which the rhyming element happens to coincide phonetically with a morpheme have no bearing on the question, since "ache" is obviously not involved in the analysis of either the rhyme or the morphemes "make" and "take.") Rhyme so analyzed fits the definition of a convention (at least, the linguistic side of it) as advanced in this paper. Now to claim that rhyme is a convention without linguistic significance is to place oneself in apparent conflict with the view that rhyme is not solely an acoustic phenomenon but possesses also a grammatical and semantic value, and that this union makes it an aesthetic device. According to Lanz, this view was first advanced by J. S. Schütze in his *Versuch einer Theorie des Reimes nach Inhalt und Form* (1802).[20] For Schütze mere repetition of sound does not induce an aesthetic response; such a response is induced only when the meanings of the rhyming words are taken into account—aesthetic satisfaction results from the expression of two or more ideas by the same sound.[21] Leaving aside for the moment the aesthetic question, we can find Schütze's argument regarding the union of sound and meaning in rhyme repeated in modern discussions; thus, Wimsatt, in his treatment of the question, has shown how Pope gains effects of variety within the essential parallelism of the heroic couplet by rhyming different parts of speech or the same part of speech in different functions.[22] And Jakobson has advanced the view that "Rhyme necessarily involves the semantic relationship between rhyming units."[23] In examining the apparent conflict of views emerging from this discussion, we should notice first of all that it is not the rhyming sounds—i.e. the rhyme *per se*—which it is claimed enter into a union with meanings; it is the rhyming *words* that do so. Only in the case of homonyms (grammatical or semantic) would this union really hold. Thus, what must actually be claimed is that the acoustic fact of rhyme stimulates a heightened awareness of the words in which the rhyme occurs. This, in fact, is what Jakobson says.[24] We thus perceive that the notion of rhyme as an acoustic fact and the views of Wimsatt and Jakobson need not conflict. In a complete analysis of a poem one would no doubt wish to describe the effects that are achieved by the deployment of rhyme. As Wimsatt and Jakobson have shown, a great many enriching effects can be produced by rhyming together words that have different grammatical or semantic properties; in fact, the sameness that would follow from failure to exploit such differences would result in banality along one dimension of the poem. I think it perfectly legitimate, however, for purposes of a particular thesis, to argue that *in the first analysis* rhyme carries no cognitive meaning. This view does not rule out the possibility that rhyme may have a significance beyond that of a mere chiming of sounds. In particular, it does not rule out the claim, frequently made for rhyme, that it recurrently satisfies expectation, thus serving to unify the poem. But of this latter function of rhyme it would be improper to say that it has a meaning. What one would be entitled to say, I think, is that it has a value, and I would say that this value is an aesthetic one.

The claim that the effectiveness of rhyme depends on its union with meaning would, moreover, appear to make rhyme exceptional among the conventions. The same claim is not usually made for alliteration or assonance, for example. And yet, between alliteration or assonance and rhyme there is a difference only of degree. In going beyond the purely acoustic significance of alliteration and assonance, it is not necessary to move to the level of cognitive meaning; this fact is apparent from the various attempts to find phonaesthetic force in such repetitions. Similarly, in the case of meter one would surely not define it as *partaking* of meaning. This, of course, does not rule out the possibility that meter may interact in some way with the elements of a poem that carry cognitive meaning. In the same way, enjambement and caesura may be said to interact with syntactic transitions in a poem, but they themselves are not such transitions. To argue, thus, that rhyme is in itself non-cognitive but that it may interact with linguistic elements which are, is simply to place it on a par with the other conventions.

So far I have presented arguments to the effect that rhyme must be considered a non-cognitive phenomenon. It remains to show that on this interpretation it may still produce an aesthetic effect. Wimsatt has denied that rhyme, so understood, may in fact produce such an effect.[25] For him it is only the union of the "sensory" and the "logical" in rhyme (in our terms, the acoustic and the cognitive) that can produce the aesthetic effect. The problem here is a delicate and difficult one—the term "aesthetic effect" is by no means well defined; no doubt a considerable range of responses falls under its head. It seems reasonable, however, to separate out one level of the overall effect, one which we may call the *primary* aesthetic response.[26] This level of aesthetic response rules out by definition any cognitive stimulus. Such a response is an intuitive, precognitive matter, activated by sensory, rhythmical, and formal stimuli. Thus, acoustic chiming, regular recurrence and its consequent formal structuring are sufficient stimuli for this primary aesthetic response. Even the projection of paradigmatic series into the syntagm, the process described by Jakobson,[27] may be reckoned a formal feature of this type and thus be held to induce the aesthetic response. Of course, nothing in this account precludes the possibility that stimuli of this kind may interact with others, of a cognitive nature, to produce a response that one would also wish to call aesthetic. But that would be a response of a different order, and there is no need to adopt this larger approach.

Rhyme is, of course, just a special case of sound-repetition; alliteration and assonance are two other standard types. Because their size-level is smaller than that of rhyme, a longer distance (in some sense) would have to be gone in order to effect a union of alliteration, say, and meaning. But, in fact, this is usually not done. The attempt to find significance for alliteration beyond the acoustic and formal levels usually remains within the area of phonaesthesia.[28] Now, since alliteration and rhyme as acoustic and phonetic phenomena differ only quantitatively, the important fact being that they are both submorphemic, it is hard to see how one can justify claiming that one enters into meaning relations while the other enters only into phonaesthetic relations. To phrase the issue differently, why should rhyme be analyzed in connection with its immediate matrix but alliteration only as itself? There would seem to be something arbitrary in such a procedure. Naturally, none of the preceding discussion compromises the status of alliteration as a convention. Apart from its effects in the realm of phonaesthesia, alliteration functions acoustically, rhythmically, and formally, but without cognitive import. Even if some phonological significance could be claimed for *t-*, on the basis of relative frequency, say, or for *st-*, in terms of some rule of consonant clustering, no such significance attaches to the mere *repetition* of such sounds. Alliteration thus satisfies all the requirements of a convention.

### THE FUNCTION OF THE CONVENTIONS

The organizing and unifying function mentioned earlier as the contribution made by the conventions can be ascribed merely to the regularity of their recurrence—as, for example, in the case of meter, rhyme, or alliteration. Viewing it in this way, however, would be to see as a simple, one-dimensional process one that is really complex. If we consider the way in which the abstract metrical pattern interacts with the linguistic stresses, and the way in which enjambement and caesura interact with the syntactic movement, we see a much more profound and integrating kind of unification at work, one in which a poetic convention is opposed to and interacts with a linguistic fact. Now in this process the elements entering into the interaction are purely formal ones; they are dynamic features of two basic types, one being abstract, the other material. There is, moreover, no need to consider meaning in accounting for the tension described earlier (except in the ancillary sense in which the meanings of words may determine their stresses or the meaning of a passage determine its syntactic flow).

The poetic conventions mentioned above are completely abstract entities. Thus, meter as such is a pattern abstracted from the flow of the language in a poem. Enjambement and caesura as defined in this paper are, similarly, abstractions. It is because they are abstractions that it is possible to oppose them to actual linguistic elements in a poem and thus speak of an interaction or tension. Rhyme, however, is a different case since it is not an abstraction from linguistic material but itself consists of such material. The question is therefore raised: what, if anything, does rhyme interact with? Before attempting to answer this question we should notice that the conventions mentioned earlier all interact with formal, non-semantic linguistic elements: meter with linguistic stresses, enjambement and caesura with

junctural phenomena of various sorts. It would thus be temping to propose
for rhyme also an interaction with a purely formal linguistic feature. I
would suggest that rhyme interacts with the phonetic remainders or un-
rhyming parts of the rhyming words—thus in *roam/foam*, the rhyme interacts with the non-rhyming opposition between *r-* and *f-*.[29] The same argument can be given for alliteration and assonance. If this account is accepted,
there is a case made for an entire universe of interaction at the level
of sound alone—with no recourse to meaning. Needless to say, various semantic components of a poem can subsequently be combined with the results of this preliminary analysis and in this way a larger and richer synthesis is achieved.

Poetry differs from ordinary language in two essential respects; it permits greater liberties and it imposes additional constraints. The liberties
take the form of deviations from the grammar of the ordinary language and
primarily involve syntactic and semantic categories; the constraints consist
of the conventions. The syntactic and semantic liberties that characterize
poetry have received a good deal of attention, notably from the Formalists
of Russia and Prague, who pointed out that deviations of this sort de-
automatize the language and cause a focusing of attention on the deviant
sequences.[30] Jakobson's description of the poetic function of language as
involving a set toward the message as such is a generalization of this perspective.[31] In thus conditioning this set toward the message, it would appear that the conventions likewise play an important role. One way to explain the foregrounding effect produced by syntactic and semantic deviation
is to say that the implicit recourse to the grammar of the language that one
normally has for understanding a text does not, in the case of deviant sequences, immediately and automatically provide an interpretation; one is
thus thrown back on the text. In the case of the conventions, if what I have
said about their autonomy from the grammar is correct, a similar result is
produced for a different reason. By definition, most of the conventions entail a repetition or recurrence of identical units: for example, meter and
the various types of sound-euphony.[32] The conventions thus establish themselves in a text (poem) and require that text solely and entirely for their
"interpretation"; they exist only in the text.[33] To the foregrounding of a
poem, its detachment and establishment as a linguistic object unto itself,
the conventions thus make a major contribution.

The repetitions or recurrences mentioned above as characteristic of the
conventions all fall under the head of Jakobson's theorem stating that
"The poetic function projects the principle of equivalence from the axis of
selection into the axis of combination."[34] This projection can be of linguistic or conventional features. In the former case we get instances of syntactic
parallelism or the distribution through a poem of words related seman-

tically or morphologically. In the latter case we get devices like meter and rhyme. The former type of feature derives from the grammar of the language, the latter from outside, in some cases—as in that of meter and rhyme—from general phonetics, which lies outside the grammar of any particular language.[35]

Although grammatical deviation and the conventions both lead to a focussing or, better, a refocussing on the text, the respective refocussings have different consequences. The return to the text occasioned by grammatical deviation promotes a response of novelty, whereas the return to the text conditioned by the conventions promotes a response of unity. I take responses of this sort—along, perhaps, with others like compression, complexity, and simplicity—to make up the primordial level of the aesthetic effect. Although this response of unity can be augmented and enriched by a consideration of the cognitive elements expressed in the conventions, this augmentation is not necessary to establish their aesthetic force. In this connection we should notice that the claim that the conventions have no cognitive import is quite consistent with the claim made earlier that they derive from sources like general phonetics, which lie outside the grammar. If the view of the conventions taken here is correct, they are unique among the elements of poetry in that it is possible to argue that they function exclusively to produce an aesthetic effect.

## NOTES

1. Given the great complexity of language functions (cf., for example, the emotive, conative, affective, phatic functions), it is rare that one can say of any linguistic element or structure that its function is purely cognitive. This is particularly true of poetry. If the claims made above about the purely cognitive or purely aesthetic linguistic functions should require modification, however, this would not necessitate abandoning them—the conventional features would still stand apart; it would only be necessary to mark them as −cognitive, +aesthetic.

2. There is nothing paradoxical in the assertion that not all language patterns or structures have linguistic significance. Thus, the sequences made up of every eighth word or of all the initial consonant clusters in a text, while consisting of language elements, would have no linguistic significance. Such patternings differ from the conventions in that, although neither type has any cognitive value, only the latter has aesthetic force.

3. For representative statements of this kind see René Wellek and Austin Warren, *Theory of Literature* (New York, 1956), p. 158; W. K. Wimsatt, Jr., "One Relation of Rhyme to Reason," in *The Verbal Icon* (Lexington, Ky., 1954), pp. 165-66. The same position, with a linguistic orientation, is taken by Roman Jakobson, "Linguistics and Poetics," in *Style in Language*, ed. by Thomas A. Sebeok (New York, 1960), p. 350 and *passim*.

4. Jakobson would apparently not allow this reason. For him, "Poetics deals with problems of verbal structure, just as the analysis of painting is concerned

with pictorial structure. Since linguistics is the global science of verbal structure, poetics may be regarded as an integral part of linguistics" (*op. cit.*, p. 350). The point at issue is whether the conventions are in fact verbal structures. Since the expression "verbal structure" is equivocal, both positions can be sustained. But as I have stated above, it need not follow that all verbal structures are linguistically significant. Of course, they can be made significant by adding to the grammar or description of a language rules that cover just those structures. But the fact that elements of *language* go to make up such phenomena as meter or rhyme does not entail that the latter are necessarily *linguistic* structures. Actually, the difference between the two positions cannot, it seems to me, be decided on *a priori* grounds. It is necessary to see what the adoption of one or the other viewpoint leads to in the way of a satisfying account of poetry.

5. Almost any definition of meter expressed in a short sentence will be open to challenge, if not to contradiction. Although there might be no objection to the claim that it involves periodicity, the claim that meter is an abstract schema, though it would meet with approval in some quarters, would probably not go unchallenged in others. There is also the question of the nature of the abstraction. For Morris Halle and Samuel J. Keyser the schema comprises the pool of restricted linguistic possibilities (involving syllables and stress) selection from which results in metrical verses. By this view there is no sense in which any abstract pattern inheres in an actual line of verse—the abstract schema is inherent rather in the metrical theory. See "Chaucer and the Study of Prosody," *College English*, 28 (Dec. 1966), esp. p. 186. For a different view, see Seymour Chatman, *A Theory of Meter* (The Hague, 1965). According to Chatman (p. 103), "The meter of a poem is not some fixed and unequivocal characteristic, but rather a structure or matrix of possibilities which may emerge in different ways as different vocal renditions." Further on, he equates the abstract meter with the "derivation of common features." Thus, for Chatman, although meter is an abstraction, it is not an *a priori* abstraction but one arrived at *a posteriori*, by abstracting the common features from a group of actualizations, i.e. performances.

6. If one were being meticulous, the term "stress" would not be used for both the mark in meter and the suprasegmental feature of ordinary language. Some writers, e.g. Chatman, *op. cit.*, have used "ictus" for the former.

7. Only in perfectly regular verse, if such exists (doggerel perhaps), would this relation hold.

8. Cf. Maurice Grammont, *Le Vers français* (Paris, 1967), p. 35: "Tout vers, *sans aucune exception possible*, est suivi d'une pause plus ou moins longue."

9. To clear up what may appear to be a circularity in the argument—when we say, as earlier, that (in syllabic verse) the typographic line-end is the mark of recurrence and thus defines the meter, and here, that a meter defines the line, we are speaking from two different points of view. It is for the reader that the line defines the meter; the poet, however, must obviously *compose* the line. From his viewpoint, therefore, the meter defines the line. Another point to be mentioned is that in discussing meter we were concerned primarily with the metrical subunit (the foot, etc.), whereas here we are dealing with the larger metrical unit. The treatment of syllabic meter above dealt, to be sure, primarily with "pure" syllabic meter, the type, that is, in which no subunits (aside from possibly the hemistich) occur.

10. Since three long syllables are involved, one might wish to conclude that the line-end is signalled by linguistic means. But this would be a mistake; it is

not simply a question of three successive long syllables, since such may occur in prose or in other meters without signalling the end of the line. It is the recurrence of this succession—a recurrence which entitles us to speak of a spondee coming after five iambs—that performs the demarcative function, and this is a metrical not a linguistic fact.

11. One other possibility would be syntax. Syntax could be said to define the line for the hearer if a syntactic close, of sentence or clause dimensions, always occurred after a more or less constant number of syllables. This is the case in Serbian epic poetry, where there is a syntactic break after each ten syllables (see Roman Jakobson, "Linguistics and Poetics," in *Style in Language,* edited by Thomas A. Sebeok (New York, 1960), p. 364. In such a case, however, with line-end and syntactic break coinciding, the possibility of significant enjambement is nullified (cf. Kiril Taranovski, "The Prosodic Structure of Serbo-Croat Verse," *Oxford Slavonic Papers,* 9 (1960), p. 6. Naturally, the pauses and accentual indicators mentioned earlier are not relevant to the point in question here, since they require for their implementation some anterior signal that the line is at an end; it is the latter that we are concerned with here. Cf. the discussion of line-demarcation in Geoffrey N. Leech, *A Linguistic Guide to English Poetry* (London, 1969), pp. 114ff., where Leech cites the work of David Abercrombie, "A Phonetician's View of Verse Structure," in *Studies in Phonetics and Linguistics* (London, 1965), pp. 16-25; the latter proposes three devices that may be used in English poetry to mark the end of the line: "rhyme, or some other sound scheme; a silent final stress; a monosyllabic measure, not used anywhere else, coinciding with the last syllable of the line."

12. Cf. Jiří Levý, "A Contribution to the Typology of Accentual-Syllabic Versifications," *Poetics* (The Hague, 1961), p. 182, citing studies testifying to the difficulty of distinguishing between irregular blank verse and prose.

13. Cf. *Webster's New Collegiate Dictionary* (Springfield, Mass., 1956).

14. Cf. *Webster's New World Dictionary,* College Edition (Cleveland, Ohio, 1968); see also *Encyclopedia of Poetry and Poetics,* ed. by Alex Preminger (Princeton, N. J., 1965).

15. See John Hollander, "The Metrical Emblem," in *Essays on the Language of Literature,* ed. by Seymour Chatman and Samuel R. Levin (Boston, Mass., 1967), pp. 118-19; see also Roger Fowler, " 'Prose Rhythm' and Metre," in *Essays on Style and Language,* ed. by Roger Fowler (London, 1966), p. 87 and *passim.*

16. See Fowler, *op. cit.,* pp. 87ff. Actually, other types are possible: cf. Cummings' *win/k* (two phonemes of a word); *sud/denly* (two syllables of a word), but these and other possible types, including different kinds of phrase transition, do not alter the picture in any significant way.

17. Fowler, *op. cit.,* p. 88. Fowler, taking a different approach, offers an excellent discussion of enjambement and the question of tension in general.

18. *Encyclopedia of Poetry and Poetics.*

19. The case is clearer in classical metrics, where caesura requires that a word end within the metrical foot. Here, then, it is not only the pressure to end the line that impels a forward movement, but also the pressure to complete the foot.

20. Henry Lanz, *The Physical Basis of Rime* (Stanford, Cal., 1931), pp. 161ff.

21. *Idem.*

22. Wimsatt, *op. cit.,* pp. 157ff.

23. Jakobson, *op. cit.,* p. 367.

24. *Idem.*

25. Wimsatt, *op. cit.*, p. 165.

26. Cf. Roman Ingarden, "Aesthetic Experience and Aesthetic Object," in *Readings in Existential Phenomenology*, ed. by N. Lawrence and D. O'Connor (Englewood Cliffs, N.J., 1967), pp. 303-23, esp. pp. 309, 312, 315.

27. Jakobson, *op. cit.*, p. 358.

28. Cf. J. R. Firth, "Modes of Meaning," *Papers in Linguistics 1934-1951* (London, 1957), pp. 190-215; in the essay Firth uses "meaning" to cover a wide range of phenomena; he talks of the phonological mode of meaning, the prosodic mode, and so on. But the "meaning" of these modes, like that of the phonaesthetic, resides essentially in formal characteristics and esthetic effects.

29. This suggestion would help to explain why rhyming of homonymous words is generally avoided.

30. For Russian Formalism see V. Shklovskij, "L'art comme procédé," in *Théorie de la littérature* (Paris, 1965), a collection of Russian Formalist articles translated and edited by Tzvetan Todorov; for a Prague statement see J. Mukařovský, "Standard Language and Poetic Language," in *A Prague School Reader on Esthetics, Literary Structure, and Style* (Wash., D.C., 1964), a collection of essays translated and edited by Paul L. Garvin.

31. Jakobson, *op. cit.*, p. 356.

32. The line abstractly conceived as a unit does not of course entail repetition. But obviously the line as such is repeated in any poem. In this connection it is to be noted that (overlooking typography) caesura and enjambement as defined in this paper function precisely so as to preserve the integrity of the line and thus make it possible to speak of a repetition at all.

33. It is true that there is a tradition of the conventions, but features like rhyme, meter, etc., assert themselves quite independently of that tradition; it is sufficient for them to appear in a text for them to be registered as what they are.

34. Jakobson, *op. cit.*, p. 358.

35. For some discussion of this point see S. R. Levin, *Linguistic Structures in Poetry* (The Hague, 1962), pp. 28ff.

## DISCUSSION OF LEVIN'S PAPER

Almost the entire discussion concerned Levin's assertion that the conventions of poetry do not have linguistic significance. For example, Levin was asked if it would not be more correct to say that the conventions were not grammatical, since phonic or graphic material certainly is a part of language, and hence "linguistic" in some sense of the word. It was further noted that some linguists at least were working with written language, with handwriting, and so forth, and that a linguist should obviously be capable of saying where a line begins and ends. Levin replied that in saying that the verse line is not a linguistic unit, he did not feel committed to the proposition that linguists cannot deal with written texts. Further, he argued, not everything expressed by language has linguistic significance. All the conventions that he mentioned were composed of language, but it does not necessarily follow that everything analyzed out of this material is a linguistic unit or structure. The fact that we have recourse to phonetics in explaining certain language material does not make the units analyzed linguistically significant. We could recur to phonetics in discussing a nonsense string and give it a phonetic description, but that is all we could do with it from the linguistic point of view, since the stretch has no linguistic significance. Pure phonetic descriptions of that sort lie outside grammar. (Outside grammar, it was argued, yes, but not outside language.) Levin replied that it was outside language too. (But then one could say the same thing about grammar itself, because one can describe the grammar of a nonverbal language, for example, that of the bees. Levin's reason for ignoring phonetics could be extended to any other level, for example that of logic.)

In the same vein, it was noted that Levin used expressions like "linguistic element, phenomenon, fact, significance, relevance, structure" but that he failed to distinguish these from linguistic law and linguistic requirement. Many things appear in one's language—one can write a composition in short sentences only, or in long, or in abstract or concrete phraseology, and so on. None of these meet linguistic requirements, but all are linguistic phenomena or facts. Other phenomena also have linguistic significance, though such significance may be relatively easy to define (as in the case of phonaesthemes) or relatively hard (as in meter). Apropos of Levin's idea, for example, that the line is only typographical, not linguistic: take a page of prose, even rhythmical prose like that of Dickens, try to cut it up into iambic pentameters, and see what happens—lines end in the middle of words or on impossible weak syllables, and so on. The line has a syntactic structure as well as a standard syllable count. Similarly, one can always distinguish a genuine line of poetry from one of an equal number and disposition of syllables taken from a block of prose.

Levin defended his position by arguing that it was essential to recognize that the mere fact that something consists of phonic material does not entail the recognition that it is linguistically significant. There are a great many things that can be said about phonic material that are trivial from the linguistic point of view. As for the definition of the verse line, he recalled that he had not said that the line is defined *only* typographically; in many cases intonation is also implicit, for example, the occurrence of a pause at line-end. Or the line may be conceptually marked as well. But the pause is not necessarily significant from the linguistic point of view. For example, it may contradict what the syntax demands: the syntax may require no pause, so that the occurrence of a pause is grammatically irrelevant; it does not figure anywhere in a description of the language at large. Similarly, the metrical ictuses may mean something, but they cannot have linguistic relevance—linguistic stresses do, but not metrical ictuses. Neither caesura nor the sense of propulsion through the line is linguistically meaningful, even though these things express themselves *through* the language. They are not *of* the language, they are only transmitted through language. Jakobson may say that everything is in the linguist's domain if it is in language; but Levin would argue that that begs the question—meter, for example, is not, ultimately, a linguistic phenomenon.

It was noted that part of the disagreement may stem from an ambiguity implicit in the English word "linguistic," which is avoided in German by the use of two words—*sprachlich* and *linguistisch*, opposing that which belongs to language to that which belongs to linguistics. In this sense, Levin is arguing only that the conventions are not *linguistisch*, not that they are not *sprachlich*. Another participant wondered whether the following paraphrase might help: As far as linguistics is concerned, a poem is a set of sentences arranged for some reason in a rather odd way on the page. It also has certain acoustic effects, but these may safely be ignored. Levin agreed, providing one meant "ignored from the strict linguistic point of view," not from the critical and aesthetic point of view. He repeated his thesis that a poem derives its structures from two different systems—the linguistic system, and the system of poetic conventions. Of course the articulation of a rhyme—as, say /-om/ rather than /-im/—has linguistic significance in the sense that two different morphemes may be represented, but the *repetition* of the syllable as such has no linguistic significance. But, it was retorted, any marked repetition of a phoneme—a rhyme or echoing sound—has potential meaning or clash of meaning; consider, for example, the undesirable rhyme in non-poetic prose, discussed by Fowler's *Modern English Usage*: there the implicit meaning of similarity engendered by phonetic repetition clashes with the explicit meanings of words which are unrelated. Levin cannot say that such things have *no* linguistic relevance; there is a potential linguistic quality there that the poem often brings out.

Another way out of the impasse was suggested; namely, to say that conventions, though not linguistically relevant, are stylistically so; it is at the stylistic level that there exist direct relations between the conventions and the language. The poet always has the choice of whether or not to link the two together, to have a semantic similarity reflected by a phonetic similarity or the like.

Another participant introduced a historical consideration: the connection between syntax, verse structure, place of rhyme and so on in the *chanson de geste* was more strict than one could suppose possible at the very beginning of the development of poetic language. The extent to which poetry of the time engaged form, sense, syntax, and lexicon cannot be explained by the verse-line, since in many manuscripts, the poems are written as prose, and it is the rhymes themselves (along with caesura) that tell us where lines end. What Levin has called conventions are actually dynamic effects, effects of a system; does this not correspond to something profound in the nature of poetry?

# THE RULE AND THE NORM:
## Halle and Keyser on Chaucer's Meter

### W. K. WIMSATT

The theory of Chaucer's iambic pentameter, and by extension of the English pentameter tradition, proposed in Morris Halle and Samuel J. Keyser's article in *College English* for December 1966[1] is not one to be taken lightly. The article is intricately argued, in correct and toughly objective linguistic terms; it asks the right kind of questions about the nature of a meter, and in my opinion gives some very good answers to some of these questions. It is an interesting, a substantial, and even an important article; it demands a very close reading (such as I hope I have given it), and I must confess it commands my admiration. Nevertheless, I have some objections to urge—not so much on the score of inaccuracies in the argument, so far as the argument reaches, but on that of a certain inadequacy to the full idea of the English iambic pentameter. My aim is furthermore to conduct my conversation or debate with Halle and Keyser in such a way as to promote one perhaps paradoxical emphasis of my own concerning what for the moment I allude to, without explanation, as a not-often recognized co-presence or co-operation, in English iambic verse, of two controlling conceptions, both a *rule* and a *norm* (the latter of which is the center of the rule but not itself a rule).

It will make at least for clarity in the direction of my discourse if I begin by somewhat abruptly challenging an assertion made in the introductory paragraphs of Halle and Keyser's article.

> When to the sessions of sweet, silent thought
> I summon up remembrance of things past.

Halle and Keyser believe that in the first of these Shakespearian lines the "strict iambic theory" (i.e., the traditional theory of a "regular" iambic line) requires that the preposition *of* "receive greater stress than *sweet* in violation of the linguistic givens of spoken English." They observe, correctly, that this "strict" theory "requires that in the phrase *sweet, silent thought* the adjective *sweet* receive less stress than *silent*." But this pattern, they believe, "is in direct violation of English." They argue further that "the second line . . . would . . . be classed as irregular by the strict iambic pentameter theory, for clearly the preposition *of* has less stress than the following noun *things*." But it is difficult to say whose theory this "strict" theory is supposed to be. And I must report (1) that in my own theory, which I have always considered mainly traditional, the preposition *of* in each line is a sufficient ictus of a foot (or a sufficiently strong syllable in an ictus position) because in each instance it is clearly stronger than the preceding syllable—*sions, -brance*. And (2) that, contrary to their reading, the adjective *sweet* (though it receives more stress than *of*) does indeed receive less stress than the first syllable of *silent*—just as in the second line, *things* receives more stress than *of* but less than *past*. We are speaking here not of a sweet kind of silent thought, as opposed to a bitter kind of silent thought, but of a kind of thought which is both *sweet* and *silent*. It is a strange reading which will stress *sweet* more strongly than *silent*—and at least a forced, perhaps an impossible, reading which would try to stress them "evenly." In each of these lines then, we have an instance of a four-syllable stress sequence, two iambs, steadily rising, which is a characteristic

tensional variant (but not a violation) in English iambic verse. *-sions of*

*sweet si-; -brance of things past; Hail! to thee, blithe spirit.*[2]

## II

The moment has come for a succinct exposition of two important features of Halle and Keyser's theory.

1. Their basic unit of reference is not the syllable (the normal ten syllables to a line of the traditional or "standard" theory), but a certain something, more generalized, which nowadays is called the "position." The iambic pentameter line has ten positions, numbered by the theorist one to ten, odd and even.[3] Each position is occupied normally by one syllable. But a *zero* position can occur (in the headless—or catalectic—line)—and also several types of *disyllabic*—or elisional—positions. It is not necessary to say more about these variant positions at this moment.[4]

The degree of abstraction or non-committedness of the Halle-Keyser "positions" is, I believe, an improvement over the traditional terms of English metrical discussion; it is a device which anticipates and forestalls a number of distractions which have charateristically arisen in the discussion of both syllable and stress.

2. The mainspring and most original clause in the Halle-Keyser theory concerns stress. Halle and Keyser define something which they call Stress Maximum—a "linguistically determined" stress, on a given syllable, greater than that on either the preceding or the following syllable in the same verse.

They formulate the triple rule (1) that any even-numbered position in an iambic pentameter line may be occupied by a stress-maximum; (2) that not every even position need be thus occupied; and (3) that no odd-numbered position may be thus occupied.[5]

Halle and Keyser's "stress maximum" is a highly specific metrical concept, and hence if the sweeping assertion they make about it is correct, then this is an *interesting* assertion. It appears to me that this assertion *is* correct, or very nearly correct—in Chaucer's case, perhaps 99% correct. Certain examples give me some difficulty.[6] But for this moment at least I am disposed, for the sake of a simplified argument, to concede the validity, or nearly complete validity, of the Halle-Keyser triple rule. My own argument criticizes the rule without rejecting it.

Let us note: a correct assertion about a kind of meter is not necessarily an assertion adequate to explain the nature of, or define, that kind of meter. Thus I might formulate: "The Chaucerian iambic pentameter consists of nine or more syllables. Some of the syllables are always more heavily stressed than some other syllables." These assertions are, I believe, unexceptionable. They are safe. But it will not require the acumen of Halle and Keyser to point out immediately that I have not said enough. The assertions are not specific enough to make a theory of the iambic pentameter. Quite so. But then at what level of the specific, or in what sort of specific terms, will a definition and a theory be adequate? For I believe that Halle and Keyser's three principles, while they come closer than my mock invention to giving an adequate definition, do not in fact do so. A partial indication why this may be so may be given in the further remark that their crucial principle is after all only a negative one. Consider the two clauses: "may only occupy even positions . . . but not every even position need be . . ." This says, in effect, and says no more than: A *stress maximum never occupies an odd position*. The clause "not every even position need be so occupied" might be interpreted to mean that at least one such position will be so occupied. But apparently not even this is conceived as a metrical requirement. It is conceived rather as a perhaps unavoidable feature of English phrasing. "The only constraint is that a line in which all the even positions are unoccupied by stress maxima is highly unlikely in view of the natural stress patterns of the language."[7] It is conceivable, no doubt, that such a sheerly negative formula will sufficiently entail the positive features which are the more emphatic and operative aspects of a meter. In that case, Halle and Keyser's formula would seem to bear to the metrical fact somewhat the same relation as a negative for a photograph does to a positive print. But I do not think this formula does accomplish that much of an entailment. And if it did, this would happen by a kind of accident. As we are about to see, Halle and Keyser tend to treat stress maxima, those which they do discover in *some* of the even positions of Chaucerian lines, as an important but somehow threatening type of occurrence. The main task is to show that these occur only in positions where they do not invalidate the negative sweep of the Principle.

III

What I miss in the Halle-Keyser theory is any serious concern for the *five* stresses (or to speak generically, the five linguistic prominences, of whatever sort) which have been the traditional concern of pentameter theory. They speak of the "iambic pentameter tradition" (p. 187) and of lines which it has been "customary to identify . . . as examples of a meter called 'iambic pentameter' " (p. 189). But they seem content not to worry about the reason why it has been called "pentameter." Their central concern with "stress maximum," and not only that but, as we shall see, their concern with a very heavy degree of stress maximum, makes them content to find at best *some* of the measures in a line *syllabic-accentual*, the others simply *syllabic*. They make iambic pentameter a mixed meter.

A striking realization of the "stress maximum" rule appears in the announcement by Halle and Keyser that "in consequence" of their "definition" of stress maximum the stress in the tenth position in many Chaucerian lines is not a stress maximum. For indeed it is not followed by any syllable at all. In other lines it *is* followed by a hypermetrical and weaker syllable; and then it *is* a stress maximum. Chaucer indeed "normally places a stress-bearing syllable in the tenth position." This, however, is "related to" his "rhyming practice."[8] As a "consequence," the stress in the tenth position, even the stress maximum in the tenth position, is "without interest." "We shall ignore it in all subsequent scansions." Thus the argument in favor of a very special supposition, the importance of the stress maximum, leads immediately to our turning our backs upon something which Chaucer normally does, a normal feature of his pentameter verse. I contend that this is very curious reasoning.[9]

A broad implementation of the stress-maximum rule which has very important "consequences" (because by means of it an even greater number of Chaucer's metrical stresses can be "ignored") appears in a "fundamental" distinction between words of "major categories like Noun, Adjective, Adverb, and Verb on the one hand," and, on the other hand, words of "minor categories like conjunction, preposition, pronoun, article, and certain verbs like *to be*." Words of major categories bear stresses heavy enough to give stress maximum, but words of minor categories either do not do this, or it is very doubtful if they do. Halle and Keyser present evidence, in a footnote (20, pp. 201-2), that prepositions did receive stress in Chaucerian English—because they were subject to the Great Vowel Shift. But never mind. For purposes of stress-maximum scansion, all sequences of minor-category words will be read as having "neutral" or "level" stresses.[10] Furthermore, secondary stresses in polysyllabic words will be treated in the same way (e.g., p. 200). Only one certain stress can be provided by any one polysyllable. Metrical stresses disappear by the dozen.[11]

It is time to exhibit a small selection of their examples of scansion.[12]

> The dróghte of Márch hath pérced to the roote

> Twenty bóokes clád in blák or reed

> In Sóuthwerk at the Tábard as I lay
> > *Canterbury Prologue*, A 2, 294, 20
> > Halle and Keyser, pp. 199, 205, 200

> So dúl ys of his bestialite
> > *Troilus and Criseyde*, I. 735
> > Halle and Keyser, p. 200

The last line quoted is the minimum example of stress maxima in a single line adduced by our authors. The primary stress of the word *bestialite* comes on the last syllable, position 10 in the line, not followed by a hypermetric syllable and hence not a stress maximum. The preposition *of* is a word of "minor category" and hence cannot receive a stress. If we wish to take an initiative and supply secondary stresses for the long word, the authors remark with an air of triumph, the pattern will be $\overset{2}{\text{bes}}\overset{2}{\text{tia}}\overset{1}{\text{lite}}$, but this will not make the line an exception or "counterexample" to their rules: it will simply put it in the class of lines with stress maximum on the 2, 6, and 8 positions. Halle and Keyser are content to say that they do not know what kind of stress fell on little syllables and little words in Chaucer's day. "Since we do not at the moment see any way in which a definitive judgment can be made with respect to the relative stresses among words which belong to the minor categories, we have assumed that all of them bear the same degree of stress, whatever that may be" (p. 202). They add, again with an air of triumph, "that a modification which demands that *to*, under normal stress, be given a greater linguistic stress than *and* or *the*" does not make certain lines "exceptional." "Instead the lines need be only reclassified" (i.e., assigned one more stress maximum in an even position). But to my mind it is significant that these possible minor stress maxima (i.e. secondary stresses on polysyllables and stresses on minor words such as prepositions) should fall so readily, as Halle and Keyser point out, in the correct iambic positions. If we know where they *would* fall if they *did* fall, that is a linguistic given. And I have less reluctance than Halle and Keyser to recognize these givens. It is relevant to remark here that two of our main types of evidence for stress placements in English of long-past eras are our own pronunciation (plus the conviction that we enjoy some continuity with our own past) and the verse and rhythmic prose compositions which survive from those eras.[13]

There is one kind of illustration which Halle and Keyser make almost no use of—I mean the hypothetically constructed counterexample, the striking instance of what Chaucer *does not* do.[14] What Chaucer does not do cannot of course be illustrated from his own works. Invented examples, by the same token, do not create any extra proof of what he does not do. Such negative examples may, however, greatly clarify, or make considerably more vivid, the metrical significance of the positive evidence. But here the debate with Halle and Keyser runs into a certain kind of difficulty. As I have remarked above, the negative pattern, no stress maxima in odd positions, may come close to entailing a positive pattern, that of some degree of stress in every even position. Thus the experimenter who wishes to bring out the metrical value of a minor stress in a Chaucerian line by rewriting the line so as to eliminate that stress will be in grave danger of hearing Halle and Keyser cry: "Foul! You have created a stress maximum in an odd position. *That* is what is wrong with your rewritten line." Monroe Beardsley and I, in an essay on English meter published in 1957, manipulated a line by Pope to show that elimination of one minor stress changed the line from iambic pentameter to anapestic tetrameter.

A líttle leárning ís a dángerous thíng.

A líttle concéit is a dángerous thíng.

But this would not do for the present argument. For in eliminating the iambic stress on *is* we created, with the word *conceit*, a stress maximum in the odd position 5. It happens indeed that it is not easy to invent counter-Chaucerian examples, which, avoiding the fatal stress maximum in an odd position, yet vivify the metrical force of a minor stress in an even position

by eliminating it. The experimenter has indeed a further distinct defeat
to confess. Yet this too is a very instructive defeat.

> The droúghte of Márch hath pérced tó the róote

Suppose we attempt to bring out the metrical force of the preposition *to*
by reversing the order of (possible) minor stresses in that area of the line.

> The droughte of March will perce *under* the roote

For reasons which I believe will be clear, I choose a later place in my essay
for the important topic of the inverted stresses, even inverted major
stresses, which iambic writers, Chaucer among them, so often use in the
first foot of a line or in the first foot after a caesura (major syntactic
boundary, as Halle and Keyser express it). Here, with *under*, we confront
what I should call an inverted order of stress, in a single *minor* word, without any apparent special reason to justify it. It may seem perhaps not as
usual, or as normal, a Chaucerian stress pattern as that of the original second line of the *Canterbury Prologue*. Yet our ear, our auditory memory,
may forestall protest. Halle and Keyser themselves, without comment,
quote the following line from the *Knight's Tale* (A 1999):

> The smylere with the knyf *under* the cloke.

In the 860 lines of the *Canterbury Prologue* I count about 36 lines (aside
from some doutbful ones) which may be taken as exhibiting this pattern,
each in a single foot only.

> Whan Zephyrus *eek with* his sweete breeth    A 5
>
> Ful semely *after* hir mete she raughte    A 136
>
> And for to festne his hood *under* his chin    A 195
>
> Ful ofte time he was *Knight of* the Shire    A 358
>
> There was *also* a Reeve *and a* Millere    A 542

That is, the pattern seems definitely a repeated one (stopping here and
there perhaps just short of a full "stress maximum" in the odd position—
e.g., in "*Knight of* the Shire"),[15] yet not a frequent pattern—36 out of
8,580 stresses. How far in this direction would we have to go to produce

a line which, while avoiding the stress maximum in the odd position, yet
would be un-Chaucerian and unmetrical? The last example quoted in the
series above suggests two main available ways of weakening a line, short of
allowing stress maximum to fall in a wrong position. The two minor monosyllables *and a* in positions 7 and 8 show not only inversion of stress but an
extreme lowering of the stress level in both positions. The adverb *also*, occupying positions 3 and 4, with a dubious stress[16] (the spelling *al so* occurs
often in Chaucer) presents at least the possibility of another inverted
minor stress—i.e., two in a single line. The synthetic examples of the crip-
pled line which now follow are presented not as absolutely unmetrical but
as, at the very least, extremely weak and questionable. I include in parenthesis before each the Chaucerian line which is its distant inspiration.

> (In Southwerk at the Tabard as I lay      A 20):

> In York *under* the tree *in a* tabárd[17]

> (As ook, firr(e), birch, asp(e), alder, hólm, popler
> > *Knight's Tale*, A 2921.
> > Halle and Keyser, p. 204):

> As ook, *alder*, aspe, holm, *birch and* popler
> As ook, *alder, and the* divyn popler
> As ook, *alder and also the* popler[18]

> (So dul ys of his bestialite
> > *Troilus and Criseyde*, I. 735):

> So high he stant *and biforn* king and quene

For good measure I throw in an instance of the position 10 stress destroyed.

> (Twenty bookes clad in blak or reed    A 294):

> Twenty bookes clad in blak *and a*[19]

The point I would make about these inventions of mine is that each conforms scrupulously to Halle-Keyser rules. Each is, to invoke their own favorite expression, "perfectly regular." For each exhibits all the meager
enough positive requirements, and each manages to avoid the cardinal fault
of placing a stress maximum in an odd position. Yet each is at best a marginal attempt to write an iambic line. Such patterns of stress, if they occur

at all in Chaucer, must be very few. Any concentration of them in a short passage would kill its meter.

It would be possible to multiply lame instances such as I have invented, but the devices would be inevitably monotonous. If Chaucer's language, and no doubt our own language, makes it difficult for a poet, avoiding stress maxima in odd positions of a line of ten syllables, not to avoid also minor stresses in the same positions, this does not tell against the metrical significance of the placement of minor stresses, though it may tell in favor of the language as a metrical medium and opportunity. I am directing my challenge to the notion that a sweeping negative rule (plus a merely optional rule about major positive features) will render certain minor positive features irrelevant to a definition of a meter. Given the mountains, the foothills may be inevitable, but they are none the less important to the aesthetic character of the landscape. Or, to try another analogy: If a man is in the habit of lingering for a while each evening on one or the other of a flight of two steps going up to his front door, we may observe: (1) that he never sits on the bottom step; (2) that he sometimes, even often, sits on the top step; (3) that he often stands momentarily on the top step; and (4) that he sometimes, but not very often, stands on the bottom step. It would be difficult to argue that of these four habits, only (1) and (2), the maxima, are relevant to a concept of this man's pattern of stopping on his steps.

It is not necessary for my argument that all of Chaucer's weaker metrical stresses should be minor stress *maxima*. There is also the situation, illustrated in the lines already quoted from Shakespeare's sonnet, where, in a sequence of four escalating syllables, odd-even, odd-even, the stress of the first pair meets only the requirement of being stronger than the preceding syllable, the odd position of that foot pair. This is a fairly common and sometimes very marked sort of special effect in later iambic verse. I do not know how frequently it may occur in Chaucer. But Halle and Keyser quote (without comment) the following example from the *Pardoner's Tale* (C 604):

> Was sent to Cory*nthe in ful greet* honour.

And in the *Canterbury Prologue* I have counted at least nine examples.

> In lystes thri*es and ay slain* his foo    A 63

> Wel loved he garlek, oy*nons, and eek lek*es    A 634

> And for to drynk*en strong wyn* reed as blood.    A 635[20]

## IV

Halle and Keyser are at great pains, repeatedly throughout their article, to emphasize a distinction between a traditional way of conceiving a "strict" iambic pattern with recognized or "listed" exceptions, deviations, or "modifications," *and* on the other hand what they conceive as their own way of formulating principles so broad and accurate that everything in Chaucer's lines comes as a "consequence" of these principles, or everything is "explained" by these principles; or these principles "yield" everything needed, so that every Chaucerian line (except a very negligible few "unmetrical" lines) is thus "perfectly regular." The Halle-Keyser principles are constructed as "alternatives," and for one of these principles at least, that concerning elided or syncopated syllables, the enabling "conditions" or alternatives make an exceedingly extensive enumeration. And it may be difficult to see the radical departure in method. If we begin by throwing our empirical dragnet wide enough, we can always formulate an alternatively structured principle which will take care of everything which somebody else might wish to call an exception. Probably indeed we are all along working with implicit reference to some simpler scheme or norm (the ten syllables which are admitted to be the "normal" occupants of the ten positions). But the mere discovery or enumeration of the "complications" which occur (the kinds of adjacent syllables, for instance, which do come together in Chaucerian lines to fill single metrical positions—i.e., which *are* elided or syncopated) is not an "explanation" of *why* these complications occur. The very long, and for all I know exhaustive, sixth section of Halle and Keyser's article enumerating the "conditions for dissyllabic positions" in Chaucer's verse, therefore, raises no metrical question of general theoretical interest, beyond their claim that they are indeed "explaining" something or constructing a principle that has "consequences," in which surely their logic is backwards.

One can agree with Halle and Keyser, and even insist, that a metrical description is a "structural" description, and not a precept for a performance, or even a full description of any actual performance. And yet if there is any "explanation" for all the kinds of adjacent syllables which are elided or syncopated in Chaucer's verse, this explanation must lie somewhere in the nature of some possible performance. Elided and syncopated syllables in verse, whether or not their author and his first audience did run them together in speech, are those which both their own character and their position in the verse would make it easy for a reader to run together. When Alexander Pope constructed his neat capsule of anti-elision or the metrical fault of hiatus,

> Tho' oft the ear the open vowels tire,

he was not making a report on whether or not he or his friends were actually in the habit of eliding the vowels of *tho'* and *the* with initial vowels
of following words. He was saying, however, that there *is* an invitation to
elision inherent in the linguistic structure of his line—but that in the kind
of *metrical* situation which he here contrives there is also a contrary invitation. There is a clash of invitations. The line needs *all* the syllables. The
opposite metrical structure (or a metrical structure which invites an elision,
or a syncope, in harmony with the linguistic givens) appears in Milton's
"Above th' Aonian Mount. . . ." or in Chaucer's

> Withoute bake met(e) was never his hous

> And bathed every veyne in swich licour.
>> *Canterbury Prologue*, A 343, 5
>> Halle and Keyser, pp. 209, 207.

Under the general rubric of Metrical Positions, Halle and Keyser also
discuss the Headless Line.

> Twenty bookes clad in blak or reed.    A 294

This is the case where a "zero syllable" occurs—that is, where one of the
ten positions is vacant. We learn here, quickly and finally, that this can
happen only in the first position of a line, i.e., only in the "headless line."
By the assumption of an initial zero position, the remaining syllables of
the line "may be assigned in a one to one fashion to weak and strong positions so that only strong positions contain the stress maxima."[21]

The headless line has a stress on the first syllable (*second* position, of
course), and this, by superficial resemblance, at least, leads us back to
something Halle and Keyser have treated earlier under the rubric of Scansion—a something which has always been and no doubt will continue to
be a main stumbling-block to anybody's attempt at a perfectly streamlined
or unified explanation of the iambic pentameter. I refer to the line with
the inverted first foot, or, as Halle and Keyser would say, with a stress in
the *first* position.

> When to the sessions of sweet silent thought

> Wondring upon this word; quaking for drede
>> *Clerk's Tale*, E 358
>> Halle and Keyser, p. 203, n. 23

Here we find the concept of the stress maximum operating with its greatest éclat as an "explanation." It may indeed seem to explain something. In most accounts of iambic pentameter, the inverted stress is simply permitted in the first foot, the first two syllables, because that is where it is most often found. But why not in any other two odd-even positions? Stress maximum explains this by the special character of the first syllable of the line. It cannot be a stress maximum, because there is no weaker syllable before it; there is no syllable at all. (If we define the fish course as that which comes after the soup, then if a hostess serves fish first, it cannot be the fish course.) The weak second syllable of the line, of course, takes care of itself. The rule says only that this position *need not* have a stress maximum. I have chosen the line from Chaucer above with the purpose of illustrating also a second principle urged by Halle and Keyser—it seems to me quite correctly and very usefully. The fourth foot of this line, like the first, is inverted, and this is all right, because it comes after a "major syntactic boundary" (caesura). Syntactic boundaries cancel out, or neutralize ordinary rules of English stress. Rules do not operate *across* such boundaries—so that neither the word *word* nor the syllable *quak*—in the line above can bear a stress maximum. Each lacks one half of the needed environment. One might add that most, perhaps all, iambic lines in Chaucer, and generally in English poets, which begin with the inverted stress are also syntactic beginnings in one marked degree or another. Thus the kinship between the inverted opening of the line and the inverted opening of the second main phrase of the line is very correctly emphasized. But we may wonder a little still about the need of the stress maximum as an "explanation" of the inverted stress. We have seen how the doctrine of stress maximum operates at the other end of the line, coolly cancelling out an invarible strong stress which is much needed for the meter of the line. We have seen how the same doctrine dispenses with the more numerous, lighter internal stresses in even positions. As so often happens in various kinds of crating and packaging, a very firm sealing at one end produces a bulge or crack somewhere else. The fact that initial syllables of lines and phrases, even when in odd positions, can receive a strong stress without spoiling the meter of the line is undoubtedly connected with the fact that they *are* initial syllables and hence not strongly subject to metrical comparison with anything preceding. "Stress maximum" may be only a roundabout way of arriving at just that conclusion.[22]

v

At several places in their article, as we have already noticed, Halle and Keyser rightly urge the thesis that a description of a meter is a description of a "structure." It is not a precept for a performance of a poem—nor, I might add, even a description of such a performance. Still, a "structure" has to be a structure of something, and a meter is a structure of certain aspects of a possible performance of a poem. Hence when Halle and Keyser, again at several places in their article, expound what they call a neutral or level sequence of stresses (for instance, in the modern British stressing

of adjective-noun monosyllabic junctures—*black* $\overset{1}{bird}$, $\overset{1}{good}$ $\overset{1}{wife}$, $\overset{1}{first}$

$\overset{1}{prize}$), I am inclined to think they are talking about certain choices of stress which are offered by these situations as we may conceive them only in some very purified, abstracted, or uncommitted state. True, *black bird*, taken just like that, by itself, does not have the determinate stress of the compound *blackbird*. But then *black bird* is not very likely to be held in just this pure, tentative state in very many sentences. In almost any actualization, we are going to be concerned to convey that we are talking about a bird that is black and not blue, or on the other hand about the color black as it is found in a bird and not in a cat. I hold too that a marked choice of stress for either *black* or *bird* is going to be all the more likely if the words are part of a meter. But this raises another question about which Halle and Keyser several times assert what seems to me a basically correct yet too simple view—that the poet has to respect his linguistic givens and use them; he has to make his meter by legitimate manipulation of the givens; he cannot alter them at will or suppose them to be this way or that at his own convenience. That much I agree is basic. Yet the matter is perhaps not quite so simple as all that; the difference between the rule and something else is not quite so "sharp" as they would suppose it to be. It is not quite as if we had ironclad linguistic rules of stress, so that if we try to write a meter which does not quite illustrate these rules, we might as well write scientific prose and call it meter (p. 188). For it is a fairly prevalent view, and I think a correct one, that the metrical pattern is not quite a mere result of linguistic arrangements, a mere inert epiphenomenon. The meter establishes a certain expectancy; it exerts a certain kind of coercion and performs a certain kind of self-assistance. It has assimilative powers. A quiet "promotion" of certain weaker syllables (as Arnold Stein has put it) and a partial "suppression" (or demotion) of certain stronger ones would appear to take place in much of our reading—and according to plausible enough norms. The neutral or level choices to which we have alluded just above are junctures where if all else fails the meter itself must often have a deciding force. Either member of those level-stress adjective-noun phrases, say Halle and Keyser, may occupy either an even or an odd position (p. 204). Most likely. But not both in the same instance. And so in my reading of Chaucer I very readily decide or tilt these levels in favor of the meter and *without violence* to any linguistic given.

A góod Wif wás ther óf bisíde Báthe     A 445

The Míllere wás a stóut carl fór the nónes     A 545

A whít cote and a bléw hood wéred hé.     A 564

Add a good many choices in stress upon prepositions and conjunctive adverbs and (with an even more curious bearing on Halle and Keyser's system) a clear choice of stresses for certain major compound words.

A long surcote of pers *upón he hade*     A 617

A povre person dwellynge *úpon* lond     A 703

And *álso* war hym of a *Significavit*     A 662

Ther was *alsó* a Reve, and a Millere     A 542

He understood, and *brýmstoon* by his brother
     *Canon's Yeoman's Tale*, G 1439

Ther nas *quyk-sílver*, lytarge, ne *brymstóon*     A 629

In the last example, if they will not permit me my two chosen stresses of
*quyk-sílver* and *brymstóon* (contrary to their supposed flat rule of first-syl-
lable stresses on compounds), they will be faced with the embarrassing
consequence of a stress maximum in position 3 of the line and of another
in position 9, and with loss of stress on the rhyme syllable in position 10.[23]

Rules of language do not include rules of meter. The meter, as Halle and
Keyser well observe, is something that the poet adds to the linguistic givens,
without contravening them. But rules of meter create their own problem:
—How regular in order to be "perfectly regular?" Halle and Keyser express
considerable contempt for a certain old-fashioned "strict" supposition
about the pentameter rule: ten syllables, no more, no less; five stresses, on
the even syllables. All the rest, the inversions, the extra syllables, the headless line, conceived as exceptions to or modifications of the rule. If a poet
ever wrote strictly according to that rule, they say, he would write "doggerel." Chaucer, Shakespeare, and the others do not write doggerel. Yet
they must write by a rule. And when we encounter in their verse such
things as inverted stresses and elisional or syncopic situations (dissyllabic
positions), we must not call these exceptions to any rule, nor do they
create any "tension" with a rule. They are but "complications" of the rule.
All these situations are "consequences" of the real rules. Without being

doggerel, they are "perfectly regular." The rules "yield" these variations. Yet the iambic line, Halle and Keyser say, does "normally" consist of ten syllables. The line of ten syllables, with each even position stressed, constitutes the most "neutral" actualization of the rules. I have commented above on the absence of any real distinction in method between the old-fashioned rule qualified by a list of exceptions and the Halle-Keyser "branching" rules or "alternatively" structured "principles" and "conditions" prepared by exhaustive empirical collecting. Halle and Keyser substitute for "exceptions" or "modifications" the term "complications" (e.g., p. 197), and they argue that in this way the idea of "tension" with some straighter norm has been eliminated. I do not understand this. If "tension" can arise from "modification," it can arise also from "complication." In the context of many human activities, perhaps in most contexts, the latter term has the stronger affinity for "tension."[24]

Halle and Keyser's resolute attempt to cope with the phenomenon of modification-complication in English verse should prompt us to ponder anew the curious fact that verse *is* written and read with reference to a norm (the iambic pentameter norm is ten syllables, alternately and evenly less and more stressed), but this is a norm which is *no ideal*. A poet who observed it would possibly, as Halle and Keyser say, write doggerel. But, what is more technically relevant, he would, if he persisted, write in fact a more specific or more specialized meter than the pentameter. It would be a meter defined not simply by number of syllables and alternations of relative stress but more artificially by *even* degrees of stress in regularly repeated positions.[25] In short, the "norm" of iambic pentameter could, by being persistently actualized, become the "rule" of a different meter. This paradox of the distinction between rule or definition and norm has not, I believe, been much pondered by the prosodists. It gives rise to a further paradox, which may be a scandal to the scientifically minded:—namely, the complicated truth that we must reckon not merely with one kind of contrary to the norm, but with three (only one of which is also a contrary to the rule). This indeed we find in most sequences of *aimed* human action. Sometimes (1) the bus breaks down and we fail to get to school, sometimes (2) we have to walk the last block, almost always (3) the ride is bumpy. We contract for rides in all sorts of vehicles, but not necessarily for smooth rides, though smoothness is a norm—and sometimes too a soporific norm, as when we go to sleep driving on the thruway. Or again: the right-hand lane (*except* for passing) is the *rule*. But this rule is wider than the space approximately down the middle of it which is more or less *normally* occupied by a moving car. I have said something in this essay about (1) the breaking of the rule and about (2) the modifications or complications of it—but very little about a third thing (3), the more or less inevitable and never-failing succession of disparities that arise between the phantom neutral *norm* and the actual variations of degree in weaker and stronger syllables (arising through longer and shorter words and various syntax), not necessarily contravening the *rule,* not even involving any of the accepted *modifications* of the rule, but nevertheless constituting the most continuous source of tensions between verse and the sound of sense.

> As ook, firre, birch, ashe, alder, holm, popler
>
> *Knights Tale,* A 2921

> By superfluytee abhomynable
>
> *Pardoner's Tale,* C 471

Three words or eight, two strong stresses or seven. Always iambic pentameter. All perfectly "perfectly regular."

## NOTES

1. "Chaucer and the Study of Prosody," *College English,* XXVIII (December 1966), 187-219. Keyser's later essay "The Linguistic Basis of English Prosody" in *Modern English Studies,* ed. David A. Reibel and Sanford A. Schane (Englewood Cliffs, N.J., 1969), pp. 379-94, is a simplified and very clear exposition of the same views. Cf. below notes. Professors Halle and Keyser have prepared a general statement, "The Iambic Pentameter," to appear with other papers on English metrics, in a book on comparative prosody to be published, under my editorship, by the Modern Language Association of America.

2. I use the numbers 4, 3, 2, 1 here to refer to the relations of these syllables to one another, not to refer to anybody's system of degrees of phonemic stress. Perhaps this involves what will be called by some "allophonic" degrees of stress. Perhaps they are allophonic only if we have already overinvested in some more limited set of phonemic stresses.

3. In terms of Keyser's statement of 1969, "weak" or "strong"—i.e. positions where weak and strong syllables will in some sense normally occur.

4. The conditions for elision are meticulously explained and illustrated in a long section of the article, "Dissyllabic Positions," pp. 206-13.

5. In their own phrasing: "A stress maximum may only occupy even positions within a verse, but not every even position need be so occupied."

6. See below.

7. P. 199. Page 202 reports that they have not found such lines in Chaucer. See below note 11.

8. One presumes that the blank verse of Shakespeare or Milton normally places a stress in the tenth position for some other reason.

9. Stressed *first* syllables of lines too will obviously come under discountenance by the principle of stress maximum. For reasons which will appear, I defer discussion of this matter to a later head.

10. Supposedly neutral or level stress, either at high levels, on major words
($bl\overset{1}{a}ck$ $b\overset{1}{i}rd$), or in the minor categories, is discussed several times in the course of the article. I defer a more general comment on the issue to a later place in my own argument.

11. "There are fourteen possible combinations of even positions, 2 through 8 being occupied and/or unoccupied by stress maxima" (p. 202). Halle and Keyser are "able to find examples for eleven of those possible combinations." The three combinations for which they are unable to find examples are:

(a) lines without stress maximum in positions 2, 4, 6, 8
(b) lines without stress maximum in positions 2, 4, 6
(c) lines without stress maximum in positions 2 and 4.

"It may be that Chaucer consciously avoided lines in which the 2 and 4 positions were both unoccupied by stress maxima, perhaps because of the weak onset imparted to such lines" (p. 202). They are willing to consider the possibility of "incorporating some such stipulation" into their rules.

12. The section of their article on Scansion alone, pp. 198-205, quotes altogether 49 lines in 20 groups. I refrain from multiplying requotations, because I am not concerned to deny (1) that they have correctly shown where all the *heavy* or *major* stress maxima fall in positions 2, 4, 6, and 8 of these lines, or (2) that they say correctly that in these lines no stress maxima at all occur in odd positions.

13. See, for instance, John C. Pope, ed. *Homilies of Ælfric, A Supplementary Collection,* I (Oxford, 1967), Introduction, pp. 105-36, "Ælfric's Rhythmical Prose."

14. At two points they appeal to straight prose sentences as instances of something which might be logically considered to be metrical if meter were conceived as an *ad lib* alteration of linguistic givens, i.e., if we were not equipped with a precise metrical rule (pp. 188, 214). They follow Jespersen in altering a line by Longfellow to show how inverting the first foot of a trochaic line makes a mess of it (p. 199).

15. The stress maximum in position 7 might be escaped by making the *-e* of *time* into position 5 and *of the* into a dissyllabic position 9. But this is a forced and bad reading.

16. See below, p. 209, my discussion of stress choices.

17. See line 543 of the *General Prologue,* "In a tabárd he rode. . . ." Or, if this word seems unsatisfactory, substitute *gypon,* as in line 75. Halle and Keyser's discussion of Romance and native rules of stress in Chaucer's day (second section of their article) would seem to require a stress on the second syllable of the Romance word *tabard.* How line A 20 then avoids a stress maximum in position 7, I leave it to them to say.

18. The stress on *holm* in Chaucer's line is Halle and Keyser's scansion, the only stress maximum and hence the only metrically relevant stress in the line. The other stresses are neutralized by the "major syntactic breaks" between the items in the series. I would call attention to Chaucer's accurate use of the English word *álder* and the Romance word *poplér* for his metrical purpose, and my own counter-use or wrong placement of *álder,* with a very bad result for my three constructions, though they are still saved by Halle-Keyser rules from having any stress maxima in the odd positions. The third of my constructions might have by my rules, though I think not by theirs, a weak stress maximum in either position 5 or position 7.

19. Halle and Keyser at one point remark that Chaucer never ends a line with an article, but the significance of this seems to escape them.

20. Other examples are lines 84, 274, 428, 578, 648, 767.

21. See Keyser's essay of 1969. Halle and Keyser do not take up the question whether syntactic arrangements internal to a line may not make possible the assumption of zero positions there too. But Chaucer's successor Lydgate, I believe, is noted for this kind of thing after the caesura. And: "Break, break, break,/ On thy cold gray stones, O Sea!/ And I would that my tongue could utter/ The thoughts that arise in me."

22. Halle and Keyser (pp. 204-5) go on to invoke "neutralization" of stress by the (major?) syntactic boundaries of items in a series ("As o$\overset{1}{o}$k, fi$\overset{1}{r}$re, bi$\overset{1}{r}$ch, a$\overset{1}{s}$he, a$\overset{1}{l}$der, ho$\overset{1}{l}$m, popler"—*Knight's Tale*, A 2921), and also neutralization or level stress (without syntactic boundary) in adjective-noun phrases ("A go$\overset{2}{o}$d wi$\overset{2}{f}$ was ther of biside Bathe"—*General Prologue*, A 445). A good many of the minor stress inversions which I note in the *Canterbury Prologue* seem to me to occur without any special justification by syntactic boundary. Halle and Keyser would no doubt say either (1) the words are so minor we cannot be sure any stress is there, or (2) the inverted stress is neutralized by a preceding boundary of some degree. The invocation of the latter principle might well approach circularity of explanation. There is a boundary because there is inversion. I have difficulty, for instance, in escaping the conclusion that line 358, "Ful ofte time he was Knight of the Shire," exhibits, in stark contravention of their rule, a stress maximum in the 7th position.

23. Halle and Keyser (p. 214) actually consider a line ending with the word *brimstoon* in the *Canon's Yeoman's Tale* (G 798):

Arsenyk, sal armonyak and brimstoon

By their severe rules this line has only three stress maxima, and one of them, "in accordance with English stress subordination" in compound nouns, must be considered a "stress maximum in the ninth position in the line." The line is accordingly to be classed as "unmetrical." Never mind the fact that *-stoon* seems to rhyme with *oon* in the next line. The *brimstoon* line is one of a very small minority of "unmetrical" lines in Chaucer (less than 1.0% in a thousand)—a tolerable percentage of exceptions to the rule, in view of the exigencies of manuscript transmission, scribal error and, finally, the possibility of poetic oversight, though, in principle, the latter seems . . . a last recourse since it fails to do justice to the craftsmanship of a great poet." A poet who absentmindedly forgot that compounds *must* be stressed on the first syllable and so tried to rhyme *brimstoon* not only with *oon* but a few lines later (825) with *anoon* and in the *Canterbury Prologue* with *noon* (630). At line 1439 in the *Canon's Yeoman's Tale* he did remember to stress the first syllable of *brimstoon*, thereby avoiding a stress maximum in position 7. But at line 822 in the *Canon's Yeoman's Tale* we seem to find again (as in A 629) *quyksílver*—unless we are to suppose a stress maximum in the wrong position.

A second example of the "unmetrical" line quoted by Halle and Keyser (p. 214) occurs in a classic portrait in the *General Prologue*.

Ful wéel she sóong the servíce dyvyne    A 122

Here I must confess I have always supposed native stress rule rather than Romance and have gotten along smoothly, in a line that ought to be smooth, with *sérvicé dyvýne*. But Halle and Keyser invoke an inexorable Romance stress rule

(*servíce*) and are content to leave the lady Prioresse's song in ruins.

Chaucer and his hearers no doubt shifted easily enough between the Romance and the English stresses on the word *service*. See the instances of both cited in W. W. Skeat's Glossary in *The Complete Works* (Oxford 1894), Vol. I. The evidence I have cited just above would suggest that they shifted too for a compound like *brimstoon* when meter demanded it. It is not necessary to suppose they felt in either case any strong sense of violence to a linguistic given.

24. Later statements by Halle and Keyser move "complication" decidedly in the direction of "tension." See note 1 above.

25. J. V. Cunningham, "How Shall the Poem be Written," *Denver Quarterly*, II (Spring 1967), 45-62. English dipodic meters exhibit more complicated patterns on this principle—e.g., dee Dum, dee DUM / dee Dum, dee DUM.

# DISCUSSION OF WIMSATT'S PAPER

The first commentator accepted Wimsatt's distinction between rule and norm, but wondered about some other possibilities of breaking the rule. He noted that in living speech one can break the rule by a shift of stress; but the poet cannot shift the stress, that is, he has no access to performance. But he can create a conflict between metrical prominence (ictus) and linguistic stress: this is the metrical equivalent of the stress shift of living speech. The speaker had done some research on the relation between stress and ictus and had discovered that there were frequently semantic corollaries, such an anger, to the conflict. In respect to enjambement, too, there is often expressive breaking of the rule. For example, in examining two cycles of poems by the same poet, Heine, a serene cycle (1817-21) and a more anguished one (1853-56), he had discovered a striking increase in the number of strong enjambements in the latter, the time of Heine's *Matratzengrab*—24 percent of the lines had enjambement, compared to only 3 percent in the earlier period. The same is true of caesura. Comparing, in *Phèdre,* the speech of the serene teacher of Hippolyte, Théramène, with that of the tormented Phèdre, he discovered practically no displacements in the first, but as many as 9.3 percent in the second, an astounding figure in terms of contemporary practice. Wimsatt reminded the speaker that he had expressly excluded from consideration such matters as the value of meter and its interrelations with other poetic elements, but said that of course he agreed with him about the importance of such effects. Meter is a pattern or ordering, a formalization which enables a number of other meanings. But the purpose of his paper was to try to determine if we can distinguish 1) outright violations of the rule, 2) modifications of the rule, and 3) variations from the center or "norm" within the rule itself.

Another participant noted that the same problems about rule, norm, and metricality occurred in the analysis of French verse, for which he had proposed the following solution: there are two levels of versification—1) the grammar of verse (the structure, the set of rules which must operate if there is to be a system at all), and 2) the stylistics of verse (the set of patterns which have rules but which also permit a margin of freedom and which introduce rhythm into the metrical structure). The latter cannot be said to break the rules established by the former. The difficulty is that we often mix the two levels, trying to insert the stylistic into the grammatical pattern. Wimsatt found no disagreement and simply gave an example of what he meant by *rule* and *norm:* in highway driving the *rule* is that one must drive between the center line and the right edge of the road except when overtaking; the *norm,* however, is a space roughly equidistant between the center line and the edge. In his paper he was concerned with the problem of whether we can know what the rule *is;* if we can, then we will also be able to inquire into the narrower thing, the norm, what Halle and Keyser call the "neutral actualization," as well as those odd things we call modifications. Nobody seems to know whether the latter occur because they have some special fitness within the rule, or whether they acquire a fitness simply through having often occurred. This is a problem which Halle and Keyser make a bold attempt to solve.

Several participants commented directly on the Halle-Keyser metrical system. It was observed that it seemed negative, that it was essentially the statement of a negative principle—namely, that no stress maximum may fall on an odd syllable, while one may or may not fall on an even. That seems to leave a good deal unexplained. We are frequently interested in even syllables which have stresses other than the stress maximum, but Halle and Keyser simply lump these together with the syllables where there is no stress. They are content to pass over a good many things which have been of traditional interest to metrists, simply because, to them, these are irrelevant. But there are many ways in which a principle may be observed, and the differences between these are and should be of interest to metrics; they produce very different effects. Halle and Keyser are basically interested in protecting their theory, whereas many of us are interested in trying to find out what meter is.

Generative linguistics presumes two general requirements in a grammar: 1) the rules must be so devised that they generate all and only grammatical sentences; and 2) the rules must also provide a description for every sentence which they allow to be generated; but it is not clear that the Halle-Keyser metrical system fulfills the second requirement. Their system does present a criterion for defining metrical well-formedness, that is, for distinguishing between metrical and unmetrical lines, but it does not provide a description of the units, the metrical lines which are well-formed. One feels dissatisfied since one seems to "know" more about the meter of these lines than the rules account for. Another consequence of the strict application of the stress-maximum principle is that there appear to be a good many lines that seem metrical and yet are violations according to the Halle-Keyser principles. Perhaps the difficulty lies in attempting to devise an abstract principle that will take only individual lines and determine whether or not they are metrical; maybe the problem should be approached differently, say by statistics. But if an entire poem, a sonnet, for example, somehow establishes the sense in the reader that its meter is iambic pentameter, then there doesn't seem to be any particular reason to call any particular line unmetrical if it happens not to fall within the explanatory power of a set of rules. What Wimsatt had aptly called the assimilative power of the meter could presumably assimilate even five trochees into the framework of an iambic poem, and if that is true, it seems wrong to develop criteria for analyzing individual lines separate from the metrical contexts of entire poems. Wimsatt found himself in substantial agreement with this position, noting that Keyser had recently published a paper in which he argued that a line by Keats with two inversions in the middle was simply unmetrical. Certain lines can be very weak without being completely unmetrical; of course, a heavy concentration of such lines might change the meter. In the end, it is the general trend in the poem that establishes the meter. And, of course, the minor stresses have to be recognized in any full account. Further, there is evidence (in an unpublished paper by Samuel Levin) of iambic lines in which stress maxima *do* occur in odd positions, throwing the whole system into question. All in all, it seems that Halle and Keyser will have to modify their theory if they want to account for the entire sweep of English iambic poetry, especially the later poets.

In defense of the Halle-Keyser system, another participant noted that generative systems of this sort are useful only when one has intuitions of some sort that one wants to deal with. If it were merely a question of de-

scribing a text in the simplest way it wouldn't be very exciting. But Halle
and Keyser assume that Chaucer knew by reference to some touchstone or
register when he was writing a metrical and when an unmetrical line. And
we all assume that we, as readers, can distinguish a metrical from an unmetrical line. (It seems a little surprising that Halle and Keyser chose to
write about Chaucer, where reconstructions are necessary, rather than
about a modern poet.) But against the objection that their explanation is
circular, it must be argued that "explanation" in such cases can only be a
simple and elegant characterization of what is going on in our minds; always behind that form of explanation there is a deeper assumption about
method, namely that the human mind tends to choose the simplest explanation of co-ordinated masses of material, so that the simpler of two
theories is more likely to be correct. It cannot, of course, ignore things that
are the case, but it does seem that Wimsatt was working in accord with the
general principle of simplicity when he pointed to other lines which were
not Chaucerian but which were not excluded by the Halle-Keyser rules.
Wimsatt replied that Levin (in the unpublished paper cited above) had
found that the formal symbolization occupying a page at the end of the
Halle-Keyser article left many of the syllables in Chaucer's lines uncharac-
terized. Wimsatt had worked only from the English exposition, where the
same criticism does not apply. Thus there seems to be a hiatus between
the formalization and the English exposition.

A third commentator on the Halle-Keyser system also argued that it was
essentially a linguist's theory rather than a metrist's theory, that it was more
concerned with accounting for meter by linguistic theory than by finding
out what in fact meter is. It reminded one of certain Freudian literary
critics who seem less concerned with explaining literary genius than with
explaining it *away*. Their attitude is that a difficulty is to be accounted for
in terms of a construct, but the effort seems rather designed to dispose of
an embarrassing source of confusion than to find out more about the nature of the difficult object. One becomes more involved in defending a
theory than in discovering something new. For example, the very concept
of syllable should not be taken as given in metrics but should be one of its
subjects of inquiry; the same is true of other metrical concepts like position
and metrical prominence. Stress is a linguistic, not a metrical concept, so
that when one talks about "stress maximum" one is confusing linguistic
with metrical elements, one is saying that, because a metrical theory requires a positional definition, the intrinsic property of the thing defined is
not relevant. The fact that metrical prominence is termed "stress maximum" instead of having a purely metrical—that is non-linguistic—name like
"ictus" is symptomatic of the confusion between the two systems. The
metrical entity, ictus, may be filled or actualized by linguistic entities

(main stresses, weaker stresses, intonational elements, or however one's linguistic system has it), but it should not be defined in terms of them; that is to blur the distinction between the two systems. Thus, it is not surprising that there is a general neglect, in the Halle-Keyser articles, of general aesthetic questions like that of the principle of diversity amid regularity. Meter entails a constant, but a constant that is constantly varied, and that variation always occurs within limits. In Halle and Keyser's analysis, all that seems to go by the board because it does not fit into the narrow problem of accounting for meter by the most sophisticated linguistic theory possible. Wimsatt said that he did not follow this argument and could not agree with it. It was true that Halle and Keyser were using linguistic elements to describe the metrical theory, but he did not know what else one could do to make the description objective but use the most reliable concepts available. Every theory of meter must have theoretical constructs, and those used by Halle and Keyser seem better than the idea of ten syllables and five feet; to him the system is more flexible than any other, less committed, and more consistent. The only limitation is that Halle and Keyser have not succeeded in establishing a set of rules that describes with complete adequacy what goes on in an iambic pentameter. One can perhaps improve on it in ways that Levin has suggested, by providing a larger context, working on the basis of ten or twenty lines rather than on that of a single line. But otherwise Wimsatt would be perfectly willing to call metrics a branch of linguistics, understanding always that there must be an aesthetic account as well.

A final comment was that Wimsatt's analysis of Chaucer's meter, though convincing, seemed ahistoric. The only historic notions were that of iambus and pentameter. Chaucer's metrical system must have been a mixture of these notions with others drawn from medieval liturgical music, and from metrical symbolism. Therefore, couldn't one question the whole attempt to define his meter in conventional terms like "the iambic pentameter"? What about introducing the notion called *offbeat* (*Auftakt*) in music? On that basis, the verse could be seen not as iambic but as trochaic, and the line as nine- rather than ten-syllabled. This would fit metrical symbolism better (e.g. the nine Muses). It would also explain why the first syllable cannot have a main stress—it is the offbeat and outside the meter —and it would account for the peculiarity in classical metrics that the last syllable is optional. Couldn't this have been what Chaucer had in mind? Wimsatt said that he had never accepted musical theories of meter (as argued in America, for example, by Northrop Frye and D. W. Prall). Chaucer may have been influenced by music and metrical symbolism, but what he produced is quite different. If we look at undeniably iambic pentameter verse like that of Shakespeare we see that the rising movement of the verse would be destroyed by throwing away the first syllable. If Chaucer thought he was writing nine-syllabled trochaic verse, the actual product certainly gives little evidence of it, nor is there any evidence in the verse of Chaucer's metrical followers like the Scottish Chaucerians, the poets in Tottel's *Miscellany*, and Spenser. Like Halle and Keyser, Wimsatt was simply trying to describe what was there; Halle and Keyser are quite historical: they have a long section in which they expound the rules for stress in Middle English in terms of both the Romance and native backgrounds, and he accepted the accuracy of that analysis.

# THE TEXTUAL FUNCTION OF
# THE FRENCH ARTICLE

### HARALD WEINRICH

TRADITIONAL LINGUISTICS divided its tasks somewhat as follows: phonetics (or phonology) considered sounds (or phonemes); morphology considered morphemes; semantics, words; and syntax, clauses and sentences. As for texts, there was stylistics, but that was considered by real linguists to be a marginal discipline, a bit *fuori le mura* of linguistics. This distribution of competences reflects the notion of a science built out of small units which pass gradually into larger units, finding its limit at the level of sentence—the Hercules columns of linguistics.

For some time, however, there have been voices questioning the cogency of this view. Manifestly, elements cannot be considered simply as "given." On the contrary, the linguist has to gather them by a process of segmentation and analysis. But what are his preliminary "givens"? If nothing is given, he must necessarily start from speculative principles, and surely he will find it difficult ever to get beyond speculation. But certainly he can permit himself *one* donnée as a basis for concrete research, namely the text, either oral or written, exchanged between speaker and listener (or author and reader) in the communicational act. All linguistics—even the generative-transformational version—is obliged to start from texts which it first segments into higher and then into lower units. The "elements" do not find their proper place at the beginning but at the end of the analysis, always allowing for the possibility of reversing the process, that is starting from the elements obtained and proceeding synthetically and "generatively" to the text. If Descartes was right in considering analysis and synthesis as two aspects of the same method, texts must be the alpha and omega of the linguistic method.[1]

Consequently, linguistics is necessarily textual. Syntax, thus, should be conceived of as textual or macro-syntax. That means that there is no reason

221

to stop syntactic research at the magic border of the sentence. Units higher than the sentence are as much syntactic as those lower, the former even having a certain methodological priority because they are obtained earlier in the segmentation process. Thus texts—from a fragmentary bit of dialogue up to the well-formed tissue of a novel—belong by formal constitution to textual syntax.

We shall try to show, in an analysis of the articles in French, that the functions of this class of morphemes can only be understood in the perspective of the whole text. But first some remarks about the paradigmatic aspect of the article. Traditional grammar distinguished between definite (*le, la, les*), and indefinite (*un, une, des*) and partitive articles (*du, de la, des*). In this series, the double occurrence of *des* in indefinite and partitive classes raises a question of morphological homonymy. Without stopping to consider it in detail,[2] I propose simply that we eliminate the problem by avoiding the notion of partitives. There remain only two classes: the definite and indefinite. The form *des* is considered only as plural of the indefinite article. But what becomes of the singular partitives *du* and *de la?* We shall cite the principle of neutralization, dear to first-generation structuralists and transposed from phonology to morphology and syntax by André Martinet and others. There is nothing odd about applying the notion of neutralization to the articles. In the plural (*les, des*), there is evidently neutralization of the opposition observed in the singular between feminine and masculine. Similarly, the opposition between singular and plural can be neutralized in the article system. In effect the indefinite (but not the definite) article admits a neutralization of the opposition between singular and plural in the archimorpheme *du, de la*.

Finally, since there is neutralization of the oppositions masculine/feminine and (at least partially) singular/plural, one may ask whether there is not also neutralization of the remaining opposition, namely definite/indefinite. Indeed, this neutralization is already accounted for, since zero article has such a function. To clarify these distinctions, here is a graphic representation of the morphological system of the French article:

Let us now concentrate on the function of the opposition between definite and indefinite articles, including the partitive article in the sense discussed above. First of all, there are grave arguments against formulating the function of the articles in terms of logical or quasi-logical explanations. According to one such explanation, dear to grammarians, the definite article serves to indicate the genus ("l'homme est mortel," "man is mortal"), while the indefinite article indicates the species or individual ("un homme qui aime à rire," "a man who likes to laugh," "on cherche un homme de confiance," "we are looking for a reliable man"). These reservations are ones of method. It is important not to confuse semantics and syntax. Isolated lexical units usually indicate the generic, while lexical units, surrounded and determined more or less by context, tend, with a precision controllable by the speakers, to indicate the specific and individual. This process is semantic, as I understand the term, that is, textually semantic. Articles are not at issue here. The function of articles must be explained by syntax and not by semantics. Nevertheless, we get the impression that observations about genus, species, and individual are not entirely irrelevant to a discussion of the function of articles. Thus we must look for a syntactic explanation of the function of articles capable at the same time of explaining certain consequences of usage that prompt us to seek logical reasons.

What is a text? Among many possible definitions I choose here the simplest: a text is an ordered sequence of morphemes, the absolute lower limit being two, while the upper limit is open. A text, then, can be considered, in the definition of several linguistic schools, as a mixture, a rather regular alternation of lexical and functional morphemes.[3] Since each morpheme possesses its own meaning, all morphemes provide context for each other, and their semantic values are mutually determined. If we consider a text of several hundred morphemes and if we take the principle of mutual determination by context seriously, we arrive at a very complex network of determinants. What listener or reader could make such a message out? Indeed he could not make it out if the language had not provided, in the utterance of each message, certain indexes and signals which can be considered as sign-posts of the discourse. These elements are *deictic*, in the famous term of the Greek grammarian Apollonius Dyscolus (Second Century A.D.), taken up again in the important *Sprachtheorie* of Karl Bühler.[4] In this conception, there is a rigorous distinction between the denotative function, which connects linguistic signs to the world of objects, and the deictic or demonstrative function which establishes the relations of signs to each other and to interlocutors present in the act of communication. According to this theory, it is the various pronouns which are above all deictic—personal, demonstrative, possessive—but also certain adverbs, especially locatives, as well as verbal tenses and articles. Bühler was a psychologist; he wanted, through such elements, to anchor linguistic signs in human perception. Anchoring linguistic signs to each other was a secondary matter

to him, which he called "anaphoric deixis." With all due respect to Bühler's capacities as a linguist, we must recognize that textual linguistics
hardly shares the priorities of psychology, and it considers all deictic functions as equivalent. There is even reason methodically to favor anaphoric—
that is to say intratextual—deixis as opposed to deixis between language
and the outside world, because a text, which is a sequence of rather homogeneous signs, lends itself more easily to analysis than any life situation,
which is necessarily complex because composed of both signs and non-signs.

The following text is taken from the short story by Albert Camus called
"La Pierre qui pousse" ("The Growing Stone"). The scene is Brazil, and
the characters are d'Arrast, a recently-arrived French engineer, and Socrate,
a native who is his guide. There is a considerable failure of communication
between the well-informed Socrate and the badly-informed d'Arrast about
the nature of the place. The dialogue serves to lessen this gap. (I put the indefinite articles in italics.)

D'Arrast cherchait Socrate au milieu de la foule quand il le reçut
dans son dos.

"C'est la fête," dit Socrate en riant, et il s'appuyait sur les hautes
épaules de d'Arrast pour sauter sur place.

"Quelle fête?"

"Eh!" s'étonna Socrate qui faisait face maintenant à d'Arrast, "tu
connais pas? La fête du bon Jésus. Chaque l'année,[5] tous viennent à
la grotte avec le marteau." Socrate montrait non pas *une* grotte, mais
*un* groupe qui semblait attendre dans *un* coin du jardin.

10    "Tu vois! *Un* jour, la bonne statue de Jésus, elle est arrivée de la
mer, en remontant le fleuve. *Des* pêcheurs l'a trouvée. Que belle! Que
belle! Alors, ils l'a lavée ici dans la grotte. Et maintenant *une* pierre
a poussé dans la grotte. Chaque année, c'est la fête. Avec le marteau,
tu casses, tu casses *des* morceaux pour le bonheur béni. Et puis quoi,
elle pousse toujours, toujours tu casses. C'est le miracle."

Ils étaient arrivés à la grotte dont on apercevait l'entrée basse par-
dessus les hommes qui attendaient. À l'intérieur, dans l'ombre piquée
par *des* flammes tremblantes de bougies, *une* forme accroupie cognait
en ce moment avec un marteau. L'homme, *un* gaucho maigre aux

20    longues moustaches, se releva et sortit, tenant dans sa paume offerte
à tous *un* petit morceau de schiste humide sur lequel, au bout de
quelques secondes, et avant de s'éloigner, il referma la main avec pré-
caution. *Un* autre homme alors entra dans la grotte en se baissant.

D'Arrast se retourna. Autour de lui, les pèlerins attendaient, sans le
regarder, impassibles sous l'eau qui descendait des arbres en voiles fins.
Lui aussi attendait, devant cette grotte, sous la même brume d'eau,
et il ne savait quoi. Il ne cessait d'attendre, en vérité, depuis *un* mois
qu'il était arrivé dans ce pays. Il attendait, dans la chaleur rouge des

jours humides, sous les étoiles menues de la nuit, malgré les tâches
30  qui étaient les siennes, les digues à bâtir, les routes à ouvrir, comme si
le travail qu'il était venu faire ici n'était qu'*un* prétexte, l'occasion
d'*une* surprise, ou d'*une* rencontre qu'il n'imaginait même pas, mais
qui l'aurait attendu, patiemment, au bout du monde.

Il se secoua, s'éloigna sans que personne, dans le petit groupe, fît
attention à lui, et se dirigea vers la sortie. Il fallait retourner au fleuve
et travailler.[6]

Considering the indefinite articles, they are seventeen in number if we include the *un* in the expression *depuis un mois* ("for a month," l. 29) which
should not be assumed too early to be a numeral adjective. The definite
articles in the passage (not italicized) number forty-three. In other texts (for
example in this paper I am presenting), the number of definite articles is
considerably greater. One can say generally that the number of the definite
articles in any text is a multiple of the number of the indefinite. One could
not simply change the definite into indefinite articles in this or any other
text. That would destroy the text, not only because of the numerical difference but also because of the position of the articles in the text. Neither
of the classes of articles obeys the law of random distribution. On the contrary, one discovers clusters of definite and indefinite in certain positions in
the text. In our passage, for example, definites are found concentrated in
Socrate's speech (ll. 3-8), when he speaks of what he knows naïvely, without being troubled by d'Arrast's incomprehension, and also later in the
thoughts of d'Arrast (ll. 24-34) when he speaks to himself with as much
information as he could expect to get from Socrate. On the other hand, indefinites are found massed together when Socrate takes account of the communication gap between himself and the newcomer (ll. 10-15), and later
when it is the narrator's turn to describe the new situation to the reader
(ll. 16-23). Finally, we must note a nest of indefinites in the middle of the
engineer's interior monologue (ll. 32-33), combined with the words *surprise*
("surprise") and *rencontre* ("meet"), which mark semantically his own
paucity of information.

Before proceeding, we must reflect for a moment about the kind of observation we are making. Is this an *explication de texte*? In other words, is
it the literary intention of Albert Camus which has distributed the articles
in this way? I think not. We have not up till now crossed over into literary
interpretation, because the only aspect of the text which we have considered has been the passage of information between Socrate and d'Arrast and
thus between the narrator and the reader. By considering distribution alone,
we have found a certain relationship between the articles and different
groupings in the exchange of information between the characters. These

considerations are, again, of a linguistic order in the sense of a textual or macro-syntax.

To validate this observation, let us look briefly at a very different text, namely the story "Le Petit Chaperon rouge" ("Little Red Riding-Hood") of Perrault.[7] In this story, the number of indefinite articles rises to twenty-three, that of definite articles to fifty-two. The numeric relation thus corresponds somewhat to that of the text from Camus. If I quote only the nouns preceded by indefinite articles (in English equivalents: *a*, sing., and zero, plur.) in this universally known story (without counting formulary repetitions), I will have presented practically the entire narrative substance: "(once upon) a time," "a little girl," "a little red riding hood," "a day," "cakes," "another village," "a forest," "a wolf," "a small dish of butter," "hazel-nuts," "butterflies," "a bunch of flowers," "big arms," "big legs," "big ears," "big eyes," "big teeth." All the decisive elements are present in this series except the grandmother, who is always referred to by the possessive adjective, that is, in her familial relationship to Little Red Riding-Hood.

We may draw the following conclusions: the distribution of articles in a text is an important aspect of its semiological structure. The articles are signals which help the listener or reader comprehend the signs of the text and their interdependence. And since there are two classes of articles, there is a binary opposition between their functions, with, of course, the possibility of neutralization. Further, since the dimension of a text is always linear, there are two main directions in which the attention of the listener/reader may be directed, namely backward, that is, "pre-informatively" (anaphorically) or forwards, that is, "post-informatively" (cataphorically). But pre-information or post-information in respect to what? To answer I must introduce a new term. The article in French is always pre-positional, occurring before some other sign, normally before a noun. One can even say that the article makes the noun, that is, that it confers upon whatever sign it precedes the value of noun. Thus we may introduce the term "articulate" to designate a sign or group of signs in relation to a preceding article. The articulate can thus be a substantive (*la vache*, "the cow"), a substantive with an adjective (*la jolie vache*, "the lovely cow"), a substantive with a relative clause or present participial phrase (*la vache qui rit*, "the laughing cow") and other syntagmas. This articulate is the reference-point in respect to which the definite article directs the audience's attention toward pre-information and the indefinite article toward post-information, because, like every other sign in the spoken or written chain of the text, not only does it bear its own meaning, but it is connected to all the other signs, preceding and following, which determine and modify its meaning according to a compatibility principle. The definite article is a signal that the listener/reader must search the anterior text to determine the articulate, and that information about the sign already presented continues to hold true. His attention can thus pass rapidly over the sign and concentrate on other segments of the text. The indefinite article, on the other hand, requires his *continuing* attention, since, in order to understand the articulate exactly, he cannot trust to information already obtained in the preceding text, but must await some new determination in the text to follow.

Thus it is usual for the indefinite article to occur at decisive points in texts at which the recital of information takes a new and unexpected direction. In "Little Red Riding-Hood," the indefinite article is attributed to the little heroine only on her first appearance on the scene ("a little girl of the village"); after the reader has been informed about her, she is always referred to by the definite article ("the little red riding-hood," "the poor girl," "the little girl"). Similarly, in "La Pierre qui pousse," the indefinite article is introduced at the point in the story in which this mysterious stone is first mentioned: "Et maintenant, *une* pierre a poussé dans la grotte." In the same passage, Camus illustrates what happens when a speaker misleads his listener by making an article a false signal. D'Arrast comes upon a native celebration. Not understanding it, he awaits Socrate's explanation. Here is the passage in question:

> —C'est la fête, dit Socrate en riant, et il s'appuyait sur les hautes épaules de d'Arrast pour sauter sur place.
> —Eh! s'étonna Socrate qui faisait face maintenant à d'Arrast, tu connais pas?

For Socrate, who believes naïvely that everybody knows what he knows, the pre-information is absolutely sufficient. His answer is "C'est la fête." D'Arrast does not of course possess the requisite information. To understand the articulate *fête*, he needs supplementary information, which can only be posterior since it is not anterior. He has the right to expect an indefinite article. But since Socrate, totally absorbed in the spectacle and unconscious of his interlocutor's need for information, does not use the indefinite, d'Arrast protests. The form of protest is a question, "Quelle fête?" The interrogative clause generally has the function of sorting out the flow of information between two or more interlocutors. The one who poses the question declares himself insufficiently informed and asks for more information from the other. In this case, since the definite article (*la fête*) had falsely signalled a pre-information, the recipient of the message requests that information and thus obliges his interlocutor to complete the message by a post-information. Which Socrate does in establishing himself as a narrator: "Tu vois! *Un* jour . . ." (ll. 10-15). In his narration there are several indefinites which are later taken up and augmented by the description of the grotto, thus d'Arrast and with him the reader) finally acquires sufficient information about the growing stone. This gives him his first opportunity to look back over the things he has seen, or, to put it in semiological terms, over the bits of information he has obtained. This perspective of course requires a concentration of definite articles (ll. 24-33).

It may be interesting to measure how much of this is due to the author and how much to the language. Clearly Camus could have chosen other characters and other levels of information for his characters. He could have confronted them with another situation, and he could have otherwise arranged the movement of the dialogue and the interventions of the narrator. What he has done represents the series of choices he has made in creating this story. These choices constitute his literary creation. But in making them rather than others, he must observe certain linguistic conditions which attach inevitably to such choices. He may choose the direction, but the language imposes the road he must follow.

It was not completely accurate to say that the first mention of the growing stone occurs in the passage we have quoted. For the stone is actually first mentioned in the title, which of course the reader reads at the very outset. But the first reference to the stone in the text is by the indefinite article, while that in the title is by the definite. The story is entitled "La Pierre qui pousse." The definite is normal form for titles in French, whatever the genre. The collection of short stories to which ours belongs is *L'Exil et le royaume* (*Exile and the Kingdom*), and the stories it contains are entitled (not counting the present story and one with the proper name "Jonas" as title): "La Femme adultère" ("The Adulterous Woman"), "Le Renégat" ("The Renegade"), "Les Muets" ("The Silent Men") and "L'Hôte" ("The Guest"). For proof that the definite article is used in the great majority of titles, one need only consult any dictionary of literature or inspect the contents of the display-window of a book-store. But why is it so popular? The definite article, we have said, directs the attention of the auditor/reader to pre-information. Now the title on the cover of a book or at the top of a poem refers to no pre-information. It is itself the pre-information upon which we rather frequently decide whether or not to read or to buy the book which it introduces. That is certainly clear. But why does the title arrest our attention? How does it lure us into reading the rest? Because titles do have this power. Corneille recognized it when he said that authors must choose titles for their works which "excite the curiosity of their audience." The play in the preface of which these words appear in called *La Galerie du palais*. What palace? What gallery? The reader of this title, unless he is well-read in literary history, can know nothing about it, and as his curiosity is stimulated (as the author more or less cunningly planned), he is tempted to go to see the play. There he learns the answer. The German poet Helmut Heissenbüttel bears witness to the same phenomenon when he says in a certain poem "Büchertitel sind magisch" ("Book-titles are magical").[8]

Far from weakening the present thesis, the frequency of definite articles in titles serves to strengthen it. These titles containing definite articles *are* magical, or to put it more soberly, *suggestive*, because they refer the passer-by (it is really for him that they are made) to a pre-information which he does not effectively possess. That is what irritates him, makes him pause a moment. The title presupposes certain pre-information which (presumably) he alone does not possess. It provokes a sudden sense of lack compared to the level of knowledge which he assumes to be possessed by others; and thus, if the author's scheme bears fruit, he is transformed into a reader and purchaser of the book. The reading of the book then gives him all the information he needs to understand its title perfectly and to relieve the semiological irritation which he has experienced from his first sight of the title.

Textual linguistics does not need to consider the world as if it were a text. Only methodology confers a priority to the function of articles in a text. But sometimes a linguistic sign or group of signs is not embedded within a context of other linguistic signs but only within a non-linguistic situation, for example, in the case of someone who exclaims, with Molière's misanthrope, in presence of a rather unprepossessing character: "L'ami du genre humain n'est pas du tout mon fait" (*Misanthrope*, I, 1). But this does not present any special problems. The equivalence and interconvertibility of linguistic context and non-linguistic situation figures among the principles of linguistics, such that one can call the situation which encompasses a syntagma its "situational context." So situational context provides determinants of a syntagma just as linguistic context does. If this were not true, it would not be possible to learn a language except through another language. Now the use of articles does not depend on whether presupposed information is textual or situational. Thus the definite article is possible even without any preceding linguistic context, provided that there exists some situation from which the audience can draw the pre-information necessary to understanding the articulate.

Finally, there is the case of the syntagma which is totally isolated, that is, encompassed only by a metalinguistic context. This requires a supplementary formulation which, hopefully, can integrate traditional logic with textual linguistics. I take as an example a proposition of the sort dear to logicians such as "L'homme est mortel" ("Man is mortal"). No context except the metalinguistic is visible. Further there is no extra-linguistic situation to provide determinants. Thus there is a total absence of pre-information. Why then the definite article in French, since there is no contextual or situational pre-information to send the hearer/reader back to? Even though these two kinds of pre-information are absent, there is a third to which the definite article can refer. Because, for a communication between two speakers to take place, they must at least share the language-code. In the absence of context or situation, the function of the definite article is to point to that code. It signals that the articulate, in this case "man," must be taken in the sense it has in the language, that is to say, as a non-determinate lexical unit. Thus it stands for man in the generic sense, as a representative of the human species. Textual linguistics thus confirms the generic import of the definite article of which logicians speak, but with an important restriction. This generic value only holds when the expression is isolated, generally in a metalinguistic context. Isolation provides the limiting case, the zero context. Linguistics need not give up in the face of a limiting case, but it cannot analyze a limiting case unless it recognizes it as such.

The textual analysis of the articles in terms of an informational dimension lends itself to some specification of the syntactic typology of their use. I shall give only a schematic sketch of these in the form of analytical rules:

1) *The articulation rule* (already mentioned) states that the reference to pre- or post-information contained in the article holds for the whole articulate. The articulate can even include a relative clause, thus permitting a lengthening of the sentence. An example in the text from Camus: "les tâches qui étaient les siennes" (l. 30). Here the first definite article has as articulate the whole expression "tâches qui étaient les siennes" with, inside, a "subarticulate" preceded by a second definite article, composed only of "siennes."

2) *The framework rule* states that the framework-term is to be considered as pre-information of the components of its content. This rule is observed above all in descriptions. If a house is mentioned in a description, the components implicit in the content of the framework-term, that is, the normal inventory of things in and of a house, are introduced by the definite article. Unpredictable components, however—above all extraordinary ones which are not infrequently introduced in narrations—require the indefinite article. For example, the series "une grotte" (l. 8), "l'entrée" (l. 16), "l'intérieur" (l. 17), "l'ombre" (l. 17); but "des flammes" (l. 18), "une forme accroupie" (l. 18).

3) *The genitive* rule is a modification of the framework rule and prescribes a partial inversion of it. Theoretically, that is to say, according to the symmetry of the system, four types of combinations can be conceived: a) "la porte de la maison" ("the door of the house"), b) "une porte d'une maison" ("a door of a house"), c) "la porte d'une maison ("the door of a house"), and d) "une porte de la maison" ("a door of the house"). The first type may be fitted without difficulty into the theory so far developed. The second type almost never occurs in texts, so we needn't trouble with it.

As for types c) and d), we must set up a rule of inversion which states that in genitive constructions, there are two articulates—the first covering only the first term, the second covering the entire construction. The first article thus holds only for the "subarticulate," the second for the main articulate. Example: in "dans un coin du jardin" ("in a corner of the garden," l. 9), the entire articulate is related to pre-information; in "l'occasion d'une surprise" ("the occasion of a surprise," l. 32), the entire articulate is related to post-information. In both cases, the component precedes the framework.

4) *The explanation rule* distinguishes between the term to be explained and the one doing the explaining. The term to be explained is inserted in a line of reasoning and develops the pre-information contained therein. Thus it is normally accompanied by the definite article. The explanation, on the other hand, which often takes the form of a predication, introduces new information and requires the indefinite article: for example, "l'homme, un gaucho maigre" ("the man, a thin gaucho," l. 19). The term *homme* is inserted in a framework which has already been established, while *gaucho* introduces new information.

5) *The numeral rule* serves to integrate numeral adjectives into the theory of articles. According to this rule, it is necessary to distinguish between two series of (cardinal) numerals: the series "(un), deux, trois, quatre . . ." and the series "(le), les deux, les trois, les quatres . . ." The elements in the first series need to be analyzed as indefinite since they refer to post-information, while those in the second behave like definite articles, focussing the reader's attention on pre-information. For example, "depuis un mois qu'il était arrivé" (l. 27). The function of this kind of numeral is not clearly distinguished from that of an indefinite article.

The article offers a certain stylistic amplitude to the writer. Let me illustrate this notion with some examples from La Fontaine. It is well known that the fable is distinguished clearly from other kinds of narration, for example the short story, by the fact that it prefers to portray characters as classes rather than individuals. "Le Chêne un jour dit au Roseau . . ." ("the oak said one day to the reed . . .")—these, of course, are the species oak and reed in the universal sense of these words, as parts of Nature's System. There is no question of some particular oak or reed. Thus the reader is referred by the definite article to his lexical and cultural knowledge of oaks and reeds. These are typical oaks and reeds—the one is large and strong, the other small and weak. We only need that information, and no more. Everything else is left to be unfolded in the fable which, in the course of the narration, may include indefinite articles. Certain fables may even begin with indefinite articles, as "Une Grenouille vit un Boeuf" ("A frog saw an ox"), because in the narration these species of animals behave as if they were individuals. But careful definition is essential. Certain lexical pre-information is available to us about this species of animal, and in most of La Fontaine's fables, the wolf behaves as wolves are supposed to in lexical convention. He is a dangerous animal who devours whatever he finds—that expresses in a phrase the lexical and cultural substance of the word "wolf." But there is a fable by La Fontaine (X, 5) which begins:

> Un loup rempli d'humanité
> (S'il en est de tels dans le monde)
> Fit un jour . . .

("A wolf filled with humanity (if there is such a thing in the world) did one day . . ."). The language provides no pre-information about this exceptional, astonishingly individual wolf. The indefinite article here tells the reader that he must expect some surprising post-information. Similarly in another fable (III, 18) entitled "Le Chat et un vieux Rat" ("The Cat and an Old Rat"), the title itself suggests a certain distinction to the reader. The articles tell him that the cat will probably behave according to a conduct considered by the language to be typical of cats, while the rat will probably be different from other rats we "know." In effect, the rat is "experimental," not to be defined simply by his membership in the class of rats. It is not strange that he finally escapes from the cat.

Let us stop here. All the problems attaching to the syntax of the article in French have not been taken up in this analysis, and those taken up have certainly not been completely resolved. I could do no more than mention the import of neutralization, manifested in the zero article, of the two opposing classes of articles, which leaves suspended the articulate (the substantive not preceded by an article) between the poles of pre- and post-information. I have not discussed at all the demonstrative, possessive, and other pronouns, which need to be attached to the article-system because they are charged with particular signalling functions within the framework of the opposition between pre- and post-information. Nor have I developed very well the stylistic typology of the use of the articles made by writers. I have only tried to pursue certain lines of investigation by making a strict application of textual linguistics to a limited problem. These methods, to summarize their basis in a word, never admit the isolation of a linguistic phenomenon as something naturally given. In the area of linguistic observation, it is essential to anchor a phenomenon in a context—whether situational, linguistic, or metalinguistic. Isolation, in the rare examples we have noted, always produces a borderline case for research. The explanation of phenomena cannot be founded on such borderline cases but only on the normal textual occurrence. But, of course, textual linguistics is sufficiently powerful to explain the normal phenomenon as well as its borderline cases.

Thus, for the article in French, organized as it is into two classes with several possibilities of neutralization, normal usage is to be found in oral and written texts, wherein the articulate is determined both by preceding and by following context. The definite article has the function of directing attention to pre-information, while the indefinite article directs it to post-information. Pre-information and post-information can be of three types: linguistic context, situational context, and the code of the language. Thus we have come to a very simple conclusion. That does not sadden me. The syntax of languages is necessarily simple. For the complexities there are still semantics and stylistics.

## NOTES

1. "Tota methodus consistit in ordine et dispositione eorum ad quae mentis acies est convertenda, ut aliquam veritatem inveniamus. Atque hanc exacte servabimus, si propositiones involutas et obscuras ad simpliciores gradatim reducamus, et deinde ex omnium simplicissimarum intuitu ad aliarum omnium cognitionem per eosdem gradus ascendere tentemus." (*Œuvres de Descartes*, ed. C. Adam and P. Taunery, X, p. 379).

2. A treatment of the problem can be found in my article "In Abrede gestellt: Der Teilungsartikel in der französischen Sprache," in *Philologische Studien für Joseph M. Piel* (Heidelberg, 1969), pp. 218-23.

3. *Lexèmes* and *morphèmes* in the French terminology of André Martinet, with *monème* as a framework-term.

4. Karl Bühler, *Sprachtheorie. Die Darstellungsfunktion der Sprache* (Jena, 1934; Stuttgart, 1965, second edition). Cf. E. Egger, *Apollonius Dyscole—Essai sur l'histoire des théories grammaticales dans l'antiquité* (Paris, 1854).

5. The native guide speaks a faulty French.

6. D'Arrast was looking for Socrate in the crowd when Socrate suddenly bumped him from behind.

"It's holiday," he said, laughing, and clung to D'Arrast's tall shoulders to jump up and down.

"What holiday?"

"Why, you not know?" Socrate said in surprise as he faced D'Arrast. "The feast of good Jesus. Each year they all come to the grotto with a hammer."

Socrate pointed out, not a grotto, but a group that seemed to be waiting in a corner of the garden.

"You see? One day the good statue of Jesus, it came upstream from the sea. Some fishermen found it. How beautiful! How beautiful! Then they washed it here in the grotto. And now a stone grew up in the grotto. Every year it's the feast. With the hammer you break, you break off pieces for blessed happiness. And then it keeps growing and you keep breaking. It's the miracle!"

They had reached the grotto and could see its low entrance beyond the waiting men. Inside, in the darkness studded with the flickering flames of candles, a squatting figure was pounding with a hammer. The man, a thin gaucho with a long mustache, got up and came out holding in his open palm, so that all might see, a small piece of moist schist, over which he soon closed his hand carefully before going away. Another man then stooped down and entered the grotto.

D'Arrast turned around. On all sides pilgrims were waiting, without looking at him, impassive under the water dripping from the trees in thin sheets. He too was waiting in front of the grotto under the same film of water, and he didn't know for what. He had been waiting constantly, to tell the truth, for a month since he had arrived in this country. He had been waiting—in the red heat of humid days, under the little stars of night, despite the tasks to be accomplished, the jetties to be built, the roads to be cut through—as if the work he had come to do here were merely a pretext for a surprise or for an encounter he did not even imagine but which had been waiting patiently for him at the end of the world. He shook himself, walked away without anyone in the little group paying attention to him, and went toward the exit. He had to go back to the river and go to work. (Translated by Justin O'Brien.)

7. Perrault, "Le Petit Chaperon rouge," *Contes*, ed. G. Rouger (Paris, 1967).

8. "Kombination VIII," in *Kombinationen* (Esslingen, 1954).

# DISCUSSION OF WEINRICH'S PAPER

Weinrich was asked at the outset whether his system would work with texts of only a sentence in length, or even shorter, like proverbs. He answered that to account for such texts he preferred the concept of textual linguistics to that of intersentence (*transphrastique*) linguistics. The latter committed one to texts of at least two sentences, and Weinrich wanted to be able to start on a text without any such predetermination.

In connection with his analysis of the French articles, it was noted that English, like French, provides a third alternative, the zero article, as in "Man is mortal" as well as a use of the demonstrative in indefinite article function, a form particularly popular in jokes—"There were these two fellows and. . . ." Weinrich responded that the zero article could be accounted for under the concept of neutralization, just as the partitive in French is a neutralization of singular and plural in the indefinite article. And those are not the only neutralizations in the article systems of French and English. The zero article is the neutralization of the distinction between definite and indefinite, so that its use effects a suspension in the question of pre- vs. post-information. He felt that the use of the demonstrative article as an introductory element in jokes is related to the fact that jokes are often made about well-known types (by pre-information), for example, the stage Irishman or Scotsman, the pedant, the niggard, and so on. The problem was worth studying in relation to other linguistic constraints in the genre, for example, the obligatory use of the present tense.

In response to a question about languages like Rumanian that contain many more than two articles, Weinrich expressed regret that he did not know enough about them to comment.

With reference to the text from Camus, a participant spoke of the heavy concentration of indefinite articles in lines 8-23 and suggested that perhaps this was in compensation for the lack of information at the very beginning. He also asked whether the use of the definite article in the first, unexplained reference to "la fête" was an instance of a reliance on situational information. Weinrich answered that he understood "situational information" only to refer to anything that was non- or extra-linguistic, for example, the case of a man running into the street and shouting "Police!" It was also pointed out that there appeared to be a curious progression of articles with *grotte:* "la grotte" is first in Socrate's speech (l. 8), then "une grotte" in that of the narrator (l. 8); Weinrich said that the word had been used in the story before his extract and that therefore this initial use of the definite article was justified. A similar phenomenon was said to occur in connection with the articles used with *groupe,* that is "un groupe" (l. 9), but "les hommes" (l. 17) "un gaucho" (l. 19) and "un autre homme" (l. 23). Weinrich agreed, but noted that *groupe* was the framework-term in this text.

Was it not true, another participant asked, that the linguistic code made most of these choices obligatory, that once Camus had made his semantic choice, for example, about whether or not the reader should understand a reference, his decision to use the definite or indefinite article was constrained and automatic? Weinrich answered that most choices are obligatory in that sense. Though it is axiomatic in linguistics that the speaker can make a choice, the choice is invariably restricted by previous choices, and "preceding choices" is precisely an alternative term for "pre-information." The pre-information predetermines the choices.

Weinrich was asked whether the particular choice of article in the speech attributed to Socrate was not rather the result of the fact that he is not supposed to speak good French, that the reader cannot rely on normal cues for post- or pre-information here since the dialect confuses the situation. Weinrich admitted that the fact that Socrate spoke in dialect was a drawback, but he did not think that the usage of the article in these particular cases depended on the fact that some of the sentences in the text imitated Pidgin French. It was still Camus' French.

It was noted also that in the last three lines all the articles were definite, and it was suggested that this was because they were no longer concerned with Socrate or D'Arrast but with the reader. At the beginning there is the tantalizing unclarity of reference, then the compensation; then we become involved with the personal experience of D'Arrast, now that he has the maximum of information; but the last three lines are in a different framework entirely.

Weinrich's discussion in terms of pre- and post-information was said to invert what we ordinarily assume about the functions of the article, namely that the indefinite article is introductory or cataphoric and the definite anaphoric (right-oriented and left-oriented respectively). It was pointed out that the preposition often has the same function as the article in right-handed orientations, for example, in Spanish (*César venció a Pompeyo*). Weinrich agreed, but wondered why these should be called prepositions and not a particular form of the Spanish definite article, to be used with proper nouns.

Weinrich was asked whether the proximity in French of the two kinds of deixis (textual and referential) was not primarily morphological. It was argued that the two are really quite different things and that one cannot be taken as the smaller or larger image of the other. There seemed to be a truly fundamental semantic difference between them, precisely to the extent that referential deixis joins all linguistic elements which contain an obligatory reference or context, one that is coded in some way. Textual deixis (ana- or cataphoric) has its own specificity, which is completely different. One does not have to go any farther than changing the emphases of Karl Bühler to dissociate these two completely. Weinrich disagreed, arguing the necessity of remaining rigorously linguistic-textual as long as possible, for otherwise certain difficulties will force us to give up any pretense to rigorous method.

There followed an extensive description of the treatment of articles in contemporary British linguistics. It was argued that any account of the definite article that requires the reader to recover pre-information anaphorically in the text or in the situation or in the *code* of the language needs to be recast. Of course, the definite article does demand some kind of recovery: that is what is meant by calling it "definite"; it is a signal that information is available about the particular class to which the noun belongs. In all the other deictic elements, the information is contained in the element itself: *his*, for example, is also definite and additionally contains identificational information within itself. In *the*, the information may be in the preceding text but it may also be in the situation (in that sense British linguistics calls it "exophoric"). And it may also be *cataphoric*—that is, it may look ahead for its reference. The latter has sometimes been taken as a kind of anaphora, but consider some examples: "le code de la langue" or "la vache qui rit" ("the code of the language," "the laughing cow") : what is the function of the definite article? It seems to be to signal that the necessary information is to be sought in the rest of the nominal phrase beyond the head. "La vache qui rit" is *la . . . qui rit + vache*—that is, the definite article is cataphoric, pointing to modifying elements in the noun phrase itself to explain its reference. This is a structural relation, not post-information in the textual sense, as one says, for example, "Now the problem is this," and then goes on to explain the reference of "this." Thus, some instances that have in the past been explained by reference to the code of the language or general knowledge of the world are in fact cataphoric. There is additionally a *homophoric* use of the definite article which does relate to the code of the language or shared general experience; an example is "the moon"—we all know that there is only one moon. But many of the literary uses of the article, in titles for example, are really cataphoric. The participant said that he had done some counting of these four kinds of definite article in texts and had found that the cataphoric use was very much the most frequent. It was further observed that the various "-phoric" functions differ according to the nature of the text. In a monologue, for example, where there is no two-way communication going on, it is likely that the definite article is anaphoric and the indefinite cataphoric. In the Camus text, there seems to be a shift of focus correlated with the shift in the use of the article; at one time the speaker is A, at another B, and at a third, a mélange of the narrator and a character. Within the story, both their views may be expressed in the same sentence, as very often occurs in English fiction like that of Jane Austen, George Eliot, etc. Weinrich replied that French and English were perhaps different in their uses of the articles, and that he had said nothing about the English articles. He felt that if in English, like French, the definite article relied chiefly on pre-information and the indefinite on post-information, it would be counter to the principle of syntactic simplicity to accept a cataphoric explanation of some instances of the definite article, and that we should look for an analysis without strong exceptions like these. As for the possessive pronoun, Weinrich was not sure that it was correct to say that it contained the requisite information within itself; it too seems to go to pre-information, but in a special way, with a special restriction, namely that the possessive looks for (grammatical) persons only. He agreed that the functions of the article differ according to the nature of the text, but he argued that we must respect the restriction of simplicity in syntactic description, reserving the treatment of nuances for semantics and stylistics. It is a function of syntax to provide a rough pre-selection of possible linguistic orientation, and it is on the basis of this rough pre-selection that semantics and stylistics make their final selections.

There was some difference of opinion about the utility of the term "information." One participant said that he was always perplexed by its use; the term, of course, is a technical one in cybernetics, and its use in literary discussion is always metaphoric, but with the suggestion that it means something scientific and not metaphorical. But isn't it as intuitive as any other term? What precisely did Weinrich mean by it? How does one measure "information"? Weinrich acknowledged the danger, since the term does have so precise a meaning in terms of scientific measurement, and said that he was somewhat unhappy with it too. Perhaps it could be replaced by the term "determination." The important thing to remember, regardless of the term, is that semantics must always be textual, it must never study isolated words. And within the text, there is always the play of mutual determination.

Another participant, however, was quite content with the term "information" and praised Weinrich for having seen that the text can be defined as an informational system (*économie de l'information*). He felt that the concept of information provided the most elegant means of description that one could find (using the word "elegant" in the sense of an elegant mathematical solution). Narrative texts, for example, are based on the delay of information. A narrative is a system of information which is held back, which is, so to speak, run through a delaying circuitry. Its universally known procedure—suspense—is cruder than those which have been spoken of. The definite article in the title of a narrative has a dilatory value; it is like the holding back of the answer in a riddle. Thus it is the first sentences of a novel which provide the richest mine of information—analytical, not narrative, information. In the beginning of Ian Fleming's *Goldfinger*, for example, the first sentence is "The man approached." The article is cataphoric; it refers to information which will come afterwards, but one acts as if it were already given. Other forms can enter this pattern, for instance a proper name at the beginning of a novel, "Frédéric prit le bateau." In this example, Frédéric functions like the definite article; we are given the name as if we know who he is, but in fact we do not. This system of delayed information leads us to the paradoxical truth that literature or style is often constituted of counter- or para-information. Literature is not always communicative in the pure sense. On the contrary, it contains that kind of communication which has been sometimes called *cacographie*, that is, information containing a decided element of "noise" (in the cybernetic sense). If it did not, we would have a kind of pure mathematics. Indeed, style might be defined as the art of noise. Weinrich agreed about the importance of the first sentences of novels, and noted that there exists in German an anthology of only the first sentences of novels.[1] Very often in novels the first paragraph will be full of definite articles, but the second—where the real exposition begins—will contain many indefinite articles. But he would not call this use of the definite article cataphoric; one must recognize the existence of a false or misleading anaphoric function. He noted that especially in the nineteenth-century novel the convention was that the proper name signified the optimum of information; once it was given, there was a kind of closure of exposition, the character taken to be known, even when he really was not.

There was some discussion about the use of articles in titles. In response to a question about the function of the definite article in "La Pierre qui pousse," Weinrich answered that it referred back to the code of the language, just as it did in other environments, but that the code of the language did not sufficiently explain the title so that it awakened the expectation in the reader.

Another participant suggested that the reason that definite articles were more frequent in titles was that they were *generic* as well as definite (compared to the indefinite which had only one function). A less obvious reason is that the definite article is often used in an ambiguous function where the opposition between generic and definite is suspended (this is always the case in titles), and that opens up a good many possibilities for the author to exploit. He can keep that suspension throughout the work, at least if it is a short poem, or he can resolve it one way or another. There is a poem by Yeats called "The Lover's Song," which is ambiguous in this way:

> Bird sighs for the air
> Thought for I know not where
> For the womb the seed sighs . . .

What he is able to get out of the unmarked "bird" is possible only because of the ambiguity of the title. Weinrich commented that the definite article in titles may afford the author the opportunity of suspense, but that such suspense was not only that deriving from the suspension of the contrast between generic and definite. There are several other possibilities.

Weinrich was asked if it weren't true that the title of the play by Corneille, *La Galerie du palais*, is a proper name and therefore that it would be impossible to say "Une Galerie du palais." But there seem to be many exceptions in which it is the indefinite article that appears: *Un Amour de Swann* (vs. *La Prisonnière*), Wilde's *An Ideal Husband*, Dickens' *A Christmas Carol*, etc. Perhaps there is the suggestion in the indefinite article that the noun referred to doesn't amount to much, reducing the whole affair to the anecdotal. Weinrich replied that though it was true that *La Galerie du palais* was for Corneille's time a proper name, there have been and will be spectators of Corneille's play who are not Frenchmen of the seventeenth century, and for them the title continues to work. As for exceptions like *Un Amour de Swann,* we can observe that an author is justified in giving up the suspense implicit in the definite any time he likes, and that the theory that the definite article is generic and the indefinite is individual is widespread, and that the author's use of the indefinite may reflect this popular (if inadequate) analysis.

More generally, it was observed that Weinrich's paper argued a classical principle of stylistics, namely that the meaning or effect of a stylistic feature (like the meaning of many linguistic features) can only be secured in context. In the speech of Socrate, the definite article is a mark of naïveté, whereas it is possible to sustain the thesis, as did G. Rostrevor Hamilton in his book *The Tell-Tale Article,* that the use of the definite article in modern English poetry possesses a snob or "in"-group appeal. When Auden, for example, speaks of "the cromlech," the implication of the definite article is that his reader—"a member of the club"—of course knows what a cromlech is, and that there is no need to belabor the point. (Another participant wondered whether we had to go quite so far as to speak of snob-appeal: was it not an ordinary evocation of the speech situation, the assumption that the speaker is making about the state of the audience's knowledge? Isn't it simply that the audience is being told what role they are to play? It doesn't matter whether they know what a cromlech is, so long as they know, from the definite article, that they are supposed to take the role of an audience that does know what it is.) Weinrich agreed that the use of a definite article might function as a signal for the existence of an "in"-group; for example, it was noteworthy that the papers of scientific "in"-groups contain a relatively greater number of definite articles than do other texts. And in internal monologue, too, the frequency of definite articles is considerably higher than elsewhere—precisely what one would expect in an "in"-group of one. It is also true that the article makes a kind of appeal to an audience, assigning it its role. The narrator of a novel is of course one of the persons in the novel, but so is the reader; a dialogue between narrator and reader takes place in the text, and one of the important elements in this dialogue is the article.

### NOTE

1. *Romananfänge: Versuch einer Poetik des Romans,* ed. by Norbert Miller (Berlin, 1965). Cf. Norbert Miller, *Der empfindsame Erzähler: Untersuchungen an Romananfängen des 18. Jahrhunderts* (Munich, 1968).

# SPEECH, ACTION, AND STYLE

### RICHARD OHMANN

IN BECKETT'S NOVEL *Watt* there is a large and indigent family, the Lynch family, whose charge it is to see that when Watt's employer rejects a meal, an emaciated dog will appear and consume it. The narrator enumerates and describes this entire "fortunate family," from the patriarch, Tom, "confined to his bed with constant undiagnosed pains in the caecum," to three-year-old Larry, who is rickety, with arms and legs like sticks, and head and belly like two balloons. I quote part of the catalogue:

> And then to pass on to the next generation there was Tom's boy young Simon aged twenty, whose it is painful to relate
>
> ?
>
> and his young cousin wife his uncle Sam's girl Ann, aged nineteen, whose it will be learnt with regret beauty and utility were greatly diminished by two withered arms and a game leg of unsuspected tubercular origin, and Sam's two surviving boys Bill and Mat aged eighteen and seventeen respectively, who having come into this world respectively blind and maim were known as Blind Bill and Maim Mat respectively, and Sam's other married daughter Kate aged twenty-one years, a fine girl but a bleeder (1), and her young cousin husband her uncle Jack's son Sean aged twenty-one years, a sterling fellow but a bleeder too . . .[1]

To the announcement of Kate's malady, a footnote is appended:

> (1) Haemophilia is, like enlargement of the prostate, an exclusively male disorder. But not in this work.

I think most would agree that the style of this passage, as of the whole novel, is unusual. Several ways of talking about its distinctiveness are ready to hand.

241

The syntax is almost wholly given over to conjunction and to the relative clause and its transformational derivatives (including participial phrases and appositives). That is a stylistic fact in itself, one that may easily be amplified by setting it next to a fact of content: the sordid medical compilation here unraveled. The syntactic features have what Spitzer called a "common denominator"; they serve to itemize, label, describe—to accumulate information without sorting it, analyzing it, or reasoning about it. The neutrality of these forms lies strangely alongside the hair-raising content, which begs for syntactic acknowledgment. In speaking of syntax, one might also mark the obtrusive parallelism of structure, implying a decorum and orderliness in things which the content sharply denies.

Beckett's choices of diction, too, would bear comment: "regret," "beauty," "utility," "diminished," "unsuspected," "respectively" belong to a realm of discourse both ornamental and abstract, where periphrasis and euphemism are the favored modes of reference, where loathsome diseases or pathetic disability are concealed behind the pomp of "greatly diminished" "beauty and utility." Yet an entirely different sensibility reveals itself along with this one, through the choice of diction from another register: "a game leg," "Blind Bill," "Maim Mat," "a fine girl but a bleeder." In the world to which these terms belong, pain and ugliness are squarely, even stoically, perceived. And in general, the passage mixes styles, tones, and levels in a way that is disconcerting, if amusing. Not only does "it will be learnt with regret" sit uneasily next to "Blind Bill and Maim Mat," but there are hints of still other modes of speech, in, for instance, a phrase like "having come into this world," with its suggestion of a gossipy piety. As a consequence, it is difficult to fix the narrator, his values, or his social background. His language seems to flow from an unimaginable co-presence of feelings and perceptions, rather than from a coherent selfhood.

A stylistic commentary on the passage might also note a repeated semantic feature, the peculiar, childlike redundancy. We are given both "his young cousin" and "his uncle Sam's girl"; "respectively" three times where one would more than suffice; the unnecessary repetition of the names "Bill" and "Mat," as well as of their epithets; and the sacrifice of economy entailed by describing Sam and Kate separately, rather than as a couple ("Sam's daughter Kate and her husband, Jack's son Sean, both aged twenty-one and both bleeders"). This trait suggests a marked cognitive passivity, a reluctance to sift and combine, as well as a compulsive desire to bring every description to its logical completion.

Finally, one might run back over these same stylistic facts and weigh their likely impact on a reader, their apparent rhetorical intent. To do so would surely be to discover a baffling mixture of rhetorical inpulses and a dizzy sequence of implied emotional responses.

This sketch of a stylistic description is, I believe, representative, in that it points toward the kinds of analysis we have traditionally performed: the discovery of lexical, syntactic, and semantic regularities; the weighing of their expressive import, and of their mimetic character; and the analysis of rhetorical effect. Any inventory of definitions or descriptions of style will also correspond pretty closely to this sketch. For instance, Bernard Bloch takes style to be the message carried by frequency-distributions and transitional probabilities, and that is simply a formal way to speak of such regularities as I identified in the passage from *Watt*. They may also be examined as relations between linguistic elements in extended discourse, to choose the formulation preferred by Samuel Levin, after Archibald Hill. Another thread in the definition of style is that represented here especially by Nils Erik Enkvist and in practical stylistics by Leo Spitzer, namely the consideration of style as deviation from norms. It was extremes and oddities of construction that commanded attention in the passage at hand. Stephen Ullmann thinks of style as the consequence of *choices* among variants, and that has been the burden of my own theoretical remarks too. Such choices are implicit in any discussion, for instance, of Beckett's redundancies, or of his parataxis. These choices carry some kind of meaning, all would agree; Michael Riffaterre speaks of style as an expressive, affective, or esthetic emphasis added to the information conveyed, implying a distinction between information and expressive meaning, to which I would also subscribe (though not to the equation of style and emotion), and which is implicit in my brief comments on Beckett's diction, as well as his syntactic habits. René Wellek includes in his conception of style the way that the structure of the text represents reality, as in the analyses of Erich Auerbach, and in my comments on the different "worlds" and sensibilities implied by Beckett's shifts in diction and tone. Finally, Wellek's account of style also mentions devices that aim at rhetorical ends—that is, features of the text as we relate them to the presumed responses of readers.

Since all these conceptions are logically compatible, and since the kinds of practical criticism they point to complement one another, there is no cause to be disturbed by the multiplicity of definitions. The concept of style seems to embrace a set of instances which bear what Wittgenstein called a "family resemblance" to one another. If that is so, *no* single definition can draw a neat line around style. Our intuitive perception of style includes more features of the text and more ways of looking at those features than can be specified in a single formulation.

In a way, this is an *ex parte* argument, since it prepares the way for the main point I wish to make in this paper: namely, that there is a lacuna in the theory of style, although some applied criticism has pointed to the stylistic options I have in mind. These options play an important role in our untrained perception of style, and they deserve a sounder and more direct accounting than they have had. My aim is to make a rough beginning in this.

II

For a start, we may return to the passage from *Watt*. My survey took note of features of the text that command attention either because they are unusual or because the insistent repetition of them is unusual. I did not mention violations of the rules of English, but there *are* at least three syntactic anomalies: "whose it is painful to relate," "whose it will be learnt with regret beauty," and the gap in the sentence after "relate," filled only with a question mark. Chomsky has made clear the difference between rarity (or statistical deviance) and actual ungrammaticality. The former entails no dissonance with the rules of English, but simply an uncharacteristic application of these rules. Ungrammatical sequences, though we interpret them by reference to syntactic and semantic rules (as most notably in the case of metaphor), are not generated directly *by* those rules. Their import is usually clear, even though they are not strictly English, and they are a fairly regular occurrence in literature, especially poetry. I believe it would be a simple matter to interpret those in the Beckett passage, and that they would be found to confirm the disorientation created by the stylistic features I mentioned previously.

I wanted to establish this distinction between the ungrammatical and the merely unusual because I think it bears on another anomaly in the passage, to me the most outrageous of all, and that is the footnote: "Haemophilia is, like enlargement of the prostate, an exclusively male disorder. But not in this work." Since our narrator has just told us that Kate is a bleeder, it is at best quixotic for him to inform us now that such a condition is medically impossible. It is odder still for him to step out of his role within the novel and allude to it as a "work." What shall we say of the text? It is not exactly contradictory, since the statement about poor Kate is made within the fictive world of the novel, while that about haemophilia is outside it. (In this respect, the passage is akin to G. E. Moore's paradox —that one cannot say "It's snowing, but I don't believe it's snowing," even though the proposition "It's snowing" is not inconsistent with the proposition "I don't believe it's snowing.") Nor is it pertinent to say that the narrator has violated truth conditions: we don't *expect* a novel to tell truth in this sense. And certainly there is nothing syntactically wrong with the anomalous sequence. Yet I imagine many would share my feeling that what Beckett has written here is not simply unusual, or bizarre, or irregular, but un-English. That is to say, the passage violates some tacit rule for conducting discourse in English, some common understanding about how we will talk with one another. This understanding seems more analogous to the rule violated by "whose it will be learnt with regret beauty," than to the expectations that make "a sterling fellow but a bleeder" surprising.

Now this kind of thing has often been noticed, of course. I think, for instance, of Auerbach's excellent discussion (in *Mimesis*[2]) of the narrative anomalies in Virginia Woolf's *To the Lighthouse*. Nor are we without helpful critical concepts—Wayne Booth's *The Rhetoric of Fiction*[3] provides a background that would allow penetrating discussion of the passage at hand. But it is my contention that stylistics has no way of relating the anomaly in this passage from *Watt* to a general theory of style or method of stylistic criticism. Further, I think that the reason for this lack is an unnecessary narrowness in the general theories of language that we have normally drawn upon—a point I shall return to later.

An appropriate theoretical framework does exist. It was first developed at length by J. L. Austin in his posthumously published lectures, *How to Do Things with Words*,[4] and has been further elaborated by a number of philosophers, including especially John R. Searle in his recent book, *Speech Acts*.[5] Although Austin arrived at his subject as part of the theory of action, his ideas belong equally to the theory of language, and, I think, enrich it substantially.

III

Plainly, to speak is to *do* something, although the precise nature of speech-as-action has received little systematic study except in the context of classical rhetoric. Austin distinguishes three major kinds of act that one performs as a speaker:

1) *Locutionary acts:* Most trivially, to say something *is* to do something, namely, to say what one says. That is, a speaker produces sounds (a writer sets down graphic symbols) which are well ordered with respect to the phonological system and grammar of a particular language, and which, furthermore, carry some sense with respect to the semantic and pragmatic rules of that language.

2) *Illocutionary acts:* Beyond that, *in* saying what he says, a speaker is performing a second kind of act, by virtue of numerous conventions for the use of language in his speech community. For instance, in writing what I just wrote, I performed the act of stating (hereafter, names of illocutionary acts will be noted with broken underlining). I might instead have performed the act of making a concession, asking a question, giving an order, etc. All of these are illocutionary acts, and to perform any of them I must do more than speak (or write) in a given language. I must speak within a

framework of conventions and circumstances, and do so in prescribed ways. I may successfully perform the locutionary act of writing an imperative English sentence, but fail to accomplish the illocutionary act of giving a command—if, for instance, my sentence is "Abraham Lincoln, repeal the Emancipation Proclamation," for among the conditions for giving commands are the recipient's being able to do as ordered, his being alive, etc.

3) *Perlocutionary acts:* Finally, by saying what I say, I normally perform a third kind of act. I may intimidate you, inform you, puzzle you, sadden you, and so on. *I may* achieve one of these things, or all of them, but I have no guarantee. Perlocutionary acts include the consequences of my speaking, and I have only limited control over them. If I were now to write (not in quotation marks) *I promise to deliver a new and valid theory of literature at the end of this paper*, I would have performed thereby the illocutionary act of promising, but possibly not the perlocutionary act of getting your hopes up.

In summary, and in schematic form, consider the utterance, "Stop, or I'll shoot."

| | |
|---|---|
| Locutionary act: | Saying "Stop, or I'll shoot." |
| Illocutionary acts: | Threatening, ordering, _._._ |
| Perlocutionary acts: | Frightening, enraging, . . . |

Since I am speaking of a problem in literary theory, I should add that all three kinds of act may be performed in and through writing. The nature of the locutionary act is thereby altered in obvious ways, the illocutionary act is more or less attenuated, and the perlocutionary act is more or less delayed.

Of the three, illocutionary acts are the most elusive. Austin remarks that philosophers of language habitually slide away from illocutionary acts, toward either locutionary or perlocutionary acts, to the detriment of their study. The same holds, I believe, for us, although illocutionary acts offer rich expressive possibilities, and are deeply rooted in a system of rules quite close to the heart of our literary concerns. Let us consider, briefly, those rules. To this end, I quote Austin's criteria for the "felicity" (successful functioning) of one class of illocutionary act, *performatives* such as "I vote no," "I hereby dismiss the class," and "I bid three spades"—a particularly pure sort of speech act, since it asserts nothing true or false, but simply performs the act in question.

1) There must exist an accepted conventional procedure having a certain conventional effect, that procedure to include the uttering of certain words by certain persons in certain circumstances, and further,

2) the particular persons and circumstances in a given case must be appropriate for the invocation of the particular procedure invoked.

3) The procedure must be executed by all participants both correctly and
4) completely.
5) Where, as often, the procedure is designed for use by persons having
certain thoughts or feelings, or for the inauguration of certain conse-
quential conduct on the part of any participant, then a person participating in and so invoking the procedure must in fact have those
thoughts or feelings, and the participants must intend so to conduct
themselves, and further
6) must actually so conduct themselves subsequently.[6]

Modified slightly, these regulations apply to other illocutionary acts, including assertion. To make a statement felicitously, I must, among other things,
utter a declarative sentence (criterion 1). I must be the right person to
make the statement (2). I will not get away with stating that a memory of
your grandfather just crossed your mind. I must not mumble (3) or break
off in the middle (4). I must believe what I say (5), and I must not
ground my future conduct or speech in a contrary understanding of the
state of the world.

It is here that the Beckett passage goes awry. Either it fails on rule 5, in
that the narrator holds an improper set of beliefs for the act of stating that
Kate was a bleeder, or it fails on rule 6, in that he comports himself inappropriately afterward—namely, in writing the footnote. So one or the other
of his statements is infelicitous—breaks the contract that exists between
writer and reader. The second sentence of the footnote compounds the
breach. For behind the acts of stating is the all-encompassing illocutionary
act of telling a story, and, by rule 5, the teller always endorses the fictive
world of the story for its duration, and, again, by convention, does not acknowledge that it *is* a fiction. When Beckett's narrator admits a discrep-
ancy between his fictive world and the real world, he violates both rules.
Hence he sets the reader at odds with the text, in a way that produces
disorientation and amusement, but which, on a deeper plane, calls into
question the very possibility, or at least the reasonableness, of building
narratives and trying to make sense of human conduct, or, indeed, of
maintaining a society.

I shall return to Beckett again. For the moment, though, I want to
underline my claim that the rules for illocutionary acts are indeed rules, in
much the way that phrase-structure rules, transformations, or semantic
rules, are such: they account for some of what every speaker knows about
how linguistic transactions are carried on. Where transformations and the
rest explicate a speaker's grammatical competence, the rules for speech acts
explicate his competence in using speech to act (and be acted upon)
within the matrix of social and verbal conventions.

As even an abbreviated statement of the rules shows, that web of convention is spun with vital threads of human relationship: power, right, ob-ligation, good and bad faith, social rank, role, compacts, agreements, swear-ings, dependencies, and so on and on. Given the conventional nature of societies and the verbal nature of human beings, it is not surprising that many actions basic to the continuity of human society and intercourse are sometimes or always performed through illocutionary acts: betrothing, marrying, divorcing, christening, contracting, voting, hiring, promoting, fir-ing, inviting, refusing, forswearing, guaranteeing, threatening, promising, abdicating, joining, endorsing, etc. Nor is the range of the illocutionary act limited to *la petite histoire*. *La grande histoire*, too, is grounded in actions that have significance only through the rules of illocutionary acts, superim-posed upon our mutual knowledge of the recent past. The front page of a newspaper like *The New York Times*, except when astronauts have just landed or when a natural disaster has just occurred, is always given over to reports of illocutionary acts and their impact.

For a random example, take the *Times* of August 3, 1969. It contains eleven stories. Of these, one reports on the atmosphere of the planet Mars, and another reports on the (stated?) intention of liberal Democrats in the House of Representatives. But the other nine report illocutionary acts: Mayor Lindsay asks that the Federal Government help the cities solve their problems; the Pope consecrates a shrine in Uganda; Senator Magnuson for-mally declares his opposition to the Safeguard antiballistic missile system; President Nixon assures the Soviet Union that his visit to Rumania is a friendly one; Anatoly Kuznetsov renounces all his published works; and so on. It is a verbal world, for—however ill-observed—the norm of human in-teraction is the principle "a man's word is his bond."

## IV

A discourse is a set of grammatical structures with meanings. It is also an attempt to influence the reader. I am suggesting that these facts about the ontology of discourse have been well recognized in theories of style, but that a third—that a discourse is a series of illocutionary acts—has not, and ought to be.

In written discourse, the conditions of action are altered in obvious ways: the audience is dispersed and uncertain; there is often nothing but internal evidence to tell us whether the writer has beliefs and feelings appropriate to his acts, and nothing at all to tell us whether he conducts himself ap-propriately afterward. Nonetheless, writing is parasitic on speech in this, as in all matters.

The point is most obvious as it applies to dramatic works, which consist almost solely of alternating speech acts by the several characters, or in prose fiction that relies mainly on dialogue. A poem, too, moves on a rhythm of illocutionary acts; and that rhythm is often telling, as in Blake's "Ah, Sunflower, weary of time . . ." where the illocutionary act that encases all the rest is an apostrophe, so that the poem avoids assertion (indeed, predication of any sort), and thus hangs suspended, as it were, in an almost actionless state which accords well with its content; or Wordsworth's Immortality Ode, in which tension builds through the first sixty lines between the acts of rejoicing and lamenting, until it is resolved in the explanation—a kind of lawlike fiction for the nonce—that begins "Our birth is but a sleep and a forgetting."

But even in discursive prose the illocutionary chain is always there, and often significant. Take the following perfectly commonplace sentences from an essay by Harvey Swados:

> If we conclude that there is nothing noble about repetitive work, but that it is nevertheless good enough for the lower orders, let's say that . . . so we will at least know where we stand. But if we cling to the belief that other men are our brothers, not just Egyptians, or Israelis, or Hungarians, but *all* men, including millions of Americans who grind their lives away on an insane treadmill, then we will have to start thinking about how their work and their lives can be made meaningful. That is what I assume the Hungarians, both workers and intellectuals, have been thinking about. Since no one has been ordering us what to think, since no one has been forbidding our intellectuals to fraternize with our workers, shouldn't it be a little easier for us to admit, first, that our problems exist, then to state them, and then to see if we can resolve them?[7]

The first sentence enacts a conditional exhortation ("let's say that"), and then justifies the exhortation ("so we will at least know where we stand"). The second sentence—also conditional—performs the act of stating ("then we will have to start thinking . . .") but, through it, the more vital act of resolving—to start thinking about the lives of factory workers. Then the act of assuming (Swados is reporting his assumption, but also making it). The last sentence is more complex. It contains three statements: no one has been ordering us what to think; no one has been forbidding our intellectuals to fraternize with our workers; and our problems exist. The main force of the sentence, though, is the act of questioning, which is itself complex: through the rhetorical question, Swados urges the audience to think and act a certain way; he also chides them for not having done so, in spite of their freedom. So the acts follow one another, bound in a series whose members are to some extent interdependent—for instance, the act of assuming something about the Hungarians prepares for the act of chiding, which depends on an unflattering contrast between the audience and the Hungarians in a totalitarian state.

How does style fit in with all this? In several important ways, I think. First, the locutionary style of the passage—its pattern of syntactic and semantic choices—intermingles with the acts performed. For instance, a signal feature of locutionary style is the reliance on verbs that have (or can have) for their direct objects noun clauses reporting propositions: "conclude," "say," "know," "believe," "think," "assume," "admit," "state." The passage moves through a series of encased propositions, ideas that are offered for consideration, accepted, rejected, and so on. There is nothing noble about repetitive work; it is nevertheless good enough for the lower orders; other men are our brothers; etc.—most of the passage, in fact, consists of such material, subordinated to verbs of cognition and speech. A style that frames and weighs propositions in this way often goes with speech acts like asserting and denying, which focus directly on belief. But Swados leads us through a rather more vigorous and personal series of acts: exhorting, resolving, chiding, etc. The audience is being asked, not simply to deliberate and believe, but to position itself emotionally *vis à vis* the encased propositions, and, further, to use them as a base for social action. In short, one cannot rightly estimate the "cognitive style" of the passage without considering the brisk action that accompanies it. The two overlap in both possible ways: the syntactic style of the passage becomes a style of action; and Swados' speech acts are also, surely, a part of the style of the passage.

Second, I think that we can see in the passage a style of action quite independent of grammatical structure, though not of the structure of speech acts. Recall that, for an illocutionary act to work properly, the speaker and the circumstances must be appropriate. Then consider Swados' act of resolving, in "we will have to start thinking about how their work and their lives can be made meaningful." This is not a private resolution, of the sort one might make at New Year's, but one that incorporates the audience. Who is the appropriate person to make such a resolution? presumably one who at least commands the attention and respect of his audience—ideally one who speaks as a leader. But there is no guarantee that Swados is, at this point, such a person; his fitness for the act depends entirely on the credit he has amassed in the course of the essay. Again, the proper circumstances for a social resolution of this sort include a good deal of solidarity and cohesion among those present. This, too, depends upon how Swados has performed up to now. In short, the illocutionary act can be characterized in several ways: first, as I said before, it has rather high emotional content (as do urging and chiding, later on). Second, it brings the "we" alive, more than do most written speech acts; it seeks to build a *community* of decent intellectuals. Third, it is relatively risky—it stakes a lot on the credit and

credibility of the writer. The same can be said, I believe, of the other illocutionary acts performed in this passage, and if so, we can isolate a style
of action here that depends on the conventions for illocutionary acts, but
not on the linguistic structure of the passage. I see no reason to set this
kind of style outside the boundaries of our concept. Style borders on, and
overlaps with, action.

There is one more connection between style and illocutionary acts that
I will touch on, and for that purpose I want to return to Beckett's *Watt*.
I had remarked that, taken together, the three illocutionary acts which
arise from Kate's unfortunate malady are defective, in conflict with the
conventions. This is not a unique occurrence in the passage. Most notably,
when the text breaks off at "it is painful to relate," there is violation of
other rules than the obvious grammatical ones. The speech act of assertion
that is in progress is not executed completely, and so fails by rule 4. Of
more interest, a condition for the general speech act of telling a story is
that the teller knows, having invented, all the facts and all the sentences
contained in that story. Beckett evidently fails to meet that condition, and
the act is in violation of the rule which says the speaker must have appropriate beliefs. Perhaps we should take the *narrator*, Sam, as the speaker. In
that case, the lacuna implies his ignorance of a pertinent fact, while the
neighboring clause, "it is painful to relate," implies that he does know
Simon's failing. Furthermore, a few lines farther on the narrator mentions
the "unsuspected" tubercular origin of Ann's game leg: apparently he
knows a medical fact concealed from everyone *in* the story—that is to say,
his vantage point here is one of omniscience. (I might note parenthetically
that the same kind of omniscience would be required to know that old
Tom's undiagnosed pains were in the caecum, not an easily identifiable
source of pain.) This implied omniscience is in even sharper dissonance
with the supposition, encouraged by the gap in the text, that the narrator
is piecing his story together from defective information. In short, either
some of these subordinate speech acts are infelicitous owing to the speaker's inappropriate beliefs, or the narrator's state of knowledge is constantly
changing, or we have more than one narrator. Any of these states of affairs
would undermine the customary relation of narrator to reader, and along
with it the foundations of narrative convention.

Now, snarls like this in the web of discourse are a commonplace throughout Beckett's novel. There is still another, less striking, instance in the
same passage: the shift from the formal announcement suggested by "it
will be learnt with regret" to the sordid content of the report—and in any
case, one does not announce as a new event what is actually a continuing
state of misery. I am suggesting that the violation itself of rules by which
we talk to one another amounts to a stylistic trait of *Watt*.

At the end of the catalogue of Lynches and their woes, the narrator says,

> Five generations, twenty-eight souls, nine hundred and eighty years,
> such was the proud record of the Lynch family, when Watt entered
> Mr Knott's service (1).

Another footnote follows:

> (1) The figures given here are incorrect. The consequent calculations
> are therefore doubly erroneous.

Again the underpinnings of the narrative are smartly withdrawn, to the
confusion of all. Or, to mention one more example, at another place
Beckett or Sam leaves several lines empty except for a parenthesis: "(Hiatus in MS)." Yet our understanding all along has been that Sam heard
the story from Watt himself. The style of the book builds in part on acts
that are defective or incompatible. The social contract that exists between
writer and reader is repeatedly broken. And hence the validity of *all* social
contracts and *all* conventions is shaken. When a text violates syntactic or
semantic rules, cognitive or logical dissonance ensues. Violating the rules
for illocutionary acts also produces a kind of chaos, but, predictably, a *social* one.

The absurdity of verbal conventions that have lost their power to stabi-
lize traffic among people, thus leaving speech unanchored to that which
makes it social action, has not been overlooked by our writers. In a time
when they have sought emblems of isolation and expressions of the felt absurdity of things, many have found their way to abuses of the illocutionary
act similar to those in *Watt*. The "theater of the absurd," in particular, has
created a medium of social exchange much like the flamingoes and hedge-
hogs used as croquet mallets and balls in *Alice's Adventures in Wonder-
land,* and with similar results. And prose writers are fairly common, who,
like Borges and Barthelme, rend the particular illocutionary conventions on
which narrative is based. This is to suggest that, just as some traits of locutionary style may be discovered which a whole group of writers at a given
time have found cognitively and esthetically valid, peculiarities of illocutionary act may also figure importantly in literary fashion. It is natural that
writers should be specially sensitive to the expressive potential of those acts
that are done with words. As Frye says, ritual, "the content of action . . .
is something continuously latent in the order of words."[8]

I suspect, also—to gesture at just one more reach of this topic—that styles
of illocutionary action help to determine the most fundamental literary
types. Thus comedy, particularly as it approaches farce, is likely to estab-

lish its world through a repetitive or mechanical series of speech acts, as if in confirmation of Bergson's ideas about comedy and action. For instance, the first few pages of *The Importance of Being Earnest* consist almost entirely in an exchange of questions and assertions, on this order:

Algernon.    . . . Where have you been since last Thursday?
      Jack.    (Sitting down on the sofa.) In the country.
Algernon.    What on earth do you do there?
      Jack.    (Pulling off his gloves.) When one is in town one amuses
                  oneself. When one is in the country one amuses other
                  people. It is excessively boring.
Algernon.    And who are the people you amuse?
      Jack.    (Airily.) Oh, neighbours, neighbours.
Algernon.    Got nice neighbours in your part of Shropshire?
      Jack.    Perfectly horrid! Never speak to one of them.
Algernon.    How immensely you must amuse them! . . . By the way,
                  Shropshire is your county, is it not?

Or recall the beginning of *The Alchemist,* which is a sustained sequence of epithets and threats, hurled by Face and Subtle at each other, with Doll Common intruding now and then a plea for temperance:

      Face.    Believe't, I will.
    Subtle.    Thy worst. I fart at thee.
      Doll.    Have you your wits? why, gentlemen! for love—
      Face.    Sirrah, I'll strip you—
    Subtle.    What to do? lick figs/Out at my—
      Face.    Rogue, rogue!—out of all your sleights.
      Doll.    Nay, look ye, sovereign, general, are you madmen?
    Subtle.    O, let the wild sheep loose. I'll gum your silks
                  With good strong water, an you come.
      Doll.    Will you have/The neighbours hear you? will you betray
                  all?/Hark! I hear somebody.
      Face.    Sirrah—
    Subtle.    I shall mar/All that the tailor has made if you approach.
      Face.    You most notorious whelp, you insolent slave . . .

By contrast, tragedies are often more varied in illocutionary acts, as if to establish at the start a fuller range of human emotion and action. *Hamlet* begins with a question, a refusal, two commands, a kind of loyalty oath ("long live the king"), a question, a statement, a compliment, a statement, an order, thanks, and a complaint—all this, of course, between two guardsmen.

Frye speaks of literature as "a body of hypothetical verbal structures,"

with the polemical emphasis on the word "hypothetical." For present purposes, I would shift the focus slightly, and say that a work of literature is
also a series of hypothetical *acts*, grounded in the conventions for verbal
action that we have all thoroughly learned. In fact I would go farther, and
say that literature can be accurately *defined* as discourse in which the seem-
ing acts are hypothetical. Around them, the reader, using his elaborate
knowledge of the rules for illocutionary acts, constructs the hypothetical
speakers and circumstances—the fictional world—that will make sense of
the given acts. This performance is what we know as mimesis.[9]

It seems to me that as stylistic critics we have been less than attentive to
this side of literature and literary syle. Like linguists, we have held mainly
to a view of discourse as static, and we have conceived literature, in a spatial metaphor, as consisting in verbal structures. This is a valid perspective,
but a terribly limited one. There are signs that linguists are broadening
their perspective to include the circumstances that surround utterances,
and the continual interplay of speech with those circumstances.[10] Literary
scholars, concerned with language as a system rooted in social convention,
and tending always to estimate generously the power of words in action,
would perhaps do well to look more carefully at the exact senses in which
speech *is* action.

## NOTES

1. Samuel Beckett, *Watt* (New York, 1959), p. 102.

2. In Erich Auerbach, *Mimesis: The Representation of Reality in Western Literature*, tr. Willard Trask (Princeton, N.J., 1953).

3. Wayne C. Booth, *Rhetoric of Fiction* (Chicago, Ill., 1961).

4. J. L. Austin, *How to Do Things with Words* (Cambridge, Mass., 1962).

5. John R. Searle, *Speech Acts: An Essay in the Philosophy of Language* (Cambridge, Mass., 1969).

6. Austin, *op. cit.*, pp. 14-15.

7. Harvey Swados, "The Myth of the Happy Worker," (1957), collected in *A Radical's America* (Boston, Mass., 1962).

8. Northrop Frye, *Anatomy of Criticism* (Princeton, N.J., 1947), p. 109.

9. See my "Speech Acts and the Definition of Literature," forthcoming in *Philosophy and Rhetoric*.

10. Noam Chomsky, "Deep Structures, Surface Structures, and Semantic Interpretation" (unpublished paper).

# DISCUSSION OF OHMANN'S PAPER

Ohmann was asked if the following was not a fair paraphrase of his argument: Every sentence has both locutionary and illocutionary force no matter what its nature, and further, every sentence has potential perlocutionary force. The distinction between the first two categories is demonstrable because it is possible to devise two different sets of rules for well-formedness, ordinary grammatical rules applying to the first category and the rules given in his paper to the second. (This is very useful since it makes it possible to explain certain deviations which would be unexplainable if we had only grammar at our disposal, as well as certain stylistic relations which don't depend on deviation but are functions of illocutionary force.)

Ohmann found such a translation excellent in every respect except one: an illocutionary act does not fully and successfully occur every time anyone speaks a well-formed sentence. Suppose one were to say to a participant at this conference "I hereby divorce you"—this is clearly a failed illocutionary act, or, in other words, no illocutionary act has been achieved, for several reasons: 1) There is no convention in English for *divorcing* by illocutionary means, 2) the speaker is not married to you, 3) he obviously doesn't believe what he is saying, and so on. But, asked the questioner, doesn't the very fact that something is a declarative sentence give it illocutionary force? Ohmann felt not; in this instance, for example, the purported illocutionary force is that of divorcing, but this statement has no such illocutionary force in English. That is, in our society (unlike Islam) one cannot divorce one's wife by simply making a statement to that effect. To which the questioner responded "But the notion of illocutionary force comprehends more than just performative verbs, doesn't it?" Ohmann agreed that it did. "What are these other verbs?" Ohmann answered that *all* verbs may be comprehended. "But then every sentence has illocutionary force." Ohmann agreed, invoking a distinction between having an illocutionary force and accomplishing an illocutionary act. Every sentence does the former, but not necessarily the latter.

Ohmann's example gave rise to another comment. Isn't it true that a statement which may be absurd in conversation may be perfectly acceptable as a literary device? (Indeed, someone recalled, triumphantly, that Dick Diver in Fitzgerald's *Tender is the Night* says to his son "I hereby divorce you," or words to that effect.) Alluding to a book on speech acts and literature which he is planning, Ohmann agreed that the reason "I hereby divorce you" is less anomalous in a fiction is precisely the presence of *mimesis* as he understands that term. The theory of the imitation of reality permits an author to present sentences purporting to do all sorts of illocutionary acts. The reader, in turn, imagines or reconstructs the situations that would appropriately go with that act—he tries to create an explanation for it. But one doesn't ordinarily do that in person-to-person conversation because there is a whole history of actual relationship between speaker and addressee. If the speaker made such a statement, he would be understood to be making a joke or being ironic—and these forms of communication, of course, are very close to the ones commonly present in literature.

Substantially the same question came up in different terms no less than three times: 1) Isn't it true that all declarative sentences tend to be locutionary, while imperatives, interrogatives, and so on are illocutionary? Ohmann answered negatively: every well-formed sentence in English is the vehicle of a locutionary act and also potentially (but not necessarily) of an illocutionary act. But what is the illocutionary value of "The sky is blue," and what is the locutionary value of "Damn you!"? Ohmann replied that the illocutionary force of "The sky is blue" varies with the context; in many situations it would be the act of performing an *assertion,* but if one's interlocutor had first said "The sky is pink," the statement would additionally have the illocutionary force of *contradiction.* The non-equivalence of grammatical forms (crucial to locutionary force) and illocutionary acts is clear not only from the fact that declarative sentences can be used in all kinds of illocutionary situations, but also that a given illocutionary act can be performed by different grammatical structures; for example, the act of *commanding* can be performed with a declarative ("I would like a little salt, please"), with a question ("Would you pass me the salt?"), and with an imperative ("Pass me the salt"). In all speech both locutionary and illocutionary acts are going on constantly, and we have, therefore, these two possible perspectives on a text. But (the questioner continued) insofar as *Watt* is a failure of social contract, is it not a locutionary rather than an illocutionary failure—one that can be expressed in old-fashioned logical terms? And can one not say about the Swados passage simply that it is hortatory expression fortified by good sense and humanity, even though the urging is embedded in dependent clauses? The questioner felt a little worried about the attempt to take over the whole of discourse under the illocutionary head when various kinds of incoherence could still be distinguished as logical, that is locutionary. Ohmann answered that he did not feel that much could be done about the "nonsense" in W*att* on straight logical grounds. The contradiction between "Kate was a bleeder" and "Hemophilia is an exclusively male disorder" is not a logical failure, but a difficulty that inheres in *saying* these two things closely together. The disorder in the message is not logical but social, a breach of contract in the discourse. (But the questioner disagreed.)

2) Why call such a phenomenon "un-English" rather than an instance of "romantic irony" or the like? Isn't Beckett merely saying: "Hemophilia in my fictional world is a female characteristic; therefore this is in fact a fiction; but in this footnote I disrupt the fictional world by reminding the reader that hemophilia is an exclusively male disorder." This is a perfectly legitimate fictional method with precedents in the work of writers like Sterne and Brentano. These contracts are only such in a limited historic sense: James, for example, thought that Trollope was violating a contract by having his narrator say "I don't know whom this character is going to marry." Beckett's footnote seems a perfectly justifiable literary device for the role of grotesque humorist that he wishes to play. Ohmann responded by admitting that he wished he had a better word than "un-English" to express what he meant. He certainly didn't wish to suggest that there were no precedents for this device in literature, nor that there is anything defective or morally reprehensible about it; rather his point was simply that anyone who was accustomed to carrying on discourse in English with fellow-speakers would know that something had gone wrong if this happened. That is not to say that it has gone wrong in a moral or aesthetic sense—it may be quite the reverse; indeed, Ohmann professed great admiration for the passage in question. He was simply trying to demonstrate that the conventions of discourse were being violated in a way analogous to the way grammatical rules were being violated in a poetic phrase like "a grief ago"—nobody, obviously, *blames* Thomas for that phrase. We simply say that as commonplace as metaphor may be, every time one occurs some rules of English are being violated. "Un-English" is a very clumsy way of trying to get at these violations, but he hoped that everyone understood what he meant by it.

3) If any literary artist has the right to *lie* (as we all grant that he does), can we really apply a method such as Austin's without serious modification? Ohmann insisted on taking the dogmatic position (the word is his own) that the best way to talk about locutionary and illocutionary states of affairs is not to say that there must be a different set of rules for the literary text but to say that the writer is *using* the system of language and language acts describable by the ordinary rules, but using it in a special

way. He would prefer not to say that one has to have a different description of *"the* language of *Watt"* or *"the* language of poetry" but simply to say that poets use language in different, exciting, creative ways.

Another questioner recalled that Ohmann had based his analysis on the reader, but wondered why that was necessary since the illocutionary act is deducible from the utterance itself. For example, if one says "Close the door," an order can be deduced from the very form of the utterance and not from the fact that you may or may not close the door as a perlocutionary response. Thus it would seem that it is only the perlocutionary force which is related to the reader, not the illocutionary. Ohmann agreed that the kind of illocutionary act which the statement may perform is indeed implicit in the statement. But it is also true that a live relationship holds between the reader and the text; that becomes particularly clear when a deviance occurs. An imperative sentence in a text ("Follow my words closely") causes no difficulty; but if the text says "Stop immediately; let your thoughts wander," we have to invoke some hypothetical reader to talk about the way in which that speech act would work. The narrator is not in a position to order me to let my thoughts wander because he cannot know, for example, that my thoughts are not *already* wandering. This is the kind of thing you find in quirky sorts of narrative—they bring out rather clearly the role of the reader in the speech act.

What was Ohmann's position on deviance, since deviance seemed to be important in only one of the examples given? If the success of the *Watt* passage depended on this device, Jonson's comic dialogue involved only repetitions of perfectly felicitous speech acts. Is it really necessary to rely on the concept of deviance? Ohmann repeated the view that the stylistics of illocutionary acts is exactly analogous to that of locutionary acts, that is grammatical stylistics. There are grammatical stylistic features which are such because they are deviant and there are stylistic features which are such because of their relative prominence, rarity, repetition, and so on. The same thing is true of illocutionary stylistic features: his example from *Watt* illustrated the first, his examples from *The Importance of Being Earnest* and Jonson illustrated the second.

Finally, there was an attempt to put Ohmann's paper in historical and critical perspective. One participant found a dimension of finality (*finalité*) in the illocutionary approach which was Aristotelian; this is implicit in the relation found between the author and the reader. But, it was argued, there is also a secondary relation, that existing between the characters. We must recognize that Austin's analysis is essentially of discourse used in practical situations, but that the situation in literature is always hypothetical. Ohmann admitted that he had shifted constantly between the two and that there was perhaps an equivocation being noted.

Another attempt was to place the paper in a wider semiotic frame, citing particularly the distinctions of Carnap and Morris between syntactics (the study of relations between signs), semantics (between signs and their denotata) and pragmatics (between signs and their interpretants, their users). Ohmann's contribution was essentially to the *pragmatics* of literary style. Ohmann agreed that it was. It was suggested that this in turn relates to such notions as that of Malinowski's "phatic communion." For example, the inclusive plural in the Swados passage was surely an invitation to some kind of social solidarity. Ohmann agreed that relatively empty statements like "How are you?" are chiefly important as illocutionary acts of "greeting" or "clearing the channel."

The Austinian view, though admittedly fruitful, was said to be only one of several possible approaches to the problem. The background of stylistics studies should include other theories of communication as well—Malinowski's, Mathesius', and Bühler's, for example, as well as some of those popular in Britain: the approach through "register" (involving the personal and social relationships of speaker and hearer), the "routine" approach (certain speech routines are associated with certain kinds of discourse; they can be predicted and even "programmed"), and the "context of situation" approach. Ohmann welcomed other theoretical possibilities.

# 4
## PERIOD STYLE

# STYLE AND EXPRESSIVE REGISTER
# IN MEDIEVAL POETRY

## PAUL ZUMTHOR

MY THEORETICAL EXPOSITION is based on a procedure which I have been following for several years: that of studying medieval literature through the actual texts instead of through general historical considerations. I may be led, almost under protest, to pose certain problems which overlap the textual domain. I shall not try to solve them here, but only submit them as the products of rather narrowly limited experience. I shall abstain as much as possible from extrapolation.

It is necessary first to focus upon the corpus to be considered and the elements to be taken as representative of that corpus.

In order to obtain a sufficiently homogeneous body of material, I limit myself to what R. Dragonetti has recently called the *grand chant courtois* (the poetry of love of the French *trouvères* at the end of the twelfth and the thirteenth century).[1] This geographical, chronological, linguistic, and even thematic restriction does not prevent the consideration of a large number of texts: almost seven hundred songs, if one keeps to the corpus of Dragonetti.[2] The great stability of medieval traditions permits us to effect economies in diachronic research: I take the corpus as a homogeneous whole. The changes in the material from five quarter centuries (*c.* 1175 to 1300) are very slight and do not prevent this simplification, at least in a first analysis.

From the outset there arises a fundamental question about the very notion of style. There is a long-standing practice in medieval studies (from the mediocre work of Rennert to the fine analyses of Curtius) to identify "style" with the various processes codified in the rhetorical figures. This tendency finds apparent justification in the attitude of medieval theoreticians themselves. But it is necessary to go beyond it. I have commented on this point several times[3] and will not do so again at this time, except to make one remark. The rhetoricians of the eleventh, twelfth, and thirteenth centuries, taking up the ideas of antiquity, concentrated their attention on *amplification* and principally on the doctrine of *ornatus*, considered as the essence of writing. By organizing turns of speech which exist in a primitive state in ordinary language, they attributed a special value to them. They described these in functional terms as a code of predictable or at least highly probable locutions. The doctrine represents a profound aspiration expressed in many ways in the mentality of the time: a need to perceive, to grasp, to state not the particular thing but a sort of stable and, in principle, universal quintessence. Whence in literature (in no matter which language) the use of familiar expressive types, types which are controllable, "minted," so to speak, as elements of a system of exchange in which both author and auditor participate. Now in the elaboration of such an expressive system, the figures and commonplaces of rhetoric play the role, among others, of raw material. Their study, to keep from becoming vacuous, must be subordinated to that of *types*, as such, and of their functionings.

The many and varied expressive types that we find in the *grand chant courtois*, whether reducible or not to figures of *ornatus*, carry with them an appeal to a particular meaning. It is clear that forms of expression and forms of content do not constitute two grids which may be neatly superimposed and whose separate examination permits us to reconstitute the structure of a poetic universe. They are connected by relatively rigid links, in such a way that the analysis of one is impracticable without a simultaneous treatment of the other. Therefore, the possibilities of analysis are rather narrowly limited in two respects. On the one hand, the semantic substance to which the work gives form escapes us completely because of the historical distance from—and hence irrecoverability of—the culture of the twelfth century. This distance—until one effaces it—distorts the relation ordinarily established between author and reader by the mediation of the work.[4] This is why, in my view, stylistics of the Spitzerian type is not very useful for analyzing medieval texts. The notion of deviation, as proposed by Valéry and as rehearsed in various forms by various stylisticians,[5] is also inapplicable to twelfth- and thirteenth-century poetry. The nature of the documents remaining from that epoch does not really permit us to make out the vernacular—the "unmarked" language from which the marked, poetic language deviates—nor what sort of a deviation that is. This is a fundamental fact of life in the study of medieval poetics and stylistics.

Thus we are forced to limit ourselves to a comparison of the elements in the corpus (the various songs), and to base that comparison on an internal analysis of the constituents of the poetic language alone.

I have recently had occasion[6] to propose certain principles of this analysis, and I shall not take them up again here. I posit a rigorous distinction between three successive levels of analysis: that of connecting links in the language (phonetic and syntagmatic), that of lexicon as such, and that of *motifs* (minimal thematic constituents). The features of a text are thus observed from two perspectives: the one horizontal, distinguishing discrete elements at each level; the other vertical, taking the relations level by level. Each level, of course, produces its own special kind of meaning (or value). The total meaning is gradually specified as the analysis proceeds from the bottom (phonological) level to the top (thematic) level. By their accumulation, these diverse effects of evaluation may be seen as constituting a base upon which a referential sense, now lost to us, once rested.

If one applies this analysis to several songs, a great number of common elements become clear, not only lexical and rhetorical elements, cliché images, and so on, but also structural similarities which seem to arise from a profound unity of intention. This impression of a formal identity grows as one proceeds through the corpus; it has been sensed for a long time, but too often is described in negative terms like "monotonous," "banal," "impersonal," or (in a pejorative sense) "formalist." It is clear, on the contrary, that the *grand chant courtois* is endowed with a positive character which cannot be interpreted on the basis of superficial manifestations, and which must be considered as the effect of a powerful dynamism—but one of so particular a character that its description requires the use of specific operational concepts. The necessity of limiting our comparison to the different units in the chosen corpus promotes the recurrent elements to the rank of "style markers" (to use the term of Nils Enkvist).

At each level of the analysis, we must class all the features we uncover into two categories: recurrent and non-recurrent. Among the former we can theoretically distinguish two subclasses—features repeated only within a given song, and those repeated in several songs. In practice these subclasses often coincide; and most of the features common to as many as five or six songs will be found in the rest of the corpus as well.[7]

Within each song, recurrent elements generally predominate. Whatever it may be, their relation with non-recurrent elements is rarely one of simple juxtaposition; it seems engendered rather by a practice which is not unlike that of *amplificatio* as defined by rhetoricians. One cannot however reduce the non-recurrent elements to a purely ornamental status; they are functional, playing a role—by opposition and similarity, by effects of gradation— which I should call "modal." In effect, the non-recurrent elements are organized either in brief intercalated sequences or in mixed combinations, free modulations of the fundamental melody which ensures the coherence of the whole.

In fact, the statistical examination of recurring elements (vocabulary, topics, "privileged" syntactic turns) reveals a significant distribution:

1) Certain syntactic tendencies are constant, occurring in noticeably equal proportions. Thus I have observed among sentence-connectors an absolute predominance of causal, consecutive, and conditional forms, as well as those of opposition (more or less antithetical: *mais, ains* "but") and an almost total absence of relations of finality and concession; the fact that temporal subordination almost always marks anteriority or simultaneity but practically never posteriority; an extremely large number of negative sentences (an average of ten occurrences of *ne* per poem); a remarkable frequency of intensifiers, qualitative (*bien*, "well"; *si* "thus"), quantitative (*moult* "many, much"), and mixed (*tant*); the fact that almost all the comparatives are ones of superiority; etc.

2) The distribution of typical terms and syntactic structures bunches only at very high or very low frequencies; there are no intermediary degrees. Low frequencies are registered principally by concrete terms, which occur in comparisons, or, less often, metaphors.

We must recognize in this fact that some of the different elements of the register have a probabilistic aspect. I mean that they exist in the tradition as forms of content to which attach many varieties of expressions whose chances of occurrence are more or less great according to certain potentialities of context. Thus there are synonymic series such as *chanter-trouver* ("sing-find"), *confort-solaz* ("comfort-solace"), *douter-craindre-redouter* ("doubt-fear-dread"), *pitié-merci-gré* ("pity-mercy-gratitude"). Among these serial elements one can observe all sorts of substitution, even within one and the same poem.

I have spoken of "coherent design." This is obviously a term which a stylistics of modern literature would reject, since it can relate only to the description of individual works. But the poetry of the twelfth and thirteenth centuries presents an aspect which cannot be handled by modern criteria: the strong coherence which one observes in the individual work exists outside of it, at a hierarchically different level, namely the one at which recurrences are established. At that level, coherence constitutes one of the qualities belonging to the traditional poetic discourse which the poem exemplifies. In other words, one can say that the types are organized in systems. To designate this phenomenon, I proposed the word *register* several years ago. By this I mean poetic coherence as such, perceptible at the textual level; thus my term has no relation to the architecture of the whole.[8]

If, therefore, one agrees to call a literary work a structure, it follows that this structure is inscribed in some system, which we may conveniently call a register. From another point of view one could say that the work is deciphered in terms of a code (or subcode) utilized by the author. But it is evident that "code" in this sense must be metaphoric. That is why I prefer "register," in order to indicate clearly that there is no suggestion, properly speaking, of necessity, or if there is a necessity, it is of a special internal sort, what I should prefer to call "coherence."

To a certain extent, registral coherence can be considered a feature of "writing" (*écriture*), in the sense given to that word today—that of a state of language possessing a certain autonomy, an "interior essence" with its own generative rules, to be distinguished from language on the one hand and individual style on the other. The term "writing," of course, is some-what paradoxical in this case since what we are talking about is "song."[9] It is also useful to designate, abstractly at least, all the expressive means which the medieval poets created in their new vernaculars and which con-sequently owed to previous traditions only what is anecdotal and external. The expressive register of the *grand chant courtois* is one of these expres-sive means. It constitutes a continuous text, pre-existent and substratal of any concrete realization. Despite the "I" who grammatically controls the poem, the writing appears to be divested completely of personal origin: only the text—neutral, composite, intransitive—seems to speak (or rather to sing).

Thus there is a participatory connection between the word and its regis-ter, and this connection fills a vital function: it constitutes, to the exclusion of all others, *the* signal of poetry; it is the integrated linguistic mark of the poem which sets it in opposition to all non-poetic discourse. But it is a global and diffuse signal, which is not actualized in any specific constituent (syntactic, lexical, thematic, etc.). Its signalling function proceeds from its *convenance* ("decorum"), to use one of Dragonetti's terms again,[10] that is, its equilibrium and internal harmony. Thus the registral signal is not always clear external evidence. It is only immediately recognizable to the initiate, to a public of connoisseurs, namely the courts where this art took shape.[11]

It seems essential to present a very summary example, not so much to underpin my theory as to clarify my terminology. I have chosen (at ran-dom) the third song of the Chastelain de Coucy (end of the twelfth cen-tury), from the edition of A. Lerond. Obviously I cannot provide a com-plete interpretation. I shall limit myself to citing, in the form of brief ex-amples at each level of analysis, some of the simplest recurring elements.

I

La douce voiz du louseignol sauvage
Qu'oi nuit et jour cointoier et tentir

M'adoucist si le cuer et rassouage

4    Qu'or ai talent que chant pour esbaudir;
Bien doi chanter puis qu'il vient a plaisir
Cele qui j'ai fait de cuer lige homage;
Si doi avoir grant joie en mon corage,

8    S'ele me veut a son oez retenir.

### II

Onques vers li n'oi en faus cuer ne volage,
Si m'en devroit pour tant mieuz avenir,
Ainz l'aim et serf et aour par usage,

12    Maiz ne li os mon pensé descouvrir,
Quar sa biautez me fait tant esbahir
Que je ne sai devant li nul language;
Nis reguarder n'os son simple visage,

16    Tant en redout mes ieuz a departir.

### III

Tant ai en li ferm assis mon corage
Qu'ailleurs ne pens, et Diex m'en lait joïr!
C'onques Tristanz, qui but le beverage,

20    Pluz loiaument n'ama sanz repentir;
Quar g'i met tout, cuer et cors et desir,
Force et pooir, ne sai se faiz folage;
Encor me dout qu'en trestout mon eage

24    Ne puisse assez li et s'amour servir.

### IV

Je ne di pas que je face folage,
Nis se pour li me devoie morir,
Qu'el mont ne truis tant bele ne si sage,

28    Ne nule rienz n'est tant a mon desir;
Mout aim mes ieuz qui me firent choisir;
Lors que la vi, li laissai en hostage
Mon cuer, qui puiz i a fait lonc estage,

32    Ne ja nul jour ne l'en quier departir.

### V

Chançon, va t'en pour faire mon message
La u je n'os trestourner ne guenchir,
Quar tant redout la fole gent ombrage

36    Qui devinent, ainz qu' il puist avenir.
Les bienz d'amours (Diex les puist maleïr!).
A maint amant ont fait ire et damage;
Maiz j'ai de ce mout cruel avantage

40    Qu'il les m'estuet seur mon pois obeïr.[12]

At the first level of analysis (sound-patterns and syntactic connections), the representative features are few and less clear than at higher levels. I will make only two observations.

The rhymes on which the stanzas are constructed (twenty -age's and twenty -ir's) put into opposition a tonality that is open, large, and feminine, with one that is closed, acute, and masculine. This effect of contrast recurs, though more irregularly, in the caesuras, where there are twenty-one acute tones and nineteen non-acute. It is notable that such oppositions (with a general predominance of acute) are extremely frequent in the *grand chant courtois*, but not in other poetic forms of the period.

We have seen that the character of sentence connectors is constant too. One can point out the tendency to co-ordination or juxtaposition rather than subordination, and the slightness (whence, often the ambiguity) of the means of subordination. Though its explicit and discursive syntax may suggest an unequivocal message, in reality, the *chant* is profoundly ambiguous.

This is doubtless not much to write about; but these diffused elements are found integrated into much more clearly representative units at a higher level, namely that of vocabulary.

The formal examination of vocabulary reveals a great scattering: one finds only six derivational series on which the poet plays by means of alteration, echo, recall, etc. Now of these six series, four are so frequent in the poems as to form keys to the lexical system: *cuer-corage, chanter-chanson, joie-joïr* and *amour-amer-amant*.

Semantically almost all of the "heavy" words may be grouped into four semantic fields of unequal importance, but which connect within a central field in which they constitute zones of metaphorical transfer:

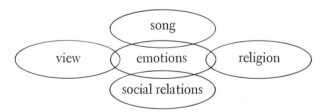

This kind of interference is characteristic of the *grand chant courtois* and constitutes one of the more obvious aspects of its register: though the vocabulary is very simple at the denotative level (the words are few and not at all ambiguous, taken by themselves), the whole, at the connotative level, is very complex. In certain poems, the terms serve to eulogize a lady, hence are integrated into this metaphoric structure. Only a few concrete words referring to external circumstances remain outside the schema.

Within each semantic field, one can identify recurrent expressions constituting topics which lend themselves to different effects of variation: *ai (grant) joie, bien doi chanter, ai talent que chant, les bien d'amours, (de cuer) fait (lige) homage*, etc. With these are connected certain key-words which are so frequent that for their original meaning, now lost, there is substituted a set of contextual values, for example, *penser* ("think") and its derivatives. Most of the figures (four metaphors and as many hyperboles) coincide with topics or key-words (thus *serf, aour, mourroie, el mont ne truis*). Most of the poems in the corpus contain figures of a similar sort, whose elements belong to the same semantic classes. This is equally true of antitheses of the type *cruel advantage*. As for the personification *chanson, va-t-en*, it is a frequent topic of the *envoi*. The only non-recurring rhetorical element in our poem is the comparison with Tristan.[13] It is noteworthy that this comparison (line 19) is connected by syntax, rhythm, and rhyme to recurring elements which surround it and which are prolonged and made resonant by an explication which is almost narrative, that is, relieved of any ambiguity. The same thing is true of non-recurrent elements (for example, the expression of fear in the second strophe); all are "placed" by and dependent on the recurrent elements.

A last remark on vocabulary. In comparison to fifty-nine semantically weighty verbs, the text contains only thirty-eight substantives and eleven adjectives (eight in figures of accumulation). This is a remarkable distribution, but one which is ubiquitous in the genre and which, in my opinion, constitutes an important factor in the register: strong verbal dominance, extreme adjectival poverty—these color the discourse in a characteristic way, operating as a preliminary sorting out of the semantic possibilities. This configuration seems related to the omnipresence of an unnamed non-substantive *I* by turns subject and object of simultaneous and successive actions. In this poem, thirty-two verbs are in the first person and fourteen in the third, and even more refer to the *I* in question (*mes ieuz firent*); there are seven instances of the objective pronouns *me* and *moi*, and ten of the possessives, *mon* and *mes*. This is probably the dominating syntactic-semantic fact of the register of the *chanson d'amour*.[14]

At the level of motifs, the number of recurrent elements is still larger. It is notable that certain poems are nothing but cumulative and programmatic catalogues of recurring motifs which elsewhere are most frequent: the earliest example is a song of Peire Vidal (number one in the Avalle edition). In the song of the Chastelain de Coucy under examination, the first stanza consists entirely of a series of assertions whose content and structure (or hierarchization) possesses a traditional character: the sequent voices of the birds, the joy of the heart, the desire to sing, unified by the syntax of a sentence of only slight complexity: *principal clause + consecu-*

*tive*—in many of the poems it is *temporal* + *principal*—and the affirmation of love, here combined with that of eternal devotion, a combination suggesting faithfulness of service.[15] The second and fifth stanzas contain various non-recurrent motifs (images and so on), nested within the sets of recurrent ones. Among these, at least three are repeated within the poem in a distribution which is difficult to interpret but cannot be fortuitous. The motif of permanent fidelity appears at the end of the first stanza, then at the beginning of the second and third, to be recalled at the end of the fourth; the motif of fear, begun in the second, returns in the fifth; the motif "sense or folly" of the third, then the fourth, is inverted in the fifth to become that of the *lozengiers* (the "others," the hostile onlookers). This is a kind of construction whose realization in the corpus exhibits innumerable variants, but which defines a certain textual mode of existence. It comprises, I think, one of the practical components of the register, a particular dispostion to knit the expressive threads in one way rather than another.

These terms must also be applied to a process in the *grand chant courtois* which is still more systematic (yet scarcely evident in the other poetic genres of the period). The actualization of the motif, the means by which the form of content and expression are welded together, permit subtle variations in the latter, developing many significant contrasts, thanks to the subtle play of verb forms. The poets utilize oppositions of time, aspect, and mode, of affirmation, negation, and interrogation in such a way as to permit the transformation of one motif into another without modifying the content. Thus a series like *ai joie* ("am joyous"), *n'ai joie* ("am not joyous"), *eusse joie* ("might have been joyous"), *aurai joie* ("shall be joyous") enables us to pass smoothly from joy to sadness, from fear to hope. In this particular poem, expression stands out against the background of a (permanent) present, by reference to which the measured past is sometimes punctual and sometimes perfective, while the future appears only as optative and conditional—with the sole exception of the imperative *va-t-en*, the instruction given to the text itself. It is clear that the possibilities of this genre are infinite. There is an affective tonality invested in the form which owes nothing to the lexicon, one which is more or less imposed by tradition.

Despite or even because of their heterogeneity, these features do not form a simple accumulation. Rather, there is a profound cohesion manifested in powerful combinatory possibilities, which embraces form and meaning inseparably, and whose realization engenders the "space" proper to this kind of discourse: a multi-dimensional and yet closed space, that of "song," that is of the language specified by a harmony called *love*, whose emblems are the bird and the flower. Whence the constant equivalence (and equivoque) between *chanter* ("sing") and *aimer* ("love"), terms which become practically interchangeable. Thus the register includes a theme, a referent unique to this expressive system—that of the genre itself.

It is not, however, without some hesitation that I use the term *space*, since it is a metaphor which is perhaps too restrictive. In a certain measure, one can speak of a framework of clear but empty contours in which is deployed, in its own rhythm and at the level of the individual poem, a literally incomparable energy. It is the abstract locus of a dynamic "convergence."

The general configuration of this space can be represented in the following diagram: .

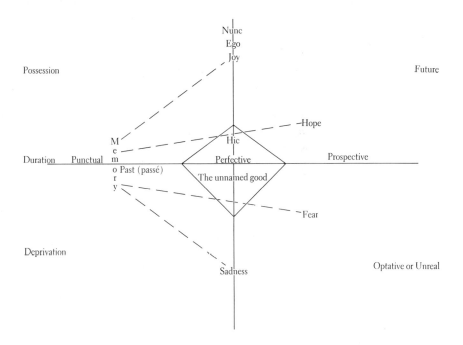

The vertical axis refers to the "I" and the "now" in reference to which the moments of the poem are defined, in its double sense of "instant of time" and "decisive element." However, the focal point determining these perspectives is a "here": the love-object is very often designated in the *grand chant courtois* by an adverb of place or equivalent locution. Normally, this *hic* is personalized as *vous* (a dilated form of *tu*), and is only rarely deleted from the level of expression.

The horizontal axis presents the chronological dimension. But the reference is to grammatical time, not necessarily real time. It is in fact rare that the tenses of the verbs (or the adverbial classes) mark out a historic succession among the other expressive elements of the poem. The alternation between past, present, and future serves generally and uniquely to evoke affective connotations. I shall return to this point later.

All stylistic features (whatever the sense given to the word) find a position within the space thus delimited (at least as long as one does not reserve the word "style" to represent the registral tradition itself). It is, in any event, in and through this kind of space that their body, their proper volume, the particular deployments of the registral framework are found. All the lexical and thematic constituents of the poem find their functional place there. Distortions are rare. This is obviously not the case with phonic elements; but it may be observed that if the opposition of grave and acute vocalic timbres has any relevence to registral style, it presents a binary opposition whose universal bearing is of the same sort as the fundamental oppositions of possession-privation, joy-sadness, hope-fear.

Finally, the rhythm (and the melody) of the verse contribute a global unity to the whole, since (as I have had occasion to explain elsewhere)[16] the expressive monad of this genre is less the whole song itself than the stanza. The latter, defined as rhythm, actualizes the registral spacing and in doing so endows it with a value.

What I have called "register" is the only perceptible referent to poetic language which the tradition provides for us, since other living cultural connections are lacking. It is what at once provokes and satisfies the reader's expectations. In the register are rooted the conventions which determine what one may call the stylistic sensibility. While in modern poetry the connotations of the work permit us to infer that extratextual thing called History, those of the *grand chant courtois* refer only to the *text*—which is the register.

It is at that level that the "classemes" of the semantic constitution are determined. Register can be formally conceived as a set of paradigms and the corpus of songs as a set of syntagmatic features. As a complex of motivations, as a pre-existent network of lexical, rhetorical, and even syntactic probabilities, as a system of pre-established equivalences, register constitutes the basis of the poetic expression of the *trouvère*: it provides him with a set of predetermined poetic requirements. If one admits the provisional designation of song as "message," one must in theory envisage two points of view: that of the performance by the *trouvère* and that of the object to be interpreted by his audience. Now my notion of register forces me to argue that these two points of view coincide: interpretation is implied in register, which in turn makes possible and justifies performance. Register contains an ideological schema; and in this way it includes the terms of the model and the value of its investment. At least this was the system originally. As long as the tradition was maintained, register was defined at the level of the encoder. But the mode of decoding changed in time; whence the ambiguity of the song thickened, within barely a century, to the extent that the genre changed profoundly. The *Razos*[17] with which certain troubadour songs of the thirteenth and fourteenth century were fitted out show clearly enough that in this later period interpretation was becoming progressively dissociated from register; it is a point in history which deserves careful study.

A set of deep structures thus underlies the surface of this corpus. In some parts of the register, these structures are so clear that the "style" of the *grand chant courtois* seems capable of formalization by strict generative rules. One discovers a dynamism analogous to that recently described by R. Pottier's terms "mega-models" and "optional models."[18] It would seem very useful to explore this ground.

Whatever the cultural model presiding over it, the register emerges as a kind of connotative language, a second level of significance which survives the centuries despite the gradual disappearance of the initial model. It is not improper to use the terminology of Halliday here,[19] to argue that the register conveys the "contextual meaning" of the message, whose "formal meaning" is established at the level of the whole poem. Inside the register, each sign in the poem is integrated in an immanent thematic projection within which it functions. A reservoir of poetic functions, the register establishes an isotopy of discourse which unfolds in the parts of the text. So true is this that in the early stages of the development of narrative, many authors continued to use expressive fragments of the lyric register in order to enable their story to utilize such an isotopy. I have recently shown this to be the case in *La Chastelaine de Vergi*; one could also cite *Flamenca* and many other works.

This is also why individual stylistic differences seem so tenuous to us in the *grand chant courtois*. We can assume that they were invisible to the contemporary audience. Comparative examination shows that the factor of personal invention can intervene effectively at the level of the whole (the context), but that it remains very weak and diffuse at that of micro-context. In other words, the individual element inheres in the distribution (within rather narrow limits) of particular features whose species and genera belong to the register which determines and makes them functional. Even if audiences of the twelfth century had some sense of what was "deviant," it would appear to them as the specific difference between the register and the current language and not as the "style of the author."[20] The essential character of register, it is necessary to repeat, is coherence: coherence which permits the audience to check, continually, the compatibility (or harmony) of the elements of the message. All the signs which make up the message find a reciprocal and common motivation in the register. Up to a certain point at least, register constitutes an integrated interpretation of this genre. I could introduce various comments by medieval aestheticians on the nature of *fictio* and on the obliquity of the poetic figures.[21] The linguistic signs assumed by register often become semantically distorted in the sense that, though they conserve their proper *semes*, the register redistributes their determining *classemes* and fixes in advance their associative possibilities. In the *grand chant courtois* this type of motivation fulfills the role played in modern poetry by what may be called "iconic motivation," that in which signs tend to become symbols.

This seems to me to be the way to describe a particular kind of poetry in a rather precisely delimited era. I do not wish to expand beyond this framework. Nevertheless I must point out, briefly and as a conclusion, the two historical axes of reference upon which the style of the *grand chant courtois* must be situated.

One is made up of the co-existing plurality of registers inherited from an archaic period of Western poetry—registers opposed to each other by their choice of formal factors, by their thematic polarization and by their different abilities to combine with non-registral elements. The other is the appearance of forms, and still more, new poetic intentions which after the end of the twelfth century began to break up registral coherence. We can distinguish, a bit summarily of course, two very noticeable tendencies after 1250. Either the contents continue to appear in more and more altered forms, or the reverse. But in both cases, it is personal invention which first gnaws and then tears asunder the *donnée* of tradition. Perhaps it is at this point that we can begin to speak about "the style of an author."

## Notes

1. *La Technique des trouvères dans la chanson courtoise* (Bruges, 1960), p. 15.

2. *Ibid.*, pp. 652 ff.

3. Most recently in a chapter to appear soon in the "new *Grundriss*" (*Grundriss der romanischen Philologie*), under the title "Stylistique et poétique latines et romanes."

4. I develop this point in my article "Testo e testura" in *Strumenti Critici* (Torino, 1968), p. 352.

5. See Nils Enkvist, "On Defining Style," in *Linguistics and Style* (Oxford, 1967), p. 28; and Michael Riffaterre, "Criteria for Style Analysis," in *Word*, XV (1959), 155.

6. See "Testo e testura," *op. cit.*

7. It is necessary to note in this connection that one observes more or less the same distribution of elements in other archaic genres, in particular the *chanson de geste*: thus we are dealing with a phenomenon of civilization, not with the law of a genre.

8. This is why the notion of register is less profitable in the analysis of narrative works, indeed scarcely usable in narratives of a historico-symbolic character, such as (generally speaking) the "novels" of the thirteenth century.

9. The gradual emergence of a written stage of literature in the twelfth and thirteenth century was an immense historical development.

10. *Op. cit.*, pp. 15-29.

11. The registral coherence of a poetic genre seems generally to be in inverse proportion to the size of its public (to the extent that one can judge these things).

12. From *Chansons attribuées au Chastelain de Couci*, ed. by Alain Lerond (Paris, 1964), pp. 68-70. To simplify, I cite only the M manuscript, without taking account of variants.

## SONG III

### I

The sweet voice of the wild nightingale which I hear warbling and echoing night and day sweetens me and calms my heart so much that I want to sing to express my joy. And I must sing because my song pleases her to whom I have sincerely rendered homage. And my heart must be joyful if she is going to keep me in her service.

### II

Never has my heart been flighty or deceitful towards her; so my fate should be better. I love her; I serve her; I adore her with constancy, but do not dare reveal my desire, for her beauty paralyzes me so much that in her presence I cannot speak and dare not even look at her innocent face, so afraid am I of having to turn aside my glance.

### III

I have fixed my heart so firmly on her that I think of no other. O God, let me enjoy her! Tristram, who drank the love potion, never loved so faithfully and ceaselessly; for I have devoted everything to her—my heart, my body, my desire, my vigor, my strength (perhaps I am mad); and yet I am afraid not to be capable, during the rest of my life, to serve her sufficiently and the love I have for her.

### IV

I swear I would never commit a foolish act even if I were about to die for her, for in all the world there is no woman so beautiful nor so good, and no other creature so inspires my desire. I love my eyes which first saw her. When I saw her, I left her my heart as hostage, which since then has long remained with her. Never, never, do I wish it to leave her!

## V

Go, song, take my message to the place which I dare not leave, and which I dare not approach, so unreasonable and suspicious are those who spy on me even before my love can be consummated. God curse them! To more than one lover have they brought trouble and sorrow; and it is painful to me that I must bow to them in spite of myself.

13. One can find a certain number of similar examples.

14. Often the second person alternated with the first, the poem unfolding as a virtual dialogue. In this respect, the poem under consideration is less typical.

15. This is a rather general fact: the initial stanzas in the songs tend to present a greater registral coherence than do the later stanzas. It is notable (although perhaps unrelated) that the theory of the *exordium* has been elaborated by the rhetoricians.

16. "Testo e testura," note four, p. 356.

17. *Razo:* a short commentary made on the contents of a *chanson*. *Razos* are added to the anthologies called *Chansonniers* (13th to 15th century).

18. "La Grammaire générative et la linguistique," in *Travaux de linguistique et de littérature*, VI (1968), 19-21.

19. Michael A. K. Halliday, "Categories of the Theory of Grammar," *Word*, XVII (1961), 244-45.

20. The remarks of S. C. Aston, "The Troubadours and the Concept of Style," in *Stil-und Formprobleme* (Heidelberg, 1959), pp. 142 ff., must be placed within this perspective.

21. See references in A. Schiaffini, *Mercanti, poeti, e un maestro* (Milan, 1969), pp. 42-43.

# DISCUSSION OF ZUMTHOR'S PAPER

Zumthor's description of the statistics of the chant was questioned; groupings of words of very high and very low frequencies with no intermediary frequencies are impossible, if the rank-frequency curves of Zipf and Mandelbrot have any validity. Zumthor replied that the most representative elements are to be found in other aspects of the analysis; it is only words heavily charged with meaning that belong to the extremes of high and low frequency; those that belong in the intermediary ranges are more colorless.

A propos of Zumthor's brief mention of the relationship between such texts and contemporaneous rhetoric, a participant wondered whether the emphasis on *amplification* to be found in Vinsauf, for example, was really an insistence on repetitious ornament, whether the theory of *amplificatio* might not allow all the variation that Zumthor was talking about—whether, in short, stereotyped *amplificatio* was not a mark of debased rhetoric, rather than of rhetoric in the best tradition. Zumthor said he considered rhetoric as only one of the components of the register. Dragonetti in his book on the trouvères probably exaggerated the importance of rhetorical elements *as such* in the chanson. The trouvères mostly use elementary figures such as metaphor, metonymy, *iteratio, personificatio*, which may well be taken as merely linguistic phenomena. The question of rhetoric in the chanson is largely a specious one.

Zumthor was questioned about his division of analysis into three levels— that of articulation, lexicon, and *motif*. Why is it necessary to distinguish between the first two, and what is unique to literature in the relation between those two which separates it from other kinds of discourse? Further, are these two levels related to the level of motif in an identical or different way from the manner in which they are related to each other? Zumthor replied that his distinctions were purely empirical. The vocabulary of medieval texts allows us, more clearly than do other texts, to distinguish among units of meaning. It is a matter of practicality to consider vocabulary as such; in the few minutes of analysis available to him he had tried to extract these units from the syntagmatic series in which they are contained and to consider them from a paradigmatic point of view. He had tried to see how the examination of their form and their semantic potential would permit us to interpret the (linear) syntagmas of the text. In theory this is difficult to do, but in practice it is rewarding. As for the level of motif, examination of the articulations furnishes the framework within which one tries to insert the vocabulary elements once they have been examined by themselves. The motifs appear at the level of textual (syntagmatic) content; therein are assembled comparatively few forms, among which the variants are distinguished by a certain degree of probability.

Another participant suggested the need for a fourth level, because in Zumthor's division there was no room for what used to be called "composition" or "syntax" (syntax not of the sentence but of the organization of the whole text, that is, its succession or structure). An analogy was suggested with Chomsky's system consisting of syntactic structure, phonological representation, and semantic interpretation. In terms of a generalized model of semiotic systems, we could envisage 1) a syntagmatic organization of the text, 2) a perceptible representation composed of concrete words, and 3) the level of motifs and themes. But beyond that there is the literary system, which uses another system, namely the language. Thus one can find within the verbal aspect the syntactic, phonetic, and lexical levels. Zumthor said that he was happy to accept this fourth level, especially in the analysis of the stanza, since the linking of the motifs in the stanza is connected to the syntactic and probably also to the rhythmic structure.

As for the concept of register itself, it was observed that the reason for its importance in the present discussion was that it raised the stylistic problem of the definition of a norm, a question utterly different from those conventionally dealt with by stylisticians. Another participant expressed agreement about the need to recognize the existence of an intermediate entity between the general literary code and the individual, idiosyncratic work. But he wondered if it wouldn't be better to call this *genre*. Wasn't "register" simply another name for genre? Not, of course, in the strict historical sense, as a combination of stylistic, thematic, and other traits, but rather in the sense of all complexes which resemble each other, all combinations of literary properties which have a certain stability and which function as models, and include the prescribed response of the reader? For we read according to a set of rules—when we read mystery novels, we follow their rules, and these differ; for example, the French *série noire* differs from the British, or Agatha Christie type. Our expectations as readers are brought into play each time the sense of genre is sufficiently acute and clear. Zumthor agreed substantially, saying that the question was simply one of terminology and that he had avoided the word *genre* because he wished to avoid its traditional associations. He wanted to add only that it is important to acknowledge the existence of a plurality of registers.

Zumthor was asked whether there were any constraints exercised by the fixed elements he had described, for example, the *reverdi's* conventional place at the beginning, or the images which tend to come at regular intervals in the poem. He answered that he did not want to insist too much on the aspect of fixity. There is a set or language of pre-existent connotations (though he hesitates to call it a system) which allows the author a very great liberty in passing from the potential to the work itself, a liberty which is not only a redistribution, in the usual sense of the word, but a re-creation, at the personal level, of the coherence implicit in the register, the potential entity. This finds a powerful reality within the text. We are in a world where the relation between the individual and the collective memory is much different from what it is today. As for Zumthor's assertion that there was little individual variation among the poems, it was argued that though individual contributions in these chants may seem minor, because in highly-stylized forms the personal element may be masked by the requirements of the genre, this appearance may be only an artifact of the analytical method used. Perhaps if other categories had been used, individual differences would have been more apparent; if the works were written by human beings, such differences must exist.

Another participant suggested that the element of coherence in the *chant* might be explained in terms of the notion of a stylistics of the reader, or more accurately, the female reader (*la lectrice*), who was essentially invented by the genre. The genre, of course, was oral; the author was transformed into a poet who was either the actual or potential lover of a mistress or mistresses who listened to him. These two elements—the female reader and the oral tradition—render the message contemporary; the poet who speaks of his love must be the lover at the moment that he is read. Zumthor found this observation to be very important, though he had spoken of the *je* as the only character (*actant*) in the little drama. It is always necessary to remember that these songs were songs of love, although they do not seem to be drawn from autobiographical material. There is an equivalence, amounting virtually to synonymy, between singing and loving, between the song and the joy of love, such that it seems as if the song has itself as object. There appears a figure which, at the level of motif, appears as *ma douce langue*.

Zumthor was asked whether he might not be confusing *courtoisie* and culture. The *chant*, after all, was part of a literature for illiterates; therefore it had to be particularly formalized, structured, coherent, just as modern spy novels and mystery stories are more highly structured, as structuralist criticism has shown, than high-brow fiction like that of Stendhal and Proust. Another participant re-emphasized the important change in the complexion of the literary audience of the Middle Ages. Originally, two groups had comprised this audience: the literate clergy, whose culture was entirely in Latin, and the secular ranks, who were essentially non-literate, even as far up as the rank of king. But this strict division disappeared with the advent of the aristocratic female reader who, though not of the clergy, was cultured, and loved the arts. Zumthor agreed, but noted that if this was a poetry for "illiterates," they were "illiterates" of a very special sort, and that there is an important coincidence between structures of the milieu and structures of the poetry.

It was remarked that such poems should never be studied apart from the melodies which accompanied them. It may very well be that the words were subordinated to the music, that the music existed first and that the words were added on the basis of simple, well-known themes. Today's popular songs are composed on similar principles; indeed, they probably inherit the tradition. Is this particular distribution of lexical units in the register characteristic only of this form? Zumthor replied that in other types of lyrical discourse, like those containing narrative elements (*chanson de toile, pas-*

*tourelle*), the distribution is completely different. In such genres, the substantives predominate. He agreed about the importance of melody, but noted, too, that the philology of music was only in its infancy, so that one had to do what one could by other means.

Zumthor was asked whether a similar method might not be applied to the corpus of less anonymous poetry—that of the Petrarchan poets of the Renaissance. Zumthor replied that, of course, the poetry he described had outlived its creators by several centuries, and what had sustained it was its system of encoding; but after the thirteenth century the manner of decoding began to change; whence a discontinuity, a growing ambiguity, in which great poets, trying to find new bearings, introduced elements which were either personal in the real sense or a form of pure court-game.

# 5
## GENRE STYLE

# THE STYLE OF AUTOBIOGRAPHY

### JEAN STAROBINSKI

A BIOGRAPHY of a person written by himself: this definition of autobiography establishes the intrinsic character of the enterprise and thus the general (and generic) conditions of autobiographical writing. But this is not merely the definition of a literary genre: in their essentials, these conditions ensure that the identity of the narrator and the hero of the narration will be revealed in the work. Further, they require that the work be a narrative and not merely a description. Biography is not portrait; or if it is a kind of portrait, it adds time and movement. The narrative must cover a temporal sequence sufficiently extensive to allow the emergence of the contour of a life. Within these conditions, autobiography may be limited to a page or extended through many volumes. It is also free to "contaminate" the record of the life with events which could only have been witnessed from a distance. The autobiographer then doubles as a writer of memoirs (this is the case of Chateaubriand); he is free also to date precisely various stages of the revisions of the text, and at the moment of composition to look back upon his situation. The intimate journal may intrude upon autobiography, and an autobiographer may from time to time become a "diarist" (this, again, is the case with Chateaubriand). Thus, the conditions of autobiography furnish only a large framework within which a great variety of particular styles may occur. So it is essential to avoid speaking of an autobiographical "style" or even an autobiographical "form," because there is no such generic style or form. Here, even more than elsewhere, style is the act of an individual. It is useful nevertheless, to insist on the fact that style will only assert itself under the conditions which we have just mentioned. It can be defined as the fashion in which each autobiographer satisfies the conditions of the genre. These conditions are of an ethical and "relational" order and require only the truthful narration of a life, leaving to the writer the right to determine his own particular modality, rhythm, span, etc. In a narrative in which the narrator takes his own past as theme, the individual mark of style assumes particular importance, since to the explicit self-reference of the narration itself the style adds the implicit self-referential value of a particular mode of speaking.

Style is currently associated with the act of writing. It is seen as resulting from the margin of liberty offered to the "author"[1] after he has satisfied the requirements of language and literary convention, and of the use he has put them to. The self-referential value of style thus refers back to the moment of writing, to the contemporary "me." But this contemporary self-reference may appear as an obstacle to the accurate grasp and transcription of past events. Critics of Rousseau and Chateaubriand have often thought that the perfection of their styles—whatever the reality of the depicted facts—rendered suspect the content of the narrative, setting up a screen between the truth of the narrated past and the present of the narrative situation. Every original aspect of style implies a redundancy which may disturb the message itself.[2] But, obviously, the past can never be evoked except with respect to a present: the "reality" of by-gone days is only such to the consciousness which, today, gathering up their present image, cannot avoid imposing upon them its own form, its style. Every autobiography—even when it limits itself to pure narrative—is a self-interpretation. Style here assumes the dual function of establishing the relation between the "author" and his own past; but also, in its orientation toward the future, of revealing the author to his future readers.

The misunderstanding of this subject is in large measure the result of conventional ideas about the nature and function of style. According to the view which sees style as a "form" added to a "content," it is logical to regard qualities of style in autobiography with suspicion. ("Too beautiful to be true" becomes a principle of systematic objection.)

This objection finds support in the ease with which a narrator may slip into fiction, a hazard which we ourselves are surely aware of from our own experiences in recounting past events. Not only (in this view) can the autobiographer lie, but the "autobiographical form" can cloak the freest fictive invention: "pseudo-memoirs" and "pseudo-biographies" exploit the possibilities of narrating purely imaginary tales in the first person. In these cases, the *I* of the narrative, "existentially" speaking, is assumed by a non-entity; it is an *I* without referent, an *I* which refers only to an arbitrary image. However, the *I* of such a text cannot be distinguished from the *I* of a "sincere" autobiographical narrative. It is easy to conclude, under this traditional conception of style, that, in autobiography or confession, despite the vow of sincerity, the "content" of the narrative can be lost, can disappear into fiction, without anything preventing its transition from one plane to another, without there even being a sure sign of that transition. Style, as an original quality, accentuating as it does the importance of the present in the act of writing, seems to serve the conventions of narrative, rather than the realities of reminiscence. It is more than an obstacle or a screen, it becomes a principle of deformation and falsification.

But if one rejects this definition of style as "form" (or dress, or ornament) superadded to a "content" in favor of one of style as deviation (*écart*), the originality in the autobiographical style—far from being suspect —offers us a system of revealing indices, of symptomatic traits. The redundancy of style is individualizing: it singles out. Hasn't the notion of stylistic deviation been elaborated precisely with a view to coming nearer to the psychic uniqueness of writers?[3] Thus the celebrated aphorism of Buffon has been rediscovered (in a slightly altered sense), and the style of autobiography now appears to bear a minimal veracity in its contemporaneousness with the life of the author. No matter how doubtful the facts related, the text will at least present an "authentic" image of the man who "held the pen."

That brings us to some observations concerning more general implications of the theory of style. Style as "form superadded to content" will be judged above all on its inevitable infidelity to a past reality: "content" is taken to be anterior to "form," and past history, the theme of the narrative, must necessarily occupy this anterior position. Style as deviation, however, seems rather to exist in a relation of fidelity to a contemporary reality. In this case, the very notion of style really obeys a system of organic metaphors, according to which expression proceeds from experience, without any discontinuity, as the flower is pushed open by the flow of sap through the stem. Conversely, the notion of "form superadded to content" implies—from its inception—discontinuity, the very opposite of organic growth, thus a mechanical operation, the intervening application of an instrument to a material of another sort. It is the image of the *stylus* with a sharp point, which tends thus to prevail over that of the *hand* moved by the writer's inner spirit. (Doubtless it is necessary to develop an idea of style which envisages both the stylus and the hand—the direction of the stylus *by* the hand.)

In a study devoted to "Temporal Relations in the French Verb," Emile Benveniste distinguishes *historic* statement (*l'énonciation historique*), a "narrative of past events," from *discourse* (*discours*), a "statement presupposing a speaker and an auditor; and in the first-named, an intention of influencing the second in some way."[4] While the narrative of past facts in historic statement uses the *passé simple* as its "typical form" in current French (which Benveniste calls "aorist"), discourse prefers to use the *passé composé*. A glance at recent autobiographies (Michel Leiris, Jean-Paul Sartre) shows us, however, that the characteristics of discourse (statement tied to a narrator named "I") may coexist with those of history (use of the aorist). Is this an archaism? Or better, aren't we dealing in autobiography with a mixed entity, which we can call *discourse-history?* This is surely a hypothesis which needs examination. The traditional form of autobiography occupies a position between two extremes: narrative in the third person[5] and pure monologue. We are very familiar with third-person narrative; it is the form of the *Commentaries* of Caesar or of the second part of the *Mémoires* of La Rochefoucauld, namely, narrative which is not distinguished from history by its form. One must learn from external information that the narrator and the hero are one and the same person. In general, such a process is expressly a depiction of a series of important events in which the editor puts himself into the scene as one of the principal actors. The effacing of the narrator (who thereby assumes the impersonal role of historian), the objective presentation of the protagonist in the third person, works to the benefit of the event, and only secondarily reflects back upon the personality of the protagonist the glitter of actions in which he has been involved. Though seemingly a modest form, autobiographical narrative in the third person accumulates and makes compatible events glorifying the hero who refuses to speak in his own name. Here the interests of the personality are committed to a "he," thus effecting a solidification by objectivity. This is quite the opposite of pure monologue, where the accent is on the me and not on the event. In extreme forms of monologue (not in the domain of autobiography but in that of lyrical fiction), the event is nothing other than the unwinding of the monologue itself, independently of any related "fact," which in the process becomes unimportant. We see the intervention of a process which is the opposite of that just described for third-person narrative: the exclusive affirmation of "I" favors the interests of an apparently vanished "he." The impersonal event becomes a secret parasite on the "I" of the monologue, fading and depersonalizing it. One need only examine the writings of Samuel Beckett to discover how the constantly repeated "first person" comes to be the equivalent of a "non-person."

Autobiography is certainly not a genre with rigorous rules. It only requires that certain possible conditions be realized, conditions which are mainly ideological (or cultural): that the personal experience be important, that it offer an opportunity for a sincere relation with someone else.[6] These presuppositions establish the legitimacy of "I" and authorize the subject of the discourse to take his past existence as theme. Moreover, the "I" is confirmed in the function of permanent subject by the presence of its correlative "you," giving clear motivation to the discourse. I am thinking here of the *Confessions* of St. Augustine: the author speaks to God but with the intention of edifying his readers.

God is the direct addressee of the discourse; the rest of mankind, on the contrary, is named in the third person as indirect beneficiary of the effusion which it has been allowed to witness. Thus the autobiographical discourse takes form by creating, almost simultaneously, two addressees, one summoned directly, the other assumed obliquely as witness. Is this a useless luxury? Shall we assume the invocation of God to be only an artifice of rhetoric? Not at all. God certainly doesn't need to receive the story of Augustine's life, since He is omniscient and sees the events of eternity at a single glance. God receives the narrator's prayer and thanksgiving. He is thanked for the intervention of His Grace in the narrator's destiny. He is the present interlocutor only because He has been the master of the narrator's previous fate: He has put him to the test, He has rescued him from error, and He is revealed to him ever more imperiously. By so openly making God his interlocutor, Augustine commits himself to absolute veracity: how could he falsify or dissimulate anything before One who can see into his innermost marrow? Here is a content guaranteed by the highest bail. The confession, because of the addressee which it presumes, avoids the risk of falsehood run by ordinary narratives. But what is the function of the secondary addressee, the human auditor who is only obliquely invoked? He comes—by his supposed presence—to legitimize the very "discursiveness" of the confession. The confession is not for God, but for the human reader who needs a narrative, a laying out of the events in their enchained succession.

The double address of the discourse—to God and to the human auditor— makes the truth discursive and the discourse true. Thus may be united, in a certain fashion, the instantaneousness of the confession offered to God and the sequential nature of the explanatory narrative offered to the human intelligence. And thereby are reconciled the edifying motivation and the transcendent finality of the confession: words addressed to God will convert or comfort other men.

Let me add this remark: one would hardly have sufficient motive to write an autobiography had not some radical change occurred in his life—conversion, entry into a new life, the operation of Grace. If such a change had not affected the life of the narrator, he could merely depict himself once and for all, and new developments would be treated as external (historical) events: we would then be in the presence of the conditions of what Benveniste has named *history*, and a narrator in the first person would hardly continue to be necessary. It is the internal transformation of the individual —and the exemplary character of this transformation—which furnishes a subject for a narrative discourse in which "I" is both subject and object.

Thus we discover an interesting fact: it is because the past "I" is different from the present "I" that the latter may really be confirmed in all his prerogatives. The narrator describes not only what happened to him at a different time in his life, but above all how he became—out of what he was—what he presently is. Here the discursive character of the narrative is justified anew, not by the addressee but by the content: it becomes necessary to retrace the genesis of the present situation, the antecedents of the moment from which the present "discourse" stems. The chain of experiences traces a path (though a sinuous one) which ends in the present state of recapitulatory knowledge.

The deviation, which establishes the autobiographical reflection, is thus double: it is at once a deviation of time and of identity. At the level of language, however, the only intruding mark is that of time. The personal mark (the first person, the "I") remains constant. But it is an ambiguous constancy, since the narrator was different from what he is today. Still, how can he keep from being recognized in the other which he was? How can he refuse to assume the other's faults? The narrative-confession, asserting the difference of identity, repudiates past errors, but does not, for all that, decline a responsibility assumed forever by the subject. Pronominal constancy is the index of this permanent responsibility, since the "first person" embodies both the present reflection and the multiplicity of past states. The changes of identity are marked by verbal and attributive elements: they are perhaps still more subtly expressed in the contamination of the discourse by traits proper to history, that is, by the treatment of the first person as a quasi-third person, authorizing recourse to the historical aorist. The aorist changes the effect of the first person. Let us remember too that the famous "rule of twenty-four hours"[7] was still generally respected in the eighteenth century, and that the evocation of past and dated events could not avoid recourse to the *passé simple* (except by using here and there the "historical" present). But it is the statements themselves, and their own *tone*, which make perfectly explicit the distance at which the narrator holds his faults, his errors, his tribulations. The figures of traditional rhetoric (and more particularly those which Fontanier defines as "figures of expression by opposition"[8]: preterition, irony, etc.) contribute something too, giving to the autobiographical style its particular color.

I shall take Rousseau as an example.

The presence of the imagined addressee strikes us even in the preamble to the *Confessions:* ". . . Qui que vous soyez que ma destinée ou ma confiance ont fait l'arbitre du sort de ce cahier. . . ."[9] Still more clearly, we find in the third paragraph of the first book, the double addressee (God, mankind) whose Augustinian prototype we have earlier tried to make precise:

> Que la trompette du jugement dernier sonne quand elle voudra;
> je viendrai ce livre à la main me présenter devant le souverain juge.
> [. . .] J'ai dévoilé mon intérieur tel que tu l'as vu toi-même. Être

éternel, rassemble autour de moi l'innombrable foule de mes sem-
blables: qu'ils écoutent mes confessions, qu'ils gémissent de mes ini-
quités, qu'ils rougissent de mes misères.[10]

To guarantee the veracity of his utterances, Rousseau, like Augustine, requires the presence of a divine gaze. But he requires it only at the outset,
and then once and for all. Within the body of the book there is scarcely
a single invocation or apostrophe to God. We note the diffuse presence of
the reader (with whom Rousseau sometimes engages in fictive dialogue), a
putative witness who is reduced most often to an indefinite *on*:[11] "It will be
thought that . . ." (*on pensera que* . . .), "One will say that . . ." (*On
dira que* . . .) Rousseau constantly assigns to this imagined interlocutor
the objections of good sense and social convention. He attributes to him
also the suspicion which he feels surrounds him. He strives to convince him
of the absolute truth of his narrative, as of the abiding innocence of his
intentions. The fact that his relation to God is looser than that of Augustine or Theresa d'Avila cannot help affecting the veracity of his statements.
The preliminary invocation, one senses, is not sufficient: truthfulness must
exist each moment, but Rousseau does not ask God to be a constant witness. In Rousseau's work the private emotions and conscience inherit some
of the functions assigned to God in traditional theological discourse. As a
consequence, the veracity of the narrative must be demonstrated with reference to intimate feeling, to the strict contemporaneity of emotion communicated in the writing. Pathos replaces the traditional address to a tran-
scendant being as the sign of reliable expression. Thus it is not surprising to
see Rousseau take from Montaigne and the Latin epistolary writers the
*quicquid in buccam venit*, and to attribute to it, this time, a quasi-ontologi-
cal value: the spontaneity of the writing, copied closely (in principle) from
the actual spontaneous sentiment (which is given as if it were an old, relived
emotion) assures the authenticity of the narration. So style, as Rousseau
himself says, takes on an importance which is not limited to the introduction of language alone, to the technical search for effects alone: it becomes
"self-referential," it undertakes to refer back to the "internal" truth within
the author. In recalling old feelings, Rousseau wants to make the present
narration strictly dependent on the "impressions" of the past:

Il faudroit, pour ce que j'ai à dire, inventer un language aussi nouveau
que mon projet: car quel ton, quel style prendre pour débrouiller ce
chaos immense de sentiments si divers, si contradictoires, souvent si
vils et quelquefois si sublimes dont je fus sans cesse agité [. . .] Je
prends donc mon parti sur le style comme sur les choses. Je ne m'at-
tacherai point à le rendre uniforme; j'aurai toujours celui qui me
viendra, j'en changerai selon mon humeur sans scrupule, je dirai chaque

chose comme je la sens, comme je la vois, sans recherche, sans gêne, sans m'embarrasser de la bigarrure. En me livrant au souvenir de l'impression reçue et au sentiment présent je peindrai doublement l'état de bon âme, savoir au moment où l'événement m'est arrivé et au moment où je l'ai écrit: mon style inégal et naturel, tantôt rapide et tantôt diffus, tantôt sage et tantôt fou, tantôt grave et tantôt gai fera lui-même partie de mon histoire.[12]

Among the diversity of styles cited by Rousseau, two particularly significant "tonalities" strike us in reading the *Confessions:* the elegiac and the picaresque.

The elegiac tone (as it is used, for example, in the celebrated lines which open the Sixth Book) expresses the feeling of lost happiness. Living in a time of affliction and menacing shadows, the writer takes refuge in the memory of the happy hours of his youth. The sojourn at Les Charmettes becomes the object of a fond regret: Rousseau is carried off by imagination, he tastes again vanished pleasures. Thus, by his imagination and at will, he fixes in writing a moment of his life in which he longs to hide. He is certain that such happiness will never come to him again:

> Mon imagination, qui dans ma jeunesse allait toujours en avant et maintenant rétrograde, compense par ces doux souvenirs l'espoir que j'ai pour jamais perdu. Je ne vois plus rien dans l'avenir qui me tente: les seuls retours du passé peuvent me flatter, et ces retours si vifs et si vrais dans l'époque dont je parle me font souvent vivre heureux malgré mes malheurs.[13]

The qualitative accent visibly favors the past, to the detriment of the present. The present in which these memories are set down is a time of disgrace; the old era which Rousseau is trying to recapture in writing is a lost paradise.

On the other hand, in narrative of the picaresque type it is the past which is "deficient": a time of weaknesses, errors, wandering, humiliations, expedients. Traditionally, the picaresque narrative is attributed to a character who has arrived at a certain stage of ease and "respectability" and who retraces, through an adventurous past, his humble beginnings at the fringes of society. *Then* he did not know the world, he was a stranger, he got by as best he could, more often for the worse than for the better, encountering on the way all the abuse, all the oppressive power, all the insolence of those above him. For the picaresque narrator, the present is the time of well-merited repose, of seeing oneself finally a winner, of finding a place in the social order. He can laugh at his former self, that obscure and needy wretch who could only respond in hang-dog fashion to the world's vanities. He can speak of his past with irony, condescension, pity, amusement. This narrative tone often requires the imaginary presence of an addressee, a confidante who is made an indulgent and amused accomplice by the playfulness with which the most outrageous behavior is recounted (the *Lazarillo de Tormès*, the prototype of the picaresque hero, is offered to the reader as a character named simply *vuestra merced*, and, pleasantly inverting the Augustinian confession, presents himself with the vow "not to be holier than my neighbors"—"confesando yo no ser mas sancto que mis vecinos"). Lazarillo's desire to begin at the beginning ("por el principio") is not without relevance to the method of Jean-Jacques' *Confessions*, for Lazarillo also wants to give a complete picture of his person ("por que se tenga entera noticia de mi persona").[14]

As a matter of fact, not only are purely picaresque episodes very numerous in the first six books of the *Confessions*, but it is not unusual to find elegiac episodes intimately mixed with picaresque, the change occurring back and forth with great rapidity. Shouldn't we recognize, here, in this full re-creation of lived experience, the equivalent of an important aspect of Rousseau's "system," a replica of his philosophy of history? According to that philosophy, man originally possessed happiness and joy: in comparison with that first felicity, the present is a time of degradation and corruption. But man was originally a brute deprived of "light," his reason still asleep; compared to that initial obscurity, the present is a time of lucid reflection and enlarged consciousness. The past, then, is at once the object of nostalgia and the object of irony; the present is at once a state of (moral) degradation and (intellectual) superiority.[15]

## Notes

1. I employ this term to designate an autobiographer independently of his quality as writer.

2. Cf Gilles–G. Granger, *Essai d'une philosophie du style* (Paris, 1968), pp. 7-8.

3. I refer, obviously, to the conception of stylistics implicit in the first period of the work of Leo Spitzer. Cf. *Linguistics and Literary History* (New York, 1962), pp. 11-14.

4. Emile Benveniste, *Problèmes de linguistique générale* (Paris, 1966), p. 242. See, also, Harald Weinrich, *Tempus. Besprochene und erzählte Welt* (Stuttgart, 1964).

5. "In the narrative, if the narrator doesn't intervene, the third person is not opposed to any other, it is truly an absence of person," *Ibid.*, p. 242.

6. On the role of autobiography in the history of culture, see Georg Misch, *Geschichte der Autobiographie* (Bern-Frankfurt-am-Main, 1949-1969), in eight volumes. See also Roy Pascal, *Design and Truth in Autobiography* (London, 1960).

7. There is an excellent discussion of this problem in Weinrich, *op. cit.*, pp. 247-53.

8. Pierre Fontanier, *Les Figures du discours*, introduction by Gérard Genette (Paris, 1968), pp. 143 ff.

9. Jean-Jacques Rousseau, *Oeuvres complètes* (Paris, 1959), I, 3:
"Whoever you may be whom my destiny or my confidence has made the arbiter of the fate of this notebook . . ."

10. *Ibid.*, p. 7:
"Let the last trump sound when it will, I shall come forward with this work in my hand, to present myself before my Sovereign Judge . . . I have bared my secret soul as Thou thyself hast seen it, Eternal Being! So let the numberless legion of my fellow men gather round me, and hear my confessions. Let them groan at my depravities, and blush for my misdeeds." Translation by J. M. Cohen (Baltimore, 1953).

11. Cf. Jacques Voisine, "Le Dialogue avec le lecteur dans *Les Confessions*," in *Jean-Jacques Rousseau et son oeuvre: Commémoration et colloque de Paris* (Paris, 1964), 23-32.

12. Jean-Jacques Rousseau, *op. cit.*, I. 1153.
"For what I have to say I need to invent a language which is as new as my project: for what tone, what style can I assume to unravel the immense chaos of sentiments, so diverse, so contradictory, often so vile and sometimes so sublime, which have agitated me without respite? . . . Thus I have decided to do the same with my style as with my content. I shall not apply myself to rendering it uniform; I shall always put down what comes to me, I shall change it according to my humor without scruple, I shall say each thing as I feel it, as I see it, without study, without difficulty, without burdening myself about the resulting mixture. In giving myself up to the memory of the received impression and the present feeling, I shall doubly paint the state of my soul, namely at the moment when the event happened to me and the moment when I wrote it: my uneven and natural style, sometimes rapid and sometimes diffuse, sometimes wise and sometimes mad, sometimes grave and sometimes gay, will itself form part of my story."

13. *Ibid.*, p. 226:
"My imagination, which in my youth always looked forward but now looks back, compensates me with these sweet memories for the hope I have lost for ever. I no longer see anything in the future to attract me; only a return into the past can please me, and these vivid and precise returns into the period of which I am speaking often give me moments of happiness in spite of my misfortunes."

14. *La Vie de Lazarillo de Tormès (édition bilingue)*, introduction by Marcel Bataillon (Paris, 1958), prologue, p. 88.

15. I refer principally to *Discours sur l'origine de l'inégalité*. Cf. preface and critical commentary in Rousseau, *op. cit.*, III.

# DISCUSSION OF STAROBINSKI'S PAPER

In connection with Starobinski's discussion of the function of the tenses in autobiography, it was noted that the *passé composé* in French is the tense which brings the past into the present and that perhaps its effect was stronger in earlier times when it contrasted even more with the *passé simple* than it does now. Starobinski replied that in Rousseau the use of the *passé composé* is a means of introducing elegiacally a nostalgic, evocative, quasi-present attitude.

An attempt was made to confirm Starobinski's idea of autobiography as a mixed entity—a discourse-history—by suggesting the possibility of the reverse, namely that of a history-discourse, as exemplified by Descartes' *Discours de la méthode*. Whereas in the confessions of St. Augustine and Rousseau, the discourse-history seeks to support the conversion, in Descartes it seeks to lessen the weight of the truth because the truth is a dangerous one. Starobinski agreed about the possibility of a history-discourse. He felt the need for a detailed study of Rousseau's style and thought that perhaps the reason for the present lack of such study was precisely that it was a style whose emotive and intellectual values send us compulsively back to the referent. There is thus an effect of concealing the style.

It was also observed that in the autobiography, as in the novel, discourse has to be interpreted in terms of the *real*. Yet discourse is not itself the real, but rather a sign of the real; there exists a semiotic relation.

The rest of the discussion turned on the importance of the pronouns, as parties of the discourse, in establishing the genre. Starobinski was asked whether the presence of a *you* (*tu*) which is addressed by an *I* is an essential element in the autobiography. It is noteworthy that autobiography is a dialogue in which the *I* does not wait for a response. His attention was drawn to an early biography, Abélard's *Historia Calamitatum* whose first sentence contains a "you" (*tu*) which is purely fictive. This pronoun gave to contemporaries the possibility of an interpretation. The first sentence of the first letter by Eloise refers to this text as a "consolation"; the consolation is a well-defined genre in the period. Historically this consolation aroused a response from the real "you" when the original "you" was fictive. Starobinski said that he was happy to have another illustration of the problem of analyzing "address" (*destination*) in the genre. Theresa of Avila could also be mentioned in this connection: she addressed herself to her confessors; again it is the addressee or audience which justifies the writing. He added that it is useful to recall that medieval authors were very conscious of the dangers of the pleasure implicit in writing; communicating something elegantly and well could be a culpable act. In *De Doctrina Christiana*, for example, Augustine offers precautions against feeling any sense of pleasure in hearing a sermon when one is supposed to be paying attention to the edifying message. The moral legitimation of autobiography can be a sort of exorcism against taking pleasure in literature, an art judged by the era and by long tradition to be capable—like the theater—of distracting one from holiness.

Concerning the analysis of the receiver or addressee (*destinataire*, or *allocutaire*), it was noted that, according to Freud, no present discursive situation can exist except in reference to a preceding discursive situation. The topic of the present utterance was necessarily the addressee of the former. The present "he" is the former "you." No discourse should be conceived as occurring for the first time.

Another participant noted that every *I* necessarily implies a *you*; the *you* is the image which one supposes the other to have of himself. As for the "I" of autobiography, there is no other definition of "I" than "the one who calls himself 'I.' " This is essentially a "shifter" definition (to use Jakobson's term); the autobiographical "I," the *auto-* in *autobiography*, is the exorcising substitute for the linguistic tautology that " 'I' is the one who says 'I.' " It tries to exorcise the tautology, to divert it, to substantivize and deformalize it. Thus it is a process of "de-shifterizing" the shifter. How? By filling this " 'I' who says 'I' " with an image, that is, someone of veracity and sincerity; he is, of course, no less imaginary than any other character in narrative. This ontologically empty "I" is filled by Rousseau with a figure possessing desire, pride, and intelligence. It is the image which Rousseau wants people to have of him. In such *littérature de signification* each episode functions as an exemplum of character, of a person. The autobiography is something which fills that which is unfillable at the level of language. It takes the whole discourse to "de-shift" this shifter. Starobinski found himself in substantial agreement, except that one must recognize that there exists for Rousseau a prior imaginary person who must be responded to and warded off, namely the persecutor. Rousseau wrote because he felt universally persecuted. It was necessary to re-establish the image of his true innocence. He needed to get others to recognize his innocence, for it was only when they did that he could be reconciled with himself.

# 6
## THE STYLES
## OF INDIVIDUAL AUTHORS
## AND TEXTS

# RIME AND REASON IN LITERATURE

### RUQAIYA HASAN

THE MOST GENERAL—and, therefore, the weakest—characterisation of stylistics can be made in a two-part statement: stylistics is a discipline concerned with the study of the language of literature;[1] and for this study, it employs a descriptive framework which is derived from some model(s) of linguistic theory. Much stronger claims have been made on behalf of the discipline, relating it to linguistics on the one hand and to rhetoric on the other. Thus Pierre Guiraud maintains: "la stylistique est une rhetorique moderne sous sa double forme, une science de l'expression et une critique des styles individuels," while, so far as Roman Jakobson is concerned, "poetics may be regarded as an integral part of linguistics."[2] There is no essential contradiction involved in holding these apparently ambivalent attitudes to stylistics: after all, the sharp division of rhetoric and grammar is itself a fairly recent phenomenon in the long history of the study of language and literature. Leaving aside the problems incumbent upon any justification of these stronger claims, I wish to concentrate here on the weaker characterisation of the subject. I would maintain that even such a general view of its scope and function raises certain fundamental questions, to which coherent answers must be supplied if stylistics is to be accorded the status of a systematic field of study. Indeed, unless these fundamental issues have been raised and satisfactory answers found, the contribution of stylistics to the study of language in general and to that of the language of literature in particular is hardly likely to merit serious consideration. I hope, too, to demonstrate during the course of the discussion that the weaker characterisation of the discipline has to be abandoned as trivial and impracticable.

One may start with the seemingly innocent question: why is stylistics concerned with the study of the language of literature? Be it noted that the emphasis in this formulation is bi-focal: not *any* language but the language of *literature* is the concern of stylistics; equally, not any other element but *only* the linguistic element of literature concerns stylistics. It is evident from this bi-focal emphasis that the answer to the question cannot lie in the status of the literary work as a "verbal structure." All texts, whether literary or non-literary, are instances of verbal structure. Not being a characteristic of literary works alone, "verbal-ness" by itself cannot provide sufficient reason for the special emphasis placed on literature as the datum that particularly concerns stylistics. Rather, it raises a doubt as to the very need for the recognition of a separate discipline: if linguistics is "the global science of verbal structure," it is reasonable to expect that it should be competent to deal with the literary verbal structures as well.[3] Unless literary verbal structures are crucially distinct[4] from non-literary ones, the discipline of stylistics is rendered superfluous by the very definition of the science of linguistics.

Such a crucial distinction may be found in the fact that, among verbal structures, the literary ones alone are also instances of art. It is significant however that stylistics shows not the slightest concern with any other instance of art; no stylistician, qua stylistician, has claimed to be able to describe or analyse the famous Mona Lisa. Moreover, we are now faced with the other side of the bi-focal emphasis in the formulation of the function of stylistics—the discipline is concerned not with *any* element of literature but solely and specifically with the *linguistic* one.

When approached in this manner, the examination of this seemingly unimportant question leads inescapably to the conclusion that this view of the function of stylistics is based upon a not very clearly articulated assumption. This emphatic isolation of the linguistic element in literary texts alone argues that the phenomena of "verbal-ness" and "art-ness" are not seen as two distinct and only accidentally related aspects of a given text; rather it is the linguistic element which has the greatest relevance to literature as art. Epigrammatically, the situation may be summed up thus: in literature, art is language, language is art. The stand being taken here would appear to be a fairly conventional one; we have known for centuries that the language of literature is "artistic," "creative," "non-communicative," "non-pragmatic," and "emotive"—and this by no means exhausts the list of epithets applied to literary language. I hope to show in the following paragraphs that what I mean by the unity of "verbal-ness" and "art-ness" in literature is somewhat different from, although does not necessarily contrast with, the description of literary language by any of the above-cited epithets.

To return to the main argument, let us grant that the postulate of the unity of "verbal-ness" and "art-ness" is fundamentally necessary for the interpretation of the function of stylistics. Such an assumption gives rise to several questions. To mention but two, one may ask a definition question: What does one mean by "the linguistic element?" And one may ask a substantial question: What is the nature of the relationship that unites the verbal to the artistic in literature? In other words, in what specific ways is the linguistic element relevant to art-ness in literature? We need to answer these questions not only because they are of theoretical interest to stylistics but also because they are of interest to any practical work in the field. "The study of language" is a phrase so inclusive that almost any operation with language as data may be justifiably regarded as some kind or instance of it. There is no exaggeration in the statement that the exhaustive linguistic study of a single major clause in English would require anything from two to four hours even for a well-trained linguist. This is in itself a chastening thought, especially in the context of works such as *The Faerie Queene*, *Paradise Lost*, and *Middlemarch*. But even if such an exhaustive study of the language of a given literary text were feasible in practice, it is to be very much doubted if the analysis of language patterns at every level and rank[5] would be of equal interest so far as the stylistic study of the text is concerned. The analysis of syllable structure in a particular lyric poem may be stylistically highly relevant; this, however, does not argue that the same would be true of another lyric poem, still less of a novel. The characterisation of stylistics as "a discipline concerned with the study of the language of literature" is thus trivial; it suffers simultaneously from both understatement and overstatement of the real concerns of the subject. Of course, no stylistician sets about studying the language of a literary text exhaustively and indiscriminately; this, however, is due to the soundness of his intuition —and probably even more due to his training in traditional literary criticism—rather than to any principled reasoning provided by the discipline for "sifting" the significant from the insignificant. We need a motivated, explicit account of those aspects of language which should have priority and significance in stylistic studies; it is reasonable to expect that such an account would be supplied by that discipline which claims recognition primarily because of its interest in such matters. The usefulness of the study of literary language for stylistic purposes does not rest on how many "facts" about the language are accumulated; it rests on how many of these facts are shown to be significant to the text as an instance of literature. This must surely follow from the basic postulate presented in the first sentence of this paragraph.

In his "Polemical Introduction," Northrop Frye remarks: "criticism cannot be a systematic study unless there is a quality in literature which enables it to be so." The remark applies equally appositely to the related discipline of stylistics. The questions raised in the previous paragraph can be answered with greater likelihood of being correct if they are based on an adequate hypothesis of the "nature" of literature: not what literature does for a community, not what it *means* (ethically, socially, economically, or philosophically), but simply what it *is* in itself. To this end, one must specify the components and those relations existing between the components which are crucial to literature and literature alone. This is not easy;[6] nonetheless it is, in my view, necessary. It is no more than a delusion to maintain that any practical study of literature—much less any valuable generalisations about it—can be made without a hypothesis regarding its nature.

Practical work presupposes some theory, no matter how weak or un-articulated it may be; no theory is possible without a hypothesis regarding the essential nature of its observed data. One specification regarding the components of literature was put forward by George Gascoigne (1575) who in his *Certayne Notes of Instruction, Etc.* presented what might be regarded as a program for the generation of literary texts. I quote here a brief passage from this document since it seems to have a direct bearing upon the question of the function of the linguistic element in literature. "The firste and most necessarie poynt that ever I founde meete to be considered in making of a delectable poeme is this, to grounde it upon some fine inuention. For it is not enough to roll in pleasant woordes, nor yet to thunder in Rym, Ram, Ruff by letter (quoth my master Chaucer), nor yet to abounde in apt vocables or epythetes, vnlesse the Inuention haue in it also aliquid salis. . . . I would exhorte you also to beware of rime without reason: my meaning is hereby that your rime leade you not from your firste Inuention."

In quoting from Gascoigne I do not imply that he demonstrates—or even claims—any originality in the views expressed by him; indeed, his parenthetical acknowledgement of Chaucerian authority is a clear disclaimer. The origin of the two hypotheses implicit in this quotation can be traced back to the very earliest works of literary criticism. That one must recognise at least two[7] distinct components in literature—those of "firste Inuention" and of "rime," in Gascoigne's formulation—has long been an established fact as is proved by the existence of a long list of pairs of terms such as plot and diction, matter and manner, content and style, "what" and "how," etc.[8] The second hypothesis, that there is some definite relationship between the two components, is again indicated at least tacitly by the presence of such old terms as "adequacy," "sincerity," and "decorum."[9] That it is ancient does not justify a hypothesis; the justification for these postulates must be found in their explanatory potential.

I am not much impressed by the warning that the recognition of two (or more) distinct components of literature contradicts the unity inherent in any instance of literature; one recognises several distinct components of language without contradicting the essential unity of these in any given instance of language. Perhaps one could offer the following points as constituting sufficient reason for the recognition of two distinct components. Sapir remarks: "literature does get itself translated and sometimes with astonishing adequacy"; the fact that translation is possible suggests that as in other uses of language, so here, too, there are some extralinguistic "facts" which are essentially independent of language, even though for their communication we must and do require the medium of language. One may compare two scientific experiments *qua* scientific experiments even though one only learns of these through language. In other words the message and the medium can theoretically be always separated from each other;[10] both the translation of a text in another language and the comparison of some part of a message with some part of another message are made possible by this quality of a symbolic medium. There exists, in literary studies, a long tradition—too predominant, one may justifiably complain—of comparing non-linguistic aspects of two or more literary texts. It is to be noted that such comparison can be and often is made not only across "genres" but also across language and culture boundaries. But perhaps most striking is the fact that there is almost no single language pattern at any level or rank which could be said to be crucially characteristic of literature; the position is somewhat different[11] in the case of other varieties of any given language. Those who have defined literature as "emotive" or "expressive" use of language are hard put to it to substantiate their claims, especially when confronted with long prose works, where the use of "emotive" and "expressive" language— no matter how these words are interpreted—is likely to be neither more consistent nor more frequent than in some other varieties such as advertising, journalese, or religious writing. This being the case, it appears reasonable to suppose that in addition to the component of "rime" some other component is required to turn an act of "riming" into the "making of a delectable poeme." This impression is further corroborated by the observation that certain figures of speech, tropes or the so-called stylistic devices which are commonly recognized as belonging to the literary register are neither restricted to literary texts alone, nor is it the case that the presence of any of these will, per se, be an indication that a given text is an instance of literature. As Aristotle remarked: "the works of Herodotus might be put into verse, and it will be a species of history, with metre no less than without it." It is difficult to see how these facts can be explained unless one is prepared to recognise the necessity of a component other than "rime" for the construction of literature; just as in the absence of such recognition, it would be difficult to see how the concept of "adequacy" is to be interpreted. This last problem is not solved by maintaining that the notion of adequacy is "evaluative" and as such does not concern stylistics. It is fallacious to argue that the suspension of all kinds of evaluation is a necessary condition for engaging in a systematic or scientific enquiry; on the contrary, nothing but advantage will flow from making explicit the basis for the evaluation of observed data while still remaining within the framework of a theory. In any

case, the concept of adequacy is so useful and powerful in the study of
literary texts that if we banish it from stylistics, as Bloomfield banished
meaning from linguistics, the concept will re-enter through the back door,
just as meaning did in Bloomfieldian linguistics—a situation which has nothing but disadvantage for literary studies.

We will grant then that a component distinct from that of "rime" is required for the construction of literature. The question still needs to be
answered: What is the nature of this component $x$? If literary verbal structures are compared with other kinds of verbal structures, the latter will also
be found to have a component which lends itself to translation and permits
intertextual comparison. Such a component is generally labelled the semantic component (or level), and it functions as a bridge between the linguistic
and the non-linguistic. On the one hand, it is related referentially to the
extralinguistic universe;[12] on the other hand, related to it realizationally are
the linguistic components of syntax, lexis, and phonology. Thus while
meanings may be said to be the property of the semantic level by virtue of
its referential relation to the extralinguistic universe, the mediation of the
meanings themselves can take place in language only through the means of
linguistic symbolization; that is, through the selection of appropriate syntactic, lexical and phonological categories (which are themselves transmitted through the phonic or graphic channel). It follows from this two-
way symbolic relationship that the semantic component can be assigned
the function of a "controlling device" in language production; amongst the
various components of language, it alone may be said to have the power to
"specify" what given concatenation of meanings is to be encoded on any
particular occasion, thus, in turn, motivating the selection of one set of
formal-phonological categories as opposed to any other. To use Gascoigne's
terms, in the production of the verbal structures of the type under focus,
the "reason" for the "rime" is furnished by the semantic level. The definition of notions such as those of appropriacy, adequacy, relevance, and
evasion, etc., depends primarily on the bringing together of the linguistic
(semantic, formal and phonological) and the extralinguistic—a principle
that is implicit in all functional theories of language.

From the foregoing comments, it might be thought that Gascoigne's
terms "firste inuention" and "rime" are perhaps no more than different
labels for what is known respectively as the "semantic" and the "formal-
phonological" component in language in general. The points of similarity
certainly seem to be striking. Thus the so-called non-linguistic[13] aspects
which are comparable intertextually and which are amenable to translation
are the "meanings" of the text, whether the text is literary or non-literary—
and meanings, as stated earlier, are the property of the semantic level. One
may note the somewhat special sense in which concepts of adequacy, ap-

propriacy, relevance, and evasion, etc. are employed in literary studies. This is due to that aspect of literature which is commonly called "fictional" or "fictitious": in literary writings, the "immediate situation" corresponding to each particular individual utterance in the text does not exist physically —indeed, not only *does not* but *need never have* existed physically in the extralinguistic universe. Since the notions under discussion are primarily defined on the basis of the relationship of the linguistic to the extralinguistic, one might question the validity of the use of these concepts in literary studies. However, such a doubt arises mainly because of a naïve interpretation of the term "immediate situation," which is equated with concrete, physical objects, entities, etc., bodily present in the real world and named through the various elements of the utterance. This, as Ellis points out, is an unsatisfactory model of "referential relation." It may very well be true that there are more things in heaven and earth than are dreamt of in some philosophies; it is truer still, however, that there are infinitely more referential resources in language than there are—or ever can be—things in heaven and earth. Consequently, the referential relation of language to extralinguistic phenomena cannot be thought of in terms of names for actually existent concrete objects, entities, events, and processes. It seems to me reasonable to suggest that that characteristic of language which permits its use for talking of events and entities *in absentia* is also the characteristic which permits its use for constructing hypotheses, for telling lies and for the making of fiction. The meanings of the hypothetical and fictive (whether lying or fiction-making) verbal structures are encoded and made available for interpretation generally in the same way as any message regarding a past experience is encoded and made available for interpretation. So long as the speaker[14] has the key to the symbols of the code, the physical "presence" or "absence" of extralinguistic processes and entities, etc., is itself immaterial,[15] both for encoding and for decoding. Needless to say, this general similarity between the four types of texts under consideration (i.e., texts (i) describing past experience, (ii) constructing hypotheses, (iii) telling lies, and (iv) making fiction) does not imply identity in every respect. I am concerned here in particular with two considerations according to which the four types can be subdivided into two groupings. First, it is in the case of hypothetical and fictive (types (ii)-(iv)) verbal structures alone, as opposed to those describing past experience (type i) that language may be said to have an essentially "creative" function: here, in the very act of reference, the categories of the language create for the speaker's contemplation those very processes, entities, etc., which they refer to:[16] the immediate situation and the thesis relevant to each individual utterance *is* only as it can be inferred from the utterance in the light of its function in the totality of the utterances of the text. On the other hand, literary texts may be set aside from the other three types (types i-iii) of texts in that it is in the latter three that the theses and immediate situations relevant to each utterance of the text are constrained to be contingent upon the actual extralinguistic universe;[17] such a constraint does not exist for the literary texts.[18] The consequence is that a literary text may be said to "contain" its own context of immediate situation in a manner which is qualitatively different, so that the use of co-textual information here does not have the same value as in the study of the other three types (i-iii). This discussion, I hope, throws some light on why the concepts of adequacy, appropriacy, relevance, etc. when applied to literary texts have somewhat different meanings. The notions as applied to given linguistic categories in literary texts are determined by reference to at least three distinct sets of criteria, which may be listed as follows:

1. The instantial symbolic function of the item in the text; i.e., the question may be asked: How does the given category "fit in" with the totality of categories in the text?—where the notion of fitting in is not limited to corroboration or contradiction of other theses only but also includes at least tenor agreement;[19]

2. The normal symbolic function of the item in the language; i.e., the question may be asked: How *would* (not *does*) the given category fit in, if there existed an actual extralinguistic context of situation for it?

3. The normal symbolic function of the item in the language of literature; i.e., the question may be asked: How is such a given category made to function normally in a literary text?

It may be noted in passing that it is the last two questions to which the Prague school concept of "structured esthetics" would be relevant. To answer these two questions, one needs sufficient knowledge of language and its functioning in different contexts of situation (cf. 2 above) as well as an awareness of existent literary traditions and conventions (cf. 3 above). To answer the first of the questions, one must have a sensitivity to language categories and their semantic functions, so that the inference of the set of immediate situations and theses is free of errors and personal limitations; and further, the bases for one interpretation as opposed to another can be made explicit. If it is the case that the meanings of a literary text are available to the reader only through the categories of language which constitute the text, and if it is the case that criteria for relevance, etc., are here dependent upon considerations of the type enumerated above, it is necessary to postulate an "ideal reader," since in practice, it is difficult if not impossible to find an actual reader who combines the maximally exhaustive knowledge of language and literature which would be required for an "ideally exhaustive" interpretation. It is beside the point that the writer of the literary text may himself not satisfy these requirements or that the ideal reader's interpretation may go beyond the writer's declared intention: in most cases of linguistic transaction, the encoder's communicative intent, as such, is no guarantee that the encoded message would be interpreted in the manner intended by him. Once transmitted, the message is in practice meaningless or meaningful according to how far the meanings are available to a decoder. An ideal reader is postulated in any literary message, for it is perhaps more true here than anywhere else that one is capable of receiving only what one can give.

However justifiable the position taken here may be, namely that the meanings of a literary text are given a particular shape and identity for a decoder according to the meanings he assigns to language categories of the text, the equation of the semantic level with Gascoigne's "firste inuention" and of the formal-phonological levels with "rime" would not be satisfactory. One would be saying no more than that two levels (or components)—one of semantic content and another of linguistic pattern selection realizing the former—can be set up for literary texts. The modification "in literary texts" would, however, be unnecessary since the condition would obtain for all texts and as such it would throw no light on the specific nature of literature. One would thus be left with the only distinguishing feature for literary texts posited above: that the immediate situations and theses relevant to the individual utterances of a literary text need not be contingent upon the actual extralinguistic ones. This feature by itself is far too weak to function as a crucial characterisation of literature; note that it can only be formulated negatively. If Gascoigne's terms are to be interpreted in this way, we would be back with the questions with which we started: what particular aspects of the language of a literary text does one *have* to study in stylistics and why? In addition, certain apparently contradictory "facts" about literary texts assume even greater proportions. Usual criteria for the assignment of a text to any register[20] fail here, since literary texts do not seem to be restricted where the selection of field, tenor, or mode of discourse is concerned, unless one indulges in the truism that the field of literature is literature and the participants of the discourse are the encoder (i.e., the author) and the decoder (i.e., the total potential reading community). Even this would not take one very far since registers are distinguished from each other crucially on the basis of some consistent and unique property of linguistic pattern selection. In literary verbal structures, on the one hand, there are no formal-phonological categories or specific combinations of these that *must* be selected in any and every work, and, on the other hand, it certainly is the case that patterns of language which pass unnoticed elsewhere are seized upon as significant here, to the extent that often efforts have been made to characterize literature by the presence of these very patterns. If the formal and phonological description of figures of speech and stylistic devices could be made precise and explicit, we would find that devices such as those of metaphor, simile, parallel structure, deviation (for which one had the more gracious term "poetic licence" till very recently), alliteration, etc., are scattered around in our non-literary use of language. Consider the sentence *Parliament promises prompt enquiry*, the alliteration of which goes unnoticed, whereas the murmurs of Tennyson's innumerable bees echo down the corridors of literary studies with a persistence which cannot be explained simply in terms of the formal or phonological properties of the device of alliteration. Nor can one's interest in figures of speech used in literary language be explained by their frequency, for it is highly doubtful if the frequency of such recognised devices in longer prose works is significantly different from that in, say, a feature article in a quality newspaper. The conclusion seems inescapable that if these devices draw attention to themselves in literary works, it is not by virtue of the fact that they can be formally or phonologically described, but that they have or acquire some additional attribute when used in such verbal structures. These comments do not imply that the language of literary works cannot be characterised at all, only that this characterisation cannot be made at the lower levels of form and phonology. Further, an accurate characterisation of literary language would gain in interest and significance if a "motivation" for it could be found. Observation would certainly bear out the truth of the assertion that literary language is marked by consistent foregrounding, a characteristic referred to also as maximal structuring or the patterning of the variability of patterns. However, motivation for this characteristic cannot be found in the fact that the literary text has the two levels of semantic content and linguistic selection.

Another apparent contradiction about literary texts concerns the theses and immediate situations that can be inferred from its individual utterance. With the exception of informal conversation—which is, in fact, a conglomeration of overlapping and interpolated texts—most non-literary texts display their unity by the unity of the topic and tenor of discourse. Briefly, for these texts, topic, and elements of topic (or sub-topic) can be defined as the "clustering" or "organising" of sets of relevant theses of the text that stand in some logical relation to each other, such as those of causality, exemplification, elaboration, etc. It is consequently true, almost by definition, that the topic of discourse in general does not vary within the boundary of the same text. If within the course of describing my friend's new car, I interrupt myself to offer you cakes or buns with your tea, this interruption is regarded as an interpolated text and forms no part of the text which it has interrupted. The observation regarding the unity of topic (in the sense in which the term topic has been used above) does not hold true for *all* literary texts. The shorter the text, the more likely it is that the topic will remain consistent. In longer texts, however, clusters of these need not stand in any of the inevitable relations which must exist between two or more sub-topics of the same non-literary text. Despite this, it would be trivial to maintain that literary texts do not display topical unity, for they are at least as highly unified as non-literary texts—if not more so. The clause by clause or sentence by sentence semanticization of literary texts will not explain the source of their unity. Where does this unity arise from? We assume that it cannot be accidental, that it is not the case that a literary writer simply reels out a string of sentences or clauses or whatever which miraculously lead to a unified text. Quite obviously there must be some regulative principle which, in the encoding activity, guides the selection of the theses and language categories that realise the latter, so that the message emerging from the totality is grasped as a structured, unified whole by the reader. It is immaterial to the present discussion whether such a regulative principle is explicitly recognised and consciously controlled by the artist—if we are to believe Plato, great poetry at least, cannot be written except under the influence of divine madness, whereas the view of the poet as the "wise mentor" leaves room for explicit recognition and conscious control. One need not dwell on these problems here; what is more to the point is the fact that if the need for such a regulative principle is recognised, then it must also inevitably be seen as a component that controls the level so far referred to as the "semantic level" of literary text, in much the same way as the latter controls the formal and phonological levels. Thus, one would be recognising at least three components as essential to the "making of a poeme": i) regulative or unifying principle; ii) sets of theses and inferred immediate situations; iii) totality of language pattern selection. From the drift of Gascoigne's Notes, it would seem justifiable to suggest that his concept of "firste inuention" is nearer to what is being referred to here as the regulative principle than it is to what might be called the semantic content in its usual sense.

It would not be true to claim that other texts do not have a regulative principle since the very fact that sub-topics must stand in some given relation to each other in order to make a unified text argues that there must be an organising principle which controls the selection and ordering of individual sentences whose clustering constitutes a sub-topic. What seems peculiar to literary texts alone is the fact that the first and the second component stand here in a symbolic relation to each other. In literature there are two layers of symbolization: the categories of the code of the language are used to symbolize a set of situations, events, processes, entities, etc. (as they are in the use of language in general); these situations, events, entities, etc., in their turn, are used to symbolize a theme or a theme-constellation. I would suggest that we have here an essential characteristic of literary verbal structures, on the ground that such a postulate provides an explanation for various observed facts regarding literature, attention to some of which has already been drawn in this paper.

So far as its own nature is concerned, the theme (or regulative principle) of a literary work may be seen as a generalisation or an abstraction, as such being closely related to all forms of hypothesis-building. A certain set of situations, a configuration of events, etc., is seen not only as itself (i.e. a particular happening) but also as a manifestation of some deep underlying principle. The Aristotelian assertions that literature proceeds from the particular to the universal and that it is more true than history because it is more probable are thus implicit in such a characterisation of literature. Its universality derives from the fact that the theme—the very governing principle—of literary works may be regarded as an hypothesis regarding the nature of the universe and man's relation to it. Its truth derives from the logical necessity inherent in any generalisation;[21] that is to say, literature is idealistic in the same sense as any scientific theory is. As Melville remarks in *Billy Budd, Sailor:* "truth (actual happening) uncompromisingly told will always have its ragged edges." The greater probability of literary truth is not based on any statistical observation, just as its idealness is not the idealness of morality; both its probability and its ideal nature derive from the fact that the governing principle of literary work is akin to a hypothesis, whether it is formulated consciously or unconsciously by the author.

It follows from this view of the relationship of the theme and the events etc. realising the theme that the latter would be seen as subservient to the former; their selection and consequently their evaluation is, to a large extent, governed by their aptness for the realisation of the theme. Equally, it is irrelevant, in itself, whether the discrete situations and characters, inferred from the language patterns of the text are actual (in the sense that they actually existed in the world) or whether they are fictitious (in the sense that they never physically existed in the universe); what is of greater importance is the consideration of what events, what propositions, and what types of characters the author has seen as the ones which would realize the governing hypothesis of his total artistic creation. Fictionality by itself does not create literature, just as the mention of a historical character in a novel does not turn it into a book on history. Considerations of accuracy or otherwise at the second level of thesis-inference are, as it were, irrelevant; the paramount consideration is the relationship of these to the first level.[22]

I hope that the drift of my argument is clear. If the double layering of symbolisation is what sets literary verbal structures apart from others—as seems to be the case—then it would follow that any aspect of language which is related to this phenomenon becomes the center of stylistic study. Two such areas come to mind readily: that area which deals with the "internal organization" of the text and that which deals with the "fit of the language" to the first and the second levels of literature, namely that which I would refer to as style. The discrete theses of the second level have to be clustered and put together in some systematic manner to show how they relate to the theme at the first level. This explains the need for the maximal structuring, the patterning of variability of language patterns and the consistent foregrounding. "The consistency manifests itself in the fact that the reshaping of the foregrounded component within a given work occurs in a stable direction" (Mukařovský). One of the most remarkable things about the use of figures of speech and stylistic devices, both traditionally recognised and new ones, is that in literature they do not occur randomly. Much is made of deviation in literary writing but a significant fact that seldom, if ever, gets mentioned in stylistic studies is the regular pattern of its occurrence within a given text. Some principle determines what kind of device, what kind of patterning of language will occur and where—to the extent that predictive statements regarding that particular text may be made.[23] A literary text has to have a code which is instantial to it, for the reason that certain discrete situations which per se do not have a given symbolic value, are assigned such a value by being placed in a certain arrangement. The maximal structuring as well as the variation in the use of the same linguistic pattern for different purposes in different texts arises from the need to signal the specific manner in which certain elements are so combined as to realize the theme. Thus, the key to what Pierre Guiraud has referred to as the *code de texte* lies within its theme. No writer, no matter how deviant he is, can afford to be randomly deviant, for the simple reason that the effect of random deviance would be meaninglessness and a total lack of communication. The consistency of foregrounding and the thematically motivated use of language patterns together ensure a reader's sensitivity to even apparently ordinary phenomena in language which might elsewhere go unnoticed. What draws attention to certain transitivity selections in Golding's *Inheritors* is not the emotive, expressive, or stylistic excellence—whatever these terms may mean—of the language pattern, per se, but the consistency with which certain text-integrating functions are performed by these selections.

In the following paragraphs a brief analysis of Yeats' poem "The Old Men Admiring Themselves in the Water" is presented. This analysis sets out to demonstrate i) that, as postulated, there do exist three levels in any literary text; ii) that they stand in a realizational relation; and iii) that the consistency of foregrounding and the patterning of specific language patterns is thematically motivated. I shall make no attempt to relate the poem to any other of Yeats' writings, nor do I intend to compare it with any contemporary works, not because I think these to be fruitless activities but because I have not sufficient time or space.

In the Macmillan edition of the *Collected Poems* of W. B. Yeats, "The Old Men Admiring Themselves in the Water" is entered under *In the Seven Woods* (1904). It is thus a poem belonging to the first stage of his productive years. The text runs as follows:

### The Old Men Admiring Themselves in the Water

1   I heard the old, old men say
2     "Everything alters,
3     And one by one we drop away."
4   They had hands like claws, and their knees
5     Were twisted like the old thorn-trees
6     By the waters.
7   I heard the old, old men say
8     "All that's beautiful drifts away
9     Like the waters."

The poem consists of nine lines, divided equally among three stanzas; each stanza corresponds to one sentence; a sentence itself is defined as a complex of clauses which are related to each other by subordination, coordination or embedding. The rhyme scheme is *aba, ccb,* and *aab* for the three stanzas respectively. All *a* and *c* lines are tetrametric while all *b* lines have only two strong syllables. One may ask then if the singling out of the *b* lines rhythmically is motivated thematically and if the rhyme variation from stanza to stanza corresponds to some function in the text. To answer these questions one must look at the set of these inferred from the clauses and clause-combinations in the text. The first sentence consisting of the first three lines may be divided primarily into two parts. The first part (line 1; rhyme [*a*]) has the contextual function of introducing quoted speech; the second part (lines 2; [*b*] and 3; [*a*]) has the function of quoted speech. We have two planes of narration for the text, direct narration and indirect. The direct plane of narration is the assertion of the *I* in the poem, while the indirect one is the assertion of the *they* (not *I*) of the poem. The relation between the quoted clauses (lines 2 and 3) should be noted. We have here the coordinating item *and;* as a coordinator at the sentence rank (i.e., when coordinating clauses to make sentences), *and* can occur between any clauses which form a list, e.g., as in *John had coffee, Joan had chocolate, and I had tea,* or stand in time sequence, e.g., as in *he arrived and we started the meeting,* or bear a cause-result relation to each other, e.g. as in *he drank the coffee and felt better,* or where the relationship is one which may be described as "non-consistent," for want of a better word, e.g. *I invited him and he didn't come* (where *and* may be read as *and yet*). The

*and* in our text does not fall into any of these categories; the two clauses
*everything alters* and *one by one we drop away* are related to each other as
would be a general statement to its particular exemplification. Thus line
2[*b*] puts forward a general proposition and line 3[*a*] offers a particular case
of the general.

There are two clauses in the second sentence (lines 4-6); the clause
boundaries do not coincide with the line boundaries. The two clauses of
the sentence stand in a list relation. Both these clauses of the sentence belong to the direct narration plane, whereas in the previous sentence the
first part that has the function of quoting belongs to the direct narration
plane, while the remaining part belongs to the indirect plane. This scheme
is repeated in the third sentence: the first part of the sentence (line 7[*a*])
is a repetition of line 1[*a*], while the second part of the sentence (lines 8[*a*]
and 9[*b*]) has the function of quoted speech, thus forming an indirect narration plane. Again the last two lines constitute one clause so that the
boundary of line 8 does not coincide with the boundary of the quoted clause
which continues into line 9. Despite this difference between the two cases
of indirect narration-plane an interesting similarity can be observed. The
relationship between lines 2 and 3:

> 2   "Everything alters,                    [b]
> 3   And one by one we drop away."   [a]

was said to be that of a generalization to its particular exemplification. Lines
8 and 9 echo this relationship:

> 8   "All that's beautiful drifts away   [a]
> 9   Like the waters."                         [b]

Line 9[*b*] is like 3[*a*] to the extent that both provide an exemplification of
some generally stated process; on the other hand, line 2[*b*] and line 8[*a*]
may be regarded as having the same kind of semantic function. The relationship of 8 and 9 does not constitute an exact reflection of the relationship between 2 and 3, for while 8 may be regarded as a general statement,
it is not so wide in its scope as the statement in line 2. This results from the
qualification of *all* by *that's beautiful*. The information regarding the rhyme
scheme and the general functions of the various parts of the sentences may
be presented together in the following manner:

$$
\begin{array}{ll}
1\,a: \text{Quoting} & \\
2\,b: \text{general} & \\
3\,a: \text{example}
\end{array}\Big\}\text{Quoted}
\quad
\begin{array}{l}
4\,c \\
5\,c \\
6\,b
\end{array}
\quad
\begin{array}{ll}
7\,a: \text{Quoting} & \\
8\,a: \text{general} & \\
9\,b: \text{example}
\end{array}\Big\}\text{Quoted}
$$

This formulation shows that there is a two-way coupling in the indirect narration: lines 2 and 8 are alike in some respects: they form the first—and the general—part of a two-part related statement while 3 and 9 are alike in that they form the other—and more specific—half. On the other hand, the coupling of the rhyme *a* in lines 3 and 9, puts together *and one by one we drop away* and *all that's beautiful drifts away*. One might consider the juxtaposition of these two lines in combination with the title of the poem, and in particular with the word *admire*[24] in mind, as well as the parallel function of *we* and *all that's beautiful*. Similarly, the coupling of the rhyme *b* for lines 2 and 9 produces a juxtaposition which is again remarkable: "*everything alters* (line 2[*b*]), *like the waters*" (line 9[*b*]). The variation in rhyme scheme ([*ba*] in the first stanza and [*ab*] in the third) is thus obviously motivated by considerations of meaning. The rhythmic regularity of the *b* lines (lines 2, 6, and 9) is remarkable when we find that in these three lines there are only three strong lexical items: *alters* (line 2), *waters* (line 6) and *waters* (line 9). The penultimate syllable of each is stressed and, as will be further corroborated by the study of the lexical selections in the text, the bringing together of *water* and *alter* is very closely related to the theme of the poem. The direct narration plane, which consists of lines 1, 4-6 and 7, is characterised by modification, qualification, and attribution, all patterns of language which normally occur in description. This general similarity is further emphasised in the selection of the actual items which realize the modifying, qualifying, and attributive elements: the semantic component common to all these realisations may be stated in one word as *decrepitude*, which sums up the meaning of the description of the *old, old men* with *hands like claws* and *knees* that were *twisted* like the *old thorn-trees*. The two planes of narration in the text are linked to each other in three ways: in the first place, to contrast with predominant description at the direct narration plane, we have one single case of qualification in *all that's beautiful* (line 8) at the direct plane of narration. This contrast is further emphasised by the selection of the item *beautiful* which may be regarded as a weak antonym of *decrepit*. (This contrast is perhaps another reason for drawing our attention to the item *admire* in the title of the poem.) The two planes are related also by the regularity of the *b* lines, which occurs in both cases, this general similarity being made more striking by the echo of the item *water* (lines 6 and 9). Apart from these two links, there is the structural link of quoting [*a*] lines to the quoted [*b/a*] and [*a/b*] lines. This explains why in the above representation I have considered it necessary to indicate two different lines of demarcation. Attention must, however, be drawn to the total lack of any explicit logical relation between the essentially descriptive lines (lines 4 to 6) and the remaining parts of the text.

At the clause rank, the two systems of options which seem to be the most relevant ones by virtue of their consistent foregrounding and their function in the internal organisation of the text, are the systems of transitivity and of mood.[25]

Disregarding the distinction of embedding, the text may be said to consist of ten major clauses, so that there are ten predictor elements (one per clause) each realized by a verbal group, each verbal group itself realizing some type of process. These verbal groups are listed below in their complete form under the separate heading of the type of process they realize. The number next to the item indicates how often the latter occurs with that particular function in the text. Within the parentheses are provided line and clause references, the latter being numbered according to the sequence in which they occur in the text.

i. process: perception
*heard* 2 (ll. 1 & 7; clause nos. 1 & 7: *I heard*)

ii. process: verbalisation
*say* 2 (ll. 1 & 7; clause nos. 1 & 7: *the old, old men say*)

iii. process: supervention
*alters* 1 (l. 2; clause no. 3: *everything alters*)
*drop away* 1 (l. 3; clause no. 4: *one by one we drop away*)
*drifts away* 1 (l. 8; clause no. 9: *all . . . drifts away like the waters*)

iv. process: relational
*had* 1 (l. 4; clause no. 5: *they had hands like claws*)
*were* 1 (l. 5; clause no. 6: *their knees were twisted like the old thorn-trees by the waters* (ll. 4-6)
*'s* 1 (l. 8; clause no. 10: *that's beautiful*)

The labels *perception* and *verbalisation* are self-explanatory; *supervention*-type process may be informally described as "action not engendered by the participant but supervising," while the *relational*-type process is one that relates a participant to some circumstance, attribute, or identity. It is remarkable that the types of process selected in this poem are mostly such that the possibility of their being undertaken voluntarily does not exist; consequently it would be abnormal to find any of the verbs listed above except *say* used in an imperative clause. It is not surprising that in an actor-goal-type analysis of transitivity for this poem we would find no items with the function of goal (or "object"), since lack of volition and intransitivity are, generally speaking, the same kind of phenomena. According to some newly suggested ways of looking at transitivity in English, we find that the subject of all of these clauses, with the exception of *say*, again, has the role of the affected participant. The element of causation, of voluntary action, is therefore missing from the poem—the participants undergo these processes. This understandably allows us to abstract the elements of passivity and total submission[26] as common to all events inferred from the text. In this context, it is interesting to note that the verb *say* (which, to my mind, like most verbalisation processes, falls mid-way between the action-type and the supervention-type of process) is embedded in a clause which itself has the transitivity function of "phenomenon" and does not involve any other participant except *the old men*; consider the similarities of *I heard them say* and *I heard a rumour*. This reduces the potentiality of the verb *say* to be regarded as actional rather than superventional.

So far as the participants and the circumstances of the processes in the text are concerned, one thing that immediately attracts our attention is the total anonymity of the participants as such: items such as *I, they, every-thing, all* are used; it would take me too much time and space to comment on the essential anonymity of the pronominal forms in the poem—suffice it to say that their interpretation could have been made specific, but the *I* remains without any attribute or identity, and the *they* remain *men* who, despite their attributes, cannot be located as a specific group of beings. Thus even those items which had the potentiality of referring to specific partici-pants are left anonymous and faceless. By this selection, the general items *everything* and *all*, coupled with the non-specificity of the use of *I* and *they*, re-inforce each other. When seen together with the factor of non-volition which is common to all processes in the poem, the anonymity and generality of the affected participants is significant. To paraphrase in most general terms: total passivity, submission and helplessness in the face of certain happenings are not characteristic of any specific, particular group of beings, but such is the case with all mankind. It is perhaps to be expected that where statements of such general applicability and universality are be-ing made, the processes would not be bound by the selection of circum-stances which stipulate a fixed time, location or even cause, since this would have the effect—semantically—of modifying the processes and thus limiting their applicability. Indeed, we do not find any such circumstances in the text; the only two to be selected are *one by one* (line 3) and *like the waters* (line 9). Both are circumstances of manner at the primary degree of deli-cacy, and due to the selection of the items which realize them, both point to the gradual but inexorable nature of the process of change.

The ten clauses of the text are alike so far as the selections from the sys-tem of mood are concerned: every clause is indicative and declarative. The unmarked contextual function of an indicative declarative clause is to make a statement. Thus, it is normally associated with the transference of infor-mation between the participants of a given discourse and may with justifica-tion be regarded as the least expressive involvement. Consequently the frequency of these clauses in the technical exposition is high even in the spoken mode. Here a set of theses is presented by the clauses of the text under focus in a manner that neither overtly invites any involvement on the part of the reader nor suggests the existence of such involvement on the part of the narrators at the two planes of narration.

Some comments have already been made regarding the nominal and the prepositional phrases in the text. Of the ten verbal phrases, two are non-finite (*say* 2 in lines 1 and 7); the remaining eight finite ones can be equally divided into two sets for their tense selection, four being simple present (*alters, drop away, 's* and *drifts away*) and four, simple past (*heard* [twice], *had, were*). Both the simple tenses are capable of indicating—and indeed, most frequently do—the habitual nature of a process; the time in the real world that they refer to transcends the moment of speaking and covers an area which is somewhat indefinite. The selection of these two tenses, to the exclusion of all others, is in agreement with the non-selection of specific time, location, or cause adjuncts, as well as with the selection of non-specific and generic nouns as participants. The universality of the processes, which are not limited by specificity of location, time, cause, or specific participants, is further emphasised by the selection of tenses which can semantically be characterised as referring to a recurrent, almost perpetual phenomenon. Again, all the verbal phrases are positive, non-emphatic, non-contrastive, and unmarked features which are in agreement with the picture of non-involvement conveyed by the uniform selection of indicative and declarative options from the mood system.

When we examine the text for those patterns of language which normally make the individual sentences of the text hang together into one coherent whole, we find that the situation is somewhat unusual. Of the four general grammatical cohesive tie-types, only one is made use of with any frequency. The four general types of grammatical cohesive ties are:

   i.  reference:  pronominal, e.g. the use of *he/she/it/they* . . . etc.
                      demonstrative, e.g. the use of *this/that/the* . . . etc.
                      comparative, e.g. the use of *better/smaller/more* . . . etc.
  ii.  substitution:  nominal, e.g. *one/ones/same/thing* . . . etc.
                      verbal, e.g. *do/do so.*
 iii.  ellipsis:  nominal, e.g. *the pink/those two/the younger* etc.
                      clausal, e.g. *he said yesterday/where?* etc.
                      verbal, e.g. *hasn't/won't/would/must* etc.
  iv.  logical connectives:  e.g. *consequently/for example/moreover* . . . etc.

The tie-type selected most frequently in the text is that of reference. As remarked earlier, the *I* is used in a very general sense and may be interpreted simply as the speaker or the encoder of the text; *they* and all forms derived therefrom refer to (*the old, old*) *men*. But the very first mention of *men* is modified by *the* in *the old, old men* (line 1). The function of the reference item *the* from this nominal phrase may not be said to be anaphoric since there is no previous mention of *men*; nor may it be regarded as a case of "immediate exophoric" usage (where the reference "requires" the listener to retrieve the relevant item from his knowledge of the immediate situation of the utterance) since it is clear that these are not some specific *men*. The use of this *the* is nearest to what may be referred to as "homophoric deictic"—a use in which *the* refers to a class generically or to a unique member class (e.g. *the farmer* when the generic class of all farmers is meant or *the moon* where there is only one member in the class). The generality of the class of men in question has already been commented upon (p. 316); from this treatment of *the old, old men*, we get the impression of a group of men who constitute a class on their own, who are non-specific and function almost as a symbol of decrepitude, since age and ugliness are the only two parameters which define this homophorically introduced quasi-generic class. Neither substitution nor ellipsis are employed as cohesive ties. Apart from the reference items discussed above, there is only one other grammatical cohesive tie, that of the selection of the item *and* (line 3). This *and* may be regarded as an instance of a logical connective. Note, however, that apart from the reference ties, no cohesive grammatical ties occur between sentences—there is no logical connective which explicitly coheres the three sentences of the text; indeed, it would be difficult to maintain that any recognized logical relationship exists between the three sentences even implicitly, unless it be the very weak one of additioning. (A logical relationship may be said to exist implicitly where two sentences bear a certain logical relationship to each other but in substance no connective is present to point explicitly to this relationship; for example, in *He didn't come to the meeting. He was ill.* Although the item *because* is not present in substance, the logical relationship of cause-effect exists implicitly.) Due to the absence of such relations between the sentences, the text can be divided into two somewhat independent parts; the theses of the two parts may be summed up in most general terms as follows: this is what the old, old men said; this is what the old, old men looked like. The entire burden of relating these two parts of the text rests upon some meaning relation between the men's comments and their appearance. This meaning relation can be brought out effectively by a consideration of the manner in which the selected patterns of rhyme, rhythm, grammar, and lexis combine (i.e., are restructured) into larger patterns.

First, however, a brief word regarding some of the notions centrally relevant to the study of the lexical organisation of texts. A well-organized text "demands" some patterning of lexical selection, which in most general terms may be said to involve both repetition and variation in the selection of the lexical types, variation, perhaps, being a more fundamental requirement than the repetition of types. The variation is however not free, since in organized texts it should be possible to conflate two (or more) types into a macro-set, the member types of any given macro-set being related to each other in one (or more) of the following ways: i) by synonymy; for example, in *drop away* and *drift away*; ii) by antonymy; for example, in *twisted, beautiful*; iii) by hyponymy; for example, in *tree, thorn-tree* or *hand, claws* or *man, knee, hand*; and iv) by morphological relationship; for example, in *beauty, beautiful* or *sail, sailor*. Again, the macro-sets formed from the individual types in a given text are themselves related to each other by some form of congruence as would be the case with two sets such as *drop away, drift away* and *alter, change*, or with *own, possess, have* and *give, take* and *make, form*. Both the repetition of a given lexical type and the possibility of relatable macro-set formation, are relevant to the lexical cohesion of a text. This is not surprising since both are largely controlled (or "prompted") by the selection of the topic or sub-topics which constitute the text. In non-literary verbal structures this fact is so transparently obvious that any comment regarding it runs the risk of being regarded as trivial. Due to the double layering of symbolisation, this relationship is not so transparent in literary verbal structures: one can predict neither the types nor their interrelations in a text whose theme is, say, mutability, since different configurations of situations can be made use of to realize the theme, as is evident from a comparison of the poem under discussion with Shakespeare's "Sea Dirge: Full Fathom Five Thy Father Lies," or with Herrick's "To Blossoms" or "To Daffodils." Situations, events, states of affairs, and characters, etc., employed in literature acquire that essential characteristic of all symbolic systems—namely, an arbitrariness within which there lies a principle of self-consistency. Therefore, in the lexical study of literary texts, the notion of "instantial equivalence" gains great significance. By instantial equivalence I mean the relating of two (or more) unrelated types or macro-sets by establishing either an identity or a similarity between the members; this identity or similarity is "instantial" in that it is valid only for that one particular text and not true of the items under consideration under all circumstances (as is the case with the members of a macro-set). As an example of identity consider *Time is two modes. The one is an effortless perception. . . . The other is a memory, a sense of shuffle, fold and coil. . . .* (Golding, *Free Fall*); and one may cite a line from Byron as an example of similarity: *she walks in beauty like the night.* Two points are evident from the examples: firstly, an instantially equivalent set is a complex symbol in the code of the text, and secondly it is based on lexico-grammatical considerations (not only lexical ones). All grammatical structures, no matter at what rank, capable of encoding the semantic features of identification, equation, attribution, and comparison can potentially introduce an instantially equivalent set, and it is more than likely that the origins of metonymy, of simile and metaphor, as well as of imagery lie in such lexico-grammatical patterns.

To return to the text under focus, we find that it contains a total of thirty-three lexical occurrences (or tokens); twenty-eight of these are specific tokens, two are tokens of an institutional-exophoric *I* and three are derived tokens of *men*, from the reference items *we, they,* and *their.* These thirty-three tokens are divided among twenty types. In view of the average type-token ratio for the text (1.65), the actual recurrence of the items *old* and *men* (both occur five times each) leads one to the conclusion that the items are "text-dominating," i.e., they are closely related to the theme of the text, while four other recurrent types *water, hear, say,* and *be* (each with 2 tokens) draw attention to themselves as non-peripheral types. Thirteen of the twenty types can be conflated into five macro-sets, as follows:

1. everything, all
2. men, hands, claws, knees
3. beautiful, twisted
4. alter, drop away, drift away
5. hear, say

The network of relationship among these patterns is tightened by the functioning of the instantially equivalent sets. An equivalence is established between *beauty* and *waters* (of lines 8-9: *all that's beautiful drifts away like the waters*) both of which are subject to change; at the same time an equivalence is established between *hands* and *claws* as also between *twisted knees* and *old thorn-trees by the waters.* The picture may be presented as follows:

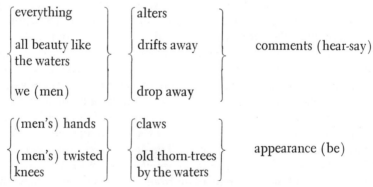

Their comments are about the inevitability of change; they see themselves as an example of this general inexorable principle of mutability. They themselves are a picture of change as seen by a third party. It is significant that all five occurrences of *old* should be found in the description of their appearance, while the item *beautiful* should appear in the old men's sayings. The *waters* reflect change in two senses: as a mirror into which old age and ugliness can marvel at itself—much "struck by amazement and admiration" at the contrast between what was and what is; at the same time, by the incessant drifting away, the waters reflect the general principle of mutability, that tendency to instability which characterises the universe. The central theme of Yeat's poem is change; the contrast between the past and present is viewed from two different points of vantage. The absence of any recognisable logical relation between the comments and the appearance of the men is well-motivated since the disjunction between the two manifests the essential difference between the points of view. To the outsider, the appearance alone is available; he sees only what things look like here and now; the insider is the sadder and the wiser for he sees the general principle of contrast: how things were, how things are, and also how things will be in time to come. It is not surprising then that the element of pathos in the poem is prominent in the insiders' (*the men's*) comments, while the spectacle of ugly decay, the here-and-now result of change, is prominent in the outsider's (*I*) description.

We can see how the details of linguistic selection fit in with the theme of the poem. The direction given to the foregrounding, and the principle governing the restructuring of the variability of the patterns of language is supplied by the theme; unless clustering of these from the text could be related to each other, the theme would not be realized with success; and if the theses are to be related to each other in some meaningful way, some regularity of pattern-selection is required. This regularity of pattern selection is the means through which is signalled the mode for the alignment of the various elements of the text. The division of the text into two planes of narration, the plasticity of the direct one (with recurrent selection of modification and of comparison, as well as with the selection of relational clauses) and the utter passivity and submission of the indirect plane of narration (with superventive clauses) are important for bringing out the different points of view.

The selection of contrasting past and present tenses together with the non-finite (and hence timeless) *say* in the poem is a manifestation at the linguistic level of the contrast between the past and the present which is the concern of the highest level of this poem. The function of the *waters* as a symbol of the principle of change provides a clue to the regularity of the [*b*] lines in the poem; as has already been pointed out *alters* and *waters* (lines 2, 6, and 9 respectively) are the only strong lexical items in these lines. The penultimate syllable of all three is salient (i.e., stressed); what strikes one as somewhat abnormal is the stress on the weak lexical item *everything* (line 2). When we see the rhyme and rhythm of the *b* lines as a complex pattern motivated by the theme of the poem, the salience of

*everything* as well as the bringing together of the items *alter* and *water* acquires a deeper significance.

I am aware that there are various aspects of the poem which remain
totally untouched in this discussion; and that at least some of these aspects
are important in that they arise from a consideration of the text as an instance of literature; for example, one could compare this text with others
with the same theme, or in the same genre; or one could place it in the
Yeats tradition. I hope, however, that the preceding analysis has sufficiently
demonstrated the essential "creativity" of language in literature—this creativity is the function of the relationship that exists between the three levels
of literature I have proposed. The "art" of a poem consists not in the selection of any particular linguistic pattern, nor in that of stylistic device; nor
does it, to my mind, consist in imagining the set of situations and hence
the language pattern—it consists rather in the symbolic, realisational relationship between the three levels, and results from an interaction of the
three. The description of literature as non-communicative or non-pragmatic
is essentially misleading. Not only do literary texts communicate, but also
part of a reader's reaction to a given literary text depends upon what he
understands it to communicate; and equally, the messages of the literature
of a community are pragmatically integrated into the life of the community
at some level. What seems to be incontrovertible is that neither communi-
cativeness nor pragmatic value is a test of the literariness of a literary text
since other verbal structures are both communicative and pragmatic. If
literature consists in the establishing of the symbolic relationship between
the various levels of the text, as discussed above, then it follows that it is
the function of language for the realisation of the internal organisation and
theme that is the primary concern of stylistics. In a sense one is doing no
more than providing an explanation of an already observed fact: in the
study and analysis of any poem we do not start from an attitude of blank-
ness; each reading of a poem is a hypothesis regarding what the poem is
about. This hypothesis may or may not be right; that is to say, one may or
may not be able to substantiate it. Nevertheless, it does motivate the selection of the facts that one chooses to present as the significant ones, as
also it guides one's ordering and arranging of these facts. There is no such
thing as an objective reader of a poem, *if* by objective reader one means a
reader who is totally without the ability to shape what he sees. Of course,
one has the right to ask that the reasoning behind the specific shaping of
the "seen" be made clear, and this is what seems to me to be the central
concern of stylistics: stylistics is the study of literary language for the purpose of showing how it is related to the internal organisation of literary
texts, how the text is made to cohere into one unity and how the elements of
this unity are brought to one's notice.

# Notes

1. There may be some disagreement here, for if stylistics is defined as the study of style and style itself is considered to be a property of all texts, then obviously even the weak characterisation being presented here would be too specific and strong. Such a position is, I think, implicit in Fowler (1966). This view of stylistics would by implication equate the subject with that part of linguistics which is concerned with the study of register. I would like to suggest here that there is some merit in making a distinction between the study of literary register and the study of literature.

2. The term "poetics" as used by Jakobson may be regarded by some as more inclusive than stylistics in its present characterisation, since poetics not only "deals . . . with what makes a verbal message a work of art," but also with the "problems of verbal structure." However, this does not materially affect the point being made here.

3. Quite obviously the characteristic of verbalness which literary texts share with other texts implies the existence of descriptive categories set up to describe non-literary texts (Halliday, 1962). This furnishes a motivation for the employment of a descriptive framework derived from some model; at the same time the special functions of language in literature make it necessary to set up certain categories which are peculiar to varieties of language sharing some characteristic of literature (Hasan, 1967).

4. It is worth pointing out that if the crucial distinction is one that can be made while remaining within linguistics, then stylistics would be only a branch of linguistics, not an autonomous field.

5. Both "level" and "rank" are used technically, as in Halliday (1961).

6. Despite the difficulty in finding an adequate means of characterising literature, I would not accept Fowler's suggestion that "contextual features may be invoked to explain why we use the label "literature" at a certain time for a certain text; to rationalise our recognition of a text as literature rather than to define absolutely what the phenomenon of literature is." The disadvantage arising from such a compromise solution of a basic problem are quite evident.

7. This is without prejudice to whether or not other levels need also be recognised; there is good reason to believe that several levels of different orders will be needed to account for the multiplicity of meanings in literary texts.

8. A more detailed discussion of some of those pairs will be found in R. Barthes' paper in this volume.

9. Often such terms for the description of some aspect of a literary text are rejected as "impressionistic" and "subjective"; nevertheless, these terms or some substitute for them will be required so long as we are interested in making statements regarding "art" in the use of language in literature.

10. This is not tantamount to maintaining that the message "exists" independent of the medium; however, once a message has been made available, certain of its properties can be examined without involving an examination of the medium as such.

11. In constructing most non-literary texts, the restriction on the selection of lexis from particular areas of the total lexicon is so evident as not to need any comment. There is good reason to believe that varieties and tenors can be

characterised by reference to collocational patterns as well as combinations of grammatical ones. By contrast, the entire lexicon of a language is available to literary texts, while none of the collocational and grammatical patterns or their combinations can be ruled out as "non-literary," with the implication that they could not be found in a literary text.

12. I do not think of the referential relation as a simple relation obtaining between existent object or property; rather an object or property exists for a given language simply because there is in that language an item that refers to it. On the notion of reference see Ellis (1966).

13. Strictly speaking, meanings cannot be regarded as "non-linguistic," if it is also maintained that meanings are the property of the semantic level. When the term "non-linguistic" is applied to translatable aspects of a text, it can only be interpreted as "non-formal."

14. For the notion "speaker" see M. A. K. Halliday's paper in this volume.

15. Any written text is essentially a text generated in the past while examples presented in metalinguistic discussions are very much like hypotheses. Both are understood because language code can operate very much like hypotheses. Both are understood because language code can operate in independence from space and time.

16. See Richard Ohmann's paper in this volume, in which he presents literature in terms of hypothetical speech acts.

17. The element of "phantasy" can therefore function as a diagnostic criterion with the effect that no reader would consider a work such as *Adventures in the Skin Trade* as an autobiography.

18. A negative formulation is necessary here since quite often—especially in certain genres of prose—a close parallelism may exist between the fictive events of the text and the extralinguistic universe. That is to say, the element of phantasy is not crucial to the definition of literature.

19. I would make a distinction between tenor and style. Tenor is a property of all varieties and is controlled by the purpose of the discourse as well as the relationship obtaining between the participants of the discourse. Style I would reserve as a relational term applicable to literature alone, where ideally it is controlled by the theme and the theme-symbolising textual events. The study of style is the study of the fit of the language of a literary text to its theme and theme-symbolising events.

20. For the set of criteria relevant to register, see Halliday *et al.* (1964) and Hasan (1970b, "Code, Register and Social Dialect," forthcoming).

21. This truth is, in effect, the truth of internal consistency which is essential to all successful hypotheses. As such, the notion of truth applies only to the central message or theme of the literary text; historical factuality or its violation in the theme-symbolising events of the text is largely irrelevant. However, see footnote 22.

22. Obviously where a literary work employs historical characters or some of the historical events—as in Shakespeare's history plays—further dimensions of relevance are added to a work, in that the modification of a historical event, etc., can function as part of the realisation of the theme.

23. See, M. A. K. Halliday's paper in this volume.

24. I am grateful to Professors Wellek, Wimsatt, and Chatman for their comments on the significance of the word *admire* in the title of this poem. Professor Chatman pointed out that the word could have been used neutrally in

its old sense of *"admirare"* meaning simply *to look in a mirror*. Professor Wimsatt drew attention to the Elizabethan use of this word where it meant, roughly,
*to be amazed* as in *"your behaviour hath struck her into amazement and admiration"* (*Hamlet:* III. 2), while Professor Wellek, accepting the contemporary sense of *admire*, pointed out that irony and pathos are created in the poem
by the tension between this word and the description of the appearance of the
old men. The use of this word is a very good example of genuine ambivalence—
that is to say, the different meanings of the word "fit" quite adequately into the
whole. There is no need to select just one meaning and ignore the others, since
a mind trained in decoding literary texts must take in all three senses of the
word if the requisite information is available.

25. Very informally, transitivity options are concerned with the encoding of
information regarding processes and the participants and circumstances of processes, while mood options are concerned with contextual speech functions; a
more detailed account of both these systems can be found in Halliday, 1970.

26. As a point of interest, consider the function of this grammatical pattern
in Golding's *Inheritors*, as described in M. A. K. Halliday's study of the novel
included in this volume.


## REFERENCES

Karl Bühler, *Sprachtheorie* (Jena, 1934).

David Daiches, *Critical Approaches to Literature* (London, 1956).

B. M. W. Dixon, *What Is Language?* (London, 1965).

Jeffrey Ellis, "On Contextual Meaning," in *In Memory of J. R. Firth*, ed.
C. Bazell, I. Catford, M. Halliday, and R. Robins; Longmans' Linguistic
Library (London, 1966).

Nils Erik Enkvist, "On Defining Style," in *Linguistics and Style*, ed. John Spencer, Language and Language Learning Series (London, 1964).

Charles J. Fillmore, *Towards a Modern Theory of Case*, The Ohio State University Research Foundation Project on Linguistic Analysis, Report 13
(Columbus, Ohio, 1966).

Roger Fowler, "Linguistic Theory and the Study of Literature," in *Essays on
Style and Language* (London, 1966).

Northrop Frye, *Anatomy of Criticism* (Princeton, N. J., 1957).

George Gascoigne, "The Making of Verse," in *Elizabethan Critical Essays*, ed.
G. Gregory Smith (Oxford, 1904).

Pierre Guiraud, *La Stylistique* (Paris, 1954).

M. A. K. Halliday, "Descriptive Linguistics in Literary Studies," in *English
Studies Today*, ed. G. I. Duthie (Edinburgh, 1962).

———, (1970a) "Relevant Models of Language," *Educational Review*, XXII
(1970).

———, (1970b) "Clause Types and Structural Functions," in *New Horizons
In Linguistics*, ed. John Lyons (Penguin Books, 1970).

———, "Notes on Transitivity and Theme in English," *Journal of Linguistics*,
IV (1968).

———, "Categories of the Theory of Grammar," *Word*, XVII (1960).

———, A. McIntosh and P. Strevens, *The Linguistic Sciences and Language
Teaching*, Longmans' Linguistic Library series (London, 1964).

Ruqaiya Hasan, "Linguistics and the Study of Literary Texts," *Études de Linguistique Appliquée*, V (1967).

———, *Grammatical Cohesion in Spoken and Written English*, Programme in Linguistics and English Teaching Series, I, Paper 7 (London, 1968).

———, (1970a) *Grammatical Cohesion in Spoken and Written English*, Part Two (forthcoming).

———, (1970b) *Code, Register and Social Dialect* (forthcoming).

Graham Hough, *An Essay on Criticism* (London, 1966).

Roman Jakobson, "Linguistics and Poetics," in *Style in Language*, ed. by Thomas A. Sebeok (New York, 1960).

Sydney M. Lamb, *Outline of Stratificational Grammar* (Washington, D.C., 1966).

Samuel R. Levin, *Linguistic Structures in Poetry*, Janua Linguarum, 23 (The Hague, 1962).

Angus McIntosh, "Graphology and Meaning," *Archivum Linguisticum*, XIII (1961).

———, "Saying," *A Review of English Literature*, VI (1965).

———, "As You Like It: A Grammatical Clue to Character," *A Review of English Literature*, IV (1966).

Herman Melville, "Billy Budd, Sailor," *Billy Budd, Sailor and Other Stories* (Penguin English Library).

Jan Mukařovský, (1964a) "Standard Language and Poetic Language," in *A Prague School Reader on Esthetics, Literary Structure and Style*, ed. by Paul L. Garvin (Washington, D.C., 1964).

———, (1964b) "The Esthetics of Language," in *A Prague School Reader on Esthetics, Literary Structure and Style*, ed. by Paul L. Garvin (Washington, D.C., 1964).

Winifred Nowottny, *The Language Poets Use* (London, 1962).

R. H. Robins, *A Short History of Linguistics*, Longmans' Linguistics Library (London, 1967).

Edward Sapir, *Language: An Introduction to the Study of Speech* (New York, 1921).

John McH. Sinclair, "Beginning the Study of Lexis," in *In Memory of J. R. Firth*, ed. C. Bazell, I. Catford, M. Halliday, and R. Robins, Longmans' Linguistic Library (London, 1966).

W. B. Yeats, *Collected Poems of W. B. Yeats* (New York, 1933).

# DISCUSSION OF HASAN'S PAPER

Miss Hasan was asked what she meant by "rime." Her answer was that "rime" (though not "reason") was a level, that it meant what she sometimes referred to as the level of linguistic execution, a level at which tables of numbers of transitive and intransitive clauses are required. Her method simply abstracts out all the patterns at these levels. "Reason" is the realizational relation holding between the level of theme and that of symbolic situation which realizes the theme; this is the reason for the need for rime.

As for her concept of "level," she was asked whether she thought that a hierarchization of levels was possible or whether they should be treated as independent. Should they be called rather "systems"? Miss Hasan replied that the levels were indeed in a hierarchy, held together by a realizational relation much like that in Sydney Lamb's stratificational model of language. Included are hypersemantics, semantics, and all levels related realizationally, so that the top one, the theme, becomes the regulative principle, just as Lamb's model needs a level higher than semantics to hook the whole language system into the cognitive system.

Another participant, though admitting that he liked the principle of nonrandom deviation, wondered whether it could account for such works as Joyce's *Finnegans Wake* where the degree of deviation is so enormous that the code itself is virtually smashed. Miss Hasan said that she used to feel that *Finnegans Wake* was either not literature, or if so, literature in an unknown language—until someone pointed out to her that it could not be understood without reference to English.

It was noted that in her analysis of levels, Miss Hasan gave predominance to ideas or subject-matter as highest level. The lexical material was taken as a sign of topic, story, theme, or whatever, and this theme would in turn be a sign of something still more general—the focal point at which all the levels converge. Did she assume this to be a general rule? Of course there is always interdependence between levels, but can't another level—say the phonic or rhythmic—be the most important in some works? Miss Hasan's reply was that the question was difficult to answer because it entailed the consideration of what literature was for, its *raison d'être*. One can get practically anything a work of literature gives in another medium except its unique literary quality, that is, the layering of symbolization and controlling of the entire pattern of selection by some theme. In other words, she would argue that theme *is* always the encoding control; of course, when one goes from the decoding direction, naturally he has to pass through lower levels to get up to the top. From one point of view, literary text has the same kind of existence as examples have in textual discussions of any kind (the point is made very clearly in an article by Angus McIntosh[1]).

The rest of the discussion concerned Miss Hasan's analysis of Yeats' poem. There was first some question about the precise meanings and implications of the title. Disagreement was expressed about Miss Hasan's view that the "the" referring to "old men" in the title was any more generalizing than say "some old men." "The old men" seems to imply not a real but an ideal or poetic group of old men, something perhaps like the named heroes of Yeats' other poems—Finn Macool, Red Hanrahan, and so on, who are not individually characterized in any real sense but are idealizations of a heroic age. These are old men who have a sense of poetry and see the mutability of things; but surely this is a rather restricted group as old men go. Miss Hasan responded that when she said that "the" was "generalized," she did not mean that it was not capable of communicating these meanings but simply that it did not mean "those specific, particular, very men." "The" is not anaphoric but borders, rather, on the institutional; it is institutionally exophoric. Another participant noted that the "the" in question positioned the reader to be the recipient of some customary wisdom, something that has always been true or something that he is supposed already to know, so that the speaker can simply allude to it, rather than saying "some old men I knew once."

A great deal of discussion was devoted to the meaning of the word "admire" in the title. Since age is not represented as a thing of beauty in the poem—the hands of the old men are claws, their knees twisted, etc.—it was argued that "admire" cannot have its normal modern sense except ironically—the old men have no reason to admire themselves, and yet they do. One view could be that the men are complacent because it is their own former beauty that they think of when they say that " 'All that's beautiful drifts away.' " But, another argument went, it is also possible to take the word in an older sense—simply "to look at," or more particularly, "to look at with wonder, to marvel over." In this view the old men are not beautiful, but they once were, as were the ladies whom they courted. Perhaps they are marvelling in a horrified way about the transformation wreaked by time. Images of ageing and decrepitude in Yeats' other poems—for example the famous "scarecrow" image—fit in very well with this idea. For other reasons too the poem must be seen in the context of the whole Yeats canon; for, more than most poets, Yeats exploited and dramatized his life, and it is difficult to read a single poem without remembering the others. Miss Hasan said she liked the "marvel over" sense the best, agreeing that one cannot ignore the reverberation of others of Yeats' poems; but, she pointed out, this also gives rise to aesthetic questions about how to account for an autonomous poem which opens out into a larger universe.

Another participant spoke of his impression that the repetition of line one in line seven, a common poetic device, here served to create a "mirror" effect consonant with the title and theme. That effect is also conveyed by the fact that the word "waters" is spoken, one time by the poet and another by the old men. The effect is clearly related to the theme of change (the men and the thorn trees ageing, the drifting away of the beautiful, etc.), set in opposition to the relative stability and permanence of the poet—a stability effected by repetitions of words and rhymes. This suggests the register of "wisdom poetry," where the speaker is established in a sort of permanent wisdom, even as he speaks of the transitory. (Compare the discussion, reported above, of the full implications of "the" in the title.)

Miss Hasan's reference to the "non-specific" verb tenses raised the question of what precisely "non-specific" means; it was argued that the simple present and simple past tenses are not "timeless" if by that one means "stretching over an unidentified time-span." The time referred to is very definite but unspecified—in "I heard the old men say," "heard" means "heard at a particular moment, but one which I will not identify in this sentence." This too gives the poem the quality of being a vignette, something which is just *there* and permanent, but not in any indefinite sense. Miss Hasan noted, by way of response, that only two of the eight simple present and past tense verbs are "specific," that is, the two occurrences of "heard."

The final comment was on the development of dissymmetry into symmetry in the poem. The poem was said to have three time-patterns, as well as metrical and semantic patterns. The metrical pattern is essentially A, B, B[1] (where B[1] means that the last three lines have the same metrical structure as the middle three); the semantic pattern, however, is A, B, A[1] (that is the semantic structure of the last three lines resembles that of the first three lines). Thus you have a conversion of dissymmetry into symmetry. Miss Hasan found nothing to disagree with in this formulation.

## NOTE

1. Angus McIntosh, "Saying," A *Review of English Literature*, VI (1965).

# LINGUISTIC FUNCTION AND LITERARY STYLE:

## An Inquiry into the Language of William Golding's *The Inheritors*

### M. A. K. HALLIDAY

My MAIN CONCERN, in this paper, is with criteria of relevance. This, it seems to me, is one of the central problems in the study of "style in language": I mean the problem of distinguishing between mere linguistic regularity, which in itself is of no interest to literary studies, and regularity which is significant for the poem or prose work in which we find it. I remember an entertaining paper read to the Philological Society in Cambridge some years ago by Professor John Sinclair, in which he drew our attention to some very striking linguistic patterns displayed in the poetry of William McGonagall, and invited us to say why, if this highly structured language was found in what we all agreed was such very trivial poetry, we should be interested in linguistic regularities at all.[1] It is no new discovery to say that pattern in language does not by itself make literature, still less "good literature": nothing is more regular than the rhythm of *Three Blind Mice*, and if this is true of phonological regularities it is likely to be true also of syntactic ones. But we lack general criteria for determining whether any particular instance of linguistic prominence is likely to be stylistically relevant or not.

This is not a simple matter, and any discussion of it is bound to touch on more than one topic, or at the least to adopt more than one angle of vision. Moreover the line of approach will often, inevitably, be indirect, and the central concern may at times be lost sight of round some of the corners. It seems to me necessary, first of all, to discuss and to emphasize the place of semantics in the study of style; and this in turn will lead to a consideration of "functional" theories of language and their relevance for the student of literature. At the same time these general points need to be exemplified;

330

and here I have allowed the illustration to take over the stage: when I re-examined for this purpose a novel I had first studied some four years ago, *The Inheritors* by William Golding, there seemed to be much that was of interest in its own right.[2] I do not think there is any antithesis between the "textual" and the "theoretical" in the study of language, so I hope the effect of this may be to strengthen rather than to weaken the general argument. The discussion of *The Inheritors* may be seen either in relation to just that one work or in relation to a general theory; I am not sure that it is possible to separate these two perspectives, either from each other or from various intermediate fields of attention such as an author, a genre, or a literary tradition.

The paper will fall into four parts: first, a discussion of a "functional theory of language"; second, a reference to various questions raised at the Style in Language conference of 1958 and in other current writings; third, an examination of certain features of the language of *The Inheritors*; and fourth, a brief résumé of the question of stylistic relevance. Of these, the third part will be the longest.

The term *function* is used, in two distinct though related senses, at two very different points in the description of language. First it is used in the sense of "grammatical" (or "syntactic") function, to refer to elements of linguistic structures such as actor and goal or subject and object or theme and rheme. These "functions" are the roles occupied by classes of words, phrases, and the like in the structure of higher units. Secondly, it is used to refer to the "functions" of language as a whole: for example in the well-known work of Karl Bühler, in which he proposes a three-way division of language function into the representational, the conative and the expressive.[3]

Here I am using "function" in the second sense, referring, however, not specifically to Bühler's theory, but to the generalized notion of "functions of language." By a functional theory of language I mean one which attempts to explain linguistic structure, and linguistic phenomena, by reference to the notion that language plays a certain part in our lives, that it is required to serve certain universal types of demand. I find this approach valuable in general for the insight it gives into the nature and use of language, but particularly so in the context of stylistic studies.

The demands that we make on language, as speakers and writers, listeners and readers, are indefinitely many and varied. They can be derived, ultimately, from a small number of very general headings; but what these headings are will depend on what questions we are asking. For example, if we were to take a broadly psychological viewpoint and consider the functions that language serves in the life of the individual, we might arrive at some such scheme as Bühler's, referred to above. If on the other hand we asked a more sociological type of question, concerning the functions that language serves in the life of the community, we should probably elaborate some framework such as Malinowski's distinction into a pragmatic and a magical function.[4] Many others could be suggested besides.

These questions are extrinsic to language; and the categorizations of language function that depend on them are of interest because, and to the extent that, the questions themselves are of interest. Such categorizations therefore imply a strictly instrumental view of linguistic theory. Some would perhaps reject this on the grounds that it does not admit the autonomy of linguistics and linguistic investigations. I am not myself impressed by that argument, although I would stress that any one particular instrumental view is by itself inadequate as a general characterization of language. But a purely extrinsic theory of language functions does fail to take into account one thing, namely the fact that the multiplicity of function, if the idea is valid at all, is likely to be reflected somewhere in the internal organization of language itself. If language is, as it were, programmed to serve a variety of needs, then this should show up in some way in an investigation of linguistic structure.

In fact this functional plurality is very clearly built into the structure of language, and forms the basis of its semantic and "syntactic" (i.e. grammatical and lexical) organization. If we set up a functional framework that is neutral as to external emphasis, but designed to take into account the nature of the internal, semantic, and syntactic patterns of language, we arrive at something that is very suggestive for literary studies, because it represents a general characterization of semantic functions—of the meaning potential of the language system. Let me suggest here the framework that seems to me most helpful. It is a rather simple catalogue of three basic functions, one of which has two sub-headings.

In the first place, language serves for the expression of content: it has a representational, or, as I would prefer to call it, an *ideational* function. (This is sometimes referred to as the expression of "cognitive meaning," though I find the term *cognitive* misleading; there is, after all, a cognitive element in all linguistic functions.) Two points need to be emphasized concerning this ideational function of language. The first is that it is through this function that the speaker or writer embodies in language his experience of the phenomena of the real world; and this includes his experience of the internal world of his own consciousness: his reactions, cognitions, and perceptions, and also his linguistic acts of speaking and understanding. We shall in no sense be adopting an extreme pseudo-Whorfian position (I say "pseudo-Whorfian" because Whorf himself never was ex-treme) if we add that, in serving this function, language lends structure to his experience and helps to determine his way of looking at things. The speaker can see through and around the settings of his semantic system; but he is aware that, in doing so, he is seeing reality in a new light, like Alice in Looking-glass House. There is, however, and this is the second point, one component of ideational meaning which, while not unrelatable to expe-rience, is nevertheless organized in language in a way which marks it off as distinct: this is the expression of certain fundamental logical relations such as are encoded in language in the form of co-ordination, apposition, modifi-cation, and the like. The notion of co-ordination, for example, as in *sun, moon, and stars,* can be derived from an aspect of the speaker's experience; but this and other such relations are realized through the medium of a particular type of structural mechanism (that of linear recursion) which takes them, linguistically, out of the domain of experience to form a func-tionally neutral, "logical" component in the total spectrum of meanings. Within the ideational function of language, therefore, we can recognize two sub-functions, the *experiential* and the *logical*; and the distinction is a sig-nificant one for our present purpose.

In the second place, language serves what we may call an *interpersonal* function. This is quite different from the expression of content. Here, the speaker is using language as the means of his own intrusion into the speech event: the expression of his comments, his attitudes, and evaluations, and also of the relationship that he sets up between himself and the listener—in particular, the communication role that he adopts, of informing, question-ing, greeting, persuading, and the like. The interpersonal function thus sub-sumes both the expressive and the conative, which are not in fact distinct in the linguistic system: to give one example, the meanings "I do not know" (expressive) and "you tell me" (conative) are combined in a single seman-tic feature, that of question, typically expressed in the grammar by an interrogative; the interrogative is both expressive and conative at the same time. The set of communication roles is unique among social relations in that it is brought into being and maintained solely through language. But the interpersonal element in language extends beyond what we might think of as its rhetorical functions. In the wider context, language is required to serve in the establishment and maintenance of all human relationships; it is the means whereby social groups are integrated and the individual is iden-tified and reinforced. It is, I think, significant for certain forms of literature that, since personality is dependent on interaction which is in turn mediated through language, the "interpersonal" function in language is both inter-actional and personal: there is, in other words, a component in language which serves at one and the same time to express both the inner and the

outer surfaces of the individual, as a single undifferentiated area of meaning potential that is personal in the broadest sense.[5]

These two functions, the ideational and the interpersonal, may seem sufficiently all-embracing; and in the context of an instrumental approach to
language they are. But there is a third function which is in turn instrumental to these two, whereby language is, as it were, enabled to meet the demands that are made on it; I shall call this the *textual* function, since it is
concerned with the creation of text. It is a function internal to language,
and for this reason is not usually taken into account where the objects of
investigation are extrinsic; but it came to be specifically associated with the
term "functional" in the work of the Prague scholars who developed Bühler's ideas within the framework of a linguistic theory (cf. their terms "functional syntax," "functional sentence perspective"). It is through this function that language makes links with itself and with the situation; and discourse becomes possible, because the speaker or writer can produce a text
and the listener or reader can recognize one. A *text* is an operational unit of
language, as a sentence is a syntactic unit; it may be spoken or written, long
or short; and it includes as a special instance a literary text, whether haiku
or Homeric epic. It is the text and not some super-sentence that is the
relevant unit for stylistic studies; this is a functional-semantic concept and
is not definable by size. And therefore the "textual" function is not limited
to the establishment of relations between sentences; it is concerned just as
much with the internal organization of the sentence, with its meaning as a
message both in itself and in relation to the context.

A tentative categorization of the principal elements of English syntax in
terms of the above functions is given in Table 1. This table is intended to
serve a twofold purpose. In the first place, it will help to make more concrete the present concept of a functional theory, by showing how the various functions are realized through the grammatical systems of the language,
all of which are accounted for in this way. Not all the labels may be self-
explanatory, nor is the framework so compartmental as in this bare outline
it is made to seem: there is a high degree of indeterminacy in the fuller
picture, representing the indeterminacy that is present throughout language,
in its categories and its relations, its types and its tokens. Secondly it will
bring out the fact that the syntax of a language is organized in such a way
that it expresses as a whole the range of linguistic functions, but that the
symptoms of functional diversity are not to be sought in single sentences or
sentence types. In general, that is to say, we shall not find whole sentences
or even smaller structures having just one function. Typically, each sentence embodies all functions, though one or another may be more prominent; and most constituents of sentences also embody more than one function, through their ability to combine two or more syntactic roles.

TABLE 1

COHESION ("above the sentence": non-structural relations)
reference; substitution & ellipsis; conjunction;
lexical cohesion

| rank: / function: | IDEATIONAL — Experiential | IDEATIONAL — Logical | INTERPERSONAL | TEXTUAL |
|---|---|---|---|---|
| CLAUSE | TRANSITIVITY types of process participants and circumstances (identity clauses) (things, facts, and reports) | condition addition report | MOOD types of speech function modality (the WH-function) | THEME types of message (identity as text relation) (identification, predication, reference, substitution) |
| Verbal GROUP | TENSE (verb classes) | POLARITY — catenation secondary tense | PERSON ("marked" options) | VOICE ("contrastive" options) |
| Nominal GROUP | MODIFICATION epithet function enumeration (noun classes) (adjective classes) | classification sub-modification | ATTITUDE attitudinal modifiers intensifiers | DEIXIS determiners "phoric" elements (qualifiers) (definite article) |
| Adverbial (incl. prepositional) GROUP | "MINOR PROCESSES" prepositional relations (classes of circumstantial adjunct) | narrowing sub-modification | COMMENT (classes of comment adjunct) | CONJUNCTION (classes of discourse adjunct) |
| WORD (incl. lexical item) | LEXICAL "CONTENT" (taxonomic organization of vocabulary) | compounding derivation | LEXICAL "REGISTER" (expressive words) (stylistic organization of vocabulary) | COLLOCATION (collocational organization of vocabulary) |
| INFORMATION UNIT | | | TONE intonation systems | INFORMATION distribution & focus |

PARATACTIC COMPLEXES (all ranks)
co-ordination
apposition

HYPOTACTIC COMPLEXES OF CAUSE, GROUP, AND WORD

335

Let us introduce an example at this point. Here is a well-known passage from *Through the Looking-Glass, and What Alice Found There*:

> "I don't understand you," said Alice. "It's dreadfully confusing!"
>
> "That's the effect of living backwards," the Queen said kindly: "it always makes one a little giddy at first—"
>
> "Living backwards!" Alice repeated in great astonishment. "I never heard of such a thing!"
>
> "—but there's one great advantage in it, that one's memory works both ways."
>
> "I'm sure *mine* only works one way," Alice remarked. "I can't remember things before they happen."
>
> "It's a poor sort of memory that only works backwards," the Queen remarked.
>
> "What sort of things do *you* remember best?" Alice ventured to ask.
>
> "Oh, things that happened the week after next," the Queen replied in a careless tone.

To illustrate the last point first, namely that most constituents of sentences embody more than one function, by combining different syntactic roles: the constituent *what sort of things* occupies simultaneously the syntactic roles of "theme," of "phenomenon" (that is, object of cognition, perception, etc.) and of "interrogation point." The theme represents a particular status in the message, and is thus an expression of "textual" function: it is the speaker's point of departure. If the speaker is asking a question he usually, in English, takes the request for information as his theme, expressing this by putting the question phrase first; here, therefore, the same element is both theme and interrogation point—the latter being an expression of "interpersonal" function since it defines the specific communication roles the speaker has chosen for himself and for the listener: the speaker is behaving as questioner. *What sort of thing* is the phenomenon dependent on the mental process *remember*; and this concept of a mental phenomenon, as something that can be talked about, is an expression of the "ideational" function of langauge—of language as content, relatable to the speaker's and the listener's experience. It should be emphasized that it is not, in fact, the syntactic role in isolation, but the structure of which it forms a part that is semantically significant: it is not the theme, for example, but the total theme-rheme structure which contributes to the texture of the discourse.

Thus the constituents themselves tend to be multivalent; which is another way of saying that the very notion of a constituent is itself rather too concrete to be of much help in a functional context. A constituent is a particular word or phrase in a particular place; but functionally the choice of an item may have one meaning, its repetition another, and its location in structure yet another—or many others, as we have seen. So, in the Queen's remark *it's a poor sort of memory that only works backwards*, the word *poor* is a "modifier," and thus expresses a subclass of its head-word *memory* (ideational); while at the same time it is an "epithet" expressing the Queen's attitude (interpersonal), and the choice of this word in this environment (as opposed to, say, *useful*) indicates more specifically that the attitude is one of disapproval. The words *it's . . . that* have here no reference at all outside the sentence, but they structure the message in a particular way (textual), which represents the Queen's opinion as if it was an "attribute" (ideational), and defines one class of *memory* as exclusively possessing this undesirable quality (ideational). The lexical repetition in *memory that only works backwards* relates the Queen's remark (textual) to *mine only works one way*, in which *mine* refers anaphorically, by ellipsis, to *memory* in the preceding sentence (textual) and also to *I* in Alice's expression of her own judgment *I'm sure* (interpersonal). Thus ideational content and personal interaction are woven together with, and by means of, the textual structure to form a coherent whole.

Taking a somewhat broader perspective, we again find the same interplay of functions. The ideational meaning of the passage is enshrined in the phrase *living backwards*; we have a general characterization of the nature of experience, in which *things that happened the week after next* turns out to be an acceptable sentence. (I am not suggesting it is serious, or offering a deep literary interpretation; I am merely using it to illustrate the nature of language.) On the interpersonal level the language expresses, through a pattern of question (or exclamation) and response, a basic relationship of seeker and guide, in interplay with various other paired functions such as yours and mine, for and against, child and adult, wonderment and judgment. The texture is that of dialogue in narrative, within which the Queen's complex thematic structures (e.g. *there's one great advantage to it, that . . .* ) contrast with the much simpler (i.e. linguistically unmarked) message patterns used by Alice.

A functional theory of language is a theory about meanings, not about words or constructions; we shall not attempt to assign a word or a construction directly to one function or another. Where then do we find the functions differentiated in language? They are differentiated semantically, as different areas of what I called the "meaning potential." Language is itself a potential: it is the totality of what the speaker can do. (By "speaker" I mean always the language user, whether as speaker, listener, writer, or reader: *homo grammaticus*, in fact.) We are considering, as it were, the dynamics of the semantic strategies that are available to him. If we represent the language system in this way, as networks of interrelated options which define, as a whole, the resources for what the speaker wants to say, we find empirically that these options fall into a small number of fairly distinct sets. In the last resort, every option in language is related to every other; there are no completely independent choices. But the total network of meaning potential is actually composed of a number of smaller networks, each one highly complex in itself but related to the others in a way that is relatively simple: rather like an elaborate piece of circuitry made up of two or three complex blocks of wiring with fairly simple interconnections. Each of these blocks corresponds to one of the functions of language.

In Table 1, where the columns represent our linguistic functions, each column is one "block" of options. These blocks are to be thought of as wired "in parallel." That is to say, the speaker does not first think of the content of what he wants to say and then go on to decide what kind of a message it is and where he himself comes into it—whether it will be statement or question, what modalities are involved and the like.[6] All these functions, the ideational, the interpersonal and the textual, are simultaneously embodied in his planning procedures. (If we pursue the metaphor, it is the rows of the table that are wired "in series": they represent the hierarchy of constituents in the grammar, where the different functions come together. Each row is one constituent type, and is a point of intersection of options from the different columns.)

The linguistic differentiation among the ideational, interpersonal and textual functions is thus to be found in the way in which choices in meaning are interrelated to one another. Each function defines a set of options that is relatively—though only relatively—independent of the other sets. Dependence here refers to the degree of mutual determination: one part of the content of what one says tends to exert a considerable effect on other parts of the content, whereas one's attitudes and speech roles are relatively undetermined by it: the speaker is, by and large, free to associate any interpersonal meanings with any content. What I wish to stress here is that all types of option, from whatever function they are derived, are meaningful. At every point the speaker is selecting among a range of possibilities that differ in meaning; and if we attempt to separate meaning from choice we are turning a valuable distinction (between linguistic functions) into an arbitrary dichotomy (between "meaningful" and "meaningless" choices). All options are embedded in the language system: the system *is* a network of options, deriving from all the various functions of language. If we take the useful functional distinction of "ideational" and "interpersonal" and rewrite it, under the labels "cognitive" and "expressive," in such a way as sharply to separate the two, equating cognitive with meaning and expressive with style, we not only fail to recognize the experiential basis of many of our own intuitions about works of literature and their impact—style as the expression of what the thing is about, at some level[7] (my own illustration in this paper is one example of this)—but we also attach the contrasting status of "non-cognitive" (whatever this may mean) to precisely these options that seem best to embody our conception of a work of literature, those whereby the writer gives form to the discourse and expresses his own individuality.[8] Even if we are on our guard against the implication that the regions of language in which style resides are the ones which are linguistically non-significant, we are still drawing the wrong line. There are no regions of language in which style does not reside.

We should not in fact be drawing lines at all; the boundaries on our map consist only in shading and overlapping. Nevertheless they are there; and provided we are not forced into seeking an unreal distinction between the "what" and the "how," we can show, by reference to the generalized notion of linguistic functions, how such real contrasts as that of denotation and connotation relate to the functional map of language as a whole, and thus how they may be incorporated into the linguistic study of style. It is through this chain of reasoning that we may hope to establish criteria of relevance, and to demonstrate the connection between the syntactic observations which we make about a text and the nature of the impact which that text has upon us. If we can relate the linguistic patterns (grammatical, lexical, and even phonological) to the underlying functions of language, we have a criterion for eliminating what is trivial and for distinguishing true foregrounding from mere prominence of a statistical or an absolute kind.

Foregrounding, as I understand it, is prominence that is motivated. It is not difficult to find patterns of prominence in a poem or prose text, regularities in the sounds or words or structures that stand out in some way, or may be brought out by careful reading; and one may often be led in this way towards a new insight, through finding that such prominence contributes to the writer's total meaning. But unless it does, it will seem to lack motivation; a feature that is brought into prominence will be "foregrounded" only if it relates to the meaning of the text as a whole. This relationship is a functional one: if a particular feature of the language contributes, by its prominence, to the total meaning of the work, it does so by virtue of and through the medium of its own value in the language—through the linguistic function from which its meaning is derived. Where that function is relevant to our interpretation of the work, the prominence will appear as motivated. I shall try to illustrate this by reference to *The Inheritors*. First, however, a few remarks about some points raised at the 1958 Style in Language Conference and in subsequent discussions, which I hope will make slightly more explicit the context within which Golding's work is being examined.

There are three questions I should like to touch on: Is prominence to be regarded as a departure from or as the attainment of a norm? To what extent is prominence a quantitative effect, to be uncovered or at least stated by means of statistics? How real is the distinction between prominence that is due to subject matter and prominence that is due to something else? All three questions are very familiar, and my justification for bringing them up once more is not that what I have to say about them is new but rather that some partial answers are needed if we are attempting an integrated approach to language and style, and that these answers will be pertinent to a consideration of our main question, which is that of criteria of relevance.

I have used the term *prominence* as a general name for the phenomenon of linguistic highlighting, whereby some feature of the language of a text stands out in some way. In choosing this term I hoped to avoid the assumption that a linguistic feature which is brought under attention will always be seen as a departure. It is quite natural to characterize such prominence as departure from a norm, since this explains why it is remarkable, especially if one is stressing the subjective nature of the highlighting effect; thus Leech, discussing what he refers to as "schemes" ("foregrounded patterns . . . in grammar or phonology"), writes "It is ultimately a matter of subjective judgment whether . . . the regularity seems remarkable enough to constitute a definite departure from the normal functions of language."[9] But at the same time it is often objected, not unreasonably, that the "departure" view puts too high a value on oddness, and suggests that normal forms are of no interest in the study of style. Thus Wellek: "The danger of linguistic stylistics is its focus on deviations from, and distortions of, the linguistic norm. We get a kind of counter-grammar, a science of discards. Normal stylistics is abandoned to the grammarian, and deviational stylistics is reserved for the student of literature. But often the most commonplace, the most normal, linguistic elements are the constituents of literary structure."[10]

Two kinds of answer have been given to this objection. One is that there are two types of prominence, only one of which is negative, a departure from a norm; the other is positive, and is the attainment or the establishment of a norm. The second is that departure may in any case be merely statistical: we are concerned not only with deviations, ungrammatical forms, but also with what we may call "deflections," departures from some expected pattern of frequency.

The distinction between negative and positive prominence, or departures and regularities, is drawn by Leech, who contrasts foregrounding in the form of "motivated deviation from linguistic, or other socially accepted norms" with foregrounding applied to "the opposite circumstance, in which a writer temporarily renounces his permitted freedom of choice, introducing uniformity where there would normally be diversity."[11] Strictly speaking this is not an "opposite circumstance," since if diversity is normal, then uniformity is a deviation. But where there is uniformity there is regularity; and this can be treated as a positive feature, as the establishment of a norm. Thus, to quote Hymes, ". . . in some sources, especially poets, style may not be deviation from but achievement of a norm."[12]

However, this is not a distinction between two types of prominence; it is a distinction between two ways of looking at prominence, depending on the standpoint of the observer. There is no single universally relevant norm, no one set of expectancies to which all instances may be referred. On the one hand, there are differences of perspective. The text may be seen as "part" of a larger "whole," such as the author's complete works, or the tradition to which it belongs, so that what is globally a departure may be locally a norm. The expectancies may lie in "the language as a whole," in a diatypic variety or register[13] characteristic of some situation type (Osgood's "situational norms"[14]), in a genre or literary form, or in some special institution such as the Queen's Christmas message; we always have the choice of saying either "this departs from a pattern" or "this forms a pattern." On the other hand, there are differences of attention. The text may be seen as "this" in contrast with "that," with another poem or another novel; stylistic studies are essentially comparative in nature, and either may be taken as the point of departure. As Hymes says, there are egalitarian universes, comprising sets of norms, and "it would be arbitrary to choose one norm as a standard from which the others depart."[15] It may be more helpful to look at a given instance of prominence in one way rather than in another, sometimes as departure from a norm and sometimes as the attainment of a norm; but there is only one type of phenomenon here, not two.

There is perhaps a limiting case, the presence of one ungrammatical sentence in an entire poem or novel; presumably this could be viewed only as a departure. But in itself it would be unlikely to be of any interest. Deviation, the use of ungrammatical forms, has received a great deal of attention, and seems to be regarded, at times, as prominence *par excellence*. This is probably because it is a deterministic concept. Deviant forms are actually prohibited by the rules of whatever is taken to be the norm; or, to express it positively, the norm that is established by a set of deviant forms excludes all texts but the one in which they occur. But for this very reason deviation is of very limited interest in stylistics. It is rarely found; and when it is found, it is often not relevant. On the contrary, if we follow McIntosh (who finds it "a chastening thought"), ". . . quite often . . . the impact of an entire work may be enormous, yet word by word, phrase by phrase, clause by clause, sentence by sentence, there may seem to be nothing very unusual or arresting, in grammar or in vocabulary. . . ."[16]

Hence the very reasonable supposition that prominence may be of a probabilistic kind, defined by Bloch as "frequency distributions and transitional probabilities [which] differ from those . . . in the language as a whole."[17] This is what we have referred to above as "deflection." It too may be viewed either as departure from a norm or as its attainment. If, for example, we meet seven occurrences of a rather specific grammatical pattern, such as that cited by Leech "*my* + noun + *you* + verb,"[18] a norm has been set up and there is, or may be, a strong local expectancy that an eighth will follow; the probability of finding this pattern repeated in eight successive clauses is infinitesimally small, so that the same phenomenon constitutes a departure. It is fairly easy to see that the one always implies the other; the contravention of one expectation is, at the same time, the ful-

TABLE 2
FREQUENCIES OF TRANSITIVITY CLAUSE TYPES

| A   Process: | ACTION intransitive movement | other | transitive movement | other | location/possession | mental process | attribution | other (equation, event) | |
|---|---|---|---|---|---|---|---|---|---|
| human { people | 9 | | 1 | 1 | 1 | 12 | | | 24 |
| human { tribe | 2 | | 1 | | | 1 | | | 4 |
| part of body | 2 | | | | 1 | 3 | 2 | | 8 |
| inanimate | 4 | | 1 | | 12 | | 3 | | 20 |
| | 17 | | 3 | 1 | 14 | 16 | 5 | | 56 |
| **B (i)** | | | | | | | | | |
| human { people | 4 | | 1 | 3* | 2 | 1 | | | 11 |
| human { tribe | 5 | | 1 | 1 | 2 | | | | 9 |
| part of body | | | | | | | | | |
| inanimate | 13 | 1 | 2 | | 5 | | | 2 | 23 |
| | 22 | 1 | 4 | 4 | 9 | 1 | | 2 | 43 |
| **B (ii)** | | | | | | | | | |
| human { people { tribe | 13 | 2 | 1 | | 2 | 4 | | | 22 |
| part of body | 3 | | | | 1 | | 2 | | 6 |
| inanimate | 3 | 1 | 1 | 2 | 4 | | 6 | 2 | 19 |
| | 19 | 3 | 2 | 2 | 7 | 4 | 8 | 2 | 47 |
| **C** | | | | | | | | | |
| human { people | 1 | | 1 | 2 | | 4 | | | 8 |
| human { tribe | 3 | 2 | 5 | 11 | 3 | 11 | 3 | 2 | 40 |
| part of body | 2 | 1 | | | | | 5 | | 8 |
| inanimate | 2 | 1 | | | 3 | | 4 | 1 | 11 |
| | 8 | 4 | 6 | 13 | 6 | 15 | 12 | 3 | 67 |

* including two passives, which are also negative and in which the actor is not explicit: *The tree would not be cajoled or persuaded.*

fillment of a different one. Either way, whether the prominence is said to consist in law-breaking or in law-making, we are dealing with a type of phenomenon that is expressible in quantitative terms, to which statistical concepts may be applied.

In the context of stylistic investigations, the term "statistical" may refer to anything from a highly detailed measurement of the reactions of subjects to sets of linguistic variables, to the parenthetical insertion of figures of occurrences designed to explain why a particular feature is being singled out for discussion. What is common to all these is the assumption that numerical data on language may be stylistically significant; whatever subsequent operations are performed, there has nearly always been some counting of linguistic elements in the text, whether of phonological units or words or grammatical patterns, and the figures obtained are potentially an indication of prominence. The notion that prominence may be defined statistically is still not always accepted; there seem to be two main counterarguments, but whatever substance these may have as stated they are not, I think, valid objections to the point at issue. The first is essentially that, since style is a manifestation of the individual, it cannot be reduced to counting. This is true, but, as has often been said before, it misses the point. If there is such a thing as a recognizable style, whether of a work, an author, or an entire period or literary tradition, its distinctive quality can in the last analysis be stated in terms of relative frequencies, although the linguistic features that show significant variation may be simple and obvious or extremely subtle and complex. An example of how period styles may be revealed in this way will be found in Josephine Miles' "Eras in English Poetry," in which she shows that different periods are characterized by a distinction in the dominant type of sentence structure, that between "the sort which emphasizes substantival elements—the phrasal and co-ordinative modifications of subject and object—and the sort which emphasizes clausal co-ordination and complication of the predicate."[19]

The second objection is that numbers of occurrences must be irrelevant to style because we are not aware of frequency in language and therefore cannot respond to it. This is almost certainly not true. We are probably rather sensitive to the relative frequency of different grammatical and lexical patterns, which is an aspect of "meaning potential"; and our expectancies, as readers, are in part based on our awareness of the probabilities inherent in the language. This is what enables us to grasp the new probabilities of the text as local norm; our ability to perceive a statistical departure and restructure it as a norm is itself evidence of the essentially probabilistic nature of the language system. Our concern here, in any case, is not with psychological problems of the response to literature but with the linguistic options selected by the writer and their relation to the total meaning of the work. If in the selections he has made there is an unexpected pattern of frequency distributions, and this turns out to be motivated, it seems pointless to argue that such a phenomenon could not possibly be significant.

What cannot be expressed statistically is foregrounding: figures do not tell us whether a particular pattern has or has not "value in the game."[20] For this we need to know the rules. A distinctive frequency distribution is in itself no guarantee of stylistic relevance, as can be seen from authorship studies, where the diagnostic features are often, from a literary standpoint, very trivial ones.[21] Conversely, a linguistic feature that is stylistically very relevant may display a much less striking frequency pattern. But there is likely to be some quantitative turbulence, if a particular feature is felt to be prominent; and a few figures may be very suggestive. Counting, as Miller remarked, has many positive virtues. Ullmann offers a balanced view of these when he writes "Yet even those who feel that detailed statistics are both unnecessary and unreliable [in a sphere where quality and context, aesthetic effects and suggestive overtones are of supreme importance] would probably agree that a rough indication of frequencies would often be help-ful."[22] A rough indication of frequencies is often just what is needed: enough to suggest why we should accept the analyst's assertion that some feature is prominent in the text, and to allow us to check his statements. The figures, obviously, do not alone constitute an analysis, interpretation, or evaluation of the style.

But this is not, be it noted, a limitation on quantitative patterns as such; it is a limitation on the significance of prominence of any kind. Deviation is no more fundamental a phenomenon than statistical deflection: in fact there is no very clear line between the two, and in any given instance the most qualitatively deviant items may be among the least relevant. Thus if style cannot be reduced to counting, this is because it cannot be reduced to a simple question of prominence. An adequate characterization of an author's style is much more than an inventory of linguistic highlights. This is why linguists were so often reluctant to take up questions of criticism and evaluation, and tended to disclaim any contribution to the appraisal of what they were describing: they were very aware that statements about linguistic prominence by themselves offer no criterion of literary value. Nevertheless some values, or some aspects of value, must be expressed in linguistic terms. This is true, for example, of metrical patterns, which linguists have always considered their proper concern. The question is how far it is also true of patterns that are more directly related to meaning: what factors govern the relevance of "effects" in grammar and vocabulary? The significance of rhythmic regularity has to be formulated linguistically, since it is a phono-logical phenomenon, although the ultimate value to which it relates is not "given" by the language—that the sonnet is a highly valued pattern is not a linguistic fact, but the sonnet itself is.[23] The sonnet form defines the relevance of certain types of phonological pattern. There may likewise be some linguistic factor involved in determining whether a syntactic or a lexical pattern is stylistically relevant or not.

Certainly there is no magic in unexpectedness; and one line of approach has been to attempt to state conditions under which the unexpected is *not* relevant—namely when it is not really unexpected. Prominence, in this view, is not significant if the linguistically unpredicted configuration is predictable on other grounds; specifically, by reference to subject matter, the implication being that it would have been predicted if we had known beforehand what the passage was about. So, for example, Ullmann warns of the danger in the search for statistically defined key-words: "One must carefully avoid what have been called contextual words whose frequency is due to the subject-matter rather than to any deep-seated stylistic or psychological tendency."[24] Ullmann's concern here is with words that serve as indices of a particular author, and he goes on to discuss the significance of recurrent imagery for style and personality, citing as an example the prominence of insect vocabulary in the writings of Sartre;[25] in this context we can see that, by contrast, the prevalence of such words in a treatise on entomology would be irrelevant. But it is less easy to see how this can be generalized, even in the realm of vocabulary; is lexical foregrounding entirely dependent on imagery?

Can we in fact dismiss, as irrelevant, prominence that is due to subject-matter? Can we even claim to identify it? This was the third and final question I asked earlier, and it is one which relates very closely to an interpretation of the style of *The Inheritors*. In *The Inheritors*, the features that come to our attention are largely syntactic, and we are in the realm of syntactic imagery, where the syntax, in Ohmann's words, "serves [a] vision of things. . . . since there are innumerable kinds of deviance, we should expect that the ones elected by a poem or poet spring from particular semantic impulses, particular ways of looking at experience."[26] Ohmann is concerned primarily with "syntactic irregularities," but syntax need not be deviant in order to serve a vision of things; a foregrounded selection of everyday syntactic options may be just as visionary, and perhaps more effective. The vision provides the motivation for their prominence; it makes them relevant, however ordinary they may be. The style of *The Inheritors* rests very much on foregrounding of this kind.

The prominence, in other words, is often due to the vision. But "vision" and "subject matter" are merely the different levels of meaning which we expect to find in a literary work; and each of these, the inner as well as the outer, and any as it were intermediate layers, finds expression in the syntax.

In Ruqaiya Hasan's words, "Each utterance has a thesis: what it is talking about uniquely and instantially; and in addition to this, each utterance has a function in the internal organization of the text: in combination with other utterances of the text it realizes the theme, structure and other aspects. . . ."[27] Patterns of syntactic prominence may reflect thesis or theme or "other aspects" of the meaning of the work; every level is a potential source of motivation, a kind of semantic "situational norm." And since the role of syntax in language is to weave into a single fabric the different threads of meaning that derive from the variety of linguistic functions, one and the same syntactic feature is very likely to have at once both a deeper and a more immediate significance, like the participial structures in Milton as Chatman has interpreted them.[28]

Thus we cannot really discount "prominence due to subject-matter," at least as far as syntactic prominence is concerned; especially where vision and subject-matter are themselves as closely interwoven as they are in *The Inheritors*. Rather, perhaps, we might think of the choice of subject-matter as being itself a stylistic choice, in the sense that the subject-matter may be more or less relevant to the underlying themes of the work. To the extent that the subject-matter is an integral element in the total meaning—in the artistic unity, if you will—to that extent, prominence that is felt to be partly or wholly "due to" the subject-matter, far from being irrelevant to the style, will turn out to be very clearly foregrounded.

To cite a small example that I have used elsewhere, the prominence of finite verbs in simple past tense in the well-known "Return of Excalibur" lines in Tennyson's *Morte d'Arthur* relates immediately to the subject-matter: the passage is a direct narrative. But the choice of a story as subject-matter is itself related to the deeper preoccupations of the work—with heroism and, beyond that, with the *res gestae*, with deeds as the realization of the true spirit of a people, and with history and historicalism; the narrative register is an appropriate form of expression, one that is congruent with the total meaning, and so the verb forms that are characteristically associated with it are motivated at every level. Similarly, it is not irrelevant to the *style* of an entomological monograph (although we may not be very interested in its style) that it contains a lot of words for insects, if in fact it does. In stylistics we are concerned with language in relation to all the various levels of meaning that a work may have.

But while a given instance of syntactic or lexical prominence may be said to be "motivated" either by the subject-matter or by some other level of the meaning, in the sense of deriving its relevance therefrom, it cannot really be said to be "due to" it. Neither thesis nor theme imposes linguistic patterns. They may set up local expectancies, but these are by no means always fulfilled; there might actually be very few insect words in the work on entomology—and there are very few in Kafka.[29] There is always choice. In *The Inheritors*, Golding is offering a "particular way of looking at experience," a vision of things which he ascribes to Neanderthal man; and he conveys this by syntactic prominence, by the frequency with which he selects certain key syntactic options. It is their frequency which establishes the clause types in question as prominent; but, as Ullmann has remarked, in stylistics we have *both* to count things *and* to look at them, one by one, and when we do this we find that the foregrounding effect is the product of two apparently opposed conditions of use. The foregrounded elements are certain clause types which display particular patterns of transitivity, as described in the next section; and in some instances the syntactic pattern is "expected" in that it is the typical form of expression for the subject-matter—for the process, participants, and circumstances that make up the thesis of the clause. Elsewhere, however, the same syntactic elements are found precisely where they would not be expected, there being other, more likely ways of "saying the same thing."

Here we might be inclined to talk of semantic choice and syntactic choice: what the author chooses to say, and how he chooses to say it. But this is a misleading distinction; not only because it is unrealistic in application (most distinctions in language leave indeterminate instances, although here there would be suspiciously many) but more because the combined effect is cumulative: the one does not weaken or cut across the other but reinforces it. We have to do here with an interaction, not of meaning and form, but of two levels of meaning, both of which find expression in form, and through the same syntactic features. The immediate thesis and the underlying theme come together in the syntax; the choice of subject-matter is motivated by the deeper meaning, and the transitivity patterns realize both. This is the explanation of their powerful impact.

The foregrounding of certain patterns in syntax as the expression of an underlying theme is what we understand by "syntactic imagery," and we assume that its effect will be striking. But in *The Inheritors* these same syntactic patterns also figure prominently in their "literal" sense, as the expression of subject-matter; and their prominence here is doubly relevant, since the literal use not only is motivated in itself but also provides a context for the metaphorical—we accept the syntactic vision of things more readily because we can see that it coincides with, and is an extension of, the reality. *The Inheritors* provides a remarkable illustration of how grammar can convey levels of meaning in literature; and this relates closely to the notion of linguistic functions which I discussed at the beginning. The foregrounded patterns, in this instance, are ideational ones, whose meaning resides in the representation of experience; as such they express not only the content of the narrative but also the abstract structure of the reality through which that content is interpreted. Sometimes the interpretation matches our own, and at other times, as in the drawing of the bow in passage A below, it conflicts with it; these are the "opposed conditions of use" referred to earlier. Yet each tells a part of the story. Language, because of the multiplicity of its functions, has a fugue-like quality in which a number of themes unfold simultaneously; each of these themes is apprehended in various settings, or perspectives, and each melodic line in the syntactic sequence has more than one value in the whole.

The Inheritors[30] is prefaced by a quotation from H. G. Wells' *Outline of History:*

> . . . We know very little of the appearance of the Neanderthal man, but this . . . seems to suggest an extreme hairiness, an ugliness, or a repulsive strangeness in his appearance over and above his low forehead, his beetle brows, his ape neck, and his inferior stature. . . . Says Sir Harry Johnston, in a survey of the rise of modern man in his *Views and Reviews:* "The dim racial remembrance of such gorilla-like monsters, with cunning brains, shambling gait, hairy bodies, strong teeth, and possibly cannibalistic tendencies, may be the germ of the ogre in folklore. . . ."

The book is, in my opinion, a highly successful piece of imaginative prose writing; in the words of Kinkead-Weekes and Gregor, in their penetrating critical study, it is a "reaching out through the imagination into the unknown."[31] The persons of the story are a small band of Neanderthal people, initially eight strong, who refer to themselves as "the people"; their world is then invaded by a group of more advanced stock, a fragment of a tribe, whom they call at first "others" and later "the new people." This casual impact—casual, that is, from the tribe's point of view—proves to be the end of the people's world, and of the people themselves. At first, and for more than nine-tenths of the book (pp. 1-216), we share the life of the people and their view of the world, and also their view of the tribe: for a long passage (pp. 137-80) the principal character, Lok, is hidden in a tree watching the tribe in their work, their ritual and their play, and the account of their doings is confined within the limits of Lok's understanding, requiring at times a considerable effort of "interpretation." At the very end (pp. 216-38) the standpoint shifts to that of the tribe, the inheritors, and the world becomes recognizable as our own, or something very like it. I propose to examine an aspect of the linguistic resources as they are used first to characterize the people's world and then to effect the shift of world-view.

For this purpose I shall look closely at three passages taken from different parts of the book; these are reproduced below (pp. 360-62). Passage A is representative of the first, and longest, section, the narrative of the people; it is taken from the long account of Lok's vigil in the tree. Passage C is taken from the short final section, concerned with the tribe; while passage B spans the transition, the shift of standpoint occurring at the paragraph division within this passage. Linguistically, A and C differ in rather significant ways, while B is in certain respects transitional between them.

The clauses of passage A [56][32] are mainly clauses of action [21], location (including possession) [14], or mental process [16]; the remainder [5] are attributive.[33] Usually the process is expressed by a finite verb in simple past tense [46]. Almost all of the action clauses [19] describe simple movements (*turn, rise, hold, reach, throw forward*, etc.); and of these the majority [15] are intransitive; the exceptions are *the man was holding the stick, as though someone had clapped a hand over her mouth, he threw himself forward,* and *the echo of Liku's voice in his head sent him trembling at this perilous way of bushes towards the island.* The typical pattern is exemplified by the first two clauses, *the bushes twitched again* and *Lok steadied by the tree,* and there is no clear line, here, between action and location: both types have some reference in space, and both have one participant only. The clauses of movement usually [16] also specify location, e.g. *the man turned sideways in the bushes, he rushed to the edge of the water*; and on the other hand, in addition to what is clearly movement, as in *a stick rose upright,* and what is clearly location, as in *there were hooks in the bone*, there is an intermediate type exemplified by [*the bushes*] *waded out,* where the verb is of the movement type but the subject is immobile.

The picture is one in which people act, but they do not act on things; they move, but they move only themselves, not other objects. Even such normally transitive verbs as *grab* occur intransitively: *he grabbed at the branches* is just another clause of movement (cf. *he smelled along the shaft of the twig*). Moreover a high proportion [exactly half] of the subjects are not people; they are either parts of the body [8] or inanimate objects [20], and of the human subjects half again [14] are found in clauses which are not clauses of action. Even among the four transitive action clauses, cited above, one has an inanimate subject and one is reflexive. There is a stress set up, a kind of syntactic counterpoint, between verbs of movement in their most active and dynamic form, that of finite verb in independent clause,[34] in the simple past tense characteristic of the direct narrative of events in a time sequence, on the one hand, and on the other hand the preference for non-human subjects and the almost total absence of transitive clauses. It is particularly the lack of transitive clauses of action with human subjects (there are only two clauses in which a person acts on an external object) that creates an atmosphere of ineffectual activity: the scene is one of constant movement, but movement which is as much inanimate as human and in which only the mover is affected—nothing else changes. The syntactic tension expresses this combination of activity and helplessness.

No doubt this is a fair summary of the life of Neanderthal man. But Passage A is not a description of the people. The section from which it is taken is one in which Lok is observing and, to a certain extent, interacting with the tribe; they have captured one of the people, and it is for the most part their doings that are being described. And the tribe are not helpless. The transitivity patterns are not imposed by the subject-matter; they are the reflexion of the underlying theme, or rather of one of the underlying themes—the inherent limitations of understanding, whether cultural or biological, of Lok and his people, and their consequent inability to survive when confronted with beings at a higher stage of development. In terms of the processes and events as we would interpret them, and encode them in our grammar, there is no immediate justification for the predominance of intransitives; this is the result of their being expressed through the medium of the semantic structure of Lok's universe. In our interpretation, a goal-directed process (or, as I shall suggest below, an externally caused process) took place: someone held up a bow and drew it. In Lok's interpretation, the process was undirected (or, again, self-caused): *a stick rose upright* and *began to grow shorter at both ends*. (I would differ slightly here from Kinkead-Weekes and Gregor, who suggest, I think, that the form of Lok's vision is perception and no more. There may be very little processing, but there surely is some; Lok has a theory—as he must have, because he has language.)

Thus it is the syntax as such, rather than the syntactic reflection of the subject-matter, to which we are responding. This would not emerge if we had no account of the activities of the tribe, since elsewhere—in the description of the people's own doings, or of natural phenomena—the intransitiveness of the syntax would have been no more than a feature of the events themselves, and of the people's ineffectual manipulation of their environment. For this reason the vigil of Lok is a central element in the novel. We find, in its syntax, both levels of meaning side by side: Lok is now actor, now interpreter, and it is his potential in both these roles that is realized by the overall patterns of prominence that we have observed, the intransitives, the non-human subjects, and the like. This is the dominant mode of expression. At the same time, in passage A, among the clauses that have human subjects, there are just two in which the subject is acting on something external to himself, and in both these the subject is a member of the tribe; it is not Lok. There is no instance in which Lok's own actions extend beyond himself; but there is a brief hint that such extension is conceivable. The syntactic foregrounding, of which this passage provides a typical example, thus has a complex significance: the predominance of intransitives reflects, first, the limitations of the people's own actions; second, the people's world view, which in general cannot transcend these limitations—but within which there may arise, thirdly, a dim apprehension of the superior powers of the "others," represented by the rare intrusion of a transitive clause such as *the man was holding the stick out to him*. Here the syntax leads us into a third level of meaning, Golding's concern with the nature of humanity; the intellectual and spiritual developments that contribute to the present human condition, and the conflicts that arise within it, are realized in the form of conflicts between the stages of that development—and, syntactically, between the types of transitivity.

Passage A is both text and sample. It is not only these particular sentences and their meanings that determine our response, but the fact that they are part of a general syntactic and semantic scheme. That this passage is representative in its transitivity patterns can be seen from comparison with other extracts.[35] It also exemplifies certain other relevant features of the language of this part of the book. We have seen that there is a strong preference for processes having only one participant: in general there is only one nominal element in the structure of the clause, which is therefore the subject. But while there are very few complements,[36] there is an abundance of adjuncts [44]; and most of these [40] have some spatial reference. Specifically, they are (a) static [25], of which most [21] are place adjuncts consisting of preposition plus noun, the noun being either an inanimate object of the immediate natural environment (e.g. *bush*) or a part of the body, the remainder [4] being localizers (*at their farthest, at the end*, etc.); and (b) dynamic [15], of which the majority [10] are of direction or non-terminal motion (*sideways, [rose] upright, at the branches, towards the island*, etc.) and the remainder [5] perception, or at least circumstantial to some process that is not a physical one (e.g. *[looked at Lok] along his shoulder, [shouted] at the green drifts*). Thus with the dynamic type, either the movement is purely perceptual or, if physical, it never reaches a goal: the nearest thing to terminal motion is *he rushed to the edge of the water* (which is followed by *and came back!*).

The restriction to a single participant also applies to mental process clauses [16]. This category includes perception, cognition, and reaction, as well as the rather distinct sub-category of verbalization; and such clauses in English typically contain a "phenomenon," that which is seen, understood, liked, etc. Here however the phenomenon is often [8] either not expressed at all (e.g. *[Lok] gazed*) or expressed indirectly through a preposition, as in *he smelled along the shaft of the twig*; and sometimes [3] the subject is not a human being but a sense organ (*his nose examined this stuff and did not like it*). There is the same reluctance to envisage the "whole man" (as distinct from a part of his body) participating in a process in which other entities are involved.

There is very little modification of nouns [10, out of about 100]; and all modifiers are non-defining (e.g. *green drifts, glittering water*) except where [2] the modifier is the only semantically significant element in the nominal, the head noun being a mere carrier demanded by the rules of English grammar (*white bone things, sticky brown stuff*). In terms of the immediate situation, things have defining attributes only if these attributes are their sole properties; at the more abstract level, in Lok's understanding the complex taxonomic ordering of natural phenomena that is implied by the use of defining modifiers is lacking, or is only rudimentary.

We can now formulate a description of a typical clause of what we may call "Language A," the language in which the major part of the book is written and of which passage A is a sample, in terms of its process, participants and circumstances:

(1) There is one participant only, which is therefore subject; this is

(a) actor in a non-directed action (action clauses are intransitive), or participant in a mental process (the one who perceives, etc.), or simply the bearer of some attribute or some spatial property;

(b) a person (*Lok, the man, he,* etc.), or a part of the body, or an inanimate object of the immediate and tangible natural environment (*bush, water, twig,* etc.);

(c) unmodified, other than by a determiner which is either an anaphoric demonstrative (*this, that*) or, with parts of the body, a personal possessive (*his, etc.*).

(2) The process is

(a) action (which is always movement in space), or location-possession (including e.g. *the man had white bone things above his eyes* = "above the man's eyes there were . . ."), or mental process (thinking and talking as well as seeing and feeling—a "cunning brain"!—but often with a part of the body as subject);

(b) active, non-modalized, finite, in simple past tense (one of a linear sequence of mutually independent processes).

(3) There are often other elements which are adjuncts, i.e. treated as circumstances attendant on the process, not as participants in it; these are

(a) static expressions of place (in the form of prepositional phrases), or, if dynamic, expressions of direction (adverbs only) or of non-terminal motion, or of directionality of perception (e.g. *peered at the stick*);

(b) often obligatory, occurring in clauses which are purely locational (e.g. *there were hooks in the bone*).

A grammar of Language A would tell us not merely what clauses occurred in the text but also what clauses could occur in that language.[37] For example, as far as I know the clause *a branch curved downwards over the water* does not occur in the book; neither does *his hands felt along the base of the rock*. But both of them could have. On the other hand, *he had very quickly broken off the lowest branches* breaks four rules: it has a human actor with a transitive verb, a tense other than simple past, a defining modifier, and a non-spatial adjunct. This is not to say that it could not occur. Each of these features is improbable, and their combination is very improbable; but they are not impossible. They are improbable in that they occur with significantly lower frequency than in other varieties of English (such as, for example, the final section of *The Inheritors*).

Before leaving this passage, let us briefly reconsider the transitivity features in the light of a somewhat different analysis of transitivity in English. I have suggested elsewhere that the most generalized pattern of transitivity in modern English, extending beyond action clauses to clauses of all types, those of mental process and those expressing attributive and other relations, is one that is based not on the notions of actor and goal but on those of cause and effect.[38] In any clause, there is one central and obligatory participant—let us call it the "affected" participant—which is inherently involved in the process. This corresponds to the actor in an intransitive clause of action, to the goal in a transitive clause of action, and to the one who perceives, etc., in a clause of mental process; *Lok* has this function in all the following examples: *Lok turned away, Fa drew Lok away, Lok looked up at Fa, Lok was frightened, curiosity overcame Lok*. There may then be a second, optional participant, which is present only if the process is being regarded as brought about by some agency other than the participant affected by it: let us call this the "agent." This is the actor in a transitive clause of action and the initiator in the various types of causative; the function of *Tuami* in *Tuami waggled the paddle in the water* and *Tuami let the ivory drop from his hands*. As far as action clauses are concerned, an intransitive clause is one in which the roles of "affected" and "agent" are combined in the one participant; a transitive clause is one in which they are separated, the process being treated as one having an external cause.

In these terms, the entire transitivity structure of Language A can be summed up by saying that there is no cause and effect. More specifically: in this language, processes are seldom represented as resulting from an external cause; in those instances where they are, the "agent" is seldom a human being; and where it is a human being, it is seldom one of the people. Whatever the type of process, there tends to be only one participant; any other entities are involved only indirectly, as circumstantial elements (syntactically, through the mediation of a preposition). It is as if doing was as passive as seeing, and things no more affected by actions than by perceptions: their role is as in clauses of mental process, where the object of perception is not in any sense "acted on"—it is in fact the perceiver that is the "affected" participant, not the thing perceived—and likewise tends to be expressed circumstantially (e.g. *Lok peered at the stick*). There is no effective relation between persons and objects: people do not bring about events in which anything other than they themselves, or parts of their bodies, are implicated.

There are, moreover, a great many, an excessive number, of these circumstantial elements; they are the objects in the natural environment, which as it were take the place of participants, and act as curbs and limitations on the process. People do not act on the things around them; they act within the limitations imposed by the things. The frustration of the struggle with the environment, of a life "poised . . . between the future and the past,"[39] is embodied in the syntax: many of the intransitive clauses have potentially transitive verbs in them, but instead of a direct object there is a prepositional phrase. The feeling of frustration is perhaps further reinforced by the constant reference to complex mental activities of cognition and verbalization. Although there are very few abstract nouns, there are very many clauses of speaking, knowing and understanding (e.g. *Lok understood that the man was holding the stick out to him*); and a recurrent theme, an obsession almost, is the difficulty of communicating memories and images (*I cannot see this picture*)—of transmitting experience through language, the vital step towards that social learning which would be a precondition of their further advance.

Such are some of the characteristics of Language A, the language which tells the story of the people. There is no such thing as a "Language B." Passage B is simply the point of transition between the two parts of the book. There is a "Language C": this is the language of the last sixteen pages of the novel, and it is exemplified by the extract shown as passage C below. But passage B is of interest because linguistically it is also to some extent transitional. There is no doubt that the first paragraph is basically in Language A and the second in Language C; moreover the switch is extremely sudden, being established in the first three words of B (ii), when Lok, with whom we have become closely identified, suddenly becomes *the red creature*. Nevertheless B (i) does provide some hints of the change to come.

There are a few instances [4] of a human "agent" (actor in a transitive clause); not many, but one of them is Lok, in *Lok . . . picked up Tanakil.* Here is Lok acting on his environment, and the object "affected" is a human being, and one of the tribe! There are some non-spatial adjuncts, such as *with an agonized squealing, like the legs of a giant.* There are abstract nominals: *demoniac activity, its weight of branches.* And there are perhaps more modifiers and complex verb forms than usual. None of these features is occurring for the first time; we have had forward-looking flashes throughout, e.g. (p. 191) *He had a picture of Liku looking up with soft and adoring eyes at Tanakil, guessed how Ha had gone with a kind of eager fearfulness to meet his sudden death* and (pp. 212-3) *"Why did you not snatch the new one?"* and *"We will take Tanakil. Then they will give back the new one,"* both spoken by the more intelligent Fa (when transitive action clauses do occur in Language A, they are often in the dialogue). But there is a greater concentration of them in B (i), a linguistic complexity that is also in harmony with the increased complexity of the events, which has been being built up ever since the tribe first impinged on the people with the mysterious disappearance of Ha (p. 65). The syntax expresses the climax of the gradual overwhelming of Lok's understanding by new things and events; and this coincides with the climax in the events themselves as, with the remainder of the people all killed or captured, Lok's last companion, Fa, is carried over the edge of the waterfall. Lok is alone; there are no more people, and the last trace of his humanity, his membership of a society, has gone. In that moment he belongs to the past.

Lok does not speak again, because there is no one to speak to. But for a while we follow him, as the tribe might have followed him, although they did not—or rather we follow *it*; there can be no *him* where there is no *you* and *me*. The language is now Language C, and the story is that of *homo sapiens*; but for a few paragraphs, beginning at B (ii), as we remain with Lok, the syntax harks back to the world of the people, just as in B (i) it was beginning to look forward. The transition has taken place; *it was a strange creature, smallish, and bowed* that we had come to know so well. But it is still the final, darkening traces of this creature's world that we are seeing, fleetingly as if in an escaping dream.

A brief sketch of B (ii): There are very few transitive clauses of action [4]; in only one of these is Lok the agent—and here the "affected" entity is a part of his own body: *it put up a hand*. The others have *the water* and *the river* as agent. Yet nearly half [22] the total number of clauses [47] have Lok as subject; here, apart from a few [4] mental process clauses, the verb is again one of simple movement or posture, and intransitive (*turn, move, crouch*, etc.; but including for the first time some with a connotation of attitude like *sidle* and *trot*; cf. *broke into a queer, loping run*). The remaining subjects are inanimate objects [19] and parts of the body [6]. But there are differences in these subjects. The horizons have widened; in addition to *water* and *river* we now have *sun* and *green sky*—a reminder that the new people walk upright; cf. (p. 143) *they did not look at the earth but straight ahead*; and there are now also human evidences and artifacts: *path, rollers, ropes*. And the parts of the body no longer see or feel; they are subjects only of intransitive verbs of movement (e.g. *its long arms swinging*), and mainly in non-finite clauses, expressing the dependent nature of the processes in which they participate. A majority [32] of the finite verbs are still in simple past tense; but there is more variation in the remainder, as well as more non-finite verbs [8], reflecting a slightly increased proportion of dependent clauses that is also a characteristic of Language C. And while in many clauses [21] we still find spatial adjuncts, these tend to be more varied and more complex (e.g. *down the rocks beyond the terrace from the melting ice in the mountains*).

This is the world of the tribe; but it is still inhabited, for a brief moment of time, by Lok. Once again the theme is enunciated by the syntax. Nature is no longer totally impenetrable; yet Lok remains powerless, master of nothing but his own body. In passages A and B taken together, there are more than fifty clauses in which the subject is Lok; but only one of these has Lok as an agent acting on something external to himself, one that has already been mentioned: *Lok picked up Tanakil*. There is a double irony here. Of all the positive actions on his environment that Lok might have taken, the one he does take is the utterly improbable one of capturing a girl of the tribe—improbable in the event, at the level of subject-matter (let us call this "level one"), and improbable also in the deeper context ("level two"), since Lok's newly awakened power manifests itself as power over the one element in the environment that is "superior" to himself. It is at a still deeper "level three" that the meaning becomes clear. The action gets him nowhere; but it is a syntactic hint that his people have played their part in the long trek towards the human condition.

By the time we reach passage C, the transition is complete. Here, for the first time, the majority of the clauses [48 out of 67] have a human subject; of these, more than half [25] are clauses of action, and most of these [19] are transitive. Leaving aside two in which the thing "affected" is a part of the body, there is still a significant increase in the number of instances [17, contrasting with 5 in the whole of A and B together] in which a human agent is acting on an external object. The world of the inheritors is organized as ours is; or at least in a way that we can recognize. Among these are two clauses in which the subject is *they*, referring to the people ("the devils": e.g. *they have given me back a changeling*); in the tribe's scheme of things, the people are by no means powerless. There is a parallel here with the earlier part. In passage A the actions of the tribe are encoded in terms of the world-view of the people, so that the predominance of intransitive clauses is interpreted at what we called "level two," although there is a partial reflection of "level one" in the fact that they are marginally less predominant when the subject-matter concerns the tribe. Similarly, in passage C references to the people are encoded in terms of the world-view of the tribe, and transitive structures predominate; yet the only member of the people who is present—the only one to survive—is the captured baby, whose infant behaviour is described in largely intransitive terms (pp. 230-31). And the references to the people, in the dialogue, include such formulations as "*They cannot follow us, I tell you. They cannot pass over water,*" which is a "level one" reassurance that, in a "level two" world of cause and effect whose causes are often unseen and unknown, there are at least limits to the devils' power.

We can now see the full complementarity between the two "languages," but it is not easy to state. In Language A there is a level-two theme, that of powerlessness. The momentary hints of potency that we are given at level one represent an antithetic variation which, however, has a significance at level three: the power is ascribed to the tribe but signifies Lok's own incipient awareness, the people's nascent understanding of the human potential. This has become a level-two theme in Language C; and in like fashion the level-two theme of Language A becomes in Language C a level-one variation, but again with a level-three significance. The people may be powerless, but the tribe's demand for explanations of things, born of their own more advanced state, leads them, while still fearfully insisting on the people's weakness in action, to ascribe to them supernatural powers.

While there are still inanimate subjects in the clause [11], as there always are in English, there is no single instance in passage C of an inanimate agent. In A and B we had *the echo of Liku's voice in his head sent him trembling . . . , the branches took her, the water had scooped a bowl out of the rock;* in C we have only *the sail glowed, the sun was sitting in it, the hills grow less.* Likewise all clauses with parts of the body as subject [8] are now intransitive, and none of them is a clause of mental process. Parts of the body no longer feel or perceive; they have attributes ascribed to them (e.g. *his teeth were wolf's teeth*) or they move (*the lips parted, the mouth was opening and shutting*). The limbs may move and posture, but only the whole man perceives and reacts to his environment. Now, he also shapes his environment: his actions have become more varied—no longer simply movements; we find here *save, obey,* and *kiss*—and they produce results. Something, or someone, is affected by them.

Just as man's relation to his environment has altered, so his perception of it has changed; the environment has become enlarged. The objects in it are no longer the *twig, stick, bush, branch* of Language A, nor even the larger but still tangible *river, water, scars in the earth.* In passage B (ii) we already had *air* and *sun* and *sky* and *wind;* in C we have *the mountain . . . full of golden light, the sun was blazing, the sand was swirling* (the last metaphorically); and also human artifacts: *the sail, the mast.* Nature is not tamed: the features of the natural environment may no longer be agents in the transitivity patterns, but neither are they direct objects. What has happened is that the horizons have broadened. Where the people were bounded by tree and river and rock, the tribe are bounded by sky and sea and mountain. Although they are not yet conquered, the features that surround them no longer circumscribe all action and all contemplation. Whereas Lok *rushed to the edge of the water and came back*, the new people *steer in towards the shore*, and *look across the water at the green hills*.

*The Inheritors* has provided a perspective for a linguistic inquiry of a kind whose relevance and significance is notoriously difficult to assess: an inquiry into the language of a full-length prose work. In this situation syntactic analysis is unlikely to offer anything in the way of new interpretations of particular sentences in terms of their subject-matter; the language as a whole is not deviant, and the difficulties of understanding are at the level of interpretation—or rather perhaps, in the present instance, re-interpretation, as when we insist on translating *the stick began to grow shorter at both ends* as "the man drew the bow." I have not, in this study, emphasized the use of linguistic analysis as a key; I doubt whether it has this function. What it can do is to establish certain regular patterns, on a comparative basis, in the form of differences which appear significant over a broad canvas. In *The Inheritors* these appear as differences within the text itself, between what we have called "Language A" and "Language C." In terms of this novel, if either of these is to be regarded as a departure, it will be Language C, which appears only briefly at the very end; but in the context of modern English as a whole it is Language A which constitutes the departure and Language C the norm. There is thus a double shift of standpoint in the move from global to local norm, but one which brings us back to more or less where we started.

The focus of attention has been on language in general, on the language system and its relation to the meanings of a literary work. In the study of the text, we have examined instances where particular syntactic options have been selected with a greater than expected frequency, a selection that is partly but not wholly explained by reference to the subject-matter; and have suggested that, by considering how the meaning of these options, taken in the context of the ideational function of language as a whole, relates to an interpretation of the meaning of the work, one can show that they are relevant both as subject-matter and as underlying theme. Each sentence in the passages that were observed in detail is thus potentially of interest both in itself and as an instance of a general trend; and we have been able to ignore other differences, such as that between dialogue and narrative, although a study of these as subvarieties would almost certainly yield further points of interest. Within the present context, the prominence that we have observed can be said to be "motivated"; it is reasonable to talk of foregrounding, here, as an explanation of stylistic impact.

The establishment of a syntactic norm (for this is what it is) is thus a way of expressing one of the levels of meaning of the work: the fact that a particular pattern constitutes a norm *is* the meaning. The linguistic function of the pattern is therefore of some importance. The features that we have seen to be foregrounded in *The Inheritors* derive from the ideational component in the language system; hence they represent, at the level at which they constitute a norm, a world-view, a structuring of experience that is significant because there is no *a priori* reason why the experience should have been structured in this way rather than in another. More particularly, the foregrounded features were selections in transitivity. Transitivity is the set of options whereby the speaker encodes his experience of the processes of the external world, and of the internal world of his own consciousness, together with the participants in these processes and their attendant circumstances; and it embodies a very basic distinction of processes into two types, those that are regarded as due to an external cause, an agency other than the person or object involved, and those that are not. There are, in addition, many further categories and subtypes. Transitivity is really the cornerstone of the semantic organization of experience; and it is at one level what *The Inheritors* is about. The theme of the entire novel, in a sense, is transitivity: man's interpretation of his experience of the world, his understanding of its processes and of his own participation in them. This is the motivation for Golding's syntactic originality; it is because of this that the syntax is effective as a "mode of meaning."[40] The particular transitivity patterns that stand out in the text contribute to the artistic whole through the functional significance, in the language system, of the semantic options which they express.

This is what we understand by "relevance"—the notion that a linguistic feature "belongs" in some way as part of the whole. The pursuit of prominence is not without significance for the understanding and evaluation of a literary work; but neither is it sufficient to be a rewarding activity in itself.[41] It has been said of phonological foregrounding that "there must be appropriateness to the nexus of sound and meaning";[42] and this is no less true of the syntactic and semantic levels, where, however, the relationship is not one of sound and meaning but one of meaning and meaning. Here "relevance" implies a congruence with our interpretation of what the work is about, and hence the criteria of belonging are semantic ones. We might be tempted to express the relevance of syntactic patterns, such as we find in *The Inheritors*, as a "unity of form and meaning," parallel to the "sound and meaning" formulation above; but this would, I think, be a false parallel. The syntactic categories are *per se* the realizations of semantic options,

and the relevance is the relevance of one set of meanings to another—a relationship among the levels of meaning of the work itself.

In *The Inheritors*, the syntax is part of the story. As readers, we are re-
acting to the whole of the writer's creative use of "meaning potential"; and
the nature of language is such that he can convey, in a line of print, a complex of simultaneous themes, reflecting the variety of functions that language is required to serve. And because the elements of the language, the
words and phrases and syntactic structures, tend to have multiple values,
any one theme may have more than one interpretation: in expressing some
content, for example, the writer may invite us at the same time to interpret it in quite a different functional context—as a cry of despair, perhaps.
It is the same property of language that enables us to react to hints, to take
offence and do all the other things that display the rhetoric of everyday
verbal interaction. A theme that is strongly foregrounded is especially likely
to be interpreted at more than one level. In *The Inheritors* it is the linguistic representation of experience, through the syntactic resources of
transitivity, that is especially brought into relief, although there may be
other themes not mentioned here that stand out in the same way. Every
work achieves a unique balance among the types and components of meaning, and embodies the writer's individual exploration of the functional diversity of language.

## APPENDIX
### Extracts from *The Inheritors*

A. (pp. 106-7.)
The bushes twitched again. Lok steadied by the tree and gazed. A head and
a chest faced him, half-hidden. There were white bone things behind the leaves
and hair. The man had white bone things above his eyes and under the mouth
so that his face was longer than a face should be. The man turned sideways in
the bushes and looked at Lok along his shoulder. A stick rose upright and there
was a lump of bone in the middle. Lok peered at the stick and the lump of
bone and the small eyes in the bone things over the face. Suddenly Lok understood that the man was holding the stick out to him but neither he nor Lok
could reach across the river. He would have laughed if it were not for the echo
of the screaming in his head. The stick began to grow shorter at both ends.
Then it shot out to full length again.
The dead tree by Lok's ear acquired a voice.
"Clop!"
His ears twitched and he turned to the tree. By his face there had grown a
twig: a twig that smelt of other, and of goose, and of the bitter berries that Lok's
stomach told him he must not eat. This twig had a white bone at the end.
There were hooks in the bone and sticky brown stuff hung in the crooks. His
nose examined this stuff and did not like it. He smelled along the shaft of the

twig. The leaves on the twig were red feathers and reminded him of goose. He was lost in a generalized astonishment and excitement. He shouted at the green drifts across the glittering water and heard Liku crying out in answer but could not catch the words. They were cut off suddenly as though someone had clapped a hand over her mouth. He rushed to the edge of the water and came back. On either side of the open bank the bushes grew thickly in the flood; they waded out until at their farthest some of the leaves were opening under water; and these bushes leaned over.

The echo of Liku's voice in his head sent him trembling at this perilous way of bushes towards the island. He dashed at them where normally they would have been rooted on dry land and his feet splashed. He threw himself forward and grabbed at the branches with hands and feet. He shouted:

"I am coming!"

B. (pp. 215-17.)
(i) Lok staggered to his feet, picked up Tanakil and ran after Fa along the terrace. There came a screaming from the figures by the hollow log and a loud bang from the jam. The tree began to move forward and the logs were lumbering about like the legs of a giant. The crumplefaced woman was struggling with Tuami on the rock by the hollow log; she burst free and came running towards Lok. There was movement everywhere, screaming, demoniac activity; the old man was coming across the tumbling logs. He threw something at Fa. Hunters were holding the hollow log against the terrace and the head of the tree with all its weight of branches and wet leaves was drawing along them. The fat woman was lying in the log, the crumpled woman was in it with Tanakil, the old man was tumbling into the back. The boughs crashed and drew along the rock with an agonized squealing. Fa was sitting by the water holding her head. The branches took her. She was moving with them out into the water and the hollow log was free of the rock and drawing away. The tree swung into the current with Fa sitting limply among the branches. Lok began to gibber again. He ran up and down on the terrace. The tree would not be cajoled or persuaded. It moved to the edge of the fall, it swung until it was lying along the lip. The water reared up over the trunk, pushing, the roots were over. The tree hung for a while with the head facing upstream. Slowly the root end sank and the head rose. Then it slid forward soundlessly and dropped over the fall.
(ii) The red creature stood on the edge of the terrace and did nothing. The hollow log was a dark spot on the water towards the place where the sun had gone down. The air in the gap was clear and blue and calm. There was no noise at all now except for the fall, for there was no wind and the green sky was clear. The red creature turned to the right and trotted slowly towards the far end of the terrace. Water was cascading down the rocks beyond the terrace from the melting ice in the mountains. The river was high and flat and drowned the edge of the terrace. There were long scars in the earth and rock where the branches of a tree had been dragged past by the water. The red creature came trotting back to a dark hollow in the side of the cliff where there was evidence of occupation. It looked at the other figure, dark now, that grinned down at it from the back of the hollow. Then it turned away and ran through the little passage that joined the terrace to the slope. It halted, peering down at the scars, the abandoned rollers and broken ropes. It turned again, sidled round a shoulder of rock and stood on an almost imperceptible path that ran along the sheer rocks. It began to sidle along the path, crouch, its long arms swinging, touching, almost

as firm a support as the legs. It was peering down into the thunderous waters but there was nothing to be seen but the columns of glimmering haze where the water had scooped a bowl out of the rock. It moved faster, broke into a queer loping run that made the head bob up and down and the forearms alternate like the legs of a horse. It stopped at the end of the path and looked down at the long streamers of weed that were moving backwards and forwards under the water. It put up a hand and scratched under its chinless mouth.

C. (pp. 228-29.)

The sail glowed red-brown. Tuami glanced back at the gap through the mountain and saw that it was full of golden light and the sun was sitting in it. As if they were obeying some signal the people began to stir, to sit up and look across the water at the green hills. Twal bent over Tanakil and kissed her and murmured to her. Tanakil's lips parted. Her voice was harsh and came from far away in the night.

"Liku!"

Tuami heard Marlan whisper to him from by the mast.

"That is the devil's name. Only she may speak it."

Now Vivani was really waking. They heard her huge, luxurious yawn and the bear skin was thrown off. She sat up, shook back her loose hair and looked first at Marlan then at Tuami. At once he was filled again with lust and hate. If she had been what she was, if Marlan, if her man, if she had saved her baby in the storm on the salt water—

"My breasts are paining me."

If she had not wanted the child as a plaything, if I had not saved the other as a joke—

He began to talk high and fast.

"There are plains beyond those hills, Marlan, for they grow less; and there will be herds for hunting. Let us steer in towards the shore. Have we water—but of course we have water! Did the women bring the food? Did you bring the food, Twal?"

Twal lifted her face towards him and it was twisted with grief and hate.

"What have I to do with food, master? You and he gave my child to the devils and they have given me back a changeling who does not see or speak."

The sand was swirling in Tuami's brain. He thought in panic: they have given me back a changed Tuami; what shall I do? Only Marlan is the same—smaller, weaker but the same. He peered forward to find the changeless one as something he could hold on to. The sun was blazing on the red sail and Marlan was red. His arms and legs were contracted, his hair stood out and his beard, his teeth were wolf's teeth and his eyes like blind stones. The mouth was opening and shutting.

"They cannot follow us, I tell you. They cannot pass over water."


## NOTES

1. J. McH. Sinclair, "Linguistic Meaning in a Literary Text." Paper read to the Philological Society, Cambridge, March 1965.

2. The results were presented in a paper read to the Conference of University Teachers of English, London (Bedford College), April 1965.

3. Karl Bühler, *Sprachtheorie* (Jena, 1934). See also Chapter 2 of Josef Vachek, *The Linguistic School of Prague* (Bloomington, Ind., and London: Indiana University Press, 1966).

4. See Bronislaw Malinowski, *Coral Gardens and their Magic*, Volume II (London: Allen & Unwin, 1935).

5. Paul Zumthor suggests (private communication) that a particular literary tradition may be characterized by the emphasis and value placed on one particular function, a shift in emphasis being associated with a major break in the tradition. Cf. Paul Zumthor's paper in the present volume (showing the orientation of medieval lyric poetry towards a particular aspect of the interpersonal function of language).

6. Nor the other way round, at least in the typical instances. There are certain linguistic activities in which one or other function is prescribed and the speaker required to supply the remainder: "language exercises" such as "Now ask your neighbour a question" (in foreign language classes) and "Write a sonnet" (in school).

7. Cf. the discussion by Tzvetan Todorov in his paper in the present volume.

8. Including those which specify types of communication role, or illocutionary force, which Richard Ohmann proposes to use in a definition of literature. See Ohmann's paper in this volume.

9. Geoffrey N. Leech, "This Bread I Break—Language and Interpretation," *A Review of English Literature*, VI (April 1965), 70.

10. René Wellek, "Closing Statement (Retrospects and Prospects from the Viewpoint of Literary Criticism)," in *Style in Language*, ed. by T. A. Sebeok (New York, 1960), pp. 417-18.

11. As n. 9 (p. 69).

12. Dell H. Hymes, "Phonological Aspects of Style: Some English Sonnets," in *Style in Language*, 109-31. Reprinted in *Essays on the Language of Literature*, ed. by Seymour Chatman and Samuel Levin (Boston, Mass., 1967), 33-53 (pp. 33-4).

13. On diatypic variation see Michael Gregory, "Aspects of Varieties Differentiation," *Journal of Linguistics*, III (1967), 177-98.

14. Charles E. Osgood, "Some Effects of Motivation on Style of Encoding," in *Style in Language*, p. 293.

15. As n. 12.

16. Angus McIntosh, "Saying," *A Review of English Literature*, VI (April 1965), 19. It is worth quoting further from the same paragraph: "It is at least clear that any approach to this kind of problem which looks at anything less than the whole text as the ultimate unit has very little to contribute. Whatever it may be in linguistic analysis, the sentence is not the proper unit here. If there are any possibilities of progress, they must, I think, be on the lines of the old recognition, e.g. by the rhetoricians, of elements or strands of something or other which permeate long stretches of text and produce a gradual build-up of effect."

17. Bernard Bloch, "Linguistic Structure and Linguistic Analysis" in A. A. Hill (ed.), *Report of the Fourth Annual Round Table Meeting on Linguistics and Language Study* (Monograph Series on Languages & Linguistics IV, Washington, D.C., 1953), pp. 40-44.

18. As n. 9 (p. 70).

19. Josephine Miles, "Eras in English Poetry" in *Essays on the Language of Literature*, pp. 175-76.

20. Cf. George A. Miller, "Closing Statement (Retrospects and Prospects from the Viewpoint of Psychology)" in *Style in Language*, p. 394.

21. See the paper by Louis Milic in the present volume, in which he suggests that the diagnostic features of an author's style are generally to be found among the "unconscious" elements.

22. See Stephen Ullmann, "Style and Personality," A *Review of English Literature*, VI (April 1965), p. 22.

23. Cf. Samuel Levin's paper in the present volume.

24. As n. 22 (p. 27).

25. As n. 22 (p. 29). See also Stephen Ullmann, *Language and Style* (Language and Style Series, Oxford, 1964), pp. 186-88.

26. Richard Ohmann, "Literature as Sentences" in *Essays on the Language of Literature*, p. 237. Originally published in *College English* (January 1966).

27. Ruqaiya Hasan, "Linguistics and the Study of Literary Texts," *Études de Linguistique Appliquée*, V (1967), pp. 109-10. See also Ruqaiya Hasan's paper in the present volume.

28. See Seymour Chatman, "Milton's Participial Style," *Publications of the Modern Language Association of America* (October 1968), 1386-99.

29. "Metamorphosis" has, I believe, only two occurrences of an insect name, although "crawl" is frequent.

30. William Golding, *The Inheritors* (London, 1955; paperback edition, 1961). The pagination is the same in both editions.

31. Mark Kinkead-Weekes and Ian Gregor, *William Golding: A Critical Study* (London, 1967).

32. Figures in square brackets show numbers of occurrences. The most important of these are summarized in Table 2.

33. For a discussion of clause types see M. A. K. Halliday, "Language Structure and Language Function," in John Lyons (ed.), *New Horizons in Linguistics* (Harmondsworth: Penguin Books, 1970), pp. 140-65.

34. Cf. M. A. K. Halliday, "Descriptive Linguistics in Literary Studies," in A. Duthie (ed.), *English Studies Today, Third Series* (Edinburgh, 1964), p. 29.

35. The other extracts examined for comparison were three passages of similar length: p. 61 from *He remembered the old woman*; pp. 102-3 from *Then there was nothing more*; p. 166 from *At that the old man rushed forward*.

36. By "complement" is understood all nominal elements other than the subject: direct object, indirect object, cognate object, and adjectival and nominal complement. "Adjuncts" are non-nominal elements (adverbs and prepositional phrases).

37. Cf. James Peter Thorne, "Stylistics and Generative Grammars," *Journal of Linguistics*, I (1965), 49-59.

38. For discussions of transitivity see Charles J. Fillmore, "The Case for Case," in Emmon Bach & Robert T. Harms (eds.), *Universals in Linguistic Theory* (New York, 1968), 1-88; M. A. K. Halliday, *Grammar, Society and the Noun* (London, 1967); M. A. K. Halliday, "Notes on Transitivity and Theme in English" (Parts I and II), *Journal of Linguistics*, III (1967), 37-81, and IV (1968), 179-215.

39. As n. 31 (p. 81).

40. See J. R. Firth, "Modes of Meaning," *Essays and Studies* (*The English Association*, 1951). Reprinted in J. R. Firth, *Papers in Linguistics 1934-1951* (London, 1957), pp. 190-215.

41. Cf. Roger Fowler, "Linguistic Theory and the Study of Literature," in *Essays on Style and Language: Linguistic and Critical Approaches to Literary Style*, ed. by Roger Fowler (London, 1966), pp. 1-28.

42. As n. 12 (p. 53).

## DISCUSSION OF HALLIDAY'S PAPER

In response to questions concerning the array in Table 1, Halliday regretted that the terms were not all self-explanatory—the table was taken from another paper containing a rather fuller discussion—and explained certain parts that were questioned. "Attitudinal modifiers" (the intersection of the rank of nominal group and the interpersonal function) are those elements in the nominal group, or noun phrase, in which the expressive force is predominant, e.g. *wonderful, horrible;* closely related to these are the "intensifiers" such as *very, absolutely,* and a host of slang or semi-slang terms. These represent the interpersonal options in the noun phrase—though the actual words do not necessarily correspond one-to-one with the underlying options. By "comment adjunct" Halliday is referring to a dozen or so sub-classes expressing such things as the speaker's sense of probability or scope, e.g. *by and large,* or degree of relevance like *by the way,* and so on, whereby the speaker intrudes his comment on the thesis of the sentence. The term "sub-modification" refers to the addition to modifiers of further elements like *so* and *too;* "deixis" is the relation to the "here and now," expressed in the noun phrase by determiners such as *this* and *that.*

In response to criticism that the terminology was opaque and difficult to remember, Halliday said that he had consulted other people, and that he never introduced or advocated new terms if others were available; at the same time if a new category is being proposed there is often no existing term to fall back on. Very little of the terminology used here was in fact new or unusual. The further criticism was made that the array did not seem logical or consistent; for example, "Textual" was not on the same footing as "Ideational" and "Interpersonal"; "Catenation" was echoed in the last column in "organization of vocabulary"; and the "Logical" sub-

division appeared without any reference to "Theme." Halliday said that
the table was an accurate though schematic representation of the underlying grammatical theory; there was certainly indeterminacy in the system—
in language itself—and this was built into the picture, but no inconsistency
in the use of terms. "Organization" was being used in a particular way
which makes it possible for it to appear in more than one column; "catenation" was being used in its normal technical sense and has no place outside
the column in which it occurs; and so on.

Most of the discussion, however, concerned Halliday's analysis of *The
Inheritors*. In reply to a question about the difference among the three passages cited, and particularly between B(i) and B(ii), Halliday pointed out
that Passage B does not represent a distinct "language"; B(i) is still in
Language A, though with a strong admixture of Language C, while B(ii)
is Language C with a strong admixture of Language A. Thus Passage B as
a whole is transitional in its syntactic properties (there are further figures
which bear this out).

It was pointed out that certain categories which Halliday did not mention seem to occur in all three passages, and perhaps generally in the novel;
for example, co-ordination on the clause and sentence level, and particularly co-ordinate verbal groups, which seem to be present in equal proportions in the three extracts. Might this not signify Golding's unconscious intention of delineating the world-view of the two tribes? Another participant
pointed out that in *Free Fall* Golding also favors co-ordinate structures, and
that in both novels these appear irrespective of changes in the situation
and of the components of the work as such; therefore one could be reasonably sure that this was a habitual trait. Halliday said that he had gone into
the question of coordination (he had compared these passages with four
other passages in the first part of the book), and his impression was that it
was not a very significant feature in the present context—it did not reveal
any systematic differences between the two parts.

Halliday was questioned about his use of the notions of "foregrounding"
and "internal motivation." At first (it was said) he seemed to be suggesting that the relevance of certain linguistic features, and the irrelevance of
others, could be seen in terms of their internal motivation: that is, of the
justification of these choices in relation to others which appear in the nearer
or further environment. For example, his reference to the fact that nine-
tenths of the book is written from the point of view of "the people" and
one-tenth from that of "the tribe" amounts to a kind of internal motivation, since an element is then considered foregrounded by virtue of the relation between it and other textual elements. But he had also said that the
foregrounding was a matter of frequency: a foregrounded element was
more frequent than one would normally expect. Are these two criteria the

same or different? Halliday answered that they were on different levels. First one observed some kind of prominence—perhaps a vague sense of more than usual frequency, a feeling of "That's rather odd—there are a lot of these things around; perhaps they form a pattern," and then one was prompted to examine and count them. Any unexpected distribution of this kind is a form of prominence. Secondly, if we have reason to think that this prominence is motivated, we recognize it as "foregrounding." We may find the motivation by reference to other linguistic factors, or to something that we may want to call the underlying theme or wider context, or indeed to any relevant aspect of the text.

Halliday was asked whether he felt part of the effect that he had described to be due to the fact that the reader seemed always to know a lot that the narrator didn't know; for example, in Passage A that the stick that grew shorter at both ends was in reality a bow. Halliday said that he had not thought of the question from this point of view and would like to consider its relation to his own analysis.

Halliday (it was noted) had raised the question of how certain forms seem to be forms of value. Was there in the stylistic selection of linguistic traits an intersection or a subordination of systems? But in such discussions it is easy to forget the presence of a third system, that of art. A literary text asks us to read with some of the interests we would have in painting or music—interests in composition, in focus and fringe, contrast and comparison, theme and variation, and so on. It is not just a matter of *res et verba* or *langue et parole* as system and individual, but it is also a matter of imitation, embodiment, artistic expression, whatever the term may be, wherein the medium (language) is used selectively (style) on certain principles relevant to expectancies in pattern and design (art).

Another participant commented that Passage A made him think of what Sartre had said about the philosophical tale. Speaking particularly of Voltaire, Sartre noted that these proceed by a decomposition of finalized acts in a time-span without finality, such that there appears a procession of external and partial aspects which become absurd precisely because finality is lacking. In this respect *The Inheritors* seems to have some link with *le conte philosophique*, and with literature like *L'Étranger* whose vision is innocent.

Finally, Halliday was applauded for considering the stylistic properties of relatively simple grammatical features. It was pointed out that we inherit from traditional rhetoric the notion that style rests on figures, specially marked forms, so we fail to study simpler features like definite vs. indefinite article, plural vs. singular noun, transitive vs. intransitive verb, etc. We need a new rhetoric which will allow us to examine these simplest, most normal features, because far from being without stylistic relevance, they contain hidden powers of style which deserve to be considered. Halliday agreed with this point and noted a remark by Angus McIntosh that some of the most striking effects are gained by language which is totally normal and undeviant. We should be alive to the stylistic potentialities of the simplest linguistic patterns. It was worth stressing here again that a feature might be significant, or stylistically "marked," not because it was deviant or unusual but merely because it occurred with unexpected frequency or regularity. This was related to the fact that, in Halliday's view, there was no essential difference between the deviation from one norm and the creation of another.

# LYRIC ATTITUDE AND PRONOMINAL STRUCTURE IN THE POETRY OF EMINESCU

ALEXANDRU NICULESCU

(*Tudor Vianu in memoriam*)

ONE CANNOT HELP being impressed when one reads, today, Shklovskij's assertion of fifty years ago that "poetic language differs from prosaic by the perceptible character of its construction."[1] For a long time it had been assumed that the poetic message was ineffable and infinite. Even a classical aesthetician like Tudor Vianu[2] interpreted the "poetic state" as an inexhaustible and unlimited metaphoric process which resists our explicative assaults and interpretations by the infinity of a symbol which remains forever open and only incompletely decodable.

To discover in a poem the precise elements which perform poetic functions is a complex and difficult operation. N. Ruwet[3] is right in assuming that one of the powers of poetic language resides in the fact that primary equivalences set up more subtle secondary ones, which in turn set up still more tenuous ones, and so on, without end. One cannot but agree with Pierre Guiraud's warning[4] that the values of style must be sought where they are hidden behind the least-analyzed forms. The fine evidence of rhetoric is outmoded: what is pertinent in poetry must be discovered in the deep structure of the expression.

In what follows, I propose to examine the poetic consequences of a distributional feature, the personal pronoun, as it participates in the equivalences and parallelisms of poetry. This pronoun is, according to Roman Jakobson,[5] a "shifter"; it belongs to the message and necessarily refers back to it. Some pronouns are "index symbols," possessing a referential function: the first- and second-person pronouns are in an existential relation

with their object. On the other hand, third-person pronouns are limited to
the linguistic context by conventional rules.

These functions confer on pronouns a significant role in poetic expression: they render explicit the aesthetic value of a poem, entering into the
fine, complex play of its structure.

The analysis of some poems by Mihail Eminescu (1859-1889), the greatest of Rumanian poets, will permit us to observe these phenomena in detail. These poems belong to his mature period (1875-1884), when the poet,
having acquired complete mastery over his tools, was filled with creative
energy. The poems are complex structures which comprehend a perfection
not only of tools but also of processes. They show a certain orientation toward German and French poetry (Heine, the Symbolists), the creators *par
excellence* of formal harmonies.

We shall consider three poems, "Peste vîrfuri," "Si dacă . . . ," and"La
steaua":

*Peste vîrfuri*
Peste vîrfuri trece lună,
Codru-şi bate frunza lin,
Dintre ramuri de arin
Melancolic cornul sună.

5    Mai departe, mai departe,
Mai încet, tot mai încet
Sufletu-mi nemîngîiet
Îndulcind cu dor de moarte.

De ce taci, cînd fermecată,
10    Inima-mi spre tine-ntorn?
Mai suna-vei, dulce corn,
Pentru mine vreodată?

*Şi dacă . . .*

Şi dacă ramuri bat în geam
    Şi se cutremur plopii,
E ca în minte să te am
    Şi încet să te apropii.

5    Şi dacă stele bat în lac
    Adîncu-i luminîndu-l
E ca durerea mea să-mpac
    Inseninîndu-mi gîndul.

Şi dacă norii deşi se duc
10 De iese-n luciu luna
E ca aminte să-mi aduc
De tine—întotdeauna.

### La steaua

La steaua care-a răsărit
E-o cale atît de lungă,
Că mii de ani i-au trebuit
Luminii să ne-ajungă.

5 Poate demult s-a stins în drum
In depărtări albastre
Dar raza ei abia acum
Luci vederii noastre

Icoana stelei ce-a murit
10 Incet pe cer se suie :
Era pe cînd nu s-a zărit,
Azi o vedem şi nu e.

Tot astfel cînd al nostru dor
Pieri în noapte-adîncă,
15 Lumina stinsului amor
Ne urmăreşte încă.[6]

Although they convey very different lyrical themes and ideas, these three poems are similar in poetic and linguistic composition. They are, essentially, metaphors or comparisons developed in homologous linguistic structures.

The first two poems are nothing but extended metaphors: nature, as it is described, represents the state of the poet's soul, and to grasp one is to find the key to the other. Nature and poet join and even blur together.

Consider the first, "Peste vîrfuri." In addition to the poet and the landscape, a third element appears, represented by a succession of verbal and pronominal forms with precise reference:

9 De ce taci, cînd fermecată,
10 Inima-mi spre tine-ntorn?
["Why art thou silent, when, enchanted, my heart turns toward thee?"]

The reference must be to the sweet horn (*dulce corn*) which appears explicitly in an apostrophe two lines later:

11      Mai suna-vei dulce corn
12      Pentru mine vreodată?
["Wilt thou again, O sweet horn, sound for me?"]

But is it only a hunting-horn that the poet addresses? Wouldn't it be more correct to suppose that in verses nine and ten the reference is also to a loved woman, though shaded down into the image of the horn? The ambiguity cannot be resolved. The syntactic structure of the poem consists of a sequence of juxtaposed clauses—the first clause stretches through verses one and two, the second through three and four, the third through nine and ten and the fourth through eleven and twelve—interrupted by the second stanza which is a modal expansion of the second clause. There are no clauses joined by conjunctions.

The same dialogue structure is used in the poem "Şi dacă . . ." the poet's description of the landscape has its *raison d'être* solely in the perspective of love and memory: if the branches knock against the window and the poplars tremble, if the stars are reflected in the lake and the moon emerges in all its splendor, it is only so that the memory of love shall never die:

11      E ca aminte să-mi aduc
12      De tine—întotdeauna.
[" . . . it is because I ever remember thee"].

Then, an unnamed element intervenes, with which the poet begins a dialogue:

3       E ca în minte să te am
4       Şi încet să te apropii
[" . . . it is that I may bear thee in mind and thou mayst come gently closer"; see also verses 11 and 12 already cited].

Unlike the first poem, the main syntactic structure here is one of subordination: a complex structure of the type *dacă* ("if" introducing a dependent clause) and *e ca* ("then," introducing the main clause) is repeated in the three stanzas of the poem with an expansion of the co-ordination:

*şi dacă*—Clause 1, $\begin{Bmatrix} şi \\ de \end{Bmatrix}$ —Clause 2, *e ca*—Clause 3, (*şi*—Clause 4). The parallelism of structure of the group *şi dacă* . . . is emphasized by the identity of Verb in the context—Noun$_1$ + *în* + Noun$_2$ in verses one (*Şi dacă ramuri bat în geam* "And if the branches knock at my window") and five (*Şi dacă stele bat în lac* "And if the stars are reflected in the lake"), as well as by the position of Noun-Article in the context Verb in verses two (*Şi se cutremur plopii* "And if the poplars tremble") and ten (*De iese-n luciu luna* "letting the moon shine forth in its splendor"). To this can be added the parallelism of Pronoun + Verb$_{sing}$ in the verses beginning with *e ca* in line three (*E ca în minte să te am* "It is that I may bear thee in mind"), seven (*E ca durerea mea să-mpac* "It is because my pain is appeased"), and eleven (*E ca aminte să-mi aduc* "It is because I remember thee"). Finally, in the second stanza, we must note the symmetry of co-ordinating gerundives in lines six (*luminîndu-l* "illuminating") and eight (*inseninîndu-mi* "turning serene").

In the third poem, the dialogue construction is not used: a fourth, generalizing person is substituted for the author and addressee. This fourth person is indeed the only personal element in the poetic statement. "La steaua" is a developed comparison in which one complex term, in all its detail and subordinated implication (*steaua care a răsărit, care s-a stins în drum*), is put in relation with a simple term—*al nostru dor* (13 "our desire"). The comparison between the two terms works by means of the adverb *tot astfel* ("so") whose semantic reference is indirect. The comparison is between *icoana stelei ce-a murit* ("the image of the star which is dead") and *lumina stinsului amor* ("the light of dead love"). Thus one obtains the series *steaua* ("star"), *icoana stelei* ("the image of the star"), *dor* ("desire"), *lumina stinsului amor* ("the light of dead love"), or, by applying the semantic oppositions "present:absent" and "visible:invisible," one ends up with the connotative equivalences *steaua* ≡ *dor* ≡ *amor* ("star ≡ desire ≡ love").

The syntactic structure of this poem is subordinative. Unlike "Peste vîrfuri," whose verses are simply juxtaposed in a loose manner, the interclausal connection if effected here by conjunctions which express logical relations of co-ordination and subordination: *E-o cale atît de lungă / Că mii de ani i-au trebuit* ("The road is very long; how many thousands of years has it taken"); *Poate demult s-a stins în drum . . . / Dar raza ei abia acum . . .* ("Perhaps it has been long since dead . . . But only now its rays . . ."); *Era pe cînd nu s-a zărit / Azi o vedem şi nu e* ("It existed when no one saw it; today we see it but it exists no longer"). "La steaua" presents a complex comparative system.

To these parallelisms, let us add another series of equivalences in the verbal construction. The structure of the three poems is based on oppositions between the verbal categories of Mode and Tense. Thus there is the significant opposition between tense forms ($\pm$ Present) in "Peste vîrfuri"— *trece* (1), *bate* (2), *sună* (3), *taci* (9), *întorn* (10) vs. *suna-vei* (11), second person future indicative; the opposition ($\pm$ Indicative) between indicative and subjunctive forms in *Şi dacă*—*bat* (1), *se cutremur* (2), vs. *să te am* (3), and *să te apropii* (9), *bat* (5) vs. *s-o împac* and *se duc* (9), and *iese* (10) vs. *să-mi aduc* (11); and finally the opposition ($\pm$ Perfect) in perfect and present indicative in "La steaua"—*a răsărit* (1), *i-au trebuit* (3) vs. *să ne ajungă* (4), and *s-a stins* (4), *luci* (8), *a murit* (9) vs. *se suie* (10) and *era* (11), *s-a zărit* (11) vs. *vedem* (11), *nu e* (11), and *pieri* (13) vs. *urmăreşte* (16). Of course, the semantic oppositon "real: not real" also enters into these oppositions.

The most important equivalences and parallelisms result from processes of pronominalization, the phenomenon which Maurice Gross has defined as an "operation which places certain morphemes called basic pronouns in nominal positions."[7] The basic pronouns are the "dialogistic" ones—first- and second-person—and the pronouns of the third person, including third-person reflexive pronouns. Between the "dialogistic" pronouns and those of the third person a whole series of differences have prompted Benveniste[8] to argue that there are two constant oppositions in the verbal expression of person: 1) an opposition between the person (*je*, "I" and *tu*, "you") on the one hand and the "non-person" (*il*, "he, it"), and within the former, 2) an opposition between *je* and *tu*.

It is within this theoretical perspective that I shall examine the distribution of basic pronouns in "Peste vîrfuri." The pronominal morphemes -*și* (2), -*mi* (8), *tine* (10), *mine* (12) are distributed through the stanzas according to the following scheme:

| | |
|---|---|
| Stanza I | Third person |
| Stanza II | First person |
| Stanza III | First and second person |
| | First person |

The personal and non-personal elements are organized into an opposition in which the first stanza is characterized by the semantic feature (— Personal) distinguishing it from the second which is characterized by the dimension (+ Personal): and both are distinguished from the third in which there occurs the interpersonal opposition (+ Subjective): (— Subjective) (first person vs. second person).

"Și dacă . . ." presents another distribution of the feature (± Personal): the pronominal occurrences are more frequent and the opposition is realized within each stanza. The pronominal forms *se* (2), *te* (3), *te* (4), -*i* (6), -*l* (6), -*o* (7), -*mi* (8), *se* (9), -*mi* (11), *tine* (12) are distributed within the stanzas in the following manner:

| | |
|---|---|
| Stanza I | Third Person |
| | Second person, second person |
| Stanza II | Third person, third person |
| | First person, third person |
| | First person |
| Stanza III | Third person |
| | First person |
| | Second person |

The opposition (+Personal) : (—Personal), repeated in each stanza, creates distributional symmetries: the first two verses of the stanza are distinguished from the others by the absence of personal forms. Verses one and two, five and six, and nine and ten contain non-personal pronouns, while three and four, seven and eight, and eleven and twelve contain personal pronouns. Just as in "Peste vîrfuri," the "dialogistic" opposition (+ Subjective) : (—Subjective) appears in the first stanza as a keystone of the poem's structure. Both are love poems in which the poet addresses his mistress.

On the other hand "La steaua" has a binary structure based exclusively on the feature (± Personal). In the first three stanzas, the first three verses of each stanza, in contrast with the fourth, contains only (—Personal) pronouns: *i-* (3), *s-* (5), *ei* (7), *se* (10), *s-* (11) vs. *ne* (4) and *noastre* (8). In symmetrical fashion, the fourth stanza includes no non-personal pronominal form, being opposed to the three preceding by the feature (+Personal) : *nostru* (11), *ne* (11), *ne* (15). (We shall assume, with Benveniste,[9] that the fourth is an "amplified person," as opposed to the "strict person" by the opposition *plural : singular*.) The distribution of the basic personal and non-personal pronouns are:

| Stanza I | Third person |
| | Amplified first person |
| Stanza II | Third person |
| | Third person |
| | Amplified first person |
| Stanza III | Third person |
| | Third person |
| Stanza IV | Amplified first person |
| | Amplified first person |

The opposition (—Personal) : (+Personal) is indicated categorically at the end of the poem: the third stanza includes no personal form, while the fourth includes no non-personal form. Eminescu's poem augments the contrastive tension at the end.

The distributional schemas presented above may raise a legitimate question: to what extent is the distribution of basic pronouns in the analyzed verses due to *constraint* and to what extent does it result from *choice?*

It is interesting to observe that the majority of these pronominal usages are obligatory. There are a few non-obligatory ones in "Peste vîrfuri": in verse eight *sufletu-mi nemîngîiet*, in verse ten *Inima-mi spre tine-ntorn*, both of which could have occurred without pronouns. In "Şi dacă" the following are non-obligatory: in verse four *Şi încet să te apropii*, in verse six *Adîncu-i luminîndu-l*, and in verse seven *E ca durerea mea să-mpac*. Finally, in "La steaua," verse seven, *Dar raza ei abia acum*, the pronoun could also have been replaced. Outside these cases, the distribution of pronouns does not undergo relevant modification. The poet has been able to assign expressive values even to the syntactic constraints of the poetic statement, proving himself master of a highly organized poetic form.

Taking into consideration verbal persons which are not expressed pronominally does not modify the personal structure of two of the analyzed poems. Here is a display of verbal as against pronominal forms in "Peste vîrfuri":

| Basic Pronominal Forms | | Verbal Persons | |
|---|---|---|---|
| Stanza I | Third person | Stanza I | Third person |
| Stanza II | First person | | Third person |
| Stanza III | First person, second person | | Third person |
| | First person | Stanza III | Second person |
| | | | First person |
| | | | Second person |

In "Şi dacă . . .":

| Basic Pronominal Forms | | Verbal Persons | |
|---|---|---|---|
| Stanza I | Third person | Stanza I | Third person |
| | Second person, second person | | Third person |
| Stanza II | Third person, third person | | First person |
| | First person, third person | | First person |
| | First person | Stanza II | Third person |
| Stanza III | Third person | | First person |
| | First person | Stanza III | Third person |
| | Second person | | Third person |
| | | | First person |

"La steaua" is the only poem in which verbal persons and pronominal forms show the normal structural relations. Thus:

| Basic Pronominal Forms | | Verbal Persons | |
|---|---|---|---|
| Stanza I | Third person | Stanza I | Third person |
| | Amplified first person | | Third person |
| Stanza II | Third person | | Third person |
| | Third person | | Third person |
| | Amplified third person | Stanza II | Third person |
| Stanza III | Third person | | Third person |
| | Third person | Stanza III | Third person |
| Stanza IV | Amplified third person | | Third person |
| | Amplified third person | | Third person |
| | | | First person |
| | | | Third person |
| | | Stanza IV | Third person |
| | | | Third person |

This shows two different structures. From the point of view of the grammatical persons selected by the verb, the opposition (—Personal) : (+Personal) which appears in the distribution of the basic pronominal forms disappears. The results of the two analyses cannot be superimposed.

This observation forces us to recognize the importance of pronominal context as an important criterion in the analysis of poetic statements. The distribution of basic pronominal forms is a means of indicating a series of concepts relevant to poetry.

Here is a list of the pronominal contexts of the three poems:

"Peste vîrfuri":
*codru-și bate frunza* (2), *sufletu-mi nemîngîiet* (7), *inima-mi spre tine-n-torn* (10), *mai suna-vei, dulce corn, pentru mine, vreodată* (11-12).

"Și dacă . . .":
*se cutremur plopii* (2), *în minte să te am* (3), *încet să te apropii* (4), *adîncu-i luminîndu-l* (6), *durerea mea să-mpac* (7), *inseninîndu-mi gîndul* (8), *norii deși se duc* (9), *aminte să-mi aduc de tine-întotdeauna* (11-12).

"La steaua":
*mii de ani i-au trebuit* (3), *luminii să ne-ajungă* (4), *demult s-a stins* (5), *raza ei* (7), *vederii noastre* (8), *pe cer se suie* (10), *nu s-a zărit* (11), *al nostru dor* (13), *lumina stinsului amor ne urmărește încă* (15-16).

Examining the pronominal contexts of the first and second persons, one observes that the nominal and verbal segments accompanied by such pronouns represent the *central lyrical concepts* of the analyzed poems. In "Peste vîrfuri," the construction is based on the elements *suflet* ("soul," 1. 7), *inimă* ("heart," 1. 10), *corn* ("horn," 1. 11), *a se înturna* ("return," 1. 10), *a suna* ("sound," 1.11). Similarly in "Și dacă . . ." the line of lyrical intensity passes through *a avea în minte* ("remember," 1. 3), *a se apropia* ("approach," 1. 4), *durerea* ("pain," 1. 7), *a însenina* ("turn serene again," 1. 8), *a-și aduce* ("remember," 1. 11). And in *La steaua*, the "arrival" of the light, *vederea noastră* ("our sight," 1. 8), *al nostru dor* ("our desire," 1. 13), the "pursuit" of dead love constitute, generally, the skeleton of the poem. All these syntagmas of $\begin{Bmatrix} \text{Noun} \\ \text{Verb} \end{Bmatrix}$ + Pronoun$_{1,2\text{Pers}}$ are combinatory processes to which is attributed the semantic feature (+Personal). They are in effect the bearers of the marks of lyrical subjectivity.

A similar lyrical structure appears in some poems of Heinrich Heine which Eminescu knew and appreciated. Literary historians and critics often point out similarities of theme and expression in the two poets. An examination of some poems by Heine, as H. Weinrich has suggested, shows the frequent use of the"dialogistic" pronouns. Here are three examples:

| | |
|---|---|
| Wenn ich an deinem Hause | 1 pers. |
| Des Morgens vorübergeh', | 1 pers., 2 pers. |
| So freut's mich, du liebe Kleine | 3 pers., 1 pers., 2 pers. |
| Wenn ich dich am Fenster seh'. | 1 pers., 2 pers. |
| | |
| Mit deinen schwarzbraunen Augen | 2 pers. |
| Siehst du mich forschend an: | 2 pers., 1 pers. |
| "Wer bist du und was fehlt dir, | 2 pers., 2 pers. |
| Du fremder, kranker Mann?" | 2 pers. |

| | |
|---|---|
| Du bist wie eine Blume | 2 pers. |
| So hold und schön und rein; | 1 pers., 2 pers. |
| Ich schau' dich an, und Wehmut | 1 pers. |
| Schleicht mir ins Herz hinein. | 1 pers. |
| | |
| Mir ist, als ob ich die Hände | 1 pers., 1 pers. |
| Aufs Haupt dir legen sollt', | 2 pers. |
| Betend, dass Gott dich erhalte | 2 pers. |
| So rein und schön und hold. | |

| | |
|---|---|
| Entflieh mit mir und sei mein Weib | 1 pers., 1 pers. |
| Und ruh an meinem Herzen aus; | 1 pers. |
| Fern in der Fremde sei mein Herz | 1 pers. |
| Dein Vaterland und Vaterhaus. | 2 pers. |
| | |
| Gehst du nicht mit, so sterb' ich hier | 2 pers., 1 pers. |
| Und du bist einsam und allein; | 2 pers. |
| Und bleibst du auch im Vaterhaus, | 2 pers. |
| Wirst doch wie in der Fremde sein.[10] | |

One notes the infrequency of non-personal pronouns and, implicitly, the absence of the opposition (+Personal) : (−Personal). Even when the third person forms *er, es* are used, as in the stanza

Braver Mann! er schafft mir zu lesen!
Will es ihm nie und nimmer vergessen!
Schade, dass ich ihn nicht küssen kann!
Denn ich bin selbst dieser brave Mann. . . .[11]

the pronominal expansion is made rather in the direction of (+Animate) (+Human). The lyrics of Heine seem to be more personal, more subjective than those of Eminescu.

Consequently the correlation between *ich* and *du* seems in Heine to be characterized by a high functional output. This phenomenon can be explained by the syntactic structure of German, which imposes a whole series of constraints on the occurrence of personal pronouns (for example, on the pronoun as subject in subordinate clauses), but also by the expansion of Romantic poetic processes (for example, the antithesis *Gehst du nicht mit, so sterb' ich hier* "If thou goest not with me, I shall die here," 1. 21). Heine's lyric is explicitly addressed to a mistress: *du liebe Kleine* ("thou beloved small one," 1. 3), *du bist wie eine Blume* ("thou art like a flower," 1. 11), *entflieh mit mir und sei mein Weib* ("flee with me and be my wife," 1. 1), an *envoi*, like the poems of the troubadours.

In this analysis, we have traced the use of pronominal forms of the first and second person as indicators of lyrical intensity in poetic statements. The contexts in which these dialogistic forms appear can be considered to represent the maximal points of lyrical relevance in poetic expression.

The first and second personal pronouns establish a particular relation between poetic expression and its content by personalizing the discourse and adding to it the feature (+Subjective). Tzvetan Todorov has pointed out the existence in the narrative of adverbial first-person and pronominal "shifters" which signal that the discourse is "personal" by identifying the narrator as a character.[12] In the same way, in poetry the contexts containing subjective pronouns allow the poet to establish himself as "subject," to become the *ego* who *says ego*.[13]

The examination of the pronominal structure of a poem can thus uncover the elements of lyrical attitude converted into poetry.

## NOTES

1. V. Shklovskij, *Poetika, sborniki po teori poeticeskogo jazyka* (Petrograd, 1919), p. 19.
2. Tudor Vianu, *Problemele metaforei și alte studii de stilistică* (București, 1957), p. 117.
3. Nicholas Ruwet, "Limites de l'analyse linguistique en poétique," in *Linguistique et littératures, Langages,* XII (1968), 57-70.
4. Pierre Guiraud, in discussion at the present conference.
5. Roman Jakobson, *Essais de linguistique générale* (Paris, 1963), pp. 178-79.
6.
"Over the Peaks"
"Over the peaks passes the moon, the frost trembles in its leafage: among the branches of the alder sounds the melancholy horn. Farther,

farther, fainter, fainter, caressing my soul, sweetening it with a longing for death. Why art thou silent, when, enchanted, my heart turns toward thee? Wilt thou again, O sweet horn, sound for me?"

### "And if . . . "

"And if branches knock against my window, and if the poplars tremble, it is that I may bear thee in mind and thou mayst come gently closer. And if the stars are reflected in the lake, illuminating its depths, it is because my pain is appeased, my thoughts turning serene again. And if the thick clouds depart letting the moon shine forth in its splendor, it is because I ever remember thee."

### "Up to the Star"

"Up to the star which is risen, the road is very long; how many thousands of years has it taken for the light to reach us! Perhaps on the way it went dead long ago in the faraway blue. But only now do its rays shine brightly in our eyes. The image of the star which is dead rises slowly in the sky; it existed when no one saw it; today we see it, but it exists no longer. So, though our desire has disappeared into the dark night, the light of dead love still pursues us."

7. See *Grammaire transformationelle du francais: Syntaxe du verbe* (Paris, 1968), p. 50.

8. Émile Benveniste, "Structure des relations de personne dans le verbe" in *Problèmes de linguistique générale* (Paris, 1966), p. 235.

9. *Ibid.*, pp. 234-35.

10. "When I go by your house in the morning, dear little girl, I am happy if I see you at the window.

With your black-brown eyes you look at me searchingly: 'Who are you and what is wrong with you, you strange, sick man?' "

\*      \*      \*

"You are like a flower, so lovely, beautiful and pure; I look at you and melancholy creeps into my heart.

I feel as though I should lay my hands upon your head, praying that God may preserve you so pure and beautiful and lovely."

\*      \*      \*

"Run away with me and be my wife and rest against my heart; in a far country let my heart be your fatherland and paternal home.

If you will not come with me, I will die here and you will be lonely and alone; and even if you remain in your father's house, you will be as though in a foreign land."

11. "Good man! He gets me things to read! I'll never, never forget the favor! A shame I can't kiss him! For I myself am this good man. . . ."

12. Tzvetan Todorov, *Littérature et signification* (Paris, 1968), pp. 79-85.

13. Émile Benveniste, "La nature des pronoms," in *op. cit.* (1966), pp. 259-60.

## DISCUSSION OF NICULESCU'S PAPER

In connection with Niculescu's observation of French influence on Eminescu, one participant found himself reminded of Verlaine; only he would not call Verlaine a Symbolist, but rather an impressionist. One can identify three styles in the poetry of that period—Symbolism (things are other things), Impressionism (things are exactly what they seem), and Surrealism (things are other than what they seem). One can find exactly the same stylistic processes in Verlaine as in Eminescu: for example, the use of the present in an actual meaning, never in the omnitemporal sense, characteristic of the Symbolists.

Niculescu was asked why he did not include in his formulation first-person verbal forms which occurred *without* the pronoun (a possibility in Rumanian as in Italian). Niculescu answered that he did not want to discuss the expression vs. the non-expression of the pronominal form for reasons of prudence. It would have complicated the distribution scheme of pronouns unduly to treat this matter too. Another participant agreed that it was more interesting to start with the opposition person: non-person, than with that of full pronoun: zero pronoun.

It was suggested that it would be interesting to make a comparable study of an Italian poet like Ungaretti; at first glance, his short poems seem to entail a similar personalization of the utterance. (As an example, someone recalled the verse "M'illumino d'immenso.")

As for the discussion of the role of the pronouns in these poems, a participant was struck by the fact that the third person referred almost uniquely to nature, to inanimate objects. Another observed that since theme is not simply image but relation, the personal pronoun is necessarily the vector of theme. In connection with theme, if one were to give a thematic rather than a stylistic analysis of these three poems, one would certainly observe the typical Romantic opposition between the impassive world and the sensitive and suffering person (as in Vigny). Did Niculescu

conceive of the freedom of position of the pronouns and of the use of "I"
as a sort of diagrammatic design which reproduced the thematic opposition? When Niculescu answered that he did, it was pointed out that that
made his explication theoretically shaky because it left intact a kind of
thematic primacy. Other observations were made about the significance of
pronouns in poetry—that the validity of Jakobson's separation of the first
from the other two is somewhat debatable, and that for some analysts the
third person is not a grammatical- but rather a non-person.

One participant, recalling that Eminescu had been heavily influenced by
Heine, noted that in a famous essay, Lukacs had attempted to explain
Heine's ironic poetry as the legitimization of the dying bourgeoisie with
its subjective idealism in the face of economic and concrete reality. Here
the first and second person would represent middle-class subjectivity, while
the third person would represent the objectivity of society. Thus irony is
achieved, according to Lukacs, by the opposition between the first and second person on the one hand, and the third person on the other. The irony
is in a kind of compensation in the unification of the first and second person against the third person. How could one expect to find this kind of
compensation so well expressed in the nineteenth century after Heine?

It was noted, finally, that though Niculescu said that the application of
linguistics to literary analysis had limits, Todorov had said quite the
contrary.

# THE STYLE OF MONTAIGNE:
## Word-Pairs and Word-Groups

### R. A. SAYCE

THOUGH THIS PAPER will inevitably be concerned with facts of language, I must stress from the outset that the approach to them will be made from the point of view of literature and not from that of a professional linguist. The dividing line between linguistic and literary stylistics is, it is true, very hard to draw, since both are working from the same set of facts. And, of course, the line can be crossed: some students of style possess the fortunate capacity to pass from one to the other, to combine the methods of both. However, the difference remains a formidable one and can be stated roughly in terms of the system to which each belongs. In linguistics the phenomena and effects of style are a necessary part of the study of language, or rather perhaps a parallel system in which the elements of language are examined from the point of view of choice and expressive or emotional values. For literary studies, style is a component of, and must be considered in relation to, a quite different system, which is not strictly linguistic, which indeed transcends language as ordinarily understood: theme, plot, structure (in a wider sense), character, above all aesthetic significance, whatever sense we may attach to that phrase. From this aspect the details of style, of language, are important for the light they throw on these larger matters, the confirmation or contradiction they bring to conclusions which can be derived from a much more generalized apprehension. This summary leaves a good deal out of account, in particular the order of the operations involved (do we start, as we logically should, with the details and go on to the generalities, or the other way round?). As a matter of observable fact, it may be doubted whether anyone embarks on the stylistic study of a work of literature which he has not already grasped in its general sense. It leaves out of account also the inescapable truth that these larger entities themselves are conveyed by means of language, but this difficulty would lead us too far. At any rate these remarks may be illustrated by the survey of a limited but nonetheless central area of Montaigne's style, one in which phonetics, semantics, and syntax are closely associated.

The most immediately obvious feature of Montaigne's style, even to a casual reader, is the doubling of words, usually, though not always, synonyms or near-synonyms, and applied to all the principal parts of speech (nouns, adjectives, verbs, adverbs). The feature appears already in the preface "Au lecteur":

> je ne m'y suis proposé aucune fin, que *domestique et privée*[1] ["I have set myself no goal but a domestic and private one"],

and if it is objected that the preface was written at a fairly late stage we can take the opening sentence of the first essay:

> La plus commune façon d'amollir les cœurs de ceux qu'on a offensez . . . c'est de les esmouvoir par submission *à commiseration et à pitié* (p. 11). ["The commonest way of softening the hearts of those we have offended . . . is by submission to move them to commiseration and pity"].

From this point on such pairs occur so frequently as to verge on the innumerable, and it would be merely tedious to give strings of examples of this simple form.

Needless to say, the usage is not confined to Montaigne. It is characteristic of, and perhaps originated in, the traditional language of law and administration: *à ses risques et périls* ["at his risks and perils"], *last will and testament, grace and favour* (an expression which in its French form appears in Montaigne's translation of Sabunde).[2] Its presence in legal documents may be attributed to the need for precision, even more perhaps, as has been suggested, to the custom of charging according to the number of words written. At any rate it is tempting to conjecture that Montaigne's predilection for it reflects his legal training, which otherwise has left few traces in his style. It is frequent too in sixteenth-century prose-writers generally. To give one or two examples, Calvin uses it, a little stiffly, for emphasis, especially to suggest the infinite qualities of God:

> le Seigneur par sa *douceur & bonté* nous a receus en *grace & amour*[3] ["the Lord by his *kindness and goodness* has received us in *grace and love*"],

> son conseil *éternel et immuable*[4] ["his *eternal* and *immutable* counsel"].

We find nine cases in fifteen lines of Amyot:

*cruds & imparfaicts, bons & francs, l'utilité & le besoing, les loix & la iustice, servir & honorer, fonder & regir, benignité & bonté, la structure & fabrication, de vain ny de friuole*[5] ["crude and imperfect," "good and sound" (fruit), "utility and need," "laws and justice," "serve and honour," "found and rule," "benignity and goodness," "structure and making," "vain nor frivolous"].

But such a heavy concentration seems to be exceptional. Shakespeare's use of the form is too well known to need much illustration: Polonius's

The *origin* and *commencement* of his grief[6]

is a good straightforward example. How it can be made to produce supreme poetic effect appears in Antony's meeting with Cleopatra:

when such a mutual pair
And such a twain. . . .[7]

Meaning and rhetorical form echo and re-echo each other in a way which is both simple and highly complex. It may be doubted whether Montaigne quite reaches these heights. Still, even these few examples (they could be multiplied indefinitely) are enough to show that Montaigne's characteristic procedure is also characteristic of his time. We must now look more closely at what he does with the form, in the hope of defining its particular functions in his style.

The most striking effect of the single pair taken in isolation, and one we have already seen in Calvin, is that of weight and emphasis, the reinforcement of a notion by sheer repetition in a different form:

*d'une vifve et vehemente esperance,*[8] *avec prudence et precaution,*[9] *plus pressant et plus poisant,*[10] *on faict fructifier et foisonner le monde*[11] ["keen and vehement hope," "with prudence and precaution," "tighter and more oppressive," "they make the world fructify and teem [with . . .]"].

It is easy to see that *avec prudence et precaution* conveys the timidity of inferior friendship, *plus pressant et plus poisant* the weight of social obligation, *fructifier et foisonner* the burgeoning of dispute in the world, in each case far more powerfully than the single word could do. All these examples are alliterative and this is true in a high proportion, perhaps even a majority, of cases. We have here the first distinguishing characteristic of Montaigne's use of the word-pair and it may be dealt with briefly, in parentheses, at this point. Clearly alliteration binds the two words of the pair more firmly in a single unit; it also has more extensive rhythmical consequences, to which I shall return. But it is not indispensable that the two parts should present a total unity of impact. Sometimes the effect is of rising force or crescendo, as in the horrifying description of Alexander's treatment of Betis:

> le fit ainsi trainer tout vif, *deschirer et desmembrer* au cul d'une charrete[12] ["had him thus dragged alive, torn, and dismembered behind a cart"].

*Deschirer* is bad enough but the full horror is only revealed with *desmembrer*. In all these cases, however, especially the alliterative, the word-pair forms a unity, sometimes stressed by a singular verb with a noun-pair:

> *La consideration et le respect* . . . reboucha . . . la pointe de sa cholere[13] ["Consideration and respect . . . took the edge off his anger"].

Though this is normal sixteenth-century usage, there can be no doubt that consideration and respect are welded into a single concept by the singular verb.

Nonetheless, the contrary is also true: a single concept is diversified by the doubling of its expression. The frequency of the word-pair in Montaigne, established literary device though it is, is closely associated with the (ostensibly) conversational or colloquial tone of his writing: in conversation it is natural to try out different words for the same thing, to fumble and hesitate; the writer normally excises what is superfluous, to leave only the *mot juste*. But there is more than this. Montaigne's thinking proceeds by a series of the finest distinctions.

> *Distingo* est le plus universel membre de ma logique[14]
> ["*Distinguo* is the most universal member of my logic"],

and the word-pair is one of the instruments by which distinctions are made. For example

> peu de choses me *touchent*, ou, pour mieux dire, me *tiennent*[15]
> ["few things touch me, or, to put it better, hold me"].

The alliteration still binds the two verbs in a pair although the inserted phrase separates them and marks a preference for the second. A similar case, with separation and alliteration, occurs when, speaking of his borrowings, he says:

> Mais je n'entends pas qu'ils me *couvrent* et qu'ils me *cachent*[16]
> ["But I do not intend that they should cover and hide me"],

the second verb introducing both an extension and a distinction of meaning. But of course such distinctions are present even in perfectly straightforward pairs:

> *trèsinepte et trèsinique*[17] ["very inept and very iniquitous"], une beauté *délicate et cachée*[18] ["a delicate and hidden beauty"].

In each case the second term of the pair, while maintaining unity, introduces a fresh and perceptible *nuance*; or in one of the most beautiful of these pairs, describing the effects of poetry on the judgment, *elle le ravit et ravage*,[19] not only "ravishes" or "carries away" but "ravages, profoundly transforms and devastates." In these cases of duplication based on distinction we can see an essential quality of Montaigne's mind which might be called, literally, duplicity, the tendency to polarize, to see everything from two points of view at once (seen on a larger scale, for example, in the double argument for and against suicide of *Coustume de l'isle de Cea*).

When we consider the form of the word-pair we soon see that its complexity goes well beyond the simple alliteration we have already observed. Very common is the use of identical prefixes, *me transpercer et transporter*,[20] *de nous entredeffaire et entretuer*[21] ["to transfix and transport me," "of undoing and killing one another"]; less common is the use of like endings, *abastardisse et estourdisse*,[22] *un peu plus grassement et gracieusement*[23] ["depraves and stupefies," " with more gusto and with better grace"], where both beginning and end are phonetically identical. A further stage is the rhyming pair, rarer but highly characteristic: *de crainte et de contrainte*,[24] *seurs et purs*,[25] *les larmes . . . ou feintes ou peintes*[26] ["of fear and constraint," "sure and pure," "tears . . . feigned or painted"]; these rhymes seem to occur mostly in the final additions of the Bordeaux Copy. The consequences to be drawn from these alliterations, assonances, echoes, are clear enough: once again, they establish the unity of the pair even more securely; and they are, especially rhyme, essentially poetic devices.

They also reveal an interest which we associate with Rabelais or Joyce or Queneau rather than with Montaigne, in playing tricks with language, in mastering the code to the point of making pirouettes round it and even altering it (and of course this conscious and literary treatment of language as something existing in itself is bound to cast doubt on the view of Montaigne's style which he himself propagates, as merely recorded talk, *tel sur le papier qu'à la bouche*). At any rate certain kinds of word-play are so closely associated with the word-pair as to be virtually inseparable from it (and in Montaigne's style as in his work generally different features tend to be linked with each other in an indissoluble chain). The most obviously connected word-play is a type of paronomasia, in which two words have different senses but very similar sounds (subtly but importantly different from the pun, where the sounds are identical). This figure occurs with considerable frequency, though all the examples I have noted come from the later phases of the text (post-1580). A few instances will suffice to show the mechanism, which generally depends on the substitution (addition, subtraction) of one or two phonemes:

> à mascher, comme à marcher,[27] autant songneuse d'en esteindre l'une que d'estendre l'autre,[28] ny les choses qui nous oignent, au pris de celles qui nous poignent,[29] Tout ce qui plaist ne paist pas[30] ["To chew, as well as to walk," "as anxious to extinguish the one as to extend the other," "nor [do we feel] the things that charm us compared with those that harm us," "Not all that entertains us sustains us"],

or best of all perhaps, speaking of Tacitus,

> qu'il nous peinct et qu'il nous pinse[31]
> ["that he is describing and decrying us"],

where he is particulary apt and telling. All this bears a strong resemblance to the tricks of euphuism and may reasonably be accounted a mannerist feature in Montaigne's style. His near-contemporary, the rhetorician Peacham, remarks on the element of affectation in paronomasia:

> This figure ought to be sparingly used, and especially in grave and weightie causes, both in the respect of the light and illuding forme, and also forasmuch as it seemeth not to be found without meditation and affected labor.[32]

The same is true of word-plays which are not quite paronomasia like *Platon en sa plus verte vertu* ["Plato in his most verdant virtue"],[33] or very similar, on the women of Sparta, *assez couvertes de leur vertu sans vertu-gade*[34] ["sufficiently covered by their virtue not to need petticoats"]. Sometimes we find the repetition of a word in a different form, *ce que la divinité nous en a si divinement exprimé* ["What the Divinity has so divinely told us about it"],[35] where, as in Calvin, divinity is magnified by the doubling, while, more subtly, its mode of existence is expressed by the adverb, or (about a piece of string equally strong in its whole length) *il est impossible de toute impossibilité qu'elle rompe . . .* ["it is impossible by all impossibility that it should break"],[36] where the effect is of intensification and dramatization. It is a short step to the extraordinary circular ingenuity (mannerist or baroque?) of *Nous veillons dormans, et veillans dormons* ["Sleeping we are awake, and waking asleep"].[37]

Of other figures in the same spectrum the most important are oxymoron (*si vilement victorieuses*[38] ["so vilely victorious"] said of the Spanish conquests, expressing deep and intense indignation, or *Les Ægyptiens, d'une impudente prudence*[39] ["The Egyptians with impudent prudence"]), and syllepsis (*Ceux qui courent un benefice ou un lievre*[40] ["Those who run after a benefice or a hare"]). In both cases we find the cultivation of deep paradox and the union of contraries: style and thought, as usual, are inseparable.[41]

It will be seen that all these are variations on the basic form of the word-pair, that all, including the alliterative and rhyming pairs, contain a strong element of mannerist artifice and, as we have seen, a professional writer's concern with language and what can be done with it. Yet it is also true to say that in Montaigne—and this is what distinguishes him from most of his euphuistic or mannerist contemporaries—such devices are never merely verbal tricks: always, I think, as in the case of *qu'il nous peinct et qu'il nous pinse*, phonetic variation is a means of sharpening and intensifying a thought drawn from direct experience of reality. It is important in this connection to grasp the difference, already mentioned, between Montaigne's form and the pun, between phonetic variation and phonetic identity. Both are playful, both have something of Peacham's *illuding forme*, and certainly Montaigne plays with ideas and with life as well as with words. Yet this side of him can be, has been, overstressed, and should not be allowed to blind us to the profound seriousness which underlies it. It is in this light that phonetic variation must be regarded. The pun brings about a union of contraries in identity, a sudden surprise, laughter, even sometimes a poetic effect, but usually at a superficial level: the symmetry is too perfect and the purely linguistic aspect too obvious. With paronomasia, when, to give a new example, Montaigne speaks of *subjets graves et qui grevent*[42] (an approximate rendering would be "subjects which are grave and which grieve"), though unity remains, the slight differentiation of sound confirms a significant difference of idea, and above all, the thought progresses instead of turning back on itself: we have here therefore one more factor in the forward movement of Montaigne, the *peinture du passage*, which is absolutely central to an understanding of what he does.

So far the picture has been simplified and to some extent falsified because for the purposes of analysis each pair has been considered in isolation. In fact, however, such pairs are often multiplied within a sentence or passage, and it is impossible to neglect this multiplicity and its consequences. The simplest case is naturally the straightforward accumulation of pairs in close proximity, as in:

> Je ne veux debvoir ma seureté, ny à la *bonté et benignité* des grands,
> qui s'aggréent de ma *legalité et liberté,* ny . . . [43]
> ["I do not want to owe my safety either to the *kindness* and *benignity*
> of the great, who approve of my obedience to the *laws* and my *inde-*
> *pendence,* nor . . . "].

Here, apart from the double alliteration, the omission of article or possessive before the second noun strengthens the unity of the pair. But this,
though it adds weight to both sense and rhythm, is not much more than
automatic amplification, almost a tic. Slightly more intricate effects arise
when one pair derives from another, for example an adjectival pair qualifying the second term of a noun pair in (speaking of animals):

> Ils ne sont pas exempts *de nos jalousies* et *d'envies extremes et ir-*
> *reconciliables*[44]
> ["They are not exempt *from our jealousies,* or *from extreme and ir-*
> *reconcilable* envy"].

Most often, however, we find combinations of pairs, usually based on different parts of speech, which are too complex to be reduced to any set pattern. To illustrate their interaction, longer quotations are necessary, and
therefore a few outstanding examples must suffice. One consequence of
such groups, which does not emerge from the study of single pairs, is the
slowing down of the movement of thought, particularly appropriate when,
as often, hesitation or dubiety forms the essence of what is to be expressed:

> De se tenir *chancelant et mestis,* de tenir son affection *immobile et*
> *sans inclination* aus *troubles de son pays et en une division publique,*
> je ne le trouve *ny beau ny honneste*[45] ["To keep oneself *wavering and*
> *half-and-half,* to keep one's allegiance *motionless and without inclina-*
> *tion* in one's *country's troubles and* in *civil dissensions,* I consider
> *neither handsome nor honorable"*].

Four pairs in a short sentence: neutrality in civil dissension stands con-
demned, of course, but the language conveys this neutrality perfectly. A
much richer example of the delaying mechanism argues the need of damp-
ing down rather than heightening the activity of the intellect, supported
by an elaborate comparison with the martial music of the Spartans, sooth-
ing rather than inflammatory:

> Ainsi, comme la vaillance Lacedemonienne avoit besoing *de modera-*
> *tion et du son doux et gratieux* du jeu des flutes . . . de peur qu'elle
> ne se jettat *à la temerité et à la furie,* là où toutes autres nations . . .
> employent *des sons et des voix aiguës et fortes* qui *esmouvent et qui*

*eschauffent* . . . le courage des soldats, il me semble . . . qu'en l'usage de nostre esprit nous avons . . . plus besoing de plomb que d'ailes, *de froideus et de repos* que *d'ardeur et d'agitation*[46] ["Thus, as the Lacedaemonian valor needed *moderation and the soft and gracious notes* of the flute . . . for fear it should fling itself into *recklessness and fury*, whereas all other nations . . . use shrill and *powerful sounds and voices* that *arouse and inflame* . . . the courage of the soldiers, it seems to me . . . that in using our minds we have . . . more need of lead than of wings, *of coolness and repose* than of *ardor and agitation*"].

Here one sentence contains eight pairs: nouns, verbs, and adjectives. Though it would be an exaggeration to say that they express the theme, they certainly support it (*doux et gratieux* is particularly striking from this point of view). We may also see a connection between this slow unfolding of thought and Montaigne's declared aim of painting the changes of mood and mind not from age to age but from minute to minute.[47]

In general, then, the multiple pair is above all a rhythmical device. However, its effects are subtler and more varied than merely slowing down the tempo: in fact it may do virtually the opposite. If we take another short sentence (on friendly conversation) which is crammed with word-pairs almost to the point of parody:

Pouvons nous pas mesler au tiltre de la *conference et communication* les devis *pointus et coupez* que *l'alegresse et la privauté* introduict entre les amis, *gossans et gaudissans plaisamment et vifvement* les uns les autres?[48] ["May we not include under the title of *discussion and communication* the *sharp, abrupt* repartee which *good spirits and familiarity* introduce among friends, *bantering and joking wittily and keenly* with one another?"]

The five pairs (two strongly alliterative) create a dancing rhythm of cheerfulness, a two-way communication (emphasized by the final reciprocity of *les uns les autres*, as well as by the rising pitch of the question form). Usually these groups seem to correspond to a heightening of emotion as well as of rhythm:

oyons *le plus grand, le plus victorieux* Empereur et *le plus puissant* qui fust onques [Augustus], *se jouant, et mettant en risée, très-plaisamment et très-ingenieusement*, plusieurs batailles hazardées *et par mer et par terre, le sang et la vie* de cinq cens mille hommes qui suivirent sa fortune, et *les forces et richesses* des deux parties du monde espuisées pour le service de ses entreprinses[49] ["Let us listen to *the greatest, the most victorious* emperor, and *the most powerful* that ever was, *very comically and very cleverly making sport and a laughing-stock* of many battles hazarded *on land and sea, the blood and the lives* of five hundred thousand men who followed his fortunes, and the *power and riches* of both parts of the world exhausted in the service of his enterprises"].

Here the rhythm is complicated by a disguised group of three (*le plus grand, le plus victorieux . . . et le plus puissant*), but the generally binary movement, culminating in *des deux parties du monde*, ends by embracing the whole world in a series of backward and forward strokes.

The word-pair, then, is essentially a conventional form and its generally synonymous character prevents it, as a rule, from surprising: in fact, the very expectedness of the second term is often part of the effect and its delaying power derives to some extent from the fact that it marks time, so to speak. It is true that the combinations of pairs are frequently unexpected, and this is particularly true when the pair takes the form of paronomasia or oxymoron. Still, the word-pair remains on the whole a static element in Montaigne's style. The group of three, of which we have just seen one example, is very different.[50] The replacement of an even by an odd number is enough in itself to break the perfect symmetry, and now a dynamic and liberating energy comes into play. This seems to remain true even when the three terms are near-synonyms, which is much less often the case. As with the pair, all the main parts of speech are involved, though adjectives tend to predominate. This certainly happens with Proust, who is probably the other great master of the group of three in French prose: *odeurs . . . casanières, humaines et renfermées, gelée exquise, industrieuse et limpide . . .*[51] ["homely, human and shut-in smells, an exquisite, industrious and limpid jelly"]. Proust is indeed very like Montaigne in the way he achieves surprising collocations. Again as with the pair, these groups occur far more frequently in the Third Book and in the additions of the Bordeaux Copy, and the quality of strangeness or surprise is more clearly present.

Taking first of all examples of near-synonymous groups:

> selon son estre *insatiable, vagabond et versatile.*[52]
> Et telles autres circonstances nous *amusent, divertissent et destournent* de la consideration de la chose en soy.[53]
> Tousjours la variation *soulage, dissout et dissipe.*[54] ["according to its *insatiable, erratic,* and *versatile* nature," "And other such circumstances *occupy, divert,* and *distract* us from consideration of the thing in itself," "Variation always *solaces, dissolves,* and *dissipates*"].

In each case the two final terms are linked by alliteration, producing a climax. In the last two cases the theme of the essay ("De la diversion") is heavily stressed, an excellent example of Montaigne's use of keywords as landmarks in the apparently formless progression of his thought. In all cases, the three words not only impress the meaning more forcibly, but squeeze out the full meaning by using the full range of possible synonyms, or at least suggesting it. A further stage is reached when the first two words are synonymous but the last introduces a new conception and a new dimension, a totally unforeseen leap from the springboard of the synonymous pair:

C'est une art, comme dict Platon, *legere, volage, demoniacle*[55] ["It is an art, as Plato says, *light, flighty, daemonic*"].

Though he has taken it from Plato it has become his own. Or (part of a much longer enumeration describing the sexual act)

cette morgue *grave, severe et ecstatique* en une action si fole[56] ["that *grave, severe,* and *ecstatic* countenance in so silly an action"],

where the sudden transition from gravity and severity to ecstasy brings out dramatically the contradictions which Montaigne sees in human love, as in so much else.

When the terms are not synonymous we move into an area of much greater freedom and stronger poetic effect. A simple early example, but one which strikes a particularly fine note of plangent regret (he is recalling the feelings of his youth) is:

la teste pleine *d'oisiveté, d'amour et de bon temps,* comme moy[57] ["his head full of *idleness, love, and a good time,* like myself"],

or the description of the armour of Caesar's soldiers:

il aymoit qu'ils fussent richement armez, et leur faisoit porter des harnois *gravez, dorez et argentez* . . .[58] ["he liked them to be richly armed, and had them wear *engraved, gilded, and silver* armor . . ."]

where the abstract notion of richness enunciated in the opening clause is fully concretized in the group of three past participles. Sometimes the three words make three separate images, as in the enumeration of the difficulties conventionally attached to virtue:

et y peut on justement attacher *ces escueils, ces haliers et ces monstres*[59] ["*these reefs, these thickets and these monsters*"].

(The remarkable interpolation of the Bordeaux Copy in which this occurs includes a whole series of groups of three). However, freedom is most marked in groups of adjectives, for instance in the characteristics of erotic pleasure:

> son goust est plus momentanée, fluide et caduque[60]
> ["the taste of it is more momentary, fleeting and insubstantial"],

or very similarly, at the end of the last essay:

> nos *necessiteuses* commoditez, *fluides et ambigues*[61]
> ["our *meagre* comforts, *fleeting and ambiguous*"].

Fluidity and ambiguity are vital elements in Montaigne's thought as in his style, and the group of three with its broken symmetry and freer rhythm is ideally fitted to convey them. Like the pair, the group of three can be doubled: the Gascon language is

> autant *nerveux, puissant et pertinant,* comme le François est *gratieus, delicat et abondant*[62] ["as *sinewy, powerful, and pertinent* as French is *graceful, delicate, and abundant*"];

or, on pleasures once more and notable for the splendour of the language:

> Je ne les veux pas tant *magnanimes, magnifiques et fastueuses,* comme je les veux *doucereuses, faciles et prestes*[63] ["I do not so much want them *noble, magnificent, and ostentatious,* as *sweet, easy, and ready at hand*"].

Of course in these cases symmetry is more than re-established.

Yet although perfect symmetry is generally broken in the group of three, it has not been eliminated, there is still a residual organization (the 1 + 2 arrangement of the alliterative examples offers especially striking confirmation). The next stage is enumeration proper, where symmetry has probably gone altogether in the majority of cases, though of course structure remains, since all the items of the enumeration normally stand in the same syntactical relation to the rest of the sentence and belong to the same part of speech. Within the limits imposed by this structure freedom is more or less absolute, in semantic content as well as in the number of possible items. To mark the extreme limit in Montaigne, we have the Rabelaisian series of sixty-eight verbs in the first person plural illustrating the language of gesture (*nous requerons, nous promettons, appellons* . . .[64] ["We beg, we promise, call . . ."]). This series is too celebrated to be worth analyzing in detail here, though the identity of the final syllable in each word may cast some doubt on what I have said about the disappearance of symmetry (a pale reflection, incidentally, may be found in the nineteen adjectives which express Mme de Sévigné's surprise at the news of the Lauzun marriage[65]). But though this is an extreme case in Montaigne, there are many others which work on the same principle, though often in a more complex fashion than the straightforward alignment of identical verb-forms. Of course, enumeration itself is one of the most familiar of stylistic devices, frequently studied, though not very much in Montaigne.[66] Still, it will hardly be necessary to dwell on the more simple and ordinary manifestations: our main purpose must be to seek those functions and forms which are specially characteristic.

Among the simple forms one of the most frequent is a long string of abstract nouns, often indicating qualities he dislikes or prizes (and thus establishing in brief compass a whole moral attitude):

> l'inconstance, l'irresolution, l'incertitude, le deuil, la superstition, la solicitude des choses à venir . . . l'ambition, l'avarice, la jalousie, l'envie, les appetits desreglez, forcenez et indomptables, la guerre, la mensonge, la desloyauté, la detraction et la curiosité[67] ["inconstancy, irresolution, uncertainty, grief, superstition, worry over things to come . . . ambition, avarice, jealousy, envy, unruly, frantic, and untameable appetites, war, falsehood, disloyalty, detraction, and curiosity"].

Here there are sixteen abstractions, which pretty well exhaust the pessimistic view of human nature expressed at this point. Or, on the other hand, in the more optimistic Third Book:

> la bonté, la moderation, l'equabilité, la constance[68]
> ["goodness, moderation, equability, constancy"].

More interestingly, and especially in the *Apologie de Raimond Sebond*, abstract enumerations are used for philosophical or scientific purposes, as in, appropriately, the discussion of the powers of abstraction of the human mind:

> l'espesseur, la longueur, la profondeur, le poids, la couleur, l'odeur, l'aspreté, la pollisseure, la dureté, la mollesse et tous accidents sensibles . . .[69] ["their thickness, length, depth, weight, color, odor, roughness, smoothness, hardness, softness and all accidents of sense . . ."].

This might be thought to prefigure Descartes, but of course Descartes reduces all these qualities to two, and even in his abstractions Montaigne conveys in enumerations like these the sense of an infinite diversity in the universe. The *Apologie* is largely concerned with discrediting the contradictory opinions of philosophers, and, dismissing each in a phrase, the enumeration is a marvellous (though not in this case original) instrument for the purpose:

> ou les idées de Platon, ou les atomes d'Epicurus, ou le plain et le vuide de Leucippus . . .[70] ["of the ideas of Plato, or the atoms of Epicurus, of the fullness and void of Leucippus . . ."]

and so on through thirteen items until we reach the final *ou toute autre opinion*, embracing everything else.

Even in these cases abstraction is somehow endowed with a concrete feeling (*l'odeur, l'aspreté, la pollisseure*), to which the multiplication of nouns contributes a great deal, and Montaigne's enumerations, of a piece with his style and imagination generally, are for the most part highly concrete. Examples are numerous, but one or two will make the matter clear. A simple one describes our robbing of animals for clothing:

> nous cacher soubs leur despouille, laine, plume, poil, soye[71] ["to hide ourselves beneath their spoils—wool, feathers, fur, silk"].

Incidentally, we are perhaps beginning to see in cases like these something of what distinguishes Montaigne's use of enumeration. It is neither the uninhibited, unlimited flow of Rabelais nor the carefully organized sequence of Bossuet. Rather the impression given is one of completeness, everything is included that is necessary. A more complex example occurs in a caricature of medical practice:

> le nombre imper de leurs pillules, la destination de certains jours et festes de l'année, la distinction des heures à cueillir les herbes de leurs ingrediens, et cette grimace rebarbative et prudente de leur port et contenance . . .[72] ["their pills in uneven numbers, the appointment of certain days and festivals of the year, the distinguishing of certain hours for plucking the herbs of their ingredients, and that surly and solemn twist of their bearing and countenance . . ."].

Variation is clearly a much more important element of enumeration than of the word-pair: here it illustrates the extravagance and absurdity of the doctors. A slight change of register without any change of form is enough to effect a transposition from the caricatural to the poetic. Here are the trifles which can overthrow man in his pride:

> Un souffle de vent contraire, le croassement d'un vol de corbeaux, le faux pas d'un cheval, le passage fortuite d'un aigle, un songe, une voix, un signe, une brouée matiniere . . .[73] ["A contrary breath of wind, the

croaking of a flight of ravens, a horse's stumbling, the chance passing of
an eagle, a dream, a voice, a sign, a morning mist . . ."].

The progression here is notable (four precise phrases, three rapid, vague
and sinister nouns, the final delicate picture of a morning mist), but even
more striking is the variation, the inexplicable collocation of disparate phenomena. Or, as with abstracts and again particularly in the *Apologie*, concrete enumeration can be used to bring a vast area of experience within a
single conspectus; for example:

> ce branle admirable de la voute celeste, la lumiere eternelle de ces
> flambeaux roulans si fierement sur sa teste, les mouvemens espouvan-
> tables de cette mer infinie . . .[74] ["that admirable motion of the celes-
> tial vault, the eternal light of those torches rolling so proudly above his
> head, the fearful movements of that infinite sea . . ."].

This multiplication of subjects expresses, in an almost Pascalian vision, the
immensity of the universe which crushes man. And we have here (and in
any number of other cases which might be cited) what is no doubt the
principal function of enumeration in Montaigne: the direct grasp of the
physical world, of tangible reality, so organized as to be manageable and
to receive a structured form. The examples given have been limited in
scale, chiefly because they are quotable, but the same principles apply,
though the element of variation and extraordinary collocations is naturally
even more pronounced, to such large-scale enumerations as the series of (if
the count is correct) forty-three clauses beginning with *où* which constitute
in "De la coustume" the main statement of the variability and relativity of
human behaviour and moral codes,[75] or the thirty direct objects (approximately) of the verb *rencontre* in the description of American customs.[76]
Though hardly an objectively verifiable stylistic feature, the immense enjoyment of passages like these is most powerfully communicated, a mind
playing (but playing seriously) with the whole of nature and human
existence.

So far the examples have mostly taken a simple linear form, but this is
by no means true of all, and the form of the enumeration deserves close
attention, though it will have to be brief. As with the word-pair, double and
multiple enumeration are common. Here is a case of double enumeration
of nouns and adjectives:

> *La santé, la conscience, l'authorité, la science, la richesse, la beauté* et
> leurs contraires se despouillent à l'entrée, et reçoivent de l'ame nou-
> velle vesture, et de la teinture qu'il lui plaist: *brune, verte, claire, ob-
> scure, aigre, douce, profonde, superficielle* . . .[77] ["*Health, conscience,*

*authority, knowledge, riches, beauty,* and their opposites—all are
stripped on entry and receive from the soul new clothing, and the
coloring that she chooses—*brown, green, bright, dark, bitter, sweet,
deep, superficial* . . ."].

The profundity of the thought (the transformation of experience by the
mind) would require long elucidation, but stylistically the point seems to
lie in the wholly poetic contrast between the familiar and comfortable abstracts (health, conscience, wealth) and the dismayingly unexpected adjectives (brown, green, bitter) which qualify them in their transformed
state. Multiple enumeration is difficult to illustrate without quotations of
inordinate length: a simple case (the adventures of Scipio) will at least
show how one enumeration springs from another:

> pour se commettre en terre ennemie, *à la puissance d'un Roy barbare,
> à une foy incognue, sans obligation, sans hostage,* sous la seule seureté
> *de la grandeur de son propre courage, de son bon heur et de la promesse
> de ses hautes esperances*[78] ["to entrust himself in enemy country *to the
> power of a barbarian king and to an untried faith—without obligation,
> without a hostage,* under the sole security of *the greatness of his own
> courage, his good fortune, and the promise of his high hopes*"].

Especially characteristic of Montaigne is the negative enumeration. One
very famous example, the passage from "Des Cannibales" imitated in *The
Tempest,* may suffice to show how it works:

> C'est une nation, diroy je à Platon, en laquelle il n'y a aucune espece
> de trafique; nulle cognoissance de lettres; nulle science de nombres; nul
> nom de magistrat, ny de superiorité politique; nul usage de service, de
> richesse ou de pauvreté; nuls contrats; nulles successions; nuls partages;
> nulles occupations qu'oysives; nul respect de parenté que commun; nuls
> vestemens; nulle agriculture; nul metal; nul usage de vin ou de bled[79]
> ["This is a nation, I should say to Plato, in which there is no sort of
> traffic, no knowledge of letters, no science of numbers, no name for a
> magistrate, or for political superiority, no custom of servitude, no
> riches or poverty, no contracts, no successions, no partitions, no occu-
> pations but leisure ones, no care for any but common kinship, no
> clothes, no agriculture, no metal, no use of wine or wheat"].

The sentence includes fourteen items (with one subsidiary enumeration,
*de service, de richesse ou de pauvreté*) and it is immediately followed by
another enumeration of seven items, positive but negated by the last word:

> Les paroles mesmes qui signifient la mensonge, la trahison, la dissimu-
> lation, l'avarice, l'envie, la detraction, le pardon, *inouïes* ["The very

words that signify lying, treachery, dissimulation, avarice, envy, belit-
tling, pardon—*unheard of*"].

It will probably be agreed that all these negations together give a very positive picture of the life and character of the American Indians, but equally
important is the condemnation of European society: they are not what we
are. The negative enumeration thus permits a double view, ambiguity, comparison, and relativity once more.

From the syntactical point of view there is an important difference between polysyndeton and asyndeton.[80] Most of the examples quoted have
been of asyndeton, which no doubt makes for a sense of pressure or urgency, especially when the article is also omitted, as in this list of remedies
inflicted by his doctors on their helpless patient:

> tant de puans breuvages, cauteres, incisions, suées, sedons, dietes . . .[81]
> ["all the stinking potions, cauteries, incisions, sweatings, setons,
> diets . . ."].

All these ills come crowding in at once. But on the same page we have a
very different picture of the restoration to health:

> avant qu'on vous aye rendu l'usage de l'air, *et* du vin, *et* de vostre
> femmes, *et* des melons . . .[82] ["before they have given you back the
> enjoyment of fresh air, and wine, and your wife, and melons . . ."].

Polysyndeton is evidently one more delaying device, one way, as in this
case, of savouring enjoyment and making it last as long as possible, which
in this same essay ("De l'experience") Montaigne declares to be his attitude
to time.[83] Polysyndeton with *ou* (as in *ou les idées de Platon* . . . , already
quoted) is obviously a vehicle for the expression of skeptical alternatives
and doubts.

I said earlier that the items of an enumeration normally stand in the
same syntactical relation to the rest of the sentence but it is also characteristic of Montaigne that this normal rule is often broken. To take a short
example (though longer ones offer more extreme anacolutha):

> Me voylà pris et rendu, retiré dans l'espais d'une forest voisine, des-
> monté, devalizé, mes cofres fouilletz, ma boyte prise, chevaux et es-
> quipage desparty a nouveaux maistres[84] ["There I was, seized and made
> a prisoner, withdrawn into the thick of a neighboring forest, forced to
> dismount, my valises seized, my coffers searched, my money box taken,
> horses and equipment divided among new masters"].

The vivid narration is conducted by means of discontinuous incidents; the
syntactical change from simple past participle to the absolute construction

reinforces this discontinuity. More generally, inconsequent syntax not only suggests the spoken word, it is a principal contributor to the depiction of moving thought, a pointer to the paths of the labyrinth, *les profondeurs opaques de ses replis internes.*

A final example brings most of these qualities together:

> En lui sont d'autres Dieux, *la terre, la mer, les astres, qui s'entretiennent d'une harmonieuse et perpetuelle agitation et danse divine, tantost se rencontrans, tantost s'esloignans, se cachans, se montrans, changeans de rang,* ores davant et ores derriere[85] ["In it are other gods, *the earth, the sea, the stars, which entertain each other with a perpetual harmonious agitation and divine dance, now meeting, now separating, hiding, appearing, changing order,* now in front and now behind"].

Enumerations and word-pairs combine in patterns which reflect the dance of the universe in the dance of the sentence.

These word-clusters, then, occupy a central position in Montaigne's style and they present us with a series of complementary oppositions: between the conversational character of his writing and the profound sense of form, even sometimes the highly developed artifice, which underlies it; between the playfulness which juggles with language and the serious grasp of the world which this play expresses; above all (and it is here that word-pair and enumeration are particularly effective) between the infinite diversity of things and the unity of vision which can subordinate diversity to dominant linguistic structures. If a wider conclusion can be drawn, it is that in the study of style, phonetics, semantics and syntax are hard to separate.

## NOTES

1. *Œuvres complètes,* ed. Rat (Paris, 1962, reprinted 1965), p. 9. All quotations are from this edition unless otherwise stated. Translations are predominantly those of Donald M. Frame, *The Complete Essays of Montaigne* (Stanford, 1948).

2. Montaigne, *Œuvres complètes,* ed. Armaingaud, X (1935), p. 368. The Latin is rather different, with chiasmus: *nova gratia et adiutorio novo* (Lyons, 1540, f.225$^r$).

3. *Commentaires sur S. Paul* ([Geneva], Conrad Badius, 1561), f.8$^r$.

4. *Institution de la religion chrestienne,* ed. Pannier (Paris, 1938), III, 62.

5. Plutarch, *Œuvres morales,* Paris, 1575, f.101$^v$.

6. *Hamlet,* III, i.

7. *Antony and Cleopatra,* I, i.

8. III, xiii, p. 1095.

9. I, xxviii, p. 188.

10. III, ix, p. 944.

11. III, xiii, p. 1043.
12. I, i, p. 14.
13. I, i, p. 11.
14. II, i, p. 319.
15. III, x, p. 980.
16. III, xii, p. 1033.
17. II, xxxvii, p. 744.
18. III, xii, p. 1013.
19. I, xxxvii, p. 228.
20. *Loc. cit.*
21. II, xii, p. 452.
22. I, xxvi, p. 165.
23. III, xiii, p. 1086.
24. I, xxvi, p. 161.
25. *Loc. cit.*
26. II, xi, p. 409.
27. III, xiii, p. 1085.
28. III, xiii, p. 1091.
29. III, x, p. 999.
30. III, xii, p. 1016.
31. III, viii, p. 920.
32. *The Garden of Eloquence* (1593), ed. Crane (Gainesville, Fla., 1954), p. 56. Mrs. Carol E. Clark notes that the use of the figure may be derived from Seneca ("Seneca's Letters to Lucilius as a Source of Some of Montaigne's Imagery," *Bibliothèque d'Humanisme et Renaissance*, XXX (1968), 265-66). See also Joseph Coppin, "Quelques procédés de style de Montaigne," *Revue de philologie française*, XL (1928), 190-201.
33. II, xx, p. 656.
34. III, v, p. 838.
35. III, ix, p. 922.
36. II, xiv, p. 595.
37. II, xii, p. 581.
38. III, vi, p. 888.
39. II, xii, p. 497.
40. III, ix, p. 955.
41. On antithesis and skepticism see Margot Recksiek, *Montaignes Verhältnis zu Klassik und Manierismus* (Bonn, 1966), p. 298.
42. III, v, p. 818.
43. III, ix, p. 943.
44. II, xii, p. 450.
45. III, i, p. 770.
46. III, iii, p. 799. On the generally slow tempo of the *Essais* see Floyd Gray, *Le Style de Montaigne* (Paris, 1958), pp. 70 ff.
47. III, ii, p. 782.
48. III, viii, p. 917.
49. II, xii, p. 453.
50. Cf. Gray, *Style*, p. 88 (a brief reference only, however).
51. *À la Recherche du temps perdu* (Paris, 1960), i, 49. On this feature of Proust's style see Yvette Louria, *La Convergence stylistique chez Proust* (Geneva and Paris, 1957).

52. III, xiii, p. 1086.

53. III, iv, p. 812.

54. III, iv, p. 813.

55. III, ix, p. 973.

56. III, v, p. 855.

57. I, xx, p. 86.

58. II, xxxiv, p. 714.

59. I, xxvi, p. 162.

60. I, xx, p. 80.

61. III, xiii, p. 1095.

62. II, xvii, p. 622.

63. III, v, pp. 819-20.

64. II, xii, p. 431.

65. *Lettres*, ed. Monmerqué (Paris, 1862), II, 25-6.

66. But see Recksiek, pp. 202 ff.; and Michel Butor, *Essais sur les Essais* (Paris, 1968), pp. 193 ff. Neither, however, analyses to any great extent.

67. II, xii, p. 465.

68. III, x, p. 999.

69. II, xii, pp. 460-61.

70. II, xii, p. 521.

71. II, xii, p. 463.

72. II, xxxvii, p. 749.

73. II, xii, pp. 453-54.

74. II, xii, p. 427.

75. I, xxiii, pp. 110-13.

76. II, xii, pp. 557-58.

77. I, l, p. 290.

78. I, xxiv, p. 129.

79. I, xxxi, p. 204.

80. Mentioned by Recksiek in a comparison with Sponde (pp. 203 ff.).

81. III, xiii, p. 1072.

82. *Loc. cit.*

83. III, xiii, pp. 1091-92.

84. III, xii, p. 1039.

85. II, xii, p. 556.

## DISCUSSION OF SAYCE'S PAPER

Forms analogous to those found by Sayce in Montaigne's style were pointed out in the style of Shakespeare, particularly where they entailed metaphors—in one scene in *Hamlet* can be found "the slings and arrows of outrageous fortune," "the whips and scorns of time," "enterprises of great pitch and moment," and "the expectancy and rose of the fair state." The form X and Y of Z or X of Y and Z is one of the richest to be found in Shakespeare, because it permits him two angles on the same metaphor with the greatest economy. It is graceful yet weighty because obviously studied. It is a good instance of the "swelling" of the blank verse line, since there is an inflation, but one that stays within the confines of meter and expression. The form is so particular that its occurrence in Keats must represent a conscious imitation of Shakespeare.

As for the linguistic aspect of the collocation of disparate phenomena, it was pointed out that unexpectedness stems not from the fact that the juxtaposed words are semantically improbable but from the fact that they have not been put together before. It is a kind of pure collocational surprise, not a semantic anomaly. For example, in Yeats' "Leda and the Swan," there is the phrase "those terrified vague fingers." There is no semantic reason why "terrified" and "vague" cannot go together, but one feels that they just have not been juxtaposed before. Did Sayce find in his study of word-pairs this underlying stratum? Sayce said that he hadn't noticed it, but wondered if there were not some historical factor to be considered. A lot of things in Shakespeare struck him as odd in a purely collocational sense, and yet in the historical context they might not be surprising. And of course poetry does tend to be more odd in its juxtapositions than prose. He was reminded of the recurrent phrase in Henry James' novels, "She vaguely wailed," which is also improbable, but funny rather than poetic.

Another participant noted that most of the word-pairs in Sayce's paper seemed to be in the predicate rather than the subject portion of the sen-

tence, either epithetic qualifications, or actions, or statements of manner or
indirect complement. Did not this sort of redoubling of the predicate coincide with the notion of *essayer*, of "trying" which, of course, is the underlying theme of the whole? It is an "essay" of thought which we see in these
various repetitions. And again we see the importance of taking stylistic
processes only in terms of the larger context or reference in which they are
embedded. Sayce agreed, saying that this expressed better than he could
what he had intended in his paper. There were, of course, occurrences of
multiplication in the subject, though they were not numerous and did not
invalidate this important point.

Sayce's distinction between linguistic stylistics and a stylistics oriented
toward the literary work was approved, but it was important not to limit the
latter to a given single work, since one can be concerned with groups of
works or epochs or indeed any kind of assemblage of works. On the term
"mannerism" Sayce was asked whether he was referring to the work of
Curtius; he answered that he was thinking rather of the term as it is used
in art history, by Pevsner and others, to refer to a movement limited to works
of the sixteenth century. As for larger stylistic groupings, they were, of
course, important and could be seen as the sum of the devices in the various works which had been discussed.

Sayce was asked whether some of the pairs in Montaigne's style might be
explained in terms of the medieval and renaissance theory of prose rhythm,
that is, the theory of the *cursus—planus, velox*, and *tardus*. Many of his examples seemed to come at the end of phrases and periods. Naturally, one
has to reintroduce the pronunciation of the mute *e*: thus the doublet *ny
beau ny honneste* seems a clear instance of *cursus planus*—◡◡—◡ . Similarly
*forces et richesses*; indeed, most of the phrases that can be seen as examples
of *cursus* are in the mode of the *planus*. Sayce found the suggestion very
interesting, though he felt there was always the question of how far the
*cursus* could be taken as operative in vernacular prose. One had also to rec-
oncile this idea with Montaigne's claim that he despised all that sort of
thing (though of course we know that he did not despise it at all).

Wasn't there a certain inconsistency in Sayce's account, to the extent
that each example was presented (it seemed) as if it had been written separately? That, of course, is a characteristic of demonstrations. But whenever one discusses a single sentence, one is deprived of the important implications of context, and one tends to overlook the fact that writing and
reading are linear processes. On this basis, their effects should be explained,
in part, at least, in terms of the principle of "dilution of information." Riffaterre's context theory, for instance, argues a progressive loss of emphasis
if a given feature is repeated often enough; the feature fades back into the
context, indeed sometimes to the point where its *non*-use may be the thing

that can be foregrounded. If this is true in the case of these multiplications in Montaigne, perhaps it would explain why other features that were mentioned—paronomasia, alliteration, like endings, and so on—came to be introduced, to bolster the emphasis of the now stereotyped doublet. Sayce agreed that the problem of context was fundamental in stylistic inquiry. If you take a single passage, it is like putting a piece of tissue under the microscope on the assumption that it is a good representative sample; but of course you cannot always be sure. If you do the work *in toto,* on the other hand, you end up with a catalog in which the style is lost. So there is a lot to be said for following individual devices.

He was then asked if he noted a coherent development in Montaigne's work in respect to this feature, for example, through the three editions of the *Essays.* He replied that he found the distribution of the shorter forms, the word-pairs, to be fairly constant, but that the more elaborate, intricate, and interesting combinations tended to come in the later stages, in the Third Book and after 1588.

Finally, in connection with his use of the expression "tic," which could be translated as "habitual stylistic feature," how widespread was the feature in Montaigne's other works, that is, could it be concluded that it was unconscious in his style? Sayce answered that the feature seemed to be considerably less frequent in Montaigne's *Journal du voyage,* which was not intended for publication, although the situation was somewhat complicated by the fact that one-third of the book had been written in Italian and another third dictated to a secretary. Still, it seemed doubtful that the feature was an unconscious part of the *homme même.*

# LIST OF CONTRIBUTORS

ROLAND BARTHES is Directeur d'études à L'École Pratique des Hautes Études, Paris. Among his many works on literature are *Le Degré zéro de l'écriture* (Paris, 1953), translated as *Writing Degree Zero*, and *S/Z* (Paris, 1970). He describes himself as "Universitaire, essayiste et critique littéraire qui a participé activement, en France, à l'élaboration de la sémiotique littéraire."

SEYMOUR CHATMAN is Professor of Rhetoric at the University of California, Berkeley. He is author of *A Theory of Meter*, "The Semantics of Style" (in *Social Science Information* and reprinted in Michael Lane, *Structuralism, A Reader*, London, 1970), and the forthcoming *The Later Style of Henry James* (to be published by Basil Blackwell, Oxford). He is currently at work on a book on narrative structure.

LUBOMÍR DOLEŽEL is Research Fellow of the Institute for Czech Literature of the Czechoslovak Academy of Sciences and Associate Professor of the Charles University in Prague. He is currently (1971) Visiting Professor in the Department of Slavic Languages and Literatures, University of Toronto. Among his publications are "Vers la stylistique structurale," in *Travaux linguistique de Prague*, Vol. I (1964), 257-66, and "A Framework for the Statistical Analysis of Style," in L. Doležel and R. W. Bailey (eds.), *Statistics and Style* (New York, 1969), 10-25. His main areas of interest are Slavic linguistics, stylistics and poetics, the structural study of fiction, and the statistical study of texts.

NILS ERIK ENKVIST is Donner Professor of English Language and Literature and former rector of the Åbo Akademi (the Swedish-speaking university of Finland). He has written on a wide range of linguistic and literary subjects; among his publications are a portion of *Linguistics and Style* (London, 1964) and an article on stylistics in Sweden and Finland in the journal *Style* (1969). He is currently working on the theory of style and on text linguistics.

IVAN FÓNAGY is Head of the Phonetics Department of the Linguistic Institute of the Hungarian Academy of Sciences and Visiting Professor of Phonetics and General Linguistics at the Institut de Phonétique de l'Université de Paris. He is the author of "Communication in Poetry" (*Word*, XVII, 1964) and "L'Information du style verbal" (*Linguistics*, IV, 1964), among many other articles and books in Hungarian, English, French, and German. His interests are, in general, style theory and phonostylistics.

PIERRE GUIRAUD is Professeur Directeur de la section de linguistique générale at the University of Nice and Professor of French and General Linguistics at Indiana University. He has written about 30 books and one hundred articles on linguistics, literary history, and stylistics. Some recent titles are *Essais de Stylistique* (Paris, 1970), *La Stylistique* (Paris, 1970), *Le Testament de Villon* (Paris, 1970), and *La Versification* (Paris, 1970). Professor Guiraud is interested in applying both statistical and structural methods to the study of lexicology and stylistics.

M. A. K. HALLIDAY is Professor of General Linguistics at the University of London, and in 1971 will become Professor of Linguistics at the University of British Columbia. Among his publications are "The Linguistic Study of Literary Texts," in S. Chatman and S. Levin, *Essays on the Language of Literature* (Boston, 1967), "Grammar, Society and the Noun" (monograph published by University College, London), "Notes on Transitivity and Theme in English," published in three parts in the *Journal of Linguistics*, and "Language Structure and Language Function," in the Penguin volume *New Horizons in Linguistics*. He is concerned with linguistics from a sociological, literary, and educational standpoint, and describes his approach to language as asking the question "What should we make language look like in order to throw light on questions of this kind?"

RUQUAIYA HASAN's most recent appointment has been Research Officer for the Nuffield Project for Sociolinguistic Study of Children's Stories, at the Sociological Research Unit, Institute of Education, University of London. Her work in linguistics includes "Linguistics and the Study of Literary Texts," *Études de Linguistique appliquée*, 5, 1967; "Syntax and Semantics," in *Biological and Social Factors in Psycholinguistics*, edited by John Morton (London, 1971); *Grammatical Cohesion in Spoken and Written English* (Papers of the Programme in Linguistics and English Teaching; London, Part 1, 1968, Part 2, forthcoming); and *Language in the Imaginative Context: A Socio-linguistic Study of Stories Told by Children* (London, forthcoming).

SAMUEL R. LEVIN is Professor of English at the City University of New York. He is author of *Linguistic Structures in Poetry* (The Hague, 1962) and co-editor with Seymour Chatman of *Essays on the Language of Literature* (Boston, 1967).

JOSEPHINE MILES is Professor of English at the University of California, Berkeley. Among her many works in stylistics are *Eras and Modes in English Poetry* (Berkeley, 1964) and *Style and Proportion* (Boston, 1967). She is interested in the formal and artistic use of language in literature.

LOUIS MILIC is Professor of English and Chairman of the English Department at the Cleveland State University. His stylistic position is described in his book on Swift, *A Quantitative Approach to the Style of Jonathan Swift* (The Hague, 1967), although a more up-to-date formulation can be found in the introductory essay of his *Stylists on Style* (New York, 1969). His emphasis has been on the study of prose from a rhetorical and linguistic point of view, stressing objective, statistical, and computer-assisted studies of style.

ALEXANDRU NICULESCU is a professor at the University of Bucharest and recently a visiting professor at the University of Padua. Among his works are "Sur un emploi particulier de l'ellipse du prédicat dans le style narratif," in *Poetics* (Warsaw, 1960) and *Individualitatea limbii române între limbile romanice— Contributii grammaticale* (Bucharest, 1965).

RICHARD OHMANN is Professor of English of Wesleyan University and former Associate Provost and Chancellor. His publications include *Shaw: The Style and the Man* (Middletown, Conn., 1962); "Generative Grammars and the Concept of Literary Style" (*Word*, 1964); and "Speech Acts and the Definition of Literature," forthcoming in *Philosophy and Rhetoric*.

RICHARD SAYCE is Reader in French Literature at Oxford University, Fellow of Worcester College, and editor of *The Library* since 1964. He is author of *Style in French Prose* (Oxford, 1953). He approaches style in the context of general literary studies.

JEAN STAROBINSKI is Professor of French Literature at the University of Geneva, Switzerland. He is Editor of the *Annales de la Société Jean-Jacques Rousseau* and author of *Rousseau* (1957); *L'Oeil vivant* (1961); *The Invention of Liberty* (1964); and *La Relation critique* (1970). He belongs to what is generally known as the "Geneva school" of literary criticism.

TZVETAN TODOROV is at the Centre National de la Recherche Scientifique, in Paris. Among his many works in stylistics and literary theory are *Littérature et signification* (Paris, 1967) and *Introduction à la littérature fantastique* (Paris, 1970). He is currently working in the fields of poetics, narrative analysis, and semiotics.

KARL D. UITTI is Professor of Romance Languages and Literatures at Princeton University. He is author of *Linguistics and Literary Theory* (Englewood Cliffs, N.J., 1969); *La Passion littéraire de Rémy de Gourmont* (Paris, 1962); and *The Concept of Self in the Symbolist Novel* (The Hague, 1961). His main interests are Romance philology, Old French narrative, and textual criticism and analysis.

STEPHEN ULLMANN is Professor of the Romance Languages in the University of Oxford and Fellow of Trinity College, Oxford. He has written three books on stylistics: *Style in the French Novel* (1957); *The Image in the Modern French Novel* (1960); *Language and Style* (1964). He is General Editor of Blackwell's "Language and Style" series and President of the Philological Society.

René Wellek is Sterling Professor of Comparative Literature at Yale University. He is co-author with Austin Warren of *Theory of Literature* (1949), and has written a *History of Modern Criticism* in four volumes (1955-65); recent works are *Concepts of Criticism* (1963), and *Discriminations* (1970). His view of stylistics is represented in the chapter "Style and Stylistics" in *Theory of Literature*, and in his "Concluding Statement" in *Style in Language*, ed. T. Sebeok (New York, 1960).

Harald Weinrich is Professor of Linguistics and Director of the Center for Interdisciplinary Research at the Universität Bielefeld. He is author of *Tempus— Besprochene und erzählte Welt* (Stuttgart, 1964, 1971) and *Linguistik der Lüge* (Heidelberg, 1964). His continuing interests are in the areas of structural and textual linguistics.

W. K. Wimsatt is Frederick Clifford Ford Professor of Literature at Yale University. His works include *The Verbal Icon* (1954), *Literary Criticism, A Short History* (with Cleanth Brooks) (1957), and *Hateful Contraries* (1965). He is currently editing a book of essays in comparative prosody by various hands for the Modern Language Association of America.

Paul Zumthor is Professor of Romance Philology, especially the French Language, at the University of Amsterdam and was recently Visiting Professor at Johns Hopkins University. His special interest is medieval literature, principally medieval stylistics. He is the author of *Langue et techniques poétiques à l'époque romane* (Paris, 1963) and has in preparation a book entitled *Essai de poétique mediévale*.

# NAME INDEX

# TITLE INDEX